# Listening to the Unconscious

# Listening to the Unconscious

*Adventures in Popular Music and Psychoanalysis*

Kenneth Smith and Stephen Overy

BLOOMSBURY ACADEMIC
NEW YORK • LONDON • OXFORD • NEW DELHI • SYDNEY

BLOOMSBURY ACADEMIC
Bloomsbury Publishing Inc
1385 Broadway, New York, NY 10018, USA
50 Bedford Square, London, WC1B 3DP, UK
29 Earlsfort Terrace, Dublin 2, Ireland

BLOOMSBURY, BLOOMSBURY ACADEMIC and the Diana logo are trademarks of
Bloomsbury Publishing Plc

First published in the United States of America 2023

Copyright © Kenneth Smith and Stephen Overy, 2023

For legal purposes the Acknowledgments on p. viii constitute an extension
of this copyright page.

Cover design by Louise Dugdale
Cover image: Edvard Munch, 1893, The Scream / National Gallery of Norway

All rights reserved. No part of this publication may be reproduced or transmitted in any
form or by any means, electronic or mechanical, including photocopying,
recording, or any information storage or retrieval system, without prior
permission in writing from the publishers.

Bloomsbury Publishing Inc does not have any control over, or responsibility for, any
third-party websites referred to or in this book. All internet addresses given in this book
were correct at the time of going to press. The author and publisher regret
any inconvenience caused if addresses have changed or sites have ceased to exist,
but can accept no responsibility for any such changes.

A catalog record for this book is available from the Library of Congress.

ISBN: PB: 978-1-5013-6846-2
HB: 978-1-5013-6845-5
ePDF: 978-1-5013-6848-6
eBook: 978-1-5013-6847-9

Typeset by Newgen KnowledgeWorks Pvt. Ltd., Chennai, India
Printed and bound in Great Britain

To find out more about our authors and books visit www.bloomsbury.com
and sign up for our newsletters.

*Dedicated to Phil Hodgson, whose English classroom was* der erste andere Schauplatz

# Contents

| | |
|---|---|
| Acknowledgments | viii |
| Introduction | 1 |

**Part 1  Core Concepts**

| | |
|---|---|
| 1  Charting Three Freudian Hypotheses with Pop Music: *The Economic, the Topographic, the Structural* | 13 |
| 2  Freud, Music, and the Psychological Condition | 45 |
| 3  Bright Eyes (and Friends), and The Antlers Meet Jacques Lacan | 85 |

**Part 2  Adventures in Popular Music and Psychoanalysis**

| | |
|---|---|
| 4  Phallocentrism, Sexuation, and the Chora: From Lacan to Kristeva; Gaga to Björk | 121 |
| 5  The Death Drive and Unconscious Production | 143 |
| 6  "Do You Want To Be the Ebb of This Great Tide?": Lacan, Freud, Nietzsche, Deleuze, and "Joy in Repetition": Prince and LCD Soundsystem | 173 |
| 7  S & M and Pop Perversion | 191 |
| 8  Polly Jean Harvey Asks, "Is This Desire [Enough]?" | 233 |
| Glossary of psychoanalytic terms | 257 |
| Bibliography | 259 |
| Index | 267 |

# Acknowledgments

The authors have only themselves (and each other) to blame.

# Introduction

## Words: "There's No Hidden Meaning"

A vignette. Your record collection probably doesn't contain F. R. David's 1981 European hit song "Words." We don't reproach you for this; neither does ours. The song reached #1 in most European charts, though it only made #2 in the UK and fared far worse in the United States. Google it, or load it into Spotify/iTunes/YouTube, and listen to the pumping, repeated, synthesized "C" chord—the "simplest" of all chords—that makes for one of the most basic and direct introductions to any song ever. There are no misdirections here, no doubts, no confusions, no obfuscations, no questions. This is as direct as music can be. A four-year-old child with a 1981 Casiotone 101 keyboard could have been trusted to play this accurately if induced with the right confectionary. And the aim of the whole song, as we soon learn when the lyrics emerge, is to offer absolutely no doubt about a seemingly simple truth—"I love you." Everything about the song conspires to present this message unambiguously. And yet, for every statement of direct intent, whether this is musical or lyrical, *something else* is betrayed—something that the performer/persona/protagonist[1] conceals; something that is always hidden from both the recipient of the message (the listener/the silent "other" addressee) and the message sender himself.

After David's jejune "introduction" (can we call a bed of repeated chords a *real* introduction?), the chorus's text offers the song's chief complaint that "words don't come eas[il]y." The melodic line delicately rises above the overtly doo-wop chord progression (listen to any doo-wop track to hear the progression when it was still interesting!),[2] breaking off as the upper note (a high *e*) reaches toward an even higher one (*f*) on the word "easy" as if to render musically the image of words being out of our reach (see Example 0.1 if a notated example is helpful). There is a deeper twist to the chord progression coming up, though. A dramatic chord change from G major to G minor (which is alien to the textbook key of C major) injects some trepidation and

---

[1] Through this book we try to maintain Allan F. Moore's distinction between performer (the person performing), persona (a real or fictional identity that the singer adopts), and protagonist (the character portrayed in the song's narrative). See Allan F. Moore, *Song Means: Analysing and Interpreting Recorded Popular Song* (Farnham: Ashgate, 2012), 179–81.

[2] The progression C-Am-Dm-G became a very prominent cliché.

**Example 0.1** The opening lines of the chorus of F. R. David's "Words" (1981).

moves further into doubt with an A major chord (also alien to C major) as the singer wonders how he can find the words to make the recipient "see, I love you."[3] There is a nervous charge in these alien chords that works in perfect sympathy with the unrest displayed in the text. The words and music seem to be harmonious.

On the immediate repeat of this phrase, however, the space left hanging after the word "words" is filled by a sinister, descending melodic "voice" from another place—another synthesizer that offers a verbally muted "response" to the singer. There is now a more complex dialogue going on here, despite the desperate attempt to control the message being transmitted. What is this voice?

In musicology we have long discussed "unsung voices"—Carolyn Abbate's seminal book on communication in classical music taught us, among many other things, to listen closely to the instrumental voices surrounding the spoken or sung melodies and the texts they cling to.[4] Our contention in this book is not that the unsung voice is the voice of the unconscious and the sung text is the voice of the conscious—though this *can* be the case on occasion; that would be far too simplistic to sustain as an argument. Throughout this book we'll show how the voice of the unconscious only ever partially comes through, but it comes from all sides. One recent philosopher of the unconscious bemoaned the fact that the unconscious is so often conceived as a basement of a multistory house, while, in reality, the unconscious is more like the drainpipes, the arterial system of ducts, vents, the hollow walls where rats crawl throughout the whole edifice.[5] But we put the cart before the horse; let's return to our "simple" song from F. R. David.

The subsequent verses follow the classic formula of beginning on a different, but related, chord—in this case F, which Western music theory calls the "subdominant," again a highly elementary move in songwriting 1.0. The lyrics here explain the fundamental communication problem: "Well, I'm just a music man / Melody's so far my best friend." Notice how the second line scans badly in English—better perhaps in French, the native language of F. R. David. Whether the words are *intended* to scan

---

[3] Together these chords form a loose impression of an alternative key—D minor.
[4] Carolyn Abbate, *Unsung Voices: Opera and Musical Narrative in the Nineteenth Century* (Princeton, NJ: Princeton University Press, 1991).
[5] Nick Land, Ray Brassier, and Robin Mackay, *Fanged Noumena: Collected Writings 1987-2007* (London: Urbanomic, 2011), 191.

badly to offer support to his main message of jumbled words, we can't tell, but he immediately declares an acknowledgment of the problem: "But my words are coming out wrong / Girl, I reveal my heart to you." The singer reveals his heart in the act of concealing it with bungled words, and his hope for the success of this strategy is registered in the follow-up line—"I hope you believe it's true." This line, above the tentative, hesitant, expectant, dark chord of F minor (a distorted version of that simple, friendly subdominant, now injecting a little pain and fear), leads back toward the simple home key of C, with naively optimistic rising scales from yet another synth lower down in the bass register, leading us ineluctably to our goal. There is a delicate game being played here. The protagonist consciously wants his message to be direct, but, recognizing that it will go awry, wants it to come through magically anyway, even as he unconsciously blows the message itself apart to make sure that it really does go awry. And this is often how a psychoanalytic patient and an analyst communicate; the recipient needs to receive the messages *in spite of* the sender.

The second verse offers still more food for thought about the whole delivery of the message. David berates his own song ("This is just a simple song"), and the upper eight-note repeated chords, all in root position, seem to comically reinforce the simplicity, as if they're saying, "Look, he really means it; he really is this basic." He hides behind modesty, declaring that he wrote the song "all on his own!" He declares the key line: "There's no hidden meaning." Here David asks us not to look for deeper meanings than the one he tries to steer us toward. But how can we not when the music constantly tells us more than *he* does? As anyone who has studied or undergone any form of psychoanalytic work will know, the fundamental premise is that deeper meanings are revealed to ourselves when we listen closer to the voices surrounding any act of enunciation than we could glean from the main voice of the speaker who tries to control the narrative, and of whom we have to be suspicious. To get the ball rolling, even before we've unpacked any of the psychoanalytical tools of this book yet, we'll offer a (nonexhaustive) list of possible deeper "meanings" below. Perhaps these are hidden from the protagonist himself, concealed by his unconscious protection mechanisms. In any case, they seem to us to break through the surface of this ultra-naive ditty as messages coming from the unconscious, that bypass the speaker, but use him as a mouthpiece nonetheless:

- Words come from outside. We will discuss the unconscious' relationship to language in our chapter on French psychoanalyst Jacques Lacan, but for now, let it be noted that the speaker believes, or *wants* to believe, that words are "outside"—they don't come to him; the melody that tries to constantly ascend to them, but never reaches its goals, gives us a portrait of words being somehow above us—in the air; we need to jump up and catch them like balloons that try to escape us. Ergo, communication is fundamentally impossible unless we can hope that the outside world of words matches the inner feelings that we want to summon forth.
- With each move away from the main chorus, which restates the loss of words— let's, rather drastically, call it *aphasia*—the other musical sections (verses,

solo, "middle 8") are made increasingly more frightening and generally more uncomfortable. At 1:25 the clean guitar "lead-in" to the chorus sounds like the Shadows when they are trying to be menacing (or think of Ennio Morricone's Western electric guitar licks in *Once Upon a Time in the West*); the bells toll as if to show "fate" or "death" in between the chorus and verses; at 2.15–2.30 we hear a "middle 8" with constantly fragmented instruments rising and fizzling out, with new synthesized sounds giving us a disturbing collage of images of musical "fallout" and failure that sounds genuinely traumatic. This increases the drama of the return to the well-known hook of the chorus, but makes it more fulfilling and ultimately more comfortable. The singer is comfortable with his inability to communicate and, therefore, hides *behind* the fallout as a way of preserving his ego. It's more comfortable to complain that you can't speak than to try to speak, even when complaining itself involves speaking.

- The problem is not only with words; music doesn't come easily either. There is a gaping hole where a guitar solo should be (according to the school of songwriting 1.0) at 1:50–2:00. A guitar solo starts off, tries again, and gives up, leading us back to the comfortable chorus. If the singer is hoping that the music will convey the message that his/her words can't, then we find (sadly) that the music is just as impossible to manipulate into articulating a clear message (unless the true intended message is indeed a declaration of sympathy-inducing impotence). What we learn from the music is that the speaker doubts his own abilities as a musician, which undercuts his/her own verbal pronouncements; thus, the unconscious misfirings of the guitar solo speak a truth that the singer doesn't acknowledge verbally. The whole idea of the words and music coming from another place, from which the artist is partially alienated, is quite profound because this place is the unconscious—the site of so much artistic production.
- What does it mean to declare love anyway? "Love" can mean almost anything. What expression of love was ever simple or direct? When we do hear the key words "I love you," they are offered as a throwaway subclause before being immediately swept away without room to breathe (or for the other to interject with a rejection?) in the melodic phrase as the emphasis returns to "words don't come easy" (see Example 0.1). What the singer is perhaps hoping for is something bigger than can be embodied in the music itself; the gesture of writing the song in the first place and the noble intention behind it are the real message. Actions speak louder than words. To this extent, the song is basically a negated placeholder; or, perhaps, we could go further and propose that the more pathetic the song, the more pathetic (and therefore loveable) the gesture of writing it. The quality of the song is thus believed to be inversely proportional to the love generated by it. He believes in his effort, not his abilities.
- F. R. David is famous for wearing sunglasses in all weathers, indoors and out. We can't assume that the protagonist in the song, who presents his ego as one thing to preserve another thing beneath, is the same persona as F. R. David who doesn't allow us to see the windows to his soul. However, as we will find in this book, it is tempting to wonder.

And by the time our readers have undertaken our "adventures"—which we believe to be a fascinating study of how we can listen to the voices of the unconscious within popular music, through its cathexes, its neuroses, its psychoses, its perversions, and many other things that we'll introduce you to—we hope to enrich your conceptions of the complex places from and mechanisms by which music and the unconscious speak to us. As you will see, the book is left open. There is no "conclusion," no cadence to wrap up the book. Instead, we'd ask you to finish your reading by listening again to F. R. David's "Words," gaze through the song, and reapply the concepts you've encountered through our adventures in psychoanalysis and popular music. If we do our job right, you'll never let it be said that David's "Words," nor any other pop song, are "simple."

## Popular Music and Psychoanalysis?

If Sigmund Freud used dreams to explore the unconscious, we contend that, were he to write today, he might rather choose popular music as his playground. Psychoanalysis as initiated by Freud at the turn of the twentieth century marked a point at which a primary assumption of philosophy—that a basic and/or universal capability of our minds is that they work according to reason—was seriously challenged. Psychoanalysis shows that underneath the conscious mind—the part that appears to be rational—there is an unconscious that is characterized by its irrationality; it is thus *ein andere Schauplatz* (another scene). This unconscious is completely different to the conscious mind. The great thinkers of psychoanalysis show us that instead of operating logically, the psyche rests on a number of processes characterized by needs or demands that are neither capable of being known nor processed via reason. Freud, the founding figure of this discipline, created a new set of terms to describe these processes within the psyche; many of these terms are tossed around casually today, but in Freud's system, they have very precise and rigorously conceived meanings. The discipline has changed dramatically over the years, but we must remember that it was one of the key intellectual revolutions of the twentieth century. While psychoanalysis is often very different to modern-day therapeutic techniques in clinical practice within psychology or psychiatry, it, nonetheless, retains its revolutionary intellectual power, touching so many branches of aesthetics and culture studies.

"Music" has always been there to support intellectual revolutions. Noted later twentieth-century philosophers of the unconscious, such as Gilles Deleuze or Slavoj Žižek, draw candidly on music, but this tends toward highbrow art-music. This is representative of a longer tradition of psychologically rich philosophy engaging with music. The modern instantiation of this focused on the nexus of Richard Wagner and philosopher Arthur Schopenhauer as the center of investigation (or on Pierre Boulez and Olivier Messiaen in Deleuze's case). Philosophers often pick up on specific musical examples to exemplify the topic under discussion, often with limited musical understanding (with the exception, perhaps, of Theodor Adorno) or precision. The post-Freudian psychoanalyst Melanie Klein famously wrote on Ravel's music to explain aggression in childhood ("Infantile Anxiety Situations Reflected in a Work of Art and in the Creative Impulse," 1929), but focused on the narrative plot of Ravel's opera, barely acknowledging the music itself (except for a passing reference to some frogs "lamenting in thirds").[6]

We find more *musical* precision in the academic discipline of musicology, which has long since adopted the psychoanalytic language of Freud (Feder 1992, Keller 2003, Wilson 2017), Jung (Donington 1963), and, more recently, Jacques Lacan (Kramer 1990, Klein 2015, Schwarz 2006), but often doesn't present the bigger picture in terms of the key role of the *unconscious* in the history (and particularly the *recent* history) of ideas, a role that has continued to evolve in philosophical discourse since the millennium; for example, theories of unconscious production run through the writings of Mark Fisher and other post-Deleuzian cybernetic theorists (Fisher 2014). Additionally, of the many Freudian innovations, the role of the unconscious is perhaps most publicly accepted, where theories such as the "Oedipus Complex," "Interpretation of Dreams," or "the Death drive" can attract resistance, often because they are taken out of context of the overarching framework of the unconscious. It is almost fair to say that even with music critics such as Hans Keller in the 1970s, musicology has been keen to take on psychological concepts selectively (however judiciously).

Psychoanalytic investigation in music has long been rooted in the tradition of Western classical art music, the implication being that only the most intricately constructed art-music, particularly opera, can register the subtle complexities of the unconscious mind. Yet, this need not be so; perhaps popular music, with its generally more modest artistic goals, less academic compositional intent, and closer resonance with the populous, can speak to us more directly—in all of the music's rawness and vitality than its classical counterparts—about the unconscious that generates it and is, in turn, generated by it. While we find that the directness of globally distributed popular music to speak from one unconscious subject to another (mediated, of course, through layers of consciousness) can in fact facilitate a clearer consideration of the concepts than perhaps more "refined" classical genres, we will, nonetheless, indicate areas of possible connection with other repertoires. In more recent times, pop music scholars have certainly been keen to engage with psychoanalytic themes, and we'll encounter some of these. And because, in the diverse musical landscape of the twenty-first century, musical subjects are speaking to us from increasingly complex psychological places and testing more and more the limits of rationality in their discourse, the psychoanalytical tools unpacked in this book can help us better understand increasingly complex musical utterances.

But "popular music" is a huge and disparate term, and authors naturally find their own musical playground. *Listening to the Unconscious* presents the fruits of collaboration between a musicologist and a philosopher, converging perspectives on shared interests in theories of the unconscious prevalent in recent discourse in both fields. And each author has stretched the other not only intellectually but also in

---

[6] Melaine Klein, "Infantile Anxiety Situations Reflected in a Work of Art and in the Creative Impulse," in *Psychoanalysis and Art: Kleinian Perspectives*, ed. Sandra Gosso (London: Karnac, 2004), 34.

terms of musical repertoire and approach. The musical "taste" of the book does not necessarily converge with either of our own individual or collective tastes (some of the music we love; some of it we downright loathe), but most of the music discussed has entered our purview because of the broad range of positive interactions with popular music in our lives. As both authors are from the UK, raised on a diet of Anglo-American popular music, and as the whole discipline of psychoanalysis itself centers on the Western imagination, we have chosen to focus on the music that we have at least *some* authority to speak about, and would not wish to imply universalization of the Western psyche into "world musics" or cultures that we have neither sufficiently studied nor been part of. We therefore retain the more modest goal of singing from a Euro-American hymn sheet, open to the possibility that some of the ideas explored could possibly be universalized, but not by us. If there is a common theme to the music we have chosen to explore, it could be music that tends to be reviewed and recommended by websites such as *Pitchfork*, *Audiogalaxy, Napster, Drowned in Sound*, the *Quietus, Pop Matters*, and so on. Such sites offer the public an ever-expanding canon of artists targeted at the intellectually stimulated and curious postmodern audiences (post-punk, post-pop, post-rock, and so on). Proliferation of a new catalog is not just a feature of the internet's capacity to distribute, but also a consequence of the transition of *criticism 1.0*, in the age of print media, to transnational multi-nodal *criticism 2.0* centered around websites. Our project offers a rigorous and psychologically thematized counterpart to "song-meaning" websites such as *songexploder.net*, which attempt to explore and unpack some of the potential hidden meanings of popular songs. While the implication with *songexploder* is often that the meaning is hidden because the songwriter has chosen to tease us by withholding the real meaning, our contention is that many (often competing) meanings are withheld from the songwriters themselves, just as the unconscious is withheld from the conscious.

Why specifically "the unconscious?" Despite the loose proliferation of psychoanalytic language in contemporary discourse, the understanding of the underlying frameworks that unite and explain such concepts is often found to be lacking. However, as engaged public theorists such as Žižek demonstrate (in his analysis of the unconscious of film: *Looking Awry*), there is a demand in readers to deepen their understanding and appreciation of theory through the artifacts of contemporary culture. The popular and influential work of the late Mark Fisher is particularly abundant in this regard— see *The Weird and the Eerie* (2017), or *Ghosts of My Life* (2014), or his *K-Punk* writings (2004–16), which use popular music throughout to help unpack the author's philosophical arguments, many of which stem from a close reading of psychoanalytic texts pertaining to the unconscious. The theorists of the unconscious called upon in our text, in tracing the structure of a generative unconscious, found not *underneath* the subject but working *through* it, provide a model for the flows of creativity and desire that precipitate the composition of innovative popular music. These residues or traces will be forensically analyzed by the authors to provide a cohesive and structured description of the components of the unconscious and the systems in which they combine.

The weakest claim we could be accused of making in this book would be that we are offering a psychoanalytic account of the genesis of the music we are considering. Essentially: that we are psychoanalyzing the composers and performers discussed. This really isn't our objective, nor is it something that would stand up to scrutiny. We are academics, not analysts, and our breezing through contemporary and recent pop music here doesn't permit the kind of slow and considered analysis that the practice of psychoanalysis entails. However, that impression of analysis taking place is certainly something that persists in this book, as it is required to set up our two stronger claims. They are, firstly, that some of the key terms and concepts in psychoanalysis can be explained with reference to popular music. This follows the recent trend in intellectual history toward popularization of ideas through pop culture, for example, Žižek's study of Hitchcock. But our final claim in the book, and the one that has energized its creation, is our belief that the process of trying to understand both music and psychoanalysis in relation to each other is rewarding. This book is a product of the age, of our age, and a product of the online proliferation of music and musical discourse since the late 1990s. There were many sources of this inspiration, ranging from para-academics, such as Popmatters' Rob Horning or K-Punk's Mark Fisher, to musicians such as Okkervil River's Will Sheff writing and hyperlinking on Audiogalaxy. These writers were not just interested in the rush of sharing their catalogs and linking similar artists and genres. They were about engagement with a song, with its meanings, and the effects it could cause on the listener. Our most sincere hope is that readers will get the same type of "theory rush" that we may have experienced, and that readers can plug into the cycle in which a deeper understanding of concepts leads to a deeper engagement with music and the casting of a wider net into the vast amount of recorded music available to us now.

Yet, while the impetus for this book is built on the legacy given to us in the formative years of our academic careers, we do believe that we have gone beyond these influences and are creating something useful in its own right here. We consider ourselves to be "good Freudians," and this text goes beyond the illustrations of isolated concepts in blog format that, though inspiring and libidinizing, were nevertheless always partial. We hope to have offered here the foundation for a more systematic approach toward using post-Freudian and post-Lacanian analysis in the understanding of popular music. Particularly with the former thinker, this is something that has been missing.

The psychoanalytic concepts and models we have chosen to illustrate in this text, much like our musical examples, should not be thought of as exhaustive or even as selected on the basis of being the most important. They are the examples about which we feel that we can offer a new or interesting perspective. As we discuss in this text, some psychoanalytic concepts are more germane to musical analysis, and others less so.

## Navigating the Book

The book has two broad sections. Part 1: Core Concepts attempts to unpack the key concepts from Freud and Lacan, providing musical examples and illustrations. Here we will establish the foundations of how musical works can intersect with, or be representative of, the human unconscious, or how they can embody that very *split* between the unconscious and the conscious. This prepares the reader to enter Part 2, where we embark on more sustained *Adventures in Popular Music and Psychoanalysis* through more refined concepts, requiring perhaps more original insights and more in-depth musical readings that require us to train our musical lenses more keenly on particular pieces of music.

The eight chapters flow along three separate streams that connect the philosophical-psychoanalytical and the musical illustrations: (1) music as an analogy of the unconscious (such as Schopenhauer's view of music as "direct copy of the *Will*"); (2) music as an account of the unconscious; (3) music as the site of unconscious production. The kind of psychoanalytic explanations that we aim for will be more thorough than those presented in musicological texts, and we want to ensure a broad readability by avoiding heavy music theory or sustained notated musical examples (where these are offered, they can be regarded as an aid to some, rather than as a barrier to others).

In the first two chapters, we shoot quick-fire musical examples from Prince to Sufjan Stevens, from Robyn to Xiu Xiu, from Radiohead to Joanna Newsom, from Dory Previn to Arcade Fire. These present core Freudian concepts and conditions from cathexis to hysteria, from narcissism to psychosis, from the superego to the pleasure principle. Each time a concept is introduced, it is entered in bold text; these keywords are contained in a list on page [000–000], which refers the reader to their first place of definition or illustration within the text. The psychoanalytical themes explored in the songs chosen become the *sine qua non* of later psychoanalytic theory under Lacan and his various critics. In Chapter 3, Lacanian theory and its limits are explored by considering the narratives of songs by Bright Eyes, and some of their milieu, before considering the key role of Lacan's "four discourses" using the Antlers album *Hospice* (with a few thoughts from Alanis Morissette where the Antlers fail us).

The second part of the book takes leave of the more foundational psychoanalytic theory and breathes the more rarefied air of post-Lacanian thought. Chapter 4 attempts to tackle one of the big issues with so much psychoanalysis from the twentieth century, particularly from the first sixty years of it—its male-centered perspective. Accordingly, we examine its "phallocentrism" and try to discern how the discipline can still speak powerfully in the modern world when so much of it was one-sided. We take a double approach by examining Lacan's theories of sexual identity, what he called *sexuation*, and then exploring a maternal view of the psyche and unconscious formation from post-Lacanian theorist Julia Kristeva. Among other examples, we draw in some depth from Lady Gaga, Joni Mitchell, and Björk.

Chapter 5 offers a genealogy of one of the most troublesome concepts in psychoanalysis—the death drive. To follow the fortunes of this drive through the writings of key thinkers is to move through the Freudian view of the drive in terms of repetition in trauma victims (illustrated by Belle and Sebastian, and Lady Gaga), through four key Lacanian twists (illustrated by Nine Inch Nails, Soft Cell, and Amy Winehouse), toward a machinic aspect of the unconscious envisioned by Gilles

Deleuze and Felix Guattari, and Jean Francois Lyotard (and illustrated by Grandaddy and Radiohead).

Chapter 6 reopens the question of repetition, so tightly bound to the death drive in Freud. We now explore its positive aspect, beginning with Prince's "Joy in Repetition." To answer a newly posed question, we examine some of the roots of the Freudian system from Nietzsche's concept of "eternal return." The main musical example comes from LCD Soundsystem's "All My Friends," from *Sounds of Silver* in our alternative model of the unconscious's need for repetition. This model is one in which an *amor fati*, found and celebrated in Nietzsche, is cybernetically inclined toward acceleration.

Chapter 7 gets down and dirty with a view of S & M in the popular imagination, revisiting Freud's notion of perversion. Deleuze, although an arch critic of psychoanalysis, offered an extremely rich study from within the same discourse, which aimed to correct Freud's false assumption that masochism and sadism were corollaries of each other. Deleuze offers two incompatible species of perversion that, we contend, play out in the darker moments of popular music. We explore what we classify as musical masochism from Tom Lehrer and Marvin Gaye, as well as from examples of sadism by Cannibal Corpse, Korn, and Raw-Rap Relationship. We then begin to break apart some of the generically kinky songs by Rihanna to examine where the boundaries become blurred. Similarly, we listen to the heart-wrenching ballad "Masochist" by Christina Aguilera, and Pendulum's instrumental track of the same name, to examine whether it is possible to switch positions between sadist and masochist.

Chapter 8 presents, in many ways, a summary case study of our entire approach. Departing from other chapters, we now place a single album under the microscope. We follow a trail left by Lori Burns and Mélisse Lafrance, who examined P. J. Harvey's 1998 album *Is This Desire?* from a Lacanian perspective, but we attempt to use the full benefits of our book-length study to answer Harvey's question by throwing as much psychoanalysis at it as it can bear, offering further considerations of psychoanalysis's formerly strained relationship with "homosexuality."

It is our ultimate hope, through our demonstration of what "hidden meanings" can be found when we trawl the unconscious, that readers and lovers of popular music will be better equipped to interrogate for themselves—with perhaps newer, or at least sharper, tools—the music that they love (or otherwise).

# Part 1

# Core Concepts

# 1

# Charting Three Freudian Hypotheses with Pop Music: *The Economic, the Topographic, the Structural*

There are at least two important things that psychoanalysis can offer to listeners and theorists of music that are not provided by other domains of thought: (i) an account of what we might call the *wanting of wanting*, and (ii) the discourse of the manifest versus the latent message of an artwork. Freud used "*der Wunsch*" to describe how the psyche aims at things it wants. In early psychoanalysis, there was quite a discussion of how this term would translate into English. James Strachey, Freud's English translator, opted for "wish," while in French it was rendered as "désir." What both try to capture is a twofold aspect. Firstly, a wish tends to point toward an object of some sort, so we always wish for a thing or a scene, and our efforts are directed toward attaining that thing. The ultimate expression of this may well be that of a child in the run-up to Christmas, who takes a series of objects (presents) and begins to construct a scheme for desiring them (and, of course, parents and other adults help build this fantasy through use of all of the iconography of Christmas). But what is interesting about this scheme of wanting is not only the object that it focuses on, be it a bike or a toy, but also the *degree* to which this wanting is present, which we call the wanting of wanting. To simply demand would be vulgar. What gives this aspect of the process of Christmas its charm is the intensity of desiring seen in the putative recipient of this gift. And this intensity is not just quantitative but, in its fullest form, always acts within a wider field of desires. To put that another way, greed is base, but desiring is humanizing. Indeed, one of the very things that makes us human is the ability to correctly desire, that is, to situate our desires within a social field.

Partisans of other theoretical frameworks may say that the work we are doing here replicates concepts in other domains. Here we particularly think of literary criticism and its use of metaphor and metonymy to "get to the bottom" of what something means; and the reader will see that, to some extent, this is true, and we do pursue this goal. But what psychoanalysis provides, that such investigations do not, is this final explanation of the wanting of wanting, of not just *what* we aim or, of what the metaphor relates to, but of the *degree* of this wanting and, even more, of the genesis of its construction.

This chapter will move quickly through many different musical examples and insights, but we might start by considering some "first principles," using the song "Visions of Gideon" by Sufjan Stevens from *Call Me by Name* (2017). This is a fairly simple song with two distinct aspects that interest us. The first is that the song tries to communicate this same wanting of wanting. Music in general is uniquely suited to this task because it can convey degrees of tension and resolution by using the qualities and relationships of its different tones, rhythms, and chord progressions. While this book will explore many parameters of musical desire, or *wanting*, the chord progressions of this song (which can be found on any guitar tablature website) have regular phrases that move from a C chord toward a G chord at the ends of phrases. To take all readers with us, we should explain one of the fundamental principles of musical chord progression, which is that there is primal tension inherent in the G chord (which is called the "dominant" in relation to C), which can only really be resolved by a move toward C (where C is called the "tonic" because it provides relief as a "key center" and feels like "coming home"). If a songwriter simply acknowledges that we are satisfied when we are given this "tonic," he or she could simply give us this in the first moment of the piece (like F. R. David did as heard in our introduction) and then let us listen to it for four minutes. This would be crass (and very boring) and would not let us feel the true nature of our desires that are always more complex. So, Sufjan Stevens, like most songwriters, offers us a four-minute narrative that runs cyclically through progressions, sometimes substituting the G for an alternative dominant of, say, E, and sometimes substituting C for a different temporary tonic, such as A. By doing this, Stevens keeps our desire flowing in a regular phrasing, taking us on a much richer journey in which C is simultaneously both a point of repose and the beginning of a new excursion. There is nothing new or novel in this musical choice as it happens in just about every piece of Western music; desire is always perpetuated and rerouted; we can't let go of it; we want to want. And, if these musical devices are simple, or even common, once we factor in the song's central question found in the lyrics, the narrative they offer becomes much richer.

Park this thought for a moment. Some time ago we said there are two things that psychoanalysis is very good at explaining, and here is the second: the difference between **latent** and **manifest** content. This is, approximately, the difference between what is *shown* and what is *meant*. Here, we can listen to "Visions of Gideon." The most common refrain in the song—"is it a video?"—is an example of manifest content. Indeed, it manifests itself repeatedly in the four minutes of the song. We can discard the hypothesis that this manifest content maps on to the latent content. It is not the case that there is an object whose qualities we are questioning and are therefore asking "is *it* a video?" (say, we are surveying a parcel of VHS tape size and heft that has come through the post and remains unopened). So what is the video, if not a physical video? Here our interpretation comes close to the art of unraveling a metaphor as described above. The video represents, in our reading, both a notion of fidelity—because of a video's ability to record reality, that is, to be true to the reality—and also a metaphor in terms of romantic fidelity. The latent content behind the video is "is it fidelity?" that is, "is it real love?" In terms of the gap between the manifest and the latent, we can also see how the psychoanalytic approach offers us an extra interpretive element, insofar as it considers not only what the metaphor is but also the work that it does. This also features in the musical chord progressions in a very specific way. The locus Romanticus of musical desire was Wagner's hypererotic, Schopenhauer-inspired epic, *Tristan and Isolde*, about which music theorists highlight what they call a "double tonic complex"[1] happening, where we are moving back and forth or, maybe, even at the same time, between two interlocking tonics, the keys of C and A minor. And the same thing is happening here, albeit in a less sophisticated way, between these same alternative tonics (well ... between C and A major, which is a similar relationship). In Wagner's world, this partially represented the duality between the world of the rational and the irrational (or day and night in Wagner's symbolism), and it may well represent the same thing here. But, given the lyrical content of "Visions of Gideon," we might wonder whether the duality is not between the more obvious, *manifest* key of C major that begins each phrase, and a "hidden" or latent key of A that always peaks through the cracks in the regular musical phrases.

In this chapter we will show how this manifest content works to assuage the psychic tension associated with the problems posed by latent content. Here, again, we have a special property of music: its suitability for catharsis; and even if we only make it or listen to it at the level of manifest content, it can still do its work. One of the striking things about music is its importance to so many people. As Shakespeare put it, "The man that hath no music in himself / Nor is not moved with concord of sweet sounds / Is fit for treasons, stratagems, and spoils." But our collective love of music, which is so crucial to our sense of identity, fashion, worldview, morals, and social networks, attests to something more than an appreciation of its abstract structures and forms. Popular music hits us "at a gut level," to such an extent that it must correspond to our desiring structures and is able to stir, play with, and stimulate them.

This chapter builds from Freud's economic hypothesis, to a topographic hypothesis, to a structural model, which together form the basis of this book. The unconscious will be shown to be very unlike consciousness and to share almost no properties with it. It is a strange or uncanny place, and it is very difficult to work back from our conscious thoughts to a conception of what is in the unconscious, which, by definition (*un*conscious), is qualitatively different from it. While the mechanisms of the unconscious are something of a mystery, even today, Freud's theories remain one of the most complete and coherent attempts to theorize its processes and components.

## Economic Hypothesis

**Cathexis or Investment**

One of the trickiest questions when discussing Freud is "where do we start?" Freud created a huge number of new concepts, models, and frameworks that tried to explain

---

[1] See Robert Bailey, *Richard Wagner, Prelude and Transfiguration from "Tristan and Isolde"* (New York: W. W. Norton, 1985).

what was being produced in the unconscious. We choose to start with **cathexis**—a relatively esoteric term, not found in everyday English. To cathect something is a process of investment in that thing. There are many senses of the term investment, and cathexis spreads out across several of them. There is an investment in a military sense, where a general has a finite number of troops to deploy in fortresses and must decide which ones to invest which forces in. On the other hand, there is a financial sense of investment, in which a person would decide how many shares to buy in which company. Finally, there is the sense that an individual can be invested in an idea—to invest in supporting a football team, or a band, or a blog, or a political party; and this goes beyond the sense of financial investment, whose aim is just to make a profit. Additionally, a cathexis investment can be made in these areas and can also be withdrawn. The psychoanalytic concept of cathexis captures both the initial investment in the concept and the possibility of withdrawing or processing this investment.

In describing cathexes or investments, Freud generally makes a distinction between the "idea" that attracts the investment and the quantity of investment in the idea.[2] The novelty and importance of this idea of cathexis or investment is that it is no longer just the nature of the idea that is of importance; it is the amount of investment attached to the idea that becomes equally—if not more—essential for understanding its effects. This is our first move in our journey into the unconscious. Something is there, a proto-idea or notion, and has been cathected with something: the system has become dynamic. Just as a growing investment in finance may become a problem (a "bubble"), or a military investment near a frontier (a buildup of forces or an "arms race") may be a precursor to conflict, so we find a potential buildup in the unconscious is of consequence. This means that we need to consider two senses of cathexis: first, the amassing of an investment, and second, the dissipation of investment when it risks becoming unsustainable. Before we move on to a discussion of the methods by which the unconscious processes cathexes, let us consider a couple of simple musical examples of how these flows of investment become charged and discharged.

The electronic dance track "Open Eye Signal" by Jon Hopkins (*Immunity*, 2013) illustrates some key features of cathexis and its relation to investments of physical and psychical energy. In the official video for this track, an American teenager (Chris Chann) rides a skateboard for a straight twenty-four-hour period. The music and video (dir. Aoife McArdle) in tandem trace the lines of psychical investment that the boy devotes to the task, which is an outlet for his intense mental state. Early on, the music appears to respond to the different concentrations of energy (investments) on his skateboard tricks demonstrated in the video. The boy sees various sights that vie for his attention—burning bushes or lines of beautiful trees—and, when the boy chooses to invest in these, as we often see from the intensity of his facial expressions, the groove of the music intensifies. As the boy focuses more on the investment of energy through vigorous skating, the layers of groove–complexity pileup and the electronic effects

---

[2] For Freud there are actually two forms of investment, the first marking the basic structural capacity of the unconscious to bear energy and to transmit it, and the second of daily energy gathering around these earlier investments.

become more threatening. With pseudo-economic language, a *Pitchfork* review of the track describes how "the track slowly bubbles and bursts"[3] as the boy suddenly stops skating near an abandoned wasteland where graffiti on a shed declares "everything must end." The dance music relaxes in intensity here as the cathected energy is rapidly drained. The boy hitches a ride on the back of a truck (*à la Back to the Future*) and the song terminates. Of course, this is an EDM track that will perhaps, more often than not, be played on headphones as listeners go about their daily lives, making their own emotional cathexes. The physicality of this introspective psychical investment is useful, however, for highlighting the energetic nature of the Freudian unconscious in its ebbs and flows.

An alternative musical illustration of this could come from Owen Pallett's "I'm Not Afraid" (*In Conflict*, 2014). The question of *what* is being cathected in this song is heard in the lyrics—the singer is investing in a more complex gender position ("I'm gonna change my body"). But for now we will refer only to the structure of the economic charge/discharge as it comes through in the sonic narrative. Pallett's method of using loop pedals to record and replay his violin in live performance means that he is constantly piling up layers and layers of musical material, which cannot be sustained for too long, and the energy created inevitably has to dissipate somehow. Psychologically, this song is an attempt to overcome fear through the assertion "I'm not afraid," while all the time, the music beneath these conscious words is offering up tropes of pure fear: the high string *Psycho* stabs and the out-of-tune pitch bends that come straight out of a 1980s horror movie. At the song's midpoint declaration of "my salvation is found in discipline," this all boils over and there is a sudden dissipation of energy into a fragmented collage of factory and electronic sounds, as well as twinkling, wistful, nostalgic piano. Much of this energy flow in popular music, and indeed in many genres, follows this pattern of energetic buildup and discharge. However, the way this happens varies from track to track, and, often in combination with the lyrical content, highlights many of the nuances of this economic model of cathexis.

**Repression**

So far we have learned that cathexes in the unconscious remain stable until they become unstable. The next part of our story will be to find out at which point they move to an unstable state, and why. Or, if they do not reach the point of becoming overcathected, what sort of agency is capable of controlling them? These agencies will become the parts of Freud's economic hypothesis—his description of the method by which the unconscious invests ideas and then processes these investments.

In "Open Eye Signal" we discussed the cathexis of an unconscious idea, finding the quantity of investment to be at a safe or controllable level, but in more complex situations, an act of repression is needed to stabilize the psyche. One can identify this in the moment of collapse in Pallett's "I Am Not Afraid" where Pallett calls upon

---

[3] Larry Fitzmaurice, "Open Eye Signal," *Pitchfork*, April 17, 2013. https://pitchfork.com/reviews/tracks/15299-jon-hopkins-open-eye-signal/.

his notion of "discipline" to be the agent that stabilizes or "represses" the chaotic investments that have been building up.

In "Someone Great" by LCD Soundsystem (*Sounds of Silver*, 2007), the singer sings of his inability to talk about a dead friend. We speak in detail about mourning in Chapter 2, but for now, we can say that some notion of a departed loved one is capable of attracting cathexis and remains in the psyche. And beyond this, "someone great" attracts an investment to the point at which LCD's James Murphy (or his unconscious!) is writing a song about it. Whenever the singer is silent (the introductions to verses and breaks in the verse/chorus structure), there is an unstable musical force bubbling beneath the surface, embodied in the seemingly randomized chaos of sampled "blips" and "blops" of synth keyboard. This seems to be a musical image of the nonverbalizable trauma that is now kept out of conscious discussion—in a word: repressed. Repression is the process by which cathected contents of the unconscious are kept stable, even if they attract significant investments. If these contents remain stable, and remain in the unconscious, they will also remain hidden from the subject. As they are below consciousness, they are hard to detect and describe—something that is repressed has been prevented from becoming spoken or manifested. The complex dialogue between the singing voice (and specifically the human subject behind it) and the repressed content (the chaotic noises bubbling just beneath the surface) seems to involve the singer trying to bring this repressed content to the table—trying to stop it from being repressed, making it available for discussion rather than being unspoken or "locked in the basement" as he describes it. This is not really possible, because there is something stopping the repressed content from reaching the surface of his consciousness. This is where control is happening; the ego is protecting itself from pain or harm. As the song develops, the repressed "bubbles" do start to underscore the vocalizations—the singer and the keyboard are heard together; that is, they coexist, but do not really interact. The repressed is present as a sedimentary layer beneath, but is inaccessible to the subject.

The Scud Mountain Boys' "A Ride" from *Massachusetts* (1996) is a fascinating example of being able to observe the effect of repression in a piece of music. Joe Pernice, the songwriter, holds a master of fine arts degree in creative writing, so it could be argued that this song is simply a poetic account of events that took place—and therefore nothing to do with the unconscious. It certainly seems, on the surface, to be an account of a series of biographical events. The lyrics describe how, in the winter of 1985, a person is called up at 1 a.m. to provide a ride.

> You hid your face in a pocket book; you had your shoes in your hand.
> The road was slick and we never spoke. I held the wheel when I should have held your hand.

This seems like a straightforward recounting of what happened, with no hidden truth buried underneath. If we consider the musical accompaniment of this section, however, a different narrative can be constructed. The picked guitar is slightly hesitant, unsure, and laden with pauses, as if the narrative is being recounted with great difficulty. There is also a low, sustained slide-guitar sound that meanders, not unlike the described country road, in the midst of the texture, as if it is trying to struggle and find its own voice amid the hesitancy of the words and accompaniment. The moment at which the song becomes truly melodic is the final line of the section quoted above, "I held the wheel when I should have held your hand," where the tension seems to slightly break, and comforting strumming begins. At this point the sliding lap-steel guitar becomes higher, more prominent, more clearly defined. This moment of admission is swiftly covered up by a return to the narrative:

> You were frail like a skeleton; all you needed from me was a greater pain to soak you up. I look back and I don't feel one thing.

The opening section of this verse reintroduces this act of *forgetting by remembering*—that is, selectively taking some of the details as salient while repressing the unconscious force or charge attached to these events. The reality of the repression is confronted by the musical (unconscious) element of the song during the final two lines, "I look back and I don't feel one thing." Again, the music becomes melodic and stable, the tension is drained, and the impression to the listener is of contentment—yet in terms of the linguistic message, this should be the most devastating part of the song.

The final section of the song, which acts as an extended "middle eight" or "bridge section," but is too long and integrated to be limited by such a formal designation, accepts the reality of this repression and takes comfort in its efficacy:

> How come I can't cross that water in my head? How come I get the feeling though part of me is dead?

The initial line here expresses some awareness that something is missing from this account. "How come I can't cross that water in my head?" is really a question like: "Why can't I access this event? Why can't I connect this memory with the full charge of affect it contains?" The success of the repression is celebrated in the repeated refrain "... me is dead." This is undoubtedly the climax of the song; yet, again, there is no musical clue that this is a negative move. Indeed, it is the culmination of the melodic structure of the song. The fact of this death of self is not to be regretted but celebrated.

The song ends by restating the narrative—reconstructing the repression—but as a more sonorous presentation, effectively showing how the process "works." However, in this section, the "repressed" slide-guitar of the first verse is now the most prominent melodic instrument at the close—this struggling, hidden voice of the repressed has broken out, though the singer seems to be unaware of it, reaffirming that his repressive mechanisms are still working.

## Reality Principle

So far we have considered several examples of cathexis, but the outcomes from this cathexis have been very different. In "Open Eye Signal," we saw that the cathected object was manifested as an interest in a process, in this case skateboarding. In "I Am

Not Afraid," we heard the dissipation of a cathexis through an action. In "Someone Great," the psychic charge of the investment seemed to become so great that a change in the musical material tries to efface the consequences of the investment. And, finally, in "A Ride," we discovered an investment that was so potentially harmful to the psyche that it could not even be known. This section will explore the reality principle and, in doing so, help explain *why* there are these different degrees of repression of cathexes.

The **reality principle** states that something must be protected from these investments that develop in the psyche. It is closely related to the notion of **ego**, as it is the ego that must be protected from these investments. For now, we can just consider ego to mean a certain sense of self (Freud called it "Ich"—literally "I" in English). Why does the self need this protection? We have seen that the items in the psyche that can be invested are representations of objects, concepts, or actions. As these become invested with energy, we can say that the psyche wants something from them (these "wants" are described in more detail in Chapter 2). However, as we will soon begin to see, there are a number of agencies within the Freudian unconscious, and these various agents or centers can come into conflict with each other. The unconsciously cathected wishes that we have hitherto described are attached to a center called the "**id**." Id is essentially the sum of these disparate and quite strange impulses. It operates according to the pleasure principle and principle of consistency, as described in the next section—these principles want to remove all cathexis in the psyche and so want to return it to a state where there is no energetic investment. The primary means of achieving this pleasure is to give in to demands to engage with objects that have been invested by the unconscious. But the reality principle asks whether this is always possible, and if not, why it is impossible. In the case of "Someone Great," the deceased friend is not there. In "A Ride," the person to whom the paean is addressed is potentially accessible, but there seems to be no question of this investment ever being cathected in such a direct way. The driver of the car will never offer to hold the hand that he let slip away on that occasion. Well, why is this? Our answer comes in the form of the reality principle deriving not from the id but from the ego. The three verses of Bright Eyes' "Take It Easy (Love Nothing)" from *Digital Ash in a Digital Urn* (2005) provide a neat model of the reality principle's workings. The first things we hear are repeated synthesized sounds, tapping away an octave apart, the upper octave a childlike, naive video-game sound, the lower one a growling, dirty sound; we are clearly facing a binary opposition in this song; we might have an angel and a demon on each shoulder, or we may have a simple opposition in between two people—one naive, one a seducer. In the first verse, we are told of a liaison that has a substantial cathexis attached to it:

> You took off your clothes, left on the light / You stood there so brave / You used to be shy / Each feature improved, each movement refined and eyes like a showroom.

However, in the second verse we witness this tryst ending with an unpleasant ingress of reality in which she writes on a cartoon notepad: "Everything is as it's always been. This never happened. Don't take it too bad it is nothing you did … You're a sweet little kid but I am a woman." Any cathexis directed toward this individual would now be futile, as not only did "this never [Happen]," but "something [has died and no one can] make it live." The singer is "a sweet little kid but [she] is a woman." The brutality of this note is such that the sense of the singer's self would be put in severer danger if, in reality, he tried to revisit his desires toward the cartoon cat pad scribbler. In such a situation, the ego, or self, blocks any attempt at cathexis that may be made by the unconscious. So, while the unconscious id remains capable of directing cathexis at the notion of this person, the ego blocks any attempts to pursue this investment. When this happens, the song's groove breaks down into stuttering, broken rhythms, which, combined with the song's mock-digital video-game aesthetic, gives the impression that the system is being hijacked. When the desires expressed in the encounter are later revisited, this encounter with reality has transformed the ego/self in such a way that it fantasizes a state of invulnerability to a repeat of such hurt.

> Now I do as I please and lie through my teeth / Someone might get hurt, but it won't be me.

The protagonist admits to being "a little bit empty" to make it difficult to get close to. S/he promises no arguments, "we will always agree," and promises a clean and "kind" breakup when the time inevitably comes. The singer reflects that "since then I've been so good at vanishing," a line sung with a new reverb that casts the voice into the distance of memory, as if the ego that could be hurt is now removed from the equation. A touching part of the song comes when Bright Eyes' singer Conor Oberst sings, "But if you stay too long inside my memory, I will trap you in a song tied to a melody and I will keep you there so you can't bother me." The system works, but it is fragile. Then we hear a musical "outro" when the voice disappears and is replaced by a melody "sung" inside the head, played on a childlike electronic synth instead of a voice. The melody, which should be beautiful (and is, in the song), is offered as a threat and becomes enacted as something violently suppressive, but suppressive against the self and the act of engagement with the beautiful melody.

The efficacy of the reality principle in such cases can be questioned—see Bright Eyes' subsequent song "Classic Cars" from *Cassadaga* (2007) in which the same scenario—the impossibility of remaining in a fixed relation with a loved object—repeats. However, the reality principle, according to Freud, is sovereign in the psyche. That which the pleasure principle (see below) invests in can be confined to the level of unconsciousness—that is, repressed—and effectively remain censored. The musically simplistic verses of "Classic Cars," therefore, flow by at a regular pace as the singer describes the past, but as soon as we focus on the present, the music hurtles toward an aggressive attempt to release trapped energy—"You can go right out of your mind trying to escape." After another return to the simple past (a past of ego-defense and adherence to the reality principle), we are finally asked to reflect on an equally unpleasant sense of the present that expresses regret and failure of this principle to bring about an effective change:

> And they keep moving at a glacial pace / Turning circles in a memory maze /

These lines clearly register the failure of the protagonist's vanishing strategy, though he seems always prepared to take it to a new level of intensity and build walls around himself.

> I made a new cast of the death mask that is going to cover my face / I had to change the combination to the safe / Hide it all behind a wall, let people wait.

Musically, the lines are once again accompanied with a damming-up and subsequent draining of pent-up energy, showing us perhaps the failure of that strategy.

## Pleasure Principle/Principle of Consistency

We have so far considered the process by which energy is invested in the unconscious. The two principles described here form the mechanism that compels the liquidation of these investments. To want zero cathected energy in the unconscious is called the **principle of consistency**. It is closely related to the **pleasure principle**, which states that the easiest way of achieving an optimal dissipation of cathexis is by allowing unconscious impulses to be acted upon—that is, to prevent their censorship and repression under the reality principle.

A classic song that speaks strongly to the pleasure principle is Bruce Springsteen's "Born to Run" (*Born to Run*, 1975). At every stage of this song, there is a new cathexis to be discharged. The protagonists search only new experiences and constantly higher levels of excitement, in which pleasure is feeding off itself, and all elements of the song are selected with pleasure as the core principle of construction. This may be registered as yet another saxophone solo, the addition of yet more instruments, a new guitar solo, a Hammond organ, an extra beat in an extra bar—everything is about the pure joy of excess. The high-speed thrill of motorcycling on "suicide machines" may speak of a reckless adult world, but the basic impulse is childlike in its simplicity; from Peter-Pan-like evocations of "Wendy" to the occasional "music box" riff, we are reminded that this is a simple imperative to enjoy. Three minutes into the song comes the only blockage—a traffic jam is described in the lyrics but the interruption was primarily a musical breakdown—a "bridge" section; what follows is an even louder celebration than before. The psyche has absorbed the negative impact and interpreted it as pleasurable. After this thrilling energetic spending spree, the song slowly calms down to the state where we can relax—this is the optimal dissipation of cathexis of the pleasure principle.

## Censorship

We are starting to build up quite a complex economic model of the psyche, and now we come to our penultimate component, which is the **censor**. Freud hypothesized that there must be an agent doing the repression, something that can determine what must be censored, and what can begin to pass from the unconscious to preconscious thought or action operating under the pleasure principle. The unconscious is going to work over the desire being repressed *just enough* to sneak it past the censor.

A song that exemplifies this process is "Hannah Hunt" by Vampire Weekend (*Modern Vampires of the City*, 2013), a song that, like "A Ride," retells a drive, this one taken with the titular Hannah Hunt. While there is no Hannah Hunt in real life, the real events that inspired the song are present: a breakup, a desire to turn that story into a romantic ballad, but the story of the actual events is excessively charged with unconscious energy, and therefore problematic for the psyche.[4] This story is therefore repressed. How does this song get written if the content is being blocked by the censor? That which is efficacious in discharging the energy stored is just about different enough in its manifest content (what is presented) from the latent content (what is meant) that it can get past the censor while still doing the work of the unconscious. So there is still a lover, a journey in time, a sense of hurt, a desire for cathexis (draining the energy associated with this memory). The solution is that none of these appear in the form that was censored. The text has been changed to retain the initial repression of these ideas.

What has not been changed as much is the musical unconscious of the song—the feeling of liberation after the moment of cathexis (the second of the repeated choruses that starts at 3:00). The way that these unconscious signs of the censored breakup events are revealed to us, and partly to the singer-speaker, is predominantly musical. The singer sings of how the magic of the world is only revealed through Hannah. The pure reliance on Hannah from the storyteller is registered in the spartan texture that he constructs (low, insecure drums, the noises of waves at the opening, incoherent and intermittent electric instruments that fade in and out of the soundscape). As he adds new elements to the song's image content, new instruments swoop in and out, always representing a distorted, detuned, dissonant version of the images he produces. When he sings of the "hidden eyes" that watch the lovers, we hear fragmented glissandi slide from a string bass to represent these unseen forces that he paranoically imagines—and which, he insists, see what he is thinking—belong to Hannah. The "hook" of song is the syncopated, out-of-time piano riff that enters whenever he sings "You and me, we got our own sense of time." These sounds all work against the gentle but direct and sugary voice of the singer to betray some of the dissonance in the relationship that his words are glossing over. Most is revealed in the chaotic instrumental break, when "our own sense of time" leads to a caterwauling of multiple instrumental voices, all very loosely fitting together. It is here that we understand that "we got our own sense of time" means a different time *each*; they are tragically not on the same wavelength, whatever the singer might be saying. The censor seems to be admitting some of the unconscious narrative into the manifest content of the lyrics, but the musical unconscious seems to be giving us deeper insights into the latent content.

**Energy/Libido**

With the economic hypothesis, Freud begins to describe the psyche as containing reserves of energy that become attached (cathected) to certain notions or impulses.

---

[4] Well, there is a Hannah Hunt, Ezra Koenig's classmate of the same name, who you can watch going on an eerily similar road trip here: www.youtube.com/watch?v=9ZW1mZPjbVM.

According to the pleasure principle, the psyche wishes to exist in a state of minimal excitement—that is, to drain all of these energies. This leads to a dualistic view of psychic life. On one side, we have the accumulation of energy or charge to certain notions; for example, you can walk around town and see someone who conjures these unhappy associations, or even just see their name on a book or billboard. On the other side, we have the quest of the psyche to drain the unpleasant energies that these encounters create in it. These charges of energy have a sexual dimension and are often termed **libido**. Indeed, for Freud, the distinction between libido and energy collapses. Libido is *always* a sexual energy, though it might not be perceived as such, particularly for Carl Gustav Jung.[5] For Freud, the term covered "all that may be comprised under the word 'love'" that exists in the unconscious.[6] Given that so many of the popular songs we are discussing are about love, or its more erotic coefficient, sex, it will come as no surprise that this energy cathexis can adopt a libidinal dimension. But we must always acknowledge that this energy is primarily psychical energy, which builds up as tension and which needs to be released, but which could be directed or redirected into sexual or ostensibly nonsexual pathways.

This energetic charge is a common idea in music, which often builds tension, before releasing it—often through harmony, pitch, and what we described earlier as "the tonic chord"—the chord that resembles the "home key." Schopenhauer's theory of the human "Will" was later recast in Freud's "drive" theory, and Schopenhauer recognized this in his chapter on musical metaphysics in *The World as Will and Representation*, describing music as a direct copy of "the Will":

> Music consists throughout in constant alternation between more of less disquieting, i.e., desire arousing, and more of less quieting and satisfying chords: just as the life of the heart (the will) is a constant alternation between greater of lesser disquietude.[7]

In a well-crafted song, this moment of release can be deferred or suspended, so that tension builds and builds. This can create a substratum of harmonic cathexis beneath what the singers are singing about. In Hannah Hunt, the first stanza has two of these "satisfying" tonic chords; they occur on the words underlined below—"believe it" and "Phoenix." The tension lasts notably for almost two lines in the first instance,

---

[5] "It would, however, be sacrificing all that we have gained hitherto from psychoanalytic observation, if we were to follow the example of Carl Gustav Jung and water down the meaning of the concept of libido itself by equating it with psychical instinctual force in general" (Sigmund Freud, "Three Essays on Sexuality," in *The Standard Edition of the Complete Psychological Works of Sigmund Freud*, vol. VII, trans. James Strachey (London: The Hogarth Press, [1905] 1953), 218.

[6] "The nucleus of what we mean by love naturally consists (and this is what is commonly called love, and what the poets sing of) in sexual love with sexual union as its aim. But we do not separate from this—what in any case has a share in the name 'love'—on the one hand, self-love, and on the other, love for parents and children, friendship and love for humanity in general, and also devotion to concrete objects and to abstract ideas." Sigmund Freud, "Group Psychology and the Analysis of the Ego," in *The Standard Edition of the Complete Psychological Works of Sigmund Freud*, vol. XVIII, trans. James Strachey (London: The Hogarth Press, [1921] 1955), 90.

[7] Arthur Schopenhauer, *The World as Will and Presentation*, vol. 2, trans. David Carus and Richard Aquila (London: Routledge, [1819] 2016), 513.

underlying the sense of mystery about what the "gardener" says, the sense of tension resolving into the affirmation of belief. In the second instance, the tension we can feel matches the textual images of "crawling vines and weeping willows," arriving at the "tonic chord" on the word "Providence."

> A gardener told me some plants move / But I could not be*lieve it* / 'Til me and Hannah Hunt / Saw crawling vines and weeping willows / As we made our way from Providence to <u>Phoenix</u>.

This creates a constant sense of repeated storing of energy reserves, chaining them with musical "cadences" that offer a point of repose. But this happens also on a macro level in many songs that release an extended tension. It is particularly common when this is combined with a sense of strong rhythmic drive. We find this even in short songs like "Hannah Hunt," which has three stages of the song: (i) building tension [0:00–03:00], (ii) a moment of anger or release [03:00–03:20], (iii) resulting "tonic" harmony [03:20–end].

Examples can be found in thousands of songs, but a good example is Arcade Fire's "Crown of Love" (*Funeral*, 2004) in which the singer betrays the constant frustration he feels with his ever-growing love. There are many "C chords" in the song, and many tense "G chords," but they do not follow in the tension-releasing order of G (tense) to C (resolution) that we would need to feel satisfied. This gives the song an unbearable sense of tension. When Win Butler sings the line "my love keeps growing," for example, he deflects from G to an ever more tense chord of E7 (the "7" indicates a particularly strong sense of tension on an E chord), before returning again to the nonresolving course he takes. There is a resolution into a different key in the chorus—the key of A minor, closely related to C as its more depressed cousin (remember the discussion of the "double tonics" at the beginning of this chapter). This happens throughout the verses, but tension grows and grows through these constant deflections and the additional layers of instruments. Butler also reaches higher to really emphasize the words the "pain of love," cranking tension still further. But the libidinal energy becomes blocked around a kind of "bridge" section (though perhaps more of a "funnel") when he sings "You gotta be the one; you gotta be the way, your name is the only word that I can say." Here we feel lots of C chords, but there is always something wrong with them—the bass isn't right (what we might call in music theory an "inversion"), and it seems as though we are never going to release this tension. However, upon the second time through this refrain, there is one of Arcade Fire's trademark releases of energy into a new state at 3:45. Here there is a huge time change from a relaxed "triple meter" (which feels quite lilting, for all of the tension) into a vast "four-to-the-floor" discobeat that arrives at a plateau of intensity that simply moves through a repeated sequence of chords and desires nothing new.

This belongs to a category of songs that have what pop music theorist Brad Osborn calls "a terminal climax."[8] Such songs move from one state of tension toward a bigger

---

[8] Brad Osborn, "Subverting the Verse–Chorus Paradigm: Terminally Climactic Forms in Recent Rock Music," *Music Theory Spectrum* 35, no. 1 (2013): 23–47.

resolution and are often described in sexualized language. But many other songs will return to their point of origin, staging this climax as a homecoming to something familiar, but something new on account of the journey we have taken away from it. In Suede's ("The London Suede" in the United States) "Asphalt World" (*Dog Man Star*, 1994) and the following "Still Life," the final song on their most acclaimed album, there are clear senses of cathexis and climactic discharges of tension, but both explore different strategies. In "Asphalt World," the libidinal charge is made all the more dramatic as the song speaks of jealousy and displays bitterness. This uncomfortable journey eventually seems to be finished at 4:30, at the close of a guitar solo from Bernard Butler with all of the music stripping back to nothing but the hum of amplifiers. However, over the next four minutes, there is a slow buildup of instrumental layers that restore energy in a new way so that it can be released into something different to break the deadlock. When we return to the main refrain, everything is stronger now and more forceful. Brett Anderson's vocals reanswer the questions he had been asking ("where does she go? And what does she do?")—"*that's* where I go, and *that's* what I do." He asserts once and for all that he exists in the girl's head; he is what she really wants. This (probably delusional) state of mind is supercharged now on account of the epic journey of the instrumental buildup that reorientates our libidinal reserves toward a revised, more acceptable version of the object of his cathexis, or at least finds a way to revitalize the moment of release.

"Still Life" also uses this release model. The song references Maurice Ravel's famous *Bolero* (1928) in the orchestral brass section at the end. Ravel's *Bolero* (also appropriated by Rufus Wainwright) is a famous piece for building layer upon layer so that, from a tiny germinal cell, a mighty orchestral edifice grows. Allan Moore coins the term "Bolero form"[9] to describe this structure, referencing also the Doves' "Satellite" as exemplar of the model. The same format pertains to "Still Life." The musical quotation from *Bolero* is highly apposite here, because each verse of "Still Life" becomes increasingly overblown in terms of instrumentation, with a full orchestra eventually backing Anderson's vocals. Again, the song ends to a mere whisper as Anderson utters "but it's still, still life." Here begins the huge outpouring of energy, through the orchestral postlude that brings about a release to the entire album's tension with full orchestra hammering out a lush, majestic, repeated chord sequence, ending with the angry but quickly elided brass of *Bolero*.

## Dreamwork

Dreams are not to be likened to the unregulated sounds that rise from a musical instrument struck by the blow of some external force instead of by a player's hand; they are not meaningless, they are not absurd; they do not imply that one portion of our store of ideas is asleep while another portion is beginning to wake.[10]

---

[9] Moore, *Song Means*, 175.
[10] Sigmund Freud, "The Interpretation of Dreams" (Part 1), in *The Standard Edition of the Complete Psychological Works of Sigmund Freud*, vol. IV, trans. James Strachey (London: The Hogarth Press, [1900] 1953), 122.

So far we have described a relatively linear path through the psyche in which a notion gains cathexis and is either manifested in some way or repressed by the regime of censorship. An obvious question may emerge—what happens to these censored notions, as they sit in the unconscious, gaining cathexis? How will their cathexis be drained? Freud gives an answer to this question in "The Interpretation of Dreams," his longest text and a crucial one in the Freudian canon.

Freud described dreams as "the royal road to a knowledge of the unconscious."[11] By this he aims to capture the possibility of dreams and their mechanisms providing a framework for understanding the general operations of the unconscious. Freud believed that psychic forces of repression were weakened in the state of sleep, and things that the waking psyche could easily repress were able to slip by the censor in sleep. This opens up a possibility for the psychoanalyst to move backward from the manifest content of the dream to the latent content that it tries to express. And that would not just open up a way to see what the dream meant, but, if we can understand the processes—the dreamwork—by which this transformation takes place, we may be able to theorize about some of the workings of the unconscious. As the unconscious is, by definition, not open to conscious introspection, plotting the dreamwork is a vital mechanism for building any understanding of how the unconscious may work.

The dream begins in the subject's daily experiences. During the day, we experience a series of images and sounds that imprint themselves on the memory. The things that are most likely to make a memory (mnemonic) imprint are those that are already associated with important content in the psyche. Things that are hypercathected in the unconscious—that is, defined as important because of the quality of unconscious investment in them and because of their links to many other hypercathected concepts. Here's an easy example: a name. It may be your name, but let's go with the name of a former partner. This proper name is going to be of much importance in the primary process, the part of the unconscious where no desire ever truly dies. It may well be the case that repression is doing its job, and nothing of the memory of this partner ever comes to consciousness—but on this one day, when you walk through a market and hear someone shout out the name … perhaps it is just shouted at a naughty child tempted to steal an apple from a grocer's display … we find that that name still holds power regardless of the context. Suddenly areas of the unconscious that may have been long dormant are now activated, teaming with energy like the power station on Mars, activated by Douglas Quaid (*Total Recall*, 1990). But there are other snippets and samples of the day of lesser power that may get retained, patches of conversation, things that you have seen, all of the textures of the day.

The easiest musical example for the working of this process is the concept of the remix. A dream is essentially a remix of the sights and sounds of the day. It may not seem like this, because this daily content is worked over by the processes of the dreamwork, described below, often to such an extent that its appearance is utterly

---

[11] Sigmund Freud, "The Interpretation of Dreams" (Part 2), in *The Standard Edition of the Complete Psychological Works of Sigmund Freud*, vol. V, trans. James Strachey (London: The Hogarth Press, [1900] 1953), 608.

unlike the thing that inspired it. For example, the song "Goth Star" by Pictureplane (*Dark Rift*, 2009) takes the Fleetwood Mac song "Seven Wonders" (*Tango in the Night*, 1987) and refashions an MOR rock song into the sound of someone on the cusp of remembering the hitherto repressed fact that tomorrow is his wife's birthday. And dreams are frustrating in this way. We often feel on the cusp of remembering a dream, or on the cusp of understanding a dream. They are fragile narratives that we understand not as a contiguous whole but as snippets and snatches that seem to anchor the rest of the text, just as snatches of the familiar anchor a remix in its original content.

As discussed in this chapter's introduction, the psychoanalytic approach to pop music offers a framework for understanding songs according to this new modality. This goes beneath traditional levels of analysis where, along with the manifest content of the song, there is a second level of content at the level of figures of speech (metaphor, etc.), in which manifest content is tied to an additional associative meaning. Psychoanalysis offers the chance to go beyond these figures of speech and discover a further layer of meaning underneath the manifest content of a text. This level of content, the latent content, represents the unconscious productions of the psyche that, though repressed, try to "speak" through the song.

We have used the terms "latent" and "manifest" already, when considering censorship and to understand the work of dreams we need to return to the same distinction. Many of the songs discussed in this chapter fall into this category by virtue of the fact that the musical content works against the sung text to produce a disjunction between the manifest content (what is said or sung) and what is latent (the truth that lies beneath the surface). Xiu Xiu's "Dear God, I Hate Myself" clearly falls into this category.[12] The singer obsessively sings "Dear God, I hate myself. I will never be happy," but the music is upbeat, happy, joyful, and anthemic of the self and the inflated ego. However, the case is not so straightforward, because it was written in response to a suicidal phone call from the singer Jamie Stewart's father in which the father berated the son. Singer Jamie Stewart recalls, "It is about the tension between feeling hopeless but also feeling as if spiritual love is possible and there for you if you want it."[13] The tension is clearly there in the song, but is not a tension given in the manifest content (the words are clearly self-destructive); it's a tension that exists *between* the manifestly pessimistic linguistic content and manifestly optimistic music. And this tension invites us to try and work back to the "true meaning" of the work, the latent impulses it tries to express.

One common feature in popular music is the inclusion of oblique elements that are not easily synthesizable in terms of any "true" meaning. Something is happening to distort and manipulate the true meanings that the songs want to express. Its most gauche manifestation is where the articulation of song words is deliberately botched, or where instrumentation is used to drown out key elements in the song (see Panda Bear's *Young Prayer*, 2004). It can also be heard in the use of a range of incongruous terms used in the song to stand for something else in such a way as to cathect the

---

[12] The analysis of this song is inspired by a superb essay written by a brilliant former student, Leo Kyle.
[13] Amrit Singh, "New Xiu Xiu Video—'Dear God, I Hate Myself,'" *Stereogum*, February 1, 2010, www.stereogum.com/112171/new_xiu_xiu_video_-_dear_god_i_hate_myself_stereog/news/.

original notion, but still hide it so much that this new articulation can pass the censor. A literal example of passing the censor via manipulation (albeit fully conscious in this instance) is the Beatles' famous attempt to sing about LSD. Their famed chorus would lose much of its musical charm if the group sung "Lysergic acid diethylamide" in place of "Lucy in the Sky with Diamonds" (although it does actually scan quite well with the song's melody; perhaps it will catch on?), but it would have been a surefire way of getting the song banned from radio. The psyche, however, achieves the same thing on an unconscious level and plays itself out most acutely in the Freudian dream world through the twin processes of **displacement** and **condensation**, to which we now turn.

## Displacement and Condensation

Condensation is a way of circumventing censorship by transferring affect from one notion to another. In cases of condensation, many affects or a single affect move to a notion that is interlinked with the original notion. Condensation describes "logical" steps aimed at circumvention of the censor, logical in the sense that we can fairly easily trace back from the manifest content they present to the latent content underneath. Displacement, on the other hand, can be a much bigger leap, in which one concept moves to another one that is harder to relate back to it.

Jacques Lacan later developed these Freudian notions, but a brief description of why there is a difference between them could involve the thought experiment of two hypothetical unconsciousness. Imagine a "big unconscious" that is shared by all of us—in which concepts link together in certain ways: either by association (Pizza–Naples) or structurally (cat–hat–mat). Moves between these concepts will be condensations. There is also a "little unconscious" that is solely individual—so if I have eaten an "important" Pizza in Paris, the link becomes "Pizza–Paris," not "Pizza–Naples." This is more like a displacement, because the link seems more arbitrary.

An example of condensation in music would be the very catchy song "Maps" sung by Karen O of the Yeah Yeah Yeahs (*Fever to Tell*, 2009). Here we have the key notion in the chorus of "maps."

> Maps / Wait, they don't love you like I love you

It would seem very unlikely that the real cause of regret here is the unloving nature of maps (unless one is seriously invested in Korzybski's notion that "the map is not the territory").[14] M.A.P.S. here stands acronymically for "My Anthony Please Stay," which is the true message. This notion is, however, subject to censorship; it cannot be sung without injuring the ego, and a solution must be found in the use of this acronym. Again, the message is just different enough from the latent message to bypass censorship. One can hear the narrowness of this distance in the vocal effects applied to "maps" as sung in the chorus. The message cannot come directly as a sung

---

[14] Alfred Korzybski, "A Non-Aristotelian System and Its Necessity for Rigor in Mathematics and Physics," *Proceedings of the American Mathematical Society*, New Orleans, LA, December 28, 1931.

"maps," but is further distorted into a melismatic "maa-aa-aa-aa-aa-aa-haa-aa-aa-ps." No other words are subject to such transformations ("say" is repeated at points but not distorted). Indeed, the words are hardly audible as "maps" unless we happen to know the title of the song we are listening to.

A number of songs by Ryan Adams (now disgraced) replace the name of a partner with their hometown. Again, the notion is closely related to the original one, but gets just far enough away from it to get past the censor. This is a form of condensation (moving down one line on the birth certificate, from "name" to "place of birth"), in which Adams tries to connect up the romantic and musical energy he used to feel, the hook line being "Love don't play any games with me anymore like she did before. But I still love you New York." The highly energetic Latin drumming and fast delivery of the words, as well as the joyous Hammond organ playing, all make this a hugely upbeat song that replaces the specifics of the relationships he had there with a general feeling of ebullience. "Dear Chicago" (*Demolition*, 2002), however, is a slightly different story. "Chicago" directly replaces the addressee of a letter, a former lover. The singer begins by saying he may have found someone new, but the letter reveals more as it progresses of his broken life, the simple major key twisting to the minor as he sings of suicidal thoughts and excessive drinking. He begins to sing to "New York City" and marks this as significant by raising the melodic register here, as if he is emphasizing to himself the perpetual reconstruction of the condensation. The song ends abruptly, telling us that condensation will continue to allow cathexis. It is interesting to note how sloppy these texts are in terms of disguising the repressed concept:

> Found myself a picture that would fit in the folds / Of my wallet and it stayed pretty good / Still amazed I didn't lose it on the roof of the place / When I was drunk and I was thinking of you

There is no way, when hearing the text, that you could consider the work or disguise well done, as the structure of these enunciations is clearly such as to be about a person and not a place. Again, the depth of the disguise is only ever just enough to mask the content so far as to escape censorship.

To return to the initial question we asked about what the psychoanalytic approach adds to our understanding of a piece of music, we can look at an example of a condensed text in the form of Clinic's track "Distortions" (*Internal Wrangler*, 2000). Fans discussing the song online can be found trying to dig down to discover the latent content under the manifest image of the condensed distortions. What is the song about? We would suggest that the mistake in interpretation would be to think that there would be just one thing, a single image that, if accessed, would explain the whole text. Instead we have a song that is capable, in its intricacy, of carrying several images at the same time. Ultimately, this gives the track far more heft, as it is capable of attaching itself to multiple formations in the unconscious and exciting them. Themes of childbirth, abortion, body dysphoria (the "Candy Says" reference in the first lines!), broken relationships and betrayal, the eighteenth-century novel—and, no doubt, others—all interplay. This is driven by an incredibly ambiguous vocal performance that sounds simultaneously like a choked scream, a sigh, and a swoon; is precise and pleading; is strong and weak; with a drum whose double register mirrors a heartbeat, a single tap its disruption. The prominent vintage synthesizer also makes the whole thing appear out of its time. This song isn't one thing but many, a multiplicity of forgotten moments all accessed by the themes it touches upon.

In the music of Pavement, we often arrive at more far-flung repressions through displacement. There is a subtle way in which the music and the spoken voice work as productive antagonists, with the spoken voice concealing a meaning that the instruments are implicated in. In "Zurich Is Stained" (*Slanted and Enchanted*, 1992), we hear Stephen Malkmus's characteristically out-of-tune voice as flat and rambling musically as his prose is a stream of consciousness, always skirting around a sense of clear, meaningful expression. Can Zurich be literally stained? If so, one would presumably need a lot of agent to stain a city. It is in fact a famously clean city. Again, we find that "Zurich" was in reality a sofa,[15] upon which an act of consummation had taken place. The result is a stain on Zurich, which can be reported and lamented in this geographical form, but not in somewhat more crass real terms. But the soiled couch is not the only stain in the song; the slide-guitar is hideously out of tune and becomes more so when Malkmus denies his "mistakes," with the guitar rising higher and higher in climactic waves. These wave patterns are so harmonically deviant that they are difficult not to hear as sexual moments as they dissolve into the upper registral joy. The constant bending of pitch sullies the purity of the melodic line, especially as the guitar and vocals are so often in unison, which is one of Pavement's trademarks (listen to the famous ballad "Here," for example). The "lead" guitar even bends skillfully when articulating phrase endings in the same way that the voice does. In fact, throughout Pavement's oeuvre, a key feature of the voice is its unusual diction and lyric scansion; its expression comes from its *Sprechgesang*—part talked, part sung—nature, finding a compromise as a detuned melody. Malkmus may be a mouthpiece of the music, but the real melody—the latent content—is somewhere beneath the surface and somewhere beyond his grasp; he can only try and summon it forth with fragmented dreamlike images. The guitar, however, is another displacement of the singer's thoughts, which represents yet another dimension in which his attempt to cover up his mistakes comes through. These musical mistakes (no-one would actually think that this sounds ok!) are artistic displacements for the unpalatable experience just as surely as the construction of Zurich that is so stained. Note the earlier condensation of the notion of "relationship" moving to the notion of the "couch." Displacements and condensations can happen in many stages and in many dimensions, until the notions have been manipulated to the point where they can pass the censor.

In Pavement's "Silence Kid" (*Crooked Rain, Crooked Rain*, 1994), the ambiguity of the words "kid" and "kit," and the song's focus on the act of drumming as an expressive device, underlie the fact that Malkmus's words are attempting to entice the "silence kid" to open up about, among other things, his troubled family. Unusually, the song

---

[15] See Danny Wright, "10 of the Best," *The Guardian*, January 6, 2016. www.theguardian.com/music/musicblog/2016/jan/06/pavement-10-of-the-best.

opens with the drums, foregrounding the drummer's rolls around the tom-toms to announce that this is a drum-driven song, and that the drum is the unsung voice, just as the melodic guitar was in "Zurich Is Stained." The drums are highlighted again as the driving force when the song breaks down its texture at 2:10 as the drummer clicks his sticks four times as if to begin the song again, now at a much slower tempo, and the lyrics describe the act: "Hand me the drumstick, snare kick, blues call upon I knew myself in / Into the spotlight, ecstasy feels so warm inside." But now the confusion arises—is the singer the "silence kid" himself? Is he a pseudotherapist? The roles are blurred, and, like the famous Freudian free association technique, Malkmus moves from the word "chewing" to its near homonym "screwing," and from that to the brutally honest admission of "screwing myself with my hand," which the entire discourse of the song seems to have tried to cover up. And now, in a moment when the instruments have dropped out to leave the singer exposed, we now have a picture of what is really going on. Whether we take this as literally as a narrative in which music is a masturbation coverup, it highlights the ego-defense of displacements and condensations that music itself provides—instead of masturbating, the drummer exchanges his penis for a drumstick. Music, then, is here more than a simple displacement activity, offering a form of **sublimation** through elevation of a base urge into something more socially and artistically acceptable. This curious moment, where the singer admits to himself the base activity underneath the obfuscating prose, is not generally accessible to us in such songs; more often than not, such underlying forces are not allowed to be passed through the censor (in this case, perhaps, it comes forth as a summons from the psychoanalytic situation—"come on kid, talk about your family").[16]

Another consequence of condensation and displacement is the tendency of certain signs to become tropes of genres of music. Any emo fan knows that no canonical album can be made in the genre without references to the "hospital," or a (probably automotive) "accident." To listen to a complete set of emo tropes in one song, see Brand New's "The Quiet Things No-One Ever Knows" (*Deja Entendu*, 2003).

## Secondary Revision; Conditions of Figurability

Two often overlooked mechanisms of the dreamwork are the **conditions of figurability** and **secondary revision**. These processes work over the fragmentary images and often discontinuous scenes that the daily residues and displacement and condensation have produced. In doing so, they create a text that is minimally coherent—as with many other processes of the unconscious, such as repression—the concept changes just enough to bypass the force that blocked it. A dream that took on this texture would be deeply

---

[16] This kind of discourse is common in Pavement. Listen to their farewell song, "Carrot Rope" from their last album *Terror Twilight* (1999). There is much online speculation over what the "carrot rope" actually is—a "joint," a "penis," or something different. Is the song about smoking, masturbation ("Carrot rope; feel my thrill"), or even childhood trauma ("hey little boy, would you like to know what's in my pocket or not?")? The song is also rich with word-associative displacements and condensations ("Harness your hopes to the folks with the liquor with the ropes, red, red ropes, periscopes").

frustrating—perhaps to the point where one of the primary requirements of sleep, that is, that it is restful, would be violated and the dreamer would awake. This process of reworking a text appears isomorphic with the notion of the *mashup*, in the works of, for example, Girl Talk, where snippets are combined in such a way as to appear whole. It can also be heard in the electronic composer Burial's work. The tie between Burial and the mashup is perhaps more pertinent than we may expect. One of the intentions of these musical texts was to invoke the feeling of walking home from a club, late at night, and having the snippets of the songs running through one's mind. This act of (recent) remembering can be compared to the nostalgia for times further passed invoked by Girl Talk.

Burial's very compositional process can be likened to the crudity of the dreamwork. The program running the compositions, Soundforge, is a relatively simple one, and the samples and fragments the text is composed from are often very basic. Their appearance in the mix is often somewhat abrupt, again being integrated to a minimal extent. Often there is surplus noise attached to these samples, yet they are again included, even though they are minimally efficacious. This process of combining the sampled elements together is the work of secondary revision, in which the transitions between various dream-parts are stitched together in such a way that a recognizable dream (song) emerges. "Come Down to Us" (*Rival Dealer*, EP, 2013) is an example of this patching together. The song ebbs and flows, with the samples joining to create distinct parts, before falling into pauses or having samples stuck over imperfections like Elastoplasts, allowing the dreamlike musical text to stumble forward to the next moment of (near) disintegration.

The conditions of figurability are more practical processes in the making of a dream. The dream text is primarily pictorial, although in this book we mainly discuss sound. The question of figurability is this—what image (sound) can the unconscious use to represent a particular concept? The McDonalds of Burial's "In McDonalds" (*Untrue*, 2017) is presumably chosen for the uncanny mélange of familiarity and impersonalness that a late-night visit to this corporate chain can engender. Burial's use of a Lana Wachowski address in "Come Down to Us" is similarly selected as it provides a form in which the underlying message of the song can be meaningfully rendered. The fragmentary messages of the song: "Don't be afraid to step into the unknown ... you are a star to me ... there's no one quite like you" could be taken for the platitudes of a love song and miss the intended mark. Hence the selection of this short speech at the end as a means of representing the intended, manifest message. Similarly, synthesized handbells are used in the same song, which conjure teenage memories of East 17's "Stay Another Day"[17] (*Steam*, 1994), pulling the listener back to a time of innocence.

## Dreamlike Texts

Dreaming has often been compared with "the ten fingers of a man who knows nothing of music wandering over the keys of a piano"; and this simile shows as well

---

[17] In itself this is a distorted text, which, though manifestly presenting as a love song, has since been explained by composer Tony Mortimer as being about the death of his brother.

as anything the sort of opinion that is usually held of dreaming by representatives of the exact sciences. On this view a dream is something wholly and completely incapable of interpretation; for how could the ten fingers of an unmusical player produce a piece of music?[18]

Freud used the study of dreams—"the royal road to a knowledge of the unconscious"—to access the workings of the unconscious. Anything that is dreamlike—that has gone through displacement and condensation, that has a different manifest meaning and latent meaning, that shows interest in childhood obsessions, that has composite and badly sketched images, that has just enough meaning to form an interpretable content—all of this points toward a text that bears the hallmarks of unconscious influence. The Neutral Milk Hotel album *In the Aeroplane over the Sea* (1998) is an example of a musical work that was inspired by and often sounds very much like a dream. Jeff Mangum's compositional process was famously tied to the dream itself. When writing *Aeroplane*, he would wake in the night after dreaming snippets of music or vivid images and run to the bathroom (because he liked the acoustics there) to try and capture the intensities of these dreams on his guitar. The songs themselves have distinctive dreamlike qualities in several modes. Foremost among them is the nature of the imagery they try and capture, which are condensed and displaced dream images centering on unfulfilled wishes or mnemonic traces. Furthermore, the compositional process itself, and the effort of stitching together fragments into one coherent text, is remarkably similar to the processes of secondary revision and conditions of figurability.

At this point we may ask: Why were these dreams so important to Mangum? Freud shows how the unconscious repeats when it returns to mnemonic traces. The mnemonic trace is a kind of image or impression that is hypercathected, in the manner of a knot or a pool, meaning that it has indelibly marked the unconscious. A point where many things all come together. We can see these mnemonic elements in the work of Neutral Milk Hotel in the repeated imagery of childhood death or mutilation. In Freudian terms, these recurring images, when they crop up, can all be considered to stem from one originary trauma. The nature of this proto-memory, perhaps just a sense of chapters, positions, or a feeling, or perhaps more fleshed out into a developed image, is uncertain for Freud, as the act that produces the trace and the qualities of the trace are not necessarily correlated. As the psyche processes and tries to stabilize the trauma, it can create false memories or add extra parts to the scene, so long as it proves efficacious in discharging cathexes that would disrupt the principle of consistency.

The material through which the mnemonic traces are presented, in the form of the songs, are drawn, just as in a dream, from varied material of everyday encounters. So the story of Anne Frank, far from being the impetus of the album *In the Aeroplane over the Sea*, is simply a wellspring of material that is suitable, because of its qualities, to be transformed into an attempt to capture the original mnemonic trace that is scarred onto the unconscious.[19]

---

[18] Freud, "The Interpretation of Dreams" (Part 1), 76.
[19] This interpretation contrasts Michael Spitzer's situation of the album as an exercise in post-memory (see "Post Memory: Anne Frank in Neutral Hotel's *In the Aeroplane over the Sea*," in *The Routledge*

*In the Aeroplane over the Sea* proved to be far from being a therapeutic working-through of an interest in the Anne Frank story and the traumas of the twentieth century. Instead, its constellation of figures and scenes that shared isomorphisms with Mangum's traumatic mnemonic traces only intensified the cathecting of and repetition of this wound. This can be seen in his post-*Aeroplane* output, songs like "Little Birds" (unreleased) that circle around the mnemonic trace without ever attempting to sublimate the energies attached to the image.[20]

Joanna Newsom's song "Emily" from *Ys* (2006) combines a dreamlike symbolic text with mythology and memory in blurred images about her sister Emily, an astrophysicist, Newsom now trying to reconnect with Emily at a point in childhood before they took different paths. She sublimates the trauma of this separation into a dreamlike song, trying to work through the loss as we listen. It is clear from the beginning that the text of this twelve-minute epic is riddled with abstruse (probably personal) displaced associations that we can only dimly appreciate the symbolism of. Ironically, the clearest part of this dreamlike text is the account of an actual dream:

> I dreamed you were skipping little stones across the surface of the water … You taught me the names of the stars overhead that I wrote down in my ledger / Though all I knew of the rote universe were those Pleiades loosed in December / I promised you I'd set them to verse so I'd always remember.

To accompany this dream of skipping stones (a "real" version of the meteorites skipping across the sky that will soon be imagined), the orchestral accompaniment is mimetic, offering us broken, fragmented rhythms. When Newsom moves into the bardlike mode and offers us her "song," she announces this on her harp (which she then relies on for her accompaniment) and closes in the same manner. This mnemonic way of remembering facts is then given to us in a stanza about meteorites. Fully dreamlike, this soon becomes a stream of consciousness once again. The whole dialogue becomes a modern reworking of the formal contrast between baroque "accompanied recitative" and "aria," though the two soon blend together and become much less distinguishable. What is truly representative of the stream of consciousness—rapidly changing images—is the surging orchestral accompaniment that produces a constant stream of novel effects. Once again, then, the music is constitutive of the underlying energy cathexis that underpins the true link between the dream images and the real events. It brims with romantic surges of energy to accompany words or phrases of high emotional

---

*Companion to Popular Music Analysis: Expanding Approaches*, ed. Kenneth Smith, Ciro Scotto, and John Brackett [New York: Routledge, 2018], 400–15).

[20] In the Pitchfork interview, Mangum gave his own explanation for why he stopped writing: "I guess I had this idea that if we all created our dream we could live happily ever after. So when so many of our dreams had come true and yet I still saw that so many of my friends were in a lot of pain … I saw their pain from a different perspective and realized that I can't just sing my way out of all this suffering." We could argue that the opposite was in fact the case—as the symbolic displacements and condensations fell away, Mangum found himself singing his way *into* suffering. Marci Fierman, "Neutral Milk Hotel," *Pitchfork*, February 1, 2002. https://pitchfork.com/features/interview/5847-neutral-milk-hotel/.

affect, sometimes consonant and full of nostalgia, at other times highly dissonant and charged with energy; at many points it fragments into pointillistic orchestral images that may immediately present word-painting such as the fall of meteorites, but on a deeper level represents the fragmented narrative.

The strand of romantic, hypercathected, emotionally intense, lush orchestration that often breaks through is particularly significant. As Newsom closes the song, she returns to her own song-within-a-song, the *mise-en-abyme* about meteorites, but this version is now elevated to the status of an apotheosis with this same type of gushing accompaniment—hyper-real and hypercathected. Perhaps this process has been more cathartic for Newsom than Mangum's constant reopening of wounds. Perhaps this is because, while Newsom's actual wounds remain unspoken, alluded only through tangential imagery ("You came and lay a cold compress upon the mess I'm in" or "In search of the midwife / Who could help me"), the sister Emily was a source of comfort rather than a source of trauma. The loss of the sister is now replaced mnemonically with musical sounds and images that fill the void left by her absence.

## Topographic Hypothesis

**Ego**

We now turn to the question of what role repression plays in the unconscious. If all of these military-like movements of investment, censorship, and repression are taking place in the unconscious, the question is "why?" What is being protected, and from what? The answer is that the ego, the sense of self, is being protected from the id, the other place of pure drive and desire that resides in the unconscious. We have seen that socialization requires a reality principle in the working of the psyche, which asks: is this notion/action/behavior something that I (=ego) can do? We now see the protagonists of this principle: the id makes demands and the ego is forced to decide on the status of these demands. Those demands that are damaging to the notion of self become repressed.

The ego is a large part of our sense of self that needs to be preserved and protected by the defenses described above. Prince's 1980s persona was the party animal par excellence. Everything about this persona—his songs about how funky he was, his famous aftershow parties, his purportedly crazy lifestyle—constructs a carefully curated ego. Doubtless, Prince the man was as fragile as any human, but this rarely gets airtime in his musical persona, and he only wrote a very small number of sad songs. One of the most "sad" performances he participated in was the famous version of "While My Guitar Gently Weeps" with a supergroup of Tom Petty, Jeff Lynne, Steve Winwood, and Dhani Harrison at the 2004 Hall-of-Fame inductions, as a memorial to George Harrison. Here, Prince lurks in the shadows hidden underneath a red hat, emerging only to perform his blinding yet interminable guitar solo, which is one of the most brazen attempts at grandstanding on record, culminating in him throwing aside his guitar and walking off. He made the event about *him*. Yet, in his own "sad songs," he admits this frailty only by making the sad songs about *someone else*. Perhaps his saddest is "Sometimes it Snows in April" (*Parade*, 1986), a song possible only because it is sung not about Prince's vulnerability (which may threaten the ego—the "Prince" figure was all about fun, sexuality, funky music, regality and purpleness, etc.) but about his alter-ego, "Christopher Tracy," the American gigolo in the French Riviera who was the main character in the film *Under the Cherry Moon*, which the album *Parade* soundtracks. One of the crucial songs from Prince's middle period that was emotionally rich and showed fragility was "Nothing Compares 2 U," which, although associated with Prince, had to be given to his alter-ego side project, "The Family" (*The Family*, 1985). It seems quite plausible, given Prince's protection of his emotional life, that the reasons behind his famous bust-up with Sinead O'Connor was that her cover version bore his soul a little too openly and broadcast it a little too widely. One could argue that there are more sad songs from Prince's early period (pre-"Symbol"), but most of the songs with sad content are descriptive and lack affect ("So Blue" [*For You*, 1978]; "If I Was Your Girlfriend" [*Sign o' the Times*, 1987], which is perhaps more of a seduction song). Others such as "Empty Room" (1985, from the *Vault Songs*, 2001) were left in the infamous vault and unreleased. "Condition of the Heart" (*Around the World in a Day*, 1985) is the exception here, as it was released and is quite devastating, although, again, this ballad has two "neutral" protagonists.

The ego often has to be shored up. Consider one of Radiohead's most famous gestures—the famous guitar crunches that signal the onset of the chorus in "Creep" (*Pablo Honey*, 1993). It was originally inserted by Jonny Greenwood as an attempt (in good Radiohead fashion) to ruin the song. Instead, this kind of addition of affect to the chorus supercharges the cathectic moment of self-loathing in which the protagonist (Yorke, or a generation of teenagers) absorbs blows and shocks to the ego and turns them into a source of pride.

The fragility of the ego can be heard in the Nine Inch Nails' song "Hurt" from *The Downward Spiral* (1994). From the outset, the ego is absorbing shocks; as singer Trent Reznor sings "I hurt myself today," the fragile guitar accompaniment features a stinging, biting dissonance that the musical "ego" has to absorb each time, perhaps the equivalent to Radiohead's distortion. Notably, in Johnny Cash's cover version, these dissonances are eradicated; perhaps Cash's own musical sense of "self" as country-favorite could not allow him to be so sacrificing of beauty in his songs as to admit jarring dissonances; perhaps he lost some of his fragility with age? As each verse of the song intensifies, particularly in the original version, the singer constructs walls around his ego to help him absorb the shocks—these walls are the evenly strummed chords, the throbbing repeated bass, the pounding drums. As the song reaches its terminal climax, Reznor sings: "If I could start again / A million miles away / I would keep myself / I would find a way." The song then dissolves into a "wall" of guitar distortion—a new figuration of the ego defense. Throughout the song, there is an admittance of vulnerability in the singer's hushed, semi-whispered voice, registering the fragility of what needs to be preserved—the human ego behind the musical walls erected to defend it.

There is a link back to the Scud Mountain Boys' "A Ride" here, discussed earlier in terms of repression, which also leads us into a discussion of the id. The part of the singer that has to die ("how come I get the feeling though part of me is dead?") is the desire in his id, and it is repressed precisely because it conflicts with the ego's image of the self. Indeed, here we can now make clear what the function of repression is: it is undertaken to protect the ego (the I) from the id (the it). The set of desires associated with "the ride" have been repressed and are no longer part of the self.

## Id

We don't want to dwell on this too much at this stage. We'll have plenty of time to see it in action. We could start with Pearl Jam's "I Got id" (*Merkin Ball*, EP, 1995). David Forrest offers us a musical analysis of this song, using a relatively recent branch of music theory (called "neo-Riemannian theory"), which examines unusual chromatic chord progressions that have often rather *outré* effects that, in conventional music theory, were hard to explain.[21] There are certainly elements of id in the track and, indeed, the whole genre—the raw energy of the psyche that tries to present immediacy without refinement. We hear this clearly in the heavy rock choruses, which break out of the more stripped-down and refined verses. But Forrest is perhaps wise to focus on alternative Freudian concept—the "Uncanny" (which he likens to the weird oscillation of two chords D and B♭, because the song essentially misdiagnoses itself: we all "got id," and it's not a sickness). The lyrics describe a lovelorn individual, clearly in extreme psychological distress, compromised in self-care, fantasizing about a would-be lover. If there is id in the song, we might say that it breaks through in those more reckless heavy choruses, when we metaphorically smash up the furniture a little when he can't get what he wants. Id represents the part of the psyche that wants the most immediate gratification, so we would only find it in a pure form in a song where unconscionable acts are described. This could be hardcore violent or hypererotic music in which normally forbidden experiences are imagined—particularly the most depraved. Thinking perhaps of Britpop band Pulp's many songs in this light, "Pencil Skirt" (*Different Class*, 1995) is a typical example, in which the singer Jarvis Cocker injuncts "watch my conscience disappear"—there is no **superego** here (see below). Cocker borders on rape fantasies in the chorus, when, amid the pounding, thumping sinister minor chords that seem to replicate violent thrusting and pounding, he whispers: "I really love it when you tell me to stop—Oh it's turning me on." This all speaks of id, which, if unchecked, unleashes destruction and harm. The id needs a force to balance and check it so that the ego can survive and the reality principle can reign—the superego.

## Superego

Do you remember the ingress of the reality principle we identified in Bright Eyes' "Take It Easy (Love Nothing)"? That resolved itself in the signer's transformation from being the one who was left to the one who does the leaving. What happens in the

---

[21] David Forrest, "PL Voice Leading and the Uncanny in Pop Music," *Music Theory Online* 23, no. 4 (December 2017). https://mtosmt.org/issues/mto.17.23.4/mto.17.23.4.forrest.html.

3 minutes, 17 seconds of the song is the incorporation of the leaver into the superego of the singer. The leaver moves from being a source of frustration and disappointment to being an example, a role model whose modus operandi is happily stolen by Mr. Oberst. So, while ego is our notion of ourselves, superego is our notion of others, those who we could be if only we could operate according to their norms.

R.E.M.'s "E-Bow the Letter" (*New Adventures in Hi-Fi*, 1996) has one of the most literal song titles in alternative music. The dominant element in the music is Peter Buck's e-bowed guitar, which accompanies Michael Stipe's semi-spoken rendition of a letter he sent to River Phoenix before the child-star's untimely death. In it, Stipe sets himself up as a superego figure, trying to guide the young Phoenix through the perils of fame and mega stardom in the nineties. Stipe reads this letter throughout the verses of the song, but the chorus—"I'm taking you over"—and frequent introjections of the same line are made by Patti Smith, offering us an image of the superego appearing to come from another place—above—with a female voice. The idea of the superego as a little voice in the head, seemingly from above, that corrects us, keeping us on the straight and narrow, is reminiscent of the sustained E-bow that floats throughout the song (the electronic guitar-bowing device).

We can hear a similar attempt to become this figure in the works of Robyn. In "Call Your Girlfriend" (*Body Talk*, 2010), she sets herself up as the prospective boyfriend's superego, inducting him into the correct methodology of orchestrating a "nice guy's" breakup. The track begins with a low, "fat" bass growl, seemingly representing the dirty world of infidelity, into which Robyn condescends to offer herself as superego, dressed in white, with a positive, upbeat, high, angelic voice—"call your girlfriend, It's time you had the talk." Of course, in this song, particularly as the accompanying video unfolds, it's clear that Robyn's (protagonist's?) actions are purely selfish (a central section of the video sees her dancing more erotically and revealing a black bra underneath her white, angelic, feathery costume); she wants the lover for herself and, as we find in post-Freudian psychoanalysis, the superego is capable of playing tricks on us. But, at least on the surface of this song, the superego/id distinction is presented between two musical worlds—the low growl of the id and the high purity of the superego.

Loss of the superego can be devastating to the psyche, and we can witness attempts to construct, shore up, or establish superego figures almost in real time, in Sufjan Stevens's *Carrie and Lowell* (2015), an album about his mother, Carrie, and his ambivalent relationship to her as a superego figure following her death. At several points, Carrie is unable to fulfill the maternal role that Stevens wishes her to take. Consider: "When I was three, three maybe four / She left us at that video store / Be my rest, be my fantasy" from "Should Have Known Better." This appeal to the mother as a fantasy is supported by the sudden injection of reverb in the high guitars to give a sense that we are entering another realm—one of motherly love and embryonic warmth. Stevens's rest does not come from this image of Carrie, because the fantasy is incapable of doing the job he wishes—to portray the full mother as present, operating as a superego regulator in the psyche. The song's failure to use the mother as a superego is manifest in its ultimate disintegration into low, rumbling, chaotic string and sound effects, much as Robyn's "Call Your Girlfriend" began.

In many ways, the most interesting feature of popular and alternative music is the power that musicians have to construct themselves as superego figures, influencing the psychic development of generations of teenagers and, indeed, generations of artists. Figures in popular music emerge as having god-like status, who hold power over the imaginations of followers to shape their own music. Consider the figure, for example, of Dr. Dre in Eminem and Hittman's "Forgot about Dre," in which the rappers create scenarios in which they ask themselves to act like Dr. Dre, erecting him as a superego in terms of gang behavior (in the lyrics) and musical influence (in their record).

## Summary: The Structural Hypothesis

Here we terminate our initial discussion of Freud at a point at which others may have been tempted to start a Freudian analysis by discussing the three parts of Freud's **structural hypothesis**: the **unconscious**, the **preconscious**, and the **conscious** parts of the psyche. The different parts of the structural model represent different qualitative states of the psyche's contents. This section of our chapter will be relatively short, not because the structural hypothesis is insignificant—the very opposite—but because you, our reader, are already a chapter into a book called *Listening to the Unconscious*. The whole premise of this book is that there is an unconscious, distinct from consciousness, and our mission so far, and through the rest of the book, is to try and show how that unconscious registers in popular music.

Let's end with a very short history of the unconscious. Notions of an unconscious part of the mind keep cropping up in the work of German philosophers, starting with Kant, perhaps the most important philosopher of modernity, and continue through Schelling, Fichte, and Schopenhauer. Freud moves the notion of the unconscious further than any of his predecessors in that he makes a firm distinction between the processes and contents of the unconscious and the parts of the psyche that are available to us (the conscious parts). Once Freud has set up this distinction, he runs into a problem similar to the one that dualists ran into two hundred years before: if we have two things that are qualitatively different (unconscious and conscious thought), how do they interact with one another? Freud's solution was to posit a transitory zone between the two, where things that start in the unconscious (the **primary process**) begin to acquire the accoutrements of conscious thought.

### Conscious

The conscious part of the psyche needs very little explication, as you, the reader, are probably experiencing its effects at this moment. What we would emphasize at this point is that this domain is not the sovereign agent in the psyche, as Cartesian and even Kantian philosophy would posit, but a secondary process that comes about after the work of the unconscious is completed. But, although the system underneath consciousness is capable of repressing and distorting a variety of truths, it is not a false self. Rather, the self is the interplay between these elements of the psyche hitherto described; both the impulses of the id, constructed across the subject's history, and the regimes it has built up to differentiate an ego, guided by "reality," from these imperatives of pure pleasure and fantasy.

## Unconscious

Before Freud, psychologists thought of the unconscious as being qualitatively similar to consciousness. The contents of the unconscious were simply the mental contents that were not being accessed by consciousness at any given time. This model is something like the effect produced on a computer game like *Doom 3*, where the player traverses a dark spaceship with a torch in hand. Whatever the torch points at is illuminated (conscious), and whatever it does not point at remains dark—yet, even when not visible, this space is "there," available for access and essentially qualitatively the same as that thing being accessed. Freud's model is different. The unconscious, the primary process, is more aptly analogous to the hardware of the computer on which the game is being run. It has no similarity with the manifest image of the game, to the point of being qualitatively nonpictorial, but is a mechanical process.

Trying to liken the products of the unconscious to a specific piece of music is therefore a challenge, as the unconscious is nothing like conscious thought and so is not comprehensible to it in any way. Indeed, this is the whole challenge of psychoanalysis— not to describe existent components in the unconscious, but to come up with models, hypotheses, and analogies that try and give us insights into what may be going on. We might remember that Freud was well aware of the speculative nature of psychoanalysis, and his texts are peppered with acknowledgments that his work is provisional,[22] metaphorical,[23] speculative,[24] or in need of a unifying "metapsychology" that would reconcile all of the various models he proposes.[25] Think of the unconscious as being

---

[22] "We must recollect that all our provisional ideas in psychology will presumably some day be based on an organic substructure" (Sigmund Freud, "On Narcissism: An Introduction," in *The Standard Edition of the Complete Psychological Works of Sigmund Freud*, vol. XIV, trans. James Strachey [London: The Hogarth Press, (1914) 1957], 78).

[23] "It is only too easy to fall into a habit of thought which assumes that every substantive has a substance behind it—which gradually comes to regard 'consciousness' as standing for some actual thing; and when we have become accustomed to make use metaphorically of spatial relations, as in the term 'sub-consciousness,' we find as time goes on that we have actually formed an idea which has lost its metaphorical nature and which we can manipulate easily as though it was real." Josef Breuer in Josef Breuer and Sigmund Freud, "Studies in Hysteria," in *The Standard Edition of the Complete Psychological Works of Sigmund Freud*, vol. II, trans. James Strachey (London: The Hogarth Press, [1893–5] 1955), 227.

[24] Sigmund Freud, "Beyond the Pleasure Principle," in *The Standard Edition of the Complete Psychological Works of Sigmund Freud*, vol. XVIII, trans. James Strachey (London: The Hogarth Press, [1920] 1955), 24.

[25] "Later on I made an attempt to produce a 'Metapsychology.' By this I meant a method of approach according to which every mental process is considered in relation to three coordinates, which I described as dynamic, topographical, and economic respectively; and this seemed to me to represent the furthest goal that psychology could attain. The attempt remained no more than a torso; after writing two or three papers—'Instincts and their Vicissitudes,' 'Repression,' 'The Unconscious,' 'Mourning and Melancholia,' etc.—I broke off, wisely perhaps, since the time for theoretical predications of this kind had not yet come." Sigmund Freud, "An Autobiographical Study," in *The*

like a factory unit in a suburban industrial park: a half brick, half metal, nondescript box, from which we know something occasionally emerges (an equally unmarked lorry), and which we suspect operates according to a set of processes and rules. If you are set the challenge of describing what goes on within, but can only see from the outside, each guess will be necessarily provisional: "I think they are fabricating double glazing; that van had a glass rack." Freud describes the properties of the unconscious in "The Unconscious" (1915):

> There are in this system no negation, no doubt, no degrees of certainty: all this is only introduced by the work of the censorship between the Ucs. [unconscious] and the Pcs [preconscious] ... In the Ucs. there are only contents, cathected with greater or lesser strength.
> 
> ...
> 
> The processes of the system *Ucs.* are *timeless*; i.e. they are not ordered temporally, are not altered by the passage of time; they have no reference to time at all. Reference to time is bound up, once again, with the work of the system *Cs*. The *Ucs.* processes pay just as little regard to reality. They are subject to the pleasure principle; their fate depends only on how strong they are and on whether they fulfil the demands of the pleasure-unpleasure regulation.[26]

Following the absolute strangeness of the unconscious posited by Freud, we must say that the unconscious is qualitatively different to anything that we can know of conscious thought. We are reminded of Wittgenstein's lion: "If a lion could talk, we could not understand him" (1953, 223). Whatever is in the unconscious is so strange that it is hard to render its demands into illustrations. When we think of the unconscious as a timeless chamber of all of the desires and wishes that the psyche has ever held, the image that comes to mind is the discovery of the alien chamber in the film *Prometheus*, in which the desires (aliens) silently and eternally rest, waiting for their chance to become manifest. Each desire individually follows the law of the pleasure principle, but they do not communicate, nor form compromises.

Does any piece of music sound like the unconscious itself? The unconscious is a zone of pure demand, and we may be best served by saying that the unconscious is not represented by a type of music, but by the general desire to listen to music—"Put something on." "Turn it up, louder." Or, perhaps, in Tom Green's comedic "The Bum Bum Song" (1999), which ends in a series of incompatible demands: "Get the poo off my bum," "I want to hear the cannon." Do such demands make sense? Are they possible? Are they even conceivable? The unconscious does not consider any of this. It passes the demand up to the next agency, which must enact it or repress it. And, although the unconscious can't be heard literally, certainly not in full, we can hear

---

*Standard Edition of the Complete Psychological Works of Sigmund Freud*, vol. XX, trans. James Strachey (London: The Hogarth Press, [1925] 1959), 59.

[26] Sigmund Freud, "The Unconscious," in *The Standard Edition of the Complete Psychological Works of Sigmund Freud*, vol. XIV, trans. James Strachey (London: The Hogarth Press, [1915] 1955), 187.

some of it speak to us through cracks and fissures in the surface of conscious thought, through all of the mechanisms described in the economic hypothesis and, indeed, in every musical example discussed in the book.

**Preconscious**

Let's go back to our model of the unconscious as being like the physical state of a computer, and the conscious as being the visible output of the computer. How does one get to become the other? This is the role of preconscious, which takes the productions of the unconscious and begins to render them into outputs—that is, as actions or things capable of being conscious. In "The Unconscious," Freud describes the preconscious as one that

> devolves upon the system Pcs. to make communication possible between the different ideational contents so that they can influence one another, to give them an order in time, and to set up a censorship or several censorships; "reality-testing" too, and the reality-principle, are in its province. Conscious memory, moreover, seems to depend wholly on the Pcs.[27]

Thus, the initial demands—so many of them and so unreasonable—are made by the unconscious, and the task of the preconscious is to respond hastily to these pressures, either passing them through to conscious action or by repressing others. It begins to apply the reality principle to what is asked of it, considering the consequences of actions.

If we look for musical models of the preconscious, they will be like some of our dreamlike music, Pictureplane's "Goth Star" with it schizzes, snatches, half-formed impulses, and imperatives that lack sufficient expressive elements to become comprehensible, or Burial's equally transitory sounds, just hovering around the threshold of unity. Perhaps, a more elaborate version of this is to consider the differences between snippets of melodies or little lines of tune that a songwriter compiles and brings to her/his producer. There is a fascinating episode of *Song Exploder* in which Vampire Weekend's Ezra Koenig discuss the song "Harmony Hall" (*Father of the Bride*, 2019), recounting how he brought such a set of recorded snatches to the studio: a baroque piano here, a melody about harmony hall, a short guitar part, and how these components were then taken by producer Ariel Rechtshaid and fashioned into the beginnings of a song. This production is the work of the preconscious, to begin to fashion the unconscious' demands into the possible and impossible, those that can be taken up and those that cannot, those that must remain in place and those that can be cathected.

## The Next Step

We now zoom into these tripartite structures and examine music that explores the more intricate workings of the psyche. Our exploration of the basic Freudian concepts

[27] Ibid., 188.

in the present chapter has prepared us now to consider aspects of ego psychology (with concepts such as narcissism, mourning and melancholia, sublimation, defense mechanisms), the qualitative unconscious (with concepts such as drive, regression, the repetition compulsion), clinical practice (examining complexes, paranoia, hysteria, and neurosis), jokes, and humor. These Freudian concepts, as we will see, all play a key role in understanding the many intense psychological mechanisms, libidinal positions, and complex cathexes that underpin much modern popular music and its consumption.

# 2

# Freud, Music, and the Psychological Condition

Freud's goal was to conceptualize the processes running the subject's psyche. His method for achieving this was to begin with cases in which the unconscious elements of the psyche could be most easily discerned. We would then see clinical patients, with various illnesses, most famously psychosis, neurosis, and hysteria, as well as conditions with less prominent symptoms such as anxieties and depression. Then we would have subclinical complexes like OCD and other obsessional disorders. Then we have parapraxes (botched actions) like slips of the tongue; at this stage, the unconscious is revealed only in tiny snippets that sneak past repression. Finally we have dreams, Freud's "royal road to a knowledge of the unconscious," albeit a road that is very hard to discern correctly, as we discussed in Chapter 1. All of these things have two commonalities. The first is the fact that there is a repression of unconscious contents, which can nevertheless be glimpsed as they avoid various forms of censorship. The second is that these formations tend to take stable, repeatable forms. By this, we mean that they are structures. They have a certain universality in that, while they might manifest in different ways in terms of the ideas that subjects are expressing, they follow a similar organizational topography across subjects. We learnt about the dreamwork in Chapter 1, the processes through which all dreams are created, but there is a similar structuration in conditions like hysteria, where prolonged repression of hypercathected elements lead to physical and mental symptoms.

In this chapter we will look further at some of the structures of the unconscious that repeat across subjects. Psychoanalysis's names for these things—narcissism, melancholia, hysteria, neurosis, psychosis—have entered the popular lexicon and taken on a life of their own. We will try to bring them back to their psychoanalytic definitions and show how these formations can be found in popular musical works. Along the way, however, we will also need to take small detours through some related concepts—obscenity, humor, and the (in)famous Oedipus complex.

## Narcissism

So far we have touched upon some of the controversies of Freudianism: the very demonstrability of an "unconscious," Freud's focus on sexual energy (libido) as the currency of that unconscious, and the persistence of drives. But in the previous chapter, set with the task of mapping out the basic areas and processes of the unconscious, we came nowhere near the most truly explosive parts of the Freudian system. In this section we will dive further into the formations that are created in that unconscious. As a result, we will begin to touch upon some of the thorniest issues in Freudianism. Our claim is simple though—Freudianism is and isn't revolutionary; Freudianism is and isn't reactionary. Both the reactionary and revolutionary elements coexist in Freud's text, and there isn't an easy way of dividing one from the other. We start with narcissism here because it demonstrates this problem in microcosm. Freud's essay "On Narcissism" begins with a discussion regarding how he began to conceptualize narcissism. The problematic cases of schizophrenics provided the jumping-off point for the observation that in such patients, the investment of "object cathexis"—that is, investment in things outside of the self—seems to be absent. Instead of an interest in the outside world and the things in it, there is a withdrawal and a fixation on the deep inner self. Freud therefore hypothesizes that there are two fundamental types of cathexis possible: cathexis of an object, and cathexis of the self or the ego. This second investment, in which one loves one's self erotically (not just in a literal sense!), becomes a narcissistic investment. Here we have the simple formulation of narcissism in popular culture: someone who loves themselves. But when we think about this in more detail, the question of narcissism is more complex than we might have imagined.

For Freud, the withdrawal of libido into the ego results in a certain disengagement from the world of objects and people. It led, in extremis, to a kind of catatonia, a nonintervention with the world that is incredibly negative for subjects who experience it (as it was for Narcissus, left listless as a flower at the edge of a pond), and this is somewhat further away from our contemporary understanding of narcissism.

The fireworks—or, perhaps more properly, the alarms—can be heard going off when Freud moves beyond speculative psychology to observations of "erotic life," "with its many kinds of differentiation in man and woman."[1] In the next few beguiling paragraphs, the modern reader is pulled between regressive and progressive thoughts. We will let Freud do most of the talking for a while. As opposed to analclitic (object) love, we find those who pick themselves as their love object—here comes the regressive step—namely "perverts and homosexuals" (more on this in Chapter 8). However, Freud's next paragraph destroys the idea of two polarized sexualities in genders:

> We have, however, not concluded that human beings are divided into two sharply differentiated groups, according as their object-choice conforms to the anaclitic or to the narcissistic type; we assume rather that both kinds of object-choice are open to each individual.[2]

That is the originary thought for a whole tree of post-Freudian feminist and queer psychoanalysis. Time for Freud to take a step back though: a comparison of the male

---

[1] Sigmund Freud, "On Narcissism: An Introduction," in *The Standard Edition of the Complete Psychological Works of Sigmund Freud*, vol. XIV, trans. James Strachey (London: The Hogarth Press, [1914] 1957), 87.
[2] Ibid., 88.

and female sexes then shows that there are fundamental differences between them in respect of their type of object choice. And it gets worse:

> Women, especially if they grow up with good looks, develop a certain self-contentment which compensates them for the social restrictions that are imposed upon them in their choice of object. Strictly speaking, it is only themselves that such women love with an intensity comparable to that of the man's love for them.[3]

before getting slightly better:

> Perhaps it is not out of place here to give an assurance that this description of the feminine form of erotic life is not due to any tendentious desire on my part to depreciate women ... I am ready to admit that there are quite a number of women who love according to the masculine type[4]

and then one last dig at the "narcissistic women":

> Even for narcissistic women, whose attitude towards men remains cool, there is a road which leads to complete object-love. In the child which they bear, a part of their own body confronts them like an extraneous object, to which, starting out from their narcissism, they can then give complete object-love.[5]

Okay, there's a lot to unpack there. Firstly, pop music is a wellspring of evidence that there is no intrinsically gendered form of love, and that any individual can take up any position regarding analclitic and narcissistic love. Be it women loving men as objects (Charli XCX's "Boys," Nicki Minaj's "Superbass"), women trying to become the object of anaclitic love (Mitski's "Your Best American Girl"), women rejecting anaclitic love (Lorde's "Royals"), men loving men narcissistically (Perfume Genius' "Queen"), or men loving objects narcissistically (The National's "All the Wine"), or men loving themselves narcissistically (The National's "Mr November"), or men refusing to gender their loved object (Sufjan Stevens's "Casimir Pulaski Day"). There are also a host of songs that further proliferate this fluidity beyond a gendered spectrum. We find another fascinating body of music that comprises songs about the very possibility of navigating this space: Against Me!'s "Transgender Dysphoria Blues"; The Smiths' "I Know It's Over" and "How Soon Is Now?"; Mazzy Star's "Flowers in December" ... we could go on and on.

We might also like to think about the supposed "pure" form of love for Freud: the analclitic love he associated with men. Consider its "desexualized" form in something like Dorrough's "Ice Cream Paint Job," where desire is cast onto a fetishized object whose selection is arbitrary. From outside of car culture, wine culture, stamp collecting,

---

[3] Ibid., 88–9.
[4] Ibid., 89.
[5] Ibid.

or trainspotting, the investment in these objects seems ludicrous. For the uninitiated, it is hard to get excited about a hue of paint or the consistency of its lacquer.

> Yea buddy! Rollin' like a big shot. Chevy tuned up like a NASCAR pit stop. Fresh paint job (check). Fresh inside (check).

Of course, Freud himself goes much further than simply taking the object as an object, and there is always a latent drive formation under the manifest content of a subject fetishizing a particular object. Nevertheless, the account in "On Narcissism" of—and its bias toward—this form of male object relations is an issue, a theme that we will return to in our very final chapter. Perhaps, an even worse thing, even at this stage, is the form of anaclitic love that loves the other as an object. You can probably guess by the repertoire of music we have used in the book so far that we might be fans of alt-J and indeed, we are. They seem very nice—and we should perhaps note that they might have taken up an ironic disposition regarding the next object of analysis. Yet, on the surface, we can see the failure in modes of the anaclitic type of love in their song "Deadcrush" (*Relaxer*, 2017), where the desire is cast onto the woman as an object, creating in our opinion a rather creepy atmosphere. This atmosphere is given immediately by the low, sinister bass, and the eerie percussive panting samples—like a crank caller—that invade us antiphonally from the left and right sides of the stereo field and become increasingly sexualized. The song is broken up into myriad small phrases, offering a postmodern bricolage of fragments, focusing in passing on characters (mostly called Anna) through history (à la Woolf's *Orlando*) as a plaything-cum-muse of men: we have Man Ray's muse, Lee Miller, Anne Boleyn ("Anna Bolina"), whose subdued screams we hear in the vocals as she is cast aside; we have L'Arlésienne, painted by Van Gogh and Gaughin, who receives the strangest musical treatment as a breakdown section that mimics early porch blues (strimmed-down, minor pentatonic fragments in the melody, rough guitar strumming, percussive finger snapping), with the sound of wolf howls (men's whistles?) in the surrounding nocturnal solitude. These fragmented vignettes all explore our fascination with "looking" at women who have already been "looked at" and thrown aside after an encounter with male narcissistic egos. If we watch the "Deadcrush" video, the first thing we notice is the proliferation of lenses. Various irises twitch and open, putting us very much in the territory of the scopic drives—those that wish to see. What do men want to see? Why women, of course—this is the so-called male gaze, which we will reexamine in Chapter 4, when we consider Jacques Lacan. Three spinning disks are quite quickly transmuted into three dancing women, who are initially featureless and faux-nude. The staccato music proceeds in a masturbatory rhythm while the women dance. Only when the lyrical content, the male fantasy about the "deadcrush," is imposed via the verses do the women take form, becoming these idealized crushes. They exist as beautiful objects for as long as attention is paid to them, before paling back to anonymity as the song moves forward. The narcissism of this situation also breaks through in the hard-to-hear (repressed?) punctuations from the phrase "watch me now," which musically alludes to the famous line from the Contours' "Do You Love Me?" as used famously in *Dirty Dancing*, as "Baby" first enters the underground dancing scene in horror at the gyrating, sweaty bodies. This suggests that a substratum of this clear investment in watching women is a suppressed narcissistic injunction—watch me! These narcissistic artists use their muses to make people watch themselves.

A final observation about narcissism is based on Freud's comments that narcissism is quite a successful strategy in some situations, and that the narcissistic personality holds some allure to others. This can be quickly confirmed by observation. It can help you get elected as the US president, despite your obvious flaws! If we listen to—and watch if possible—Prince's 1991 track "Cream," we can see these two aspects of narcissism. The musical setup is perfect for 1980s/90s sexy funk—slinky bass groove, wah-wah pedal. The lyrics place the anaclitic love on the side of the "other" who, Prince assumes, desperately wants him—"You got the horn so why don't you blow it (go on and blow it)." Narcissism is here drawn in the guitar lines that fill the spaces between his call and response melodies. Most of his vocal fragments, short, melodic statements are immediately followed by his guitar licks, as if he is admiring himself through his own guitar. More narcissistic still—the guitar sounds morph across successive iterations—we have first the distorted but precise guitar line, then we have the wah pedal in the right ear, then the lone female singer in the left, and we soon hear full backing vocals of swooning women in the entire stereo field. This is Prince making love to his guitar as an emblem of himself and then imagining that guitar becomes everyone around him. At one point (2:12) comes the break—"look up, it's your guitar"—and a collage of short, guitar sounds surrounds us, solidifying the image of the guitar presiding over the whole lovemaking episode. Maybe the guitar is also representing the "cream" that Prince keeps referring to (which we believe has a more sexualized connotation than an innocent ode to the most luxurious form of dairy). In this case, the guitar becomes a clear symbol of Prince's own sexual excitement, though imagined to be on the part of others who desperately want him. The staccato organ playing, which comes straight out of the 1970s softcore porn genre and accompanies the more intimate moments in the song, also has the kind of masturbatory intent that we found in "Deadcrush," but the organ is a new instrument in the mix, hidden in the wings, as if it represents crowds of spectators becoming onanistically active in their support for Prince. The preamble section of the extended video (a narrative set in a train station), the main body of the video in which the song is performed, and the song itself are all about Prince (as the holy trinity of *performer, persona,* and *protagonist*). People go where he goes, eat cream on cue, and dance around him so as to accentuate his importance. And, of course, the whole song consists of him singing about himself and his excellence "You're so good. Baby there ain't nobody better." And it's worth reflecting that this whole narcissistic strategy seems to work for Prince; it is one of the vital aspects of his allure—at least up to a point.

On the printed page, Prince's words of self-congratulation seem a little strange. But this record, released at the end point of Prince's imperial phase, comes at the end of a decade in which people were drawn to the narcissistic, self-interested figures of various megastars such as Jackson, Madonna, or Prince. The fact that these figures seemed only to be pleased by themselves—whether literally (Madonna's famed masturbatory gestures onstage), through only their own music (Prince and his extensive ghostwriting), or through their own company in their own theme park (Jackson)—there remained a huge throng of devotees, desperate to become an object—maybe even a subject—recognized by the narcissist as lovable-in-itself.

## Oedipus Complex

The famous "Oedipus complex" is not a psychological "condition" in itself. Readers only vaguely familiar with this complex may be surprised to learn (while doubtlessly wincing in horror) that it is one of the most "normal" situations we find in this book and is purportedly universal. A knowledge of it is necessary to understand the Freudian psyche, the poetic imagination, and the points in psychological functioning where problems emerge. We will also further refine the concept in Chapter 3, when we consider the conceptual twists that came from Jacques Lacan, and again in Chapter 7 when we explore the work of Gilles Deleuze in sadomasochism. At this early stage we will also preserve Freud's problematic male-centrism, as articulated in his 1910 essay, "A Special Type of Choice of Object Made by Men," though this will be radically challenged later by Lacan, and us in turn.

Probably the most obvious but nonetheless powerful musical explication of Freud's original concept would be the Doors' famous "Oedipal ending" of "The End" (*The Doors*, 1967), in which Jim Morrison narrates in the third person how "the killer awoke before dawn" (6:27), walks into his parents' bedrooms, tells his father he wants to kill him, and then turns to his mother, claiming, "I want to …." His screams then cover up what we presume to be a sexual declamation (7:45) as the band threaten to break down their groove through wild improvisation. At 8:50 a sexually articulated rhythm enters the texture—a palm-muted, staccato, clean guitar strike, though our perception of the beat is challenged—are we "on" or "off" the beat here? Soon this rhythmic articulation of the sexual act will merge into Morrison violently shouting "fuck" with the intensely clipped stabbing effect from before as the music works its way up to a breaking climactic wave into which everything collapses. When asked about the song's "meaning," Morrison once stated:

> Let's see … Oedipus is a Greek myth. Sophocles wrote about it. I don't know who before that. It's about a man who inadvertently killed his father and married his mother. Yeh, I'd say there was a similarity, definitely.[6]

Morrison's use of the word "inadvertently" is perfect here, because it describes two things that happened by accident. Freud, who is not a great believer in accidents, casts

---

[6] Jim Morrison, "*The Rolling Stone* Interview," *Rolling Stone*, July 26, 1969, interview with Jerry Hopkins. www.rollingstone.com/music/music-news/the-rolling-stone-interview-jim-morrison-73308/.

this myth into all our psyches and claims that the unconscious is causing this accident to happen, when a boy

> begins to desire his mother herself in the sense with which he has recently become acquainted, and to hate his father anew as a rival who stands in the way of this wish; he comes, as we say, under the dominance of the Oedipus complex.[7]

This is all unconscious. The speaker Morrison cannot admit it clearly to himself (or his listeners), preferring to cover up the word "fuck" with distorting screams. But a crucial difference between Freud and the Doors is that, in Freud, the boy passing through the complex learns that he cannot overpower his father and so represses his murderous intentions, learning to accept paternal authority that is thus manifested through fear. The child does not follow through his wishes and learns to be a responsible adult. This is healthy. Thus, the father comes to stand for authority, while the mother stands for the object of desire (but also the contradictory forces of envy and distrust for betraying the child with the father). Of course, what the child ultimately wants is to fulfill his "single wish *to be his own father*."[8] Although this mother/father dynamic is real, as are the conflicting emotions, they are more likely to be confronted later in life symbolically. And the Doors see Oedipus as a symbol for a level of restraint and civility that they want to abandon. As John Densmore recorded:

> Jim just kept saying over and over kill the father, fuck the mother, and essentially boils down to this, kill all those things in yourself which are instilled in you and are not of yourself, they are alien concepts which are not yours, they must die. Fuck the mother is very basic, and it means get back to essence, what is reality, what is, fuck the mother is very basically mother, mother-birth, real, you can touch it, it's nature, it can't lie to you.[9]

We'll think a little more deeply in future chapters about how music can be maternal, but in "The End," there are some clearly unique factors: the pseudo Indian sitar playing (actually a guitar tuned in a manner learned from Ravi Shankar) evokes the *Bhārat Mātā* (Mother India) in the Doors' aesthetic; the gentle undulation of the guitar riff becomes the breathing in and out of Brahma that creates and destroys the world; the vocal and instrumental reverberation on the recording perhaps embodies the ultimate uterine environment. And this static, timeless atmosphere of maternity is spread throughout the song.

On the literal narrative level, we don't musically hear any sounds of murdering the father except in the act of seizing the mother—the two are conceptually so entwined.

---

[7] Sigmund Freud, "A Special Type of Choice of Object Made by Men," in *The Standard Edition of the Complete Psychological Works of Sigmund Freud*, vol. XI, trans. James Strachey (London: The Hogarth Press, [1910] 1957), 171.
[8] Ibid., 173, emphasis original.
[9] John Densmore, *Riders on the Storm: My Life with Jim Morrison and the Doors* (New York: Delacorte Press, 1990), 88.

The ever-accelerating speed of the shouts of "fuck" and "yeah," the slow postclimactic musical descent into languor, all betoken violence and lovemaking in one musical gesture. While Freud maintains a ritual ordering of murdering the father, *before* sleeping with the mother, the Doors musically amalgamate into one, because musically they are symbolically identical.

However, in the musico-symbolic world, the father is murdered most obviously when the whole musical edifice or rhythm, groove, timbre, texture, and all elements of instrumental control break down. Perhaps this is the symbolic murder that lies beyond all of those Dionysian musical moments in which the patriarchal order of Western musical civilization and the remnants of the classical tradition are symbolically torn down. Perhaps this finds its symbolic apogee in the 1960s wave of instrument smashing from the Who, or Hendrix. Not entirely confined to rock-and-roll, however, in the Doors' year of 1969, we found a similar gesture within the "classical" tradition from Peter Maxwell Davies, whose *Eight Songs for a Mad King* calls for the violin to be smashed by the vocalist. Violin, as a patriarchal leader of the orchestra, is symbolically murdered when the "mad king" cannot accept paternal authority and, like the Doors, tries to break his Oedipal chains.

## Regression

The Freudian unconscious never gives up a past drive and, therefore, keeps all of its previous structures of desire in place. Freud's striking image is that it is like the various cities of Troy, all built on top of one another, so that the foundations of earlier cities remain buried under each other. Though the reality principle means that such desires are often prevented from actualizing themselves, they nevertheless retain a level of cathexis (investment). Think of those many Pulp songs like "Babies" (*His 'n' Hers*, 1994), a raunchy but raucous celebration of a childhood fantasy that loses none of its ability to excite despite the passage of time. In fact, most of the songs on Pulp's first six albums were about teenage explorations of sex; only in *This Is Hardcore* are we launched suddenly into the "grown-up" world of manufactured glamor and the porn industry.[10] In one of Cocker's most regressive songs, "I Spy" (*Different Class*, 1995), the bitter song breaks down completely as he narrates (perhaps from a time before he learnt to sing) riding around on his bicycle, "skillfully avoiding the dog turd" and imagining a "blue plaque" above his first exploration of a girl's chest. But he is not simply living in a memory; nor is this simple nostalgia; he is bringing the past with him into his present. Freud made clear that

---

[10] See Nicola Dibben, "Pulp, Pornography and Spectatorship: Subject Matter and Subject Position in Pulp's *This Is Hardcore*," *Journal of the Royal Musical Association* 126, no. 1 (2001): 83–106. See also Kenneth Smith, "Pulp: A Paradigm for Perversion in Pornosonic Pop," in *Popular Musicology and Identity: Essays in Honour of Stan Hawkins*, ed. F. Jarman, K. A. Hansen, and E. Askeroi (Oxford: Routledge, 2020), 160–77.

it is a matter of observation that people never abandon a libidinal position, not even, indeed, when a substitute is beckoning to them. This opposition can be so intense that a turning away from reality takes place and a clinging to the object through the medium of a hallucinatory wishful psychosis.[11]

Likewise Jarvis Cocker turns with great frequency to these sites of childhood loss of innocence. As far as the unconscious is concerned, a childhood fantasy is as efficacious, if not more so, than a middle-aged reality. More generally, a regression is a form of turning away from the reality of the present to a time of imagined plenitude. We find musical references to childhood in so many places in popular music, most frequently perhaps the sound of music boxes that symbolize regularity, predictability, repetition, plenitude. We often find these childhood regressions in those artists who are normally preconcerned with more troublesome sexual themes in their songs. An album project by Tindersticks' (a group of oversexed lounge lizards) frontman Stuart Staples, *Songs for the Young at Heart* (2007), features the full spectrum of adults regressing, from Jarvis Cocker reciting "Albert the Lion" (in his Sheffield drawl, describing a child being eaten, all in comedic children's verse) to Bonnie Prince Billy singing "Puff the Magic Dragon" (with the zaney singing in the chorus reminding us that the song, ostensibly about growing up, has overtones about drug abuse). We might also think of those wonderfully maternal voices that characterize "dream pop" (or "synth-pop" as it's sometimes known). One of the quirkiest and yet most disturbing aspects of David Lynch's *Twin Peaks* is the maternal, soporific voice of Julee Cruise, who sings the title song, "Falling" (1989), with its gentle rocking, undulating bass riff, and the smooth, saccharin melodies that are purely sung but barely whispered at the same time. In fact the characteristic bass notes of this particular song emphasize the melodic interval of a fourth (think—the first two notes of "Away in a Manger"), and this is also the beginning of the same song's vocal melody, as if the voice arises seamlessly out of the edgy, harsh bass sound—the memory of the mother soothes everything. We regress into her arms to escape the cruel world outside. The breathiness of the voice is then mimicked by the synth sonic envelope that surrounds us, cushions us in a fake string orchestra (i.e., not the real thing—this is a memory, an impossible regression). And yet the song is about falling in love—taking an adventure into the outside world. How does this square? We might say that the singing persona is taking the regressive thoughts into the future—clinging to the mother, refusing to renounce the earlier libidinal position despite needing to (and wanting to) form a new one. Other songs by Cruise, such as "The Nightingale," have exactly the same effect, in which the only disturbance to the perfect uterine fantasy is the occasional scale pattern in the melody that gives us a glimpse of some kind of striving away from the warmth of maternal plenitude into something new. The music basically regresses us and, given the insanity of Lynch's *Twin Peaks* world—its murders, its sexual abuse, its mysterious "Black lodge" (the

---

[11] Sigmund Freud, "Mourning and Melancholia," in *The Standard Edition of the Complete Psychological Works of Sigmund Freud*, vol. XIV, trans. James Strachey (London: The Hogarth Press, [1918] 1953), 244.

parallel universe in which evil beings live)—it's scarcely surprising that we need to regress to a happier time.

Freud situates the origin of our system of drives and desires in somatic processes—things of the body rather than of the mind. These somatic processes begin in the subject as biological needs such as eating, hearing, defecating, and so on. However, even in very young children, these needs do not stay solely in the domain of the somatic. A most basic need, Freud hypothesizes, is that of the child to feed. When the child is fed, it is happy. However, the mother is not always there to feed the child. If the excitation caused by this absence was external to the child, as in the case of a hot or cold zone, the child can move away from it. But when the excitation is internal, it cannot be escaped. The child must come up with alternative strategies. So, in the first instance, the child may fantasize about the mother, simply imagining she is feeding. If this fails, the thumb or a dummy may be sucked as a proxy. And, furthermore, the drive can reverse itself in a "vicissitude," by which satisfaction is attained by denial—the child avoids the thing that would make it happy. So, in terms of our initial desires, there are relatively few, according to Freud, focusing on bodily urges. These drives can change as the child develops—an example is the famous anal retentiveness or laxity, which is conditioned by the parents' reaction to defecation. If they praise it, however, the child offers more and offers it as a gift; psychoanalysis claims this can lead to a messy personality. If the parents condemn, the child may move to the retentive type, becoming miserly and precise. What is interesting here, in terms of regression, is that these initial phases of drive moving from the body to the mental apparatus lay down the basic pathways all later drives will be built upon. They are the boughs of the tree of drives; so, in the case of the relationship of the child to excrement, once these grand decisions about pathways are laid down, others will generally follow in their pattern. Hence, early childhood encounters with sexuality are, in the Freudian system, largely responsible for determining the basic structure on top of which later sexual drives will be laid down. This can be seen in the famous Oedipus complex, where the failure of the child to progress along the "normal" pathway leads to distinct complexes, unique to the stages in which Oedipus broke down.

Let's consider the song "Rainbow in the Dark" (*Bottoms of Barrels*, 2006) by Tilly and the Wall. Singer Kianna Alarid sings a happy-go-lucky melody over the suitably upbeat high school aesthetic of the acoustic guitar and tambourine, with additional tap-dancing sounds rather than percussion. The song describes images of childhood, but always interlaced with sinister hints of abuse—in fact, even simple, otherwise pleasant images are couched in violent terms ("I was kidnapped real young by the sweet taste of love"). An introductory riff on the electric guitar gives us sinister, chromatic twists and turns, counterbalancing the prevailingly pure vocal melody that draws from perfect arpeggios of the main chords (the melody uses only the three primary notes in some phrases, creating a very simplistic, childlike aesthetic); this replicates the cognitive dissonance in the narrative of childlike love and sinister sexual violence ("Then I met a man with a fist for a hand; Held me flat on my back, taught me how to give in").

And this childhood bleeds into the present: "Now they're drilling my teeth while I'm soiling sheets / With my lover, she's counting the diamonds on rings. And even when truth doesn't help with the sting." The sexual relationship described is suffused with images of pain (dentists) and filth (soiled sheets); the matrix of cathexes described from the child's world is present in those of the adults. Even the truth brings no release from the past—even talking these things through with Freud wouldn't necessarily help. It's clear from the final "terminal climax" of this song when a new chorus enters and all singers unite in singing "sometimes you can't hold back the river" that the flow of drives established in childhood can't be simply cast aside but remain present throughout adult life. Like Freud's hydraulic imagery of the unconscious—its flows, its dams, its reservoirs—the river here cannot be halted all of the time and needs to be let out rather than repressed.

## Obscenity, Jokes, and the Unconscious

In *Jokes and Their Relation to the Unconscious* from 1905, Freud speculates that jokes allow the telling of a story or truth that would be otherwise impossible in polite conversation—particularly with sexual or scatological topics involved. We will use this as the basis for a discussion of musical humor, and perhaps music more broadly.

For Freud, the qualities of the superego produce different forms of joke. A very strict superego would probably not allow any jokes, whereas a generous superego may allow some light humor. Freud said, "Non-tendentious jokes were described by Vischer as 'abstract' jokes. I prefer to call them 'innocent' jokes."[12] There are hundreds of these innocent musical jokes, from Mozart to Bill Bailey. But a harsher superego might allow a seriously unpalatable message to come through the sensor as a bitter sarcasm, a comic attack, or a cushion for obscenity. Time and again we find songs whose lyrics would sound downright appalling, but whose music makes it clear that the author/songwriter is attempting to be funny—or is, at least, moving his/her position outside of the words being spoken or sung to adopt an outside position of reflection on them.

One of the things we gain from an understanding of jokes through the unconscious—and this is much like the understanding of other things afforded by consideration of the unconscious, such as love or desire—is that it explains why we laugh and to what extent we laugh. In *Jokes*, Freud likes to use train metaphors to explain what is going on in the unconscious when we encounter a joke. By using two of these train metaphors, we can start to understand why jokes work, and why they have whatever force of merriment that they do. Let's start with why the joke works. One thing we know, from Chapter 1, is that there are two different qualitative spaces in the psyche, the unconscious and conscious parts. There is also a space in between, the preconscious, which somehow miraculates the transition of an impulse from one to the other. The unconscious, we learnt, was the dark, puerile, resting place of the immortal drives—inclinations toward pure pleasure that had no concern for their actionability or consequence. These drives

---

[12] Sigmund Freud, "Jokes and Their Relation to the Unconscious," in *The Standard Edition of the Complete Psychological Works of Sigmund Freud*, vol. VIII, trans. James Strachey (London: The Hogarth Press, [1905] 1960), 90.

are dangerous, so the regime of censorship keeps them in the unconscious. This force protects the upper echelons of the ego, the self, and the conscious part of the psyche from encountering the disturbing drive economy it rests on. If we want to understand what is going on in the unconscious, what the polymorphously perverse (capable of gaining pleasure from any source) drives look like, one interesting way in is the joke. In the case of a classic absurd joke: "Q: If a man can walk a mile in a fortnight, how many sticks are there in a tin of rhubarb? A: You cannot clean a window with a shovel."[13] Freud describes the switch between the two parts as a kind of jumping of a train from one track to another. In the case of the joke above, there is no real connection between the two parts, so the leap is large. In a simple double-meaning joke such as: "I don't suffer from insanity—I enjoy every minute of it," the point of ambiguity is that the listener is pulled from their expectation about where the conversation will go—"I'm not insane"—to the surprising revelation that "I am insane and I like it." The reaction of the psyche, after being made to do this leap, is to produce laughter.

In the case of an obscene joke, the source of the laughter can often be attributed to the artificial uncensoring power of the joke to reveal a formation that was actually in the unconscious, but censored. On the simplest level, someone falling over can be said to be funny because there is a sadistic drive in us that enjoys seeing someone get hurt. Other drives equally apply to people being coated in various fluids and oozes—see the trope of gunge used so often in kids TV to eke out a minimal amount of laughter. Hence the political jokes of late-night TV that have the basic structure: politician X is a Y. Remember, the id is violent and obscene and derives pleasure from all kinds of "wrong" thoughts. As Freud said, jokes are just as revealing as parapraxes—and there is a convergence between the common slip of the tongue with former UK Health Secretary (for much of 2018) Jeremy Hunt's surname and a common "humorous" political observation about him.

So laughter is about the process of jumping a train of thought to the end of an idea, or from one idea to another; and when this act of circumventing the normal passage of thought in the psyche happens, the reaction is mirth. It is a kind of breaking down of repression and a revelation of unconscious thought or potential. If we want to know about the qualitative aspect of laughter—how funny something is—we can consider how certain it was for the personal train of thought to eventually (if uncensored) reach the destination and how invested the psyche is in that type of notion.

This perhaps explains why some musical comedy can be so vicious. Consider the Ken Kaniff skits on early Eminem albums. These homophobic, scatological skits are not something that we (ego) like, but rather that it (id) likes. The same goes for much of the abusive, sexist, violent content that Eminem was famous for or, after him, acts like Odd Future. Going further in at the deep end of scatological musical humor, we find Micky Avalon—white, Jewish rapper, former sex worker and drug addict turned musician—whose "bonus track" on self-titled *Micky Avalon* (2006) is called "My Dick" (feat. Dirt Nasty and Andre Legacy). The track begins with a broken, stuttering

---

[13] This particular joke enjoyed various incarnations, but the present formulation was a favorite of one of the authors' uncle Cyril.

funk bass, "stuck in the groove" and stammering forward. It outlines a minor key through which its heavy, portentous sound soon begins to jar with the lyrics on the surface, serving, in fact, to compound the humor with mock-comi-tragic overtones. Uncannily enough, this broken musical bass line, from the beginning, seems to represent something unable to really break through into a position of articulation. And a feeling of the unconscious trying to break through is made all the more palpable when the singers enter with an extremely long series of scatological insults, in the following format:

> My dick: [positive statement about my penis's brilliance]
> Yo' dick: [negative statement about your penis's properties]

One of few printable examples:

> My dick, size of a pumpkin
> Yo' dick looks like McCauley Culkin.

The three rappers insult each other's "dicks" (or, perhaps, collectively insult an imaginary other's dick?), and the pleasure of the song lies in the liberation from repression that the musical joke affords us. The song is clearly making fun of the classic Alpha-masculinity trope of comparing penis sizes. Normally, of course, this game (highly Freudian in this phallic incarnation) plays itself out in sublimated ways—buying the biggest car, wearing the most expensive suit, and so on—but here the material is entirely directed to its most obscene and yet most open form. The *symbol* of a penis—the **phallus**—is turned back into a *literal* penis. And not only does this game become "allowed," its very permissibility becomes fun, and funny (for some). There is a pure enjoyment that we can access in this bypassing of the censor. As Freud says:

> We are now able to state the formula for the mode of operation of tendentious jokes. They put themselves at the service of purposes in order that, by means of using the pleasure from jokes as a fore-pleasure, they may produce new pleasure by lifting suppressions and repressions.[14]

Perhaps, it is no surprise that this "bonus track" became more famous than any other song from the album.

The song, and its self-consciously hypermasculine aesthetic, also spawned an interesting experiment from Awkwafina, perhaps better known in recent times from her acting roles in *Ocean's 8* and *Crazy Rich Asian*. Her 2012 "My Vag" was released, going viral as a response to Avalon, using the identical format and the same melody to discuss "my vag" vs. "your vag." Although claiming not to be pushing a feminist agenda, she acknowledged that

---

[14] Freud, "Jokes and Their Relation to the Unconscious," 137.

the existence of someone like me, especially from my earlier videos, when YouTube was a landscape where not a lot of people saw an Asian-American woman being entirely unashamed—save for Cho—is in itself provocative.[15]

However, she attracted the ire of feminists for entering this masculinist, phallogocentric world of one-up-MAN-ship. Yet, her song also deploys two aspects, which we might find offer us deeper insights into the role of musical jokes and the unconscious.

For one thing, it *clearly* is a joke and fulfills the structure of the Freudian punchline—train hopping. Where the men may well be using their comic song to mask a genuine overprotestation of masculinity, Awkwafina can hardly control her giggling as she pretends to try and look sexy while pulling huge objects out of someone's vagina. This is not an attempt to enter masculine territory—she is clearly having a joke at its expense. For another thing though, and more subliminally, we hear that she tries to critique the musical masculinity of the men's music. Gone is the low, grungy, heavy bass of the Avalon track; instead we have all of the hyperstereotyped markers of musical femininity, which seem to parody the idea of Freudian feminine lack. While the Western classical music tradition exploited gendered musical tropes, we would probably (hopefully) try and shy away from that now, but here they are in full display. The lack of any real bass places all of the emphasis onto the higher musical register, giving a lightness and grace; the men's battle with their unconscious in the stuttering, groove-stuck bassline is replaced with gentle, delicate, refined hi-hat rhythm; the heavy instrumentation is replaced with a large man playing a tiny, comic ukulele. The whole musical show is demasculinized and shown proudly to be the feminine **lack** (seen from the Freudian male's perspective) that Awkwafina is mocking by rendering in comic song.

But these are not just any joke; they are *musical* jokes. And perhaps there is something peculiar to the music itself that allows its own form of acceptance of things that otherwise would remain unacceptable or inaccessible, just like jokes. Let's think about that.

September 19, 1985. Frank Zappa, Dee Snider, and John Denver participate in the *Parents' Music Resource Center* (PMRC) hearings, headed by Tipper Gore. The end result was to be those "Parental Advisory" labels. Looking at the PMRC's list of fifteen offending songs—"the Filthy Fifteen"—in 2020, we might see the most innocuous series of artists: Cindy Lauper, Madonna, Def Leppard. Compare their sex, drugs, and rock-n-roll references to anything we see on MTV today, and we realize the failure of censorship. What we witnessed after these hearings was not a cleaned-up act from pop musicians, but a celebration of freedom. Today the "parental advisory" label is, if anything, an incitement for young people to listen, and a cover for artists to go much further into the realms of obscenity and enjoy this newly permitted space to the full.

---

[15] Dale Berning Sawa, "Awkwafina: 'I Was Just Rapping about My Genitalia—Not Making a Feminist Message,'" *The Guardian*, December 28, 2017. www.theguardian.com/film/2017/dec/28/nora-lum-awkwafina-genitalia-feminist-message.

Take a moment, if you can bear it, to look at Avalon's latest offering, a bitter attack on woke culture, with a sex-change operation resulting in blood spurting over the breasts of a scantily clad surgeon, while Avalon sings:

> I wish you woke motherfuckers would go back to sleep. It's retarded how you fags be so PC. I wish you woke motherfuckers would go back to bed. And take a plastic bag and tie it over your head.

This would clearly class as what Freud would describe as a "hostile joke":

> We are now prepared to realize the part played by jokes in hostile aggressiveness. A joke will allow us to exploit something ridiculous in our enemy which we could not, on account of obstacles in the way, bring forward openly or consciously; once again, then, the joke will evade restrictions and open sources of pleasure that have become inaccessible.[16]

Perhaps, he being the sexually ambiguous grandson of an Auschwitz survivor, we may have more time to listen to what Avalon has to say on the topic of "wokeness" than, say, to a Baptist preacher from the US bible belt, but the point is that the musical outlet for his hostile attack on political correctness barely draws a whisper. Does popular music now allow us to upload the unsayable into the "singable," bypassing sublimation just like the joke does? A "parental warning" sticker on a pop record is perhaps a musical analog to the "did you hear the one about … ?"

Equally relatable to the present political climate, consider a song by one of the greatest comedy-music duos, Flanders and Swann—their "A Song of Patriotic Prejudice" (*At the Drop of Another Hat*, 1954), which features the refrain "The English, the English, the English are best; I wouldn't give tuppence for all of the rest." The song opens thus:

> The rottenest bits of these islands of ours
> We've left in the hands of three unfriendly powers
> Examine the Irishman, Welshman or Scot
> You'll find he's a stinker, as likely as not.

The music is clearly utterly comedic and makes the text instantly positioned as humor. Each verse, in turn, describes, in ultra-stereotyped terms, "the Scotsman," "the Irishman," and "the Welshman," before leaping across the channel, where the Germans are described as "German," the Russians "red," while the Greeks and Italians are accused of eating "garlic in bed." Sure, this song is a *parody* of patriotic prejudice, and, nostrils aflare, the source of its humor is the mocking of the English sense of national pride. Yet, even with this in mind, the song makes for difficult listening post-Brexit, with the breakup of the UK seeming more possible than it ever has. Because the

---

[16] Freud, "Jokes and Their Relation to the Unconscious," 103.

musical humor doesn't exactly tell us *where* the humor lies—is the joke at the expense of the English or "Johnny foreigner"?—it could easily be made into a joke in the latter sense that expresses national pride by projecting rather than introjecting the humor (as we are supposed to if we are English). While the song clearly lampoons national pride, it undoubtedly serves as a joke that belies the truth as seen by many a nationalist, who feels otherwise unable to engage in national stereotypes. We might think of Warren Mitchell, the staunch socialist who used his character Alf Garnett to expose and mock national prejudice by portraying the misogynistic, racist, commie-hating, reactionary, but who seemed to receive doubly loud applause from the very people he was lampooning, who now used his humor as an outlet for their own inexpressible racism.

One way of resolving, or at least understanding, this and moving from an us vs. them dialectic, be it Englishman/foreigner, or politically right/wrong, is to understand how the Freudian unconscious, which powers the libido attached to such hatred, is something we all possess. The work of "civilization," as explored in Freud's later writings, is the work of repressing the base instincts of the id. We are all subjects built on dangerous flows, though in some of us these currents are closer to the surface.

Freud reserves a special place for a discussion of smutty jokes. While he associates smut with the "peasantry," he also shows us to be structurally identical to the more "refined" (we might read "middle-class") obscene jokes. Freud claims that smut masquerades as humor, but is a fairly direct mechanism for displaying to one's (assumed to be female in Freud's study) listener that the joketeller is essentially imagining the listener in a sexualized way.

> Smut is like an exposure of the sexually different person to whom it is directed. By the utterance of the obscene words it compels the person who is assailed to imagine the part of the body or the procedure in question and shows her that the assailant is himself imagining it. It cannot be doubted that the desire to see what is sexual exposed is the original motive of smut.[17]

For really low-brow musical smut, we might dig deep below the mainstream of transatlantic pop and find artist Scuzz Twittly, whose website bio boasts that his father was "the most promising upcoming armpit fartist in all of Skankbush County." After the success of "I Like Boobs" (*Yer a Homo!*, 2010), his latest offering is "She Spread Like the Covid" (2020). Scuzz apes the redneck aesthetic musically as well as visually (the cowboy hat, the Texan drawl) with bouncing chord progression, feigned, suppressed yodel-cracking, and hugely catchy, asinine tunes; he has the classic redneck lineup in the video for this "virtual" performance: Scuzz in tasteless shirt, strumming guitar; a clave player with false buck teeth, making silly faces (but singing backing vocals with near-perfect intonation); a guitarist with fake handlebar moustaches. The fourth participant is the actress, comedienne Georgie Leahy, who dances erotically in hotpants, braless

---

[17] Ibid., 98.

with a cut-off T-shirt that leaves little to the imagination. The ballad describes how Scuzz picked "her" up in a bar, took her into his pick-up, where:

> She spread like the Covid, she was only 19; when she came she exploded like you've never seen.

The lyrics, if possible, become even less edifying, as successive choruses intensify the smut:

> Cos she spread like the Covid, I tried to put up a fight. But my balls were overloaded; they needed draining that night.

Perhaps this is the kind of thing *some* men could say in small gathering in a bar and *mean it* without fear of being called out among their group of friends (though, to be clear, neither of the present authors would [we don't have friends anyway]), but not in a wide public forum, unless there was clear smokescreen of humor. But it passes the censors—the people who find it offensive, or the women they berate, can do nothing about it—and Scuzz Twittly is essentially sticking two fingers of his fretting hand up at them. And it seems to be liberating for these guys to be able to openly bring the people they berate into their hypermale fantasy space that they create; Georgie Leahy's dancing is intended to be genuinely erotic, while the three redneck misfits (and their viewers) salivate in the wings. But the perhaps more interesting question, and the raison d'etre for discussing Scuzz Twittly, is whether this is structurally the same in more high-brow musical smut. Readers (and writers) of this particular book will doubtless wag the finger at Scuzz Twittly, but are we so very different? For Freud:

> When we laugh at a refined obscene joke, we are laughing at the same thing that makes a peasant laugh at a coarse piece of smut. In both cases the pleasure springs from the same source. We, however, could never bring ourselves to laugh at the coarse smut; we should feel ashamed or it would seem to us disgusting. We can only laugh when a joke has come to our help.[18]

So let's take a more "refined obscene joke"—Frank Zappa's "Bobby Brown Goes Down." Zappa, author of the album *Does Humor Belong in Music?* (1984), had already written "Bobby Brown Goes Down" in 1979. This is a comedy song (we hope) about a fictitious, narcissistic "American Dream" student, Bobby Brown. We hear an impressive string of outlandish misogynistic and homophobic phrases and anecdotes, some of the choicest stanzas being perhaps:

> Women's liberation / Came creepin' all across the nation / I tell you, people, I was not ready / When I fucked this dyke by the name of Freddie ... She had my balls in a vice but she left the dick / I guess it's still hooked on but now it shoots too quick.

---

[18] Ibid., 101.

On the surface, these lyrics seem to be much worse (from a censor's point of view) than Scuzz Twittly's, but this comes from a more high-brow artist (influenced in no small part by the avant-garde music tradition of Stockhausen and Edgard Varese). What makes the song more palatable for an audience to enjoy? How can we listen to this without needing to wash afterwards? Or should we still wash afterwards?

Well, there are some very clear differences in the subject position adopted by the artists. Zappa mocks Bobby Brown and his narcissism from the beginning—"Hey now people I'm Bobby Brown, they say I'm the cutest guy in town." And from then on, the words belong to Bobby—Zappa distances himself from his character through a bitterly sarcastic form of irony. This comes across firmly in the music too. The laid-back, super-smooth doo-wop bassline and chord progression puts us in a surreal space for the late 1970s, and the "shiny" teeth of Bobby Brown can be visualized from Zappa's strong "zz" sounds as his voice comes through—double-tracked—in stereo, as if we are surrounded by this angelic-demon, Bobby Brown. Zappa removes himself in this pastiche; is this really Zappa, the near-serialist composer, using a four-chord trick—I, vi, IV, V progression (the classic doo-wop)? As he sings, "Oh God I am the American Dream, I do not think I'm too extreme," we hear the synthesized mock-trumpets showering him with glamor, and the myriad additional backing voices in extremely low registers highlighting his hyper-real masculinity.

Hopefully we can feel that this is a very different register to Scuzz Twittly; Zappa can't possibly (we desperately hope) be using this as joke to mask what he really wants to say or do (particularly as Bobby describes raping a cheerleader after helping with her essay). Freud must be wrong about the more refined obscene joke being the same as smut? We can perhaps reflect a little more on Freud's structure of jokes by considering the "type" of superego employed by the jokester. Scuzz's superego seems to be quite relaxed; perhaps his id is sticking two fingers up to his superego, in the same way as Scuzz's ego sticks two fingers up at the would-be censor in public. For Freud, a harsh superego allowed for a particularly biting form of sarcastic humor. And this is exactly what we find in Zappa. In the UK comedy world, we might think of Chris Morris's form of ultra-bitter humor that was so misinterpreted in 2001. His *Brass Eye* "Paedogeddon!" was a bitter attack on the media hysteria around pedophilia, but shocked viewers (and many nonviewers who heard about it) who imagined that Morris was mocking the victims of pedophilia, leading to record-breaking Ofcom complaints. Morris's musical skit on this special feature involved a chorus of young children singing "maybe tomorrow, but not today" in a mock BBC Children's Christmas party song. The tabloids were particularly horrified, seemingly trying to deflect from the real attack that was on their own hypocritical values: *The Star*, in a particularly dramatic stroke of hypocrisy, complained of Morris's "perversion" alongside an article that encouraged its readers to watch out for singer Charlotte Church, who, at fifteen, was developing an impressive bust. *The Star* hoped to see "more of her" next year. So, for Freud, the nature of the humor is highly dependent upon the nature of the superego creating it. True though, it's always difficult trying to work out whether we should/can laugh at smutty humor. So in musical humor, or musical attempts to provide an analogous mechanism for saying the unsayable, we could perhaps start by attempting to locate the superego of the musico-comedian, as well as listen to musical cues to help locate the position of the musical-joke. In Zappa's case, his musical self as persona is removed as far as possible from the offensive lyrics of his protagonist; in Scuzz's, his musical self is basically immersed in the song.

## Mourning and Melancholia

The fun stops here. The Libertines offer an example of what Freud calls **melancholia**, but which we could perhaps call "depression." Freud's *Mourning and Melancholia* is a fascinating text in which the author tries to discover the commonalities and differences between the states of "mourning" and "melancholia." This former state is fairly simple and relates to the process of grieving in our everyday language. In the work of mourning, Freud hypothesized that an object that had been a target of libidinal investment is no longer present in reality and, therefore, no longer an effective target of libidinal cathexis. The solution to this impasse is the slow disinvestment of the object. When this process happens "healthily," the invested libido becomes available for the ego to invest in new objects. But there is a condition that seems to have a similar structure to this work of mourning that goes far beyond it in severity. Freud calls this "melancholia." The symptoms of melancholia Freud lists are "painful dejection, cessation of interest in the outside world, loss of the capacity to love, inhibition of all activity, and a lowering of the self-regarding feelings to a degree that finds utterance in self-reproaches and self-revilings."[19] The difference between a psyche that falls into mourning and one into melancholia, Freud's hypothesizes, is that in mourning, the object is likely to have died, while in melancholia, a betrayal or departure is more likely. In this latter case, the investment in the object, which is no longer sustainable, is brought into the ego, that is, into the self-conception of the person. It then becomes subject to critique and reproach, but now as self-reproach, as it is part of the ego. Freud's example is of a wife who says of her husband "it must be awful for him, having to live with me," but she really means—"it is awful for me living with him."

The song Libertines' "Gunga Din" explores the nature of melancholia by presenting an unending series of attempts to escape it, which only reaffirm it and lead back to it; there does not seem any possibility for forming new investments. Everything about the song speaks of the recurring, pathological nature of this condition. The quirky chromatic chord slides downward (a classical trope of despondency in music) in reference to the "Monday blues" (a normal, healthy experience of most working people) and then the "Sunday blues" (less healthy and indicative of something all-pervasive). The chorus presents a repeated—failed—attempt at communal enjoyment, alternating with the more all-pervasive air of despondency in the verses. However, even these verses are undergirded with a ska/reggae vibe, which would normally signal a positive atmosphere of communal love, and so on. But here, in this minor key, the effect is turned inward upon itself as a perpetual reminder that their condition is permanent.

[19] Freud, "Mourning and Melancholia," 244.

Further layers of melancholic behavior are exhibited in the video of this song, which foregrounds the relations between the two vocalists who were so often at loggerheads with each other, staging a "makeup" with this song.

The apparent self-loathing in the song disguises a barb aimed toward a betrayer. In "Gunga Din," we hear a simple verse-chorus structure in which the two songwriters, Pete Doherty and Carl Barat, seem to offer verses as summaries of their failings, which segue into a chorus in which these failings (various, but including heroin addiction and extreme aggression) seem to be sublimated into reconciliation. However, on closer listening, this reconciliation—"You're a better man than I" (the final line from Kipling's poem "Gunga Din")—can be read as an exercise in melancholia, where each singer is really meaning the reverse—"I am a better man than you." The depth of the two Libertines' libidinal investment in each other was made clear in their early interviews and output, with romanticized notions of an "Albion" that both were constructing. Here, a basic reading of the Libertines' biography is particularly useful in highlighting a specific aspect of melancholia. As we have learned, Freud claimed that in the case of the object dying or being otherwise removed from existence, the subject tends to enter a state of mourning, whereas a betrayal or refusal by a still living or existing object is much more likely to go toward the melancholic. The first dissolution of the Libertines in 2003/4 followed an intense period of bonding between Barat and Doherty. In Freudian terms, this would be the establishment of a huge investment of the ego in the notion of other as object in itself. In practice, this means a huge number of important places, processes, and actions are associated in relation to this other, whose presence becomes a vital part of the consistency of the ego. After the other betrays, they can no longer be acknowledged as the object of this love—such a thing must be repressed, as it is too hurtful to the ego. But in Freud's understanding, the fixed investments of libido in this person can't be withdrawn *tout court*. Nor can they be ignored as the second libidinal investment (called the "tonic libido"), which attaches to this formation when elements in reality that are connected to it are observed, would otherwise build up to intolerable levels. The solution the psyche chooses is ingenious in its simplicity. The ego investments are detached from the person or thing associated with the betrayal and, instead, attached to the self. So when Barat thinks of Albion, the residual—and now disliked—Doherty formation in the psyche is triggered, but instead of manifesting as Doherty, it comes out as Barat's self. Vice versa with Doherty, hence the delighted chorus "you're a better man than I," where each gains some measure of melancholic satisfaction, criticizing the betrayer by using themselves as proxy.

A similar kind of aggressive inversion of the latent truth of the psyche can be seen in Pavement's "Painted Soldiers" video, where guitarist Scott Kannberg is depicted as trying to end the band when, in fact, it was singer Stephen Malkmus who harbored such expectations. Malkmus's exasperation can be clearly read in his expression as he is lifted into an ambulance in this skit.

Conversely, there's a lovely little version of mourning in LCD Soundsystem's "Someone Great." The melodic phrasing here has two registers—an antecedent phrase (a questioning phrase) is sung relatively high; the consequent (answering phrase) is sung low as if a monologue is being played as a dialogue in two registers—the latter, lower phrase coinciding with consigning memories to another place.

[High voice:] The little things that made me nervous
[Low voice:] Are gone in a moment.
[High voice:] I miss the way we used to argue,
[Low voice:] Locked in your basement

Here we can hear the gradual withdrawal of investment in the object, as the subject repeats through citations associated with the lost object. Yet, as there is no explicit betrayal, there is no censorship. James Murphy is aware that the sadness is tied to the lost object, and not himself, and is cognizant of the slow process of recuperation that his psyche is going through as notions and places associated with the lost object become less hurtful over time.

In a similar view, Sufjan Stevens' *Carrie and Lowell*, an album that concerns the death of his mother, can be considered a work of mourning, as the loss is acknowledged, and in the structure of the album, we can see a process of working-through and delibidinization of the notion of the mother. Even though there are some disturbing and depressive images in the album, Stevens as-a-subject is aware of his state of mourning and its slight melancholic tendencies. Returning to our primary example of the Libertines, we can see a clear contrast, as the Libertines do seem to believe that they wrote a magnanimous song in "Gunga Din." The rage is below the conscious level, creating a text in which the manifest and latent content is not aligned.

## Neurosis

So far we have mainly been defining components or processes in Freud's understanding of the unconscious. In this section, we move toward classifications of tendencies in the psyche into certain conditions. There are four key terms: neurosis, psychosis, hysteria, and perversion. The boundaries between them are not always clear. Hysteria, for example, can present as a mixture of psychosis and neurosis. What tends to tie these four terms together is that they are defined by their relationship to one another.

We've decided to devote the whole of Chapter 7 to perversion, but we will deal with the other three terms now. It's also worth pointing out at this stage that we will illustrate that neurosis lies beneath several songs that claim to be about hysteria or psychosis. But let's start with a definition of a neurotic thought: *one that comes from somewhere*. Let's unpack that. Coming from *somewhere* is opposed here to coming from *ourselves*, or *another*. So we don't get to neurotic ideas consciously, nor do we hear them from a recognizable other subject. Instead, they just come *upon* us, as if from somewhere else. Consider the obsessive-compulsive when they close their door. Is it locked? Should I check it again? This process isn't arrived at through reason, but arrives as a kind of demand from somewhere else. That somewhere else is the unconscious.

We can, maybe, shine a little more light on this definition by comparing neurosis to psychosis. A neurotic demand is a demand from somewhere else that we recognize as being irreal but, nevertheless, has an effect, whereas psychosis, discussed below, presents itself as a demand from somewhere else that we mistake for being real. So there is a kind of similarity, but also a kind of difference, between the neurotic and psychotic models of thinking.

What does neurosis sound like? The answer to that question is complicated by the fact that the objects of neurosis can be incredibly varied. If we consider some of the conditions that operate under the heading of the neuroses, such as anxiety, impulse control, obsessions, and phobias, we can see a commonality in which a central object is being poorly repressed. The object functions: in anxiety, as something that causes physical symptoms; in obsessions, as ideas and routines we return to; in impulse control and addictions, as objects we seek out; in phobias, as objects we avoid. Somewhere behind these objects—the manifest objects of neurosis—we have the latent objects or formations in the unconscious that have been repressed. As in the discussion of displacement and condensation, there can be a big space between the latent and the manifest.

Further complicating this picture, we can postulate that there is a difference between objects of neurosis and objects that are found aesthetically pleasing. How about Prince's love of the color purple? It could be a neurotic object that kept returning to him (with its regal associations and so on), or it could simply have been an aesthetic decision to favor this shade. It could even be a compromise between the two: the neurotic object now rationalized as an aesthetic choice. This makes neurotic markers difficult to discern in pop music, because in music there was always an aesthetic imperative.

To start from "another place," however, one of the clearest symbols of neurosis in the history of Western music, in its broadest sense, might be the famous *Symphonie fantastique: Épisode de la vie d'un artiste ... en cinq parties* by Hector Berlioz. In the first movement, the musical "program" reads:

> The author imagines that a young musician, afflicted with that moral disease that a well-known writer calls the vague des passions, sees for the first time a woman who embodies all the charms of the ideal being he has imagined in his dreams, and he falls desperately in love with her. Through an odd whim, whenever the beloved appears before the mind's eye of the artist it is linked with a musical thought whose character, passionate but at the same time noble and shy, he finds similar to the one he attributes to the beloved.
>
> This melodic image and the model it reflects pursue him incessantly like a double *idée fixe*. That is the reason for the constant appearance, in every moment of the symphony, of the melody that begins the first Allegro. The passage from this state of melancholy reverie, interrupted by a few fits of ground-less joy, to one of frenzied passion, with its movements of fury, of jealousy, its return of tenderness, its tears, its religious consolations.[20]

---

[20] Brittan Francesca, "Berlioz and the Pathological Fantastic: Melancholy, Monomania, and Romantic Autobiography," *Nineteenth Century Music* 29, no. 3 (2006): 213.

**Example 2.1** The opening of the *idée fixe* melody from Berlioz' *Symphonie fantastique*, 1830.

The melody itself is well known and always appears to come from "outside" of the orchestral setting in each movement, changing the whole course of the drama. As described by Berlioz himself, it comes from another place—the *idée fixe* (a psychological term associated with obsession, in general circulation in the nineteenth century) "pursues" him; he can't escape it.

This works well in the course of a five-movement program symphony, but how can this level of neurosis figure in popular music, with tracks generally being much shorter in duration? As noted with the Prince example, this could be a recurring idea that follows an artist throughout their career. We might think of Madonna's songs, with their religious themes—"Like a Prayer," "Like a Virgin," "Sanctuary," "Holy Water"; her list is huge. Religious imagery, especially when it contrasts the artist's more liberal, free, and sexually commanding persona, can be conceived as an outside place that makes false demands, one that the artist may consciously know to be irreal—along with her religious name Madonna—something bestowed upon her. As we come to visit Lacan in the next chapters, we'll refine our vision of neurosis as a question that we always imagined is being addressed to us from the voice of law and order; religion is a wonderful symbol of that. Sure, it's an aesthetic musical choice too, but it's one that still arguably comes from outside. We might also think of Robyn, whose obsession with robotics, cyborgs, and so on comes through consistently in songs like "The Girl and the Robot," "Fembot," "Robot Boy," to list only the most obvious. Robyn adopts a different palette of musical traits that summon up robotic aesthetics in each song. Think of the blips and interruptions, glitches and malfunctioning repetitions of "Robot Boy"; think of her generally overly simplistic "mechanical" three-chord patterns in some songs, contrasting these with some of the weird progressions in others that give what music theorists, using Freud, would call an "uncanny" feeling, in this case the "uncanniness" of Silicon Valley.[21] In both of these cases, however, it's difficult to discern how much of this is a simple aesthetic choice, how much of this is a cliché that an artist slips into and later cannot avoid repeating, and how much of this is a portrayal of something more like neurosis.

Maybe we can look to the Pixies for a slightly more sustained example. As is well known, the Pixies' gimmick was to stage a dialogue between loud music and soft music

---

[21] We're thinking here of the "slide transformations" in "The Girl and the Robot," which, according to recent music theorists, are prominent in film scores, replacing, to some extent, the "Hexatonic Pole" that Richard Cohn found to be uncanny in the classical tradition. See Richard Cohn, "Uncanny Resemblances: Tonal Signification in the Freudian Age," *Journal of the American Musicological Society* 57, no. 2 (2004): 285–324; Frank Lehman, *Hollywood Harmony* (New York: Oxford University Press, 2018), 103–5.

**Example 2.2** Comparison of the opening melodies of Modest Mouse's "3rd Planet" and the Pixies' "Where Is My Mind?"

or, more subtly, as musics that seem to come from different places—one interior, one exterior. This became a feature of Pixies-inspired bands such as Modest Mouse.[22] Let's think about a song from each artist, both similar in some regards—The Pixies' famous "Where Is My Mind?" (*Surfer Rosa*, 1988) and Modest Mouse's "3rd Planet." In the Pixies' "Where Is My Mind?" (*The Moon and Antarctica*, 2000) the layers of instrumentation build up and present a contradictory world of stability and instability to accompany the images of being turned upside down—the warm acoustic guitar, the distant, fragile voice, the rocking but distorted interval of a third in the heavy guitar, the plodding drums and bass. This all immediately stops as if we are suddenly cast into a different space where all of this noise ceases, and we have a simple bass and minimal drum continuation, while the singer voices "where is my mind?" in a semi-spoken, more comfortable, clearer register and tone. The lyrics are full of clues that outside agencies are confronting an inside world. For example, while swimming in the Caribbean, fish verbally bombard him with unreasonable and clearly irreal demands. But which is the inside world, and which is the outside?—this isn't musically clear. Is the built-up world of fragile stability the inner world, meaning that the questioning of the mind is happening outside in the social world? Or is the inner world—the calm clarity of the voice in the lower, comfortable vocal register questioning the location of his mind, which is otherwise dispersed somewhere else—lost in the noise of the outside world and its irreal demands? This inability to tell what is truly an internal or external pressure is, however, part and parcel of the neurotic experience.

Inspired by the Pixies' opening melodic gambit of descending triadic melody (see Examples 2.2), and rhythmically flexible rhythm (trying to cram as many words into the strict beats as possible), the same kickstarts Modest Mouse's "3rd Planet," whose protagonist declares that they are, like the Pixies, "falling apart." In both cases, the descent seems to support the images of things being turned upside down, and twinned with this is the feeling that this is working its way from above (air; outside) to below (ground; the inside).

The "3rd Planet" presents a sustained vision of an outside agency who watches—a mixture of God and Big Brother—while the protagonist projects his realities to speculate

---

[22] For a more thorough consideration of Modest Mouse's formal continuities and discontinuities, see Kenneth Smith, "Formal Negativities, Breakthroughs, Ruptures and Continuities in the Music of Modest Mouse," *Popular Music* 33, no. 3 (2014): 428–54.

about macrocosms and microcosms. Like the Pixies song, there is a scene of swimming that offers him food for thought, and the thought strikes him that microscopic animals are swimming around in his own body just like he is swimming in the Atlantic. He then speculates upwards that "the universe is shaped exactly like the earth; if you go straight along you're gonna end up where you were." These are ideas that take hold from outside and are presented as irreal. Such outsideness is sometimes registered with the violently interrupting guitar chords, playing rapid but intermittent punctuations every second beat as the lyrics describe "outside, naked, shivering, looking blue from the cold sunlight that's reflected off the moon," and the voice is projected (as it so often is in this track about the irreal "outside" demands) through constantly changing and novel reverberative effects.

Even before this, however, there are indications of musical neurosis. As described above, the opening line—"Everything that keeps me together is falling apart"—is given the same treatment as the opening of the Pixies' track—the gentle, rocking thirds articulated by the guitar, the thin, strained voice. But, after the second line, which is musically identical—"I got this thing that I consider my only art ..."—an instrumental nothingness takes us to a different, hollower place as he names his condition—"it's fucking people over," when the guitar and singer both offer a kind of shake or trill figure, and silence allows the reverb to sink in. Musically, this is the equivalent to the Pixies' "where is my mind?" chorus—lyrically, it marks a moment when the singer gives a name to the demand that seems to come from outside (though it is clearly irreal) and which makes him repeatedly act negatively toward others.

If neurosis is difficult to separate from normal life and artistic considerations in our task of exploring pop songs, we must remember that, for Lacan, as we will see, neurotic is the new normal. We might then say that even simple verse-chorus structures have elements of neurosis—the verse can represent an interior world of questioning and struggling through ideas by the singing subject; the chorus can often represent a more unified, fixed outside object that keeps returning, both lyrically and musically (where verses change lyrically, and bridges change musically).[23] But we will also need to keep neurosis in the back of our minds for a little while longer, because as we move into more troublesome maladies—hysteria, paranoia (and later perversion)—we will see how sometimes the popular imagination often confuses these things with more common neurosis.

## Hysteria

Freud and Josef Breuer's *Studies on Hysteria* (1895) assured their place in history. Their approach is problematic today for its focus on the condition that male psychologists could only understand as a women's disease. In the nineteenth century, various

---

[23] Two recent books deal with the differences between verses and choruses as a running concern: David Temperley, *The Musical Language of Rock* (New York: Oxford University Press, 2018); Drew Nobile, *Form as Harmony in Rock Music* (New York: Oxford University Press, 2020). See especially Nobile's summary remark that "verses are starting points, choruses are conclusions" (71).

symptoms were lumped together and associated with "women's problems" ("hystera" is Greek for uterus). Nietzsche famously emasculated Wagner by calling him a hysteric:

> Wagner's art is sick. The problems he presents on the stage—all of them problems of hysterics—the convulsive nature of his affects, his overexcited sensibility, his taste that required ever stronger spices, his instability which he dressed up as principles, not least of all the choice of his heroes and heroines—consider them as physiological types (a pathological gallery!)—all of this taken together represents a profile of sickness that permits no further doubt.[24]

Certainly Freud carried on this tradition of male fascination with the female hysteric, but at least (if we can defend him *just a little*) he tried to get to the bottom of the situation, rather than parading "hysterical women" around medical theaters as other psychologists did. He and Breuer—although differing in some ways about treatment options (hypnosis or not?)—tried to understand what psychological traumas were lurking beneath such extreme physical symptoms. Their fundamental discovery was the "psychosomatic" relation, by which a trauma that was not dealt with properly and that remained repressed would break through the surface of everyday life as a physical symptom—mental pain is "converted" into physical symptoms, which can all vary greatly.

Freud became an overnight celebrity with this book, and it was hugely inspirational to artists particularly in *fin-de-siècle* Vienna. Think of the German expressionist composers—Schoenberg, Webern, Berg, and their obsession with hysterical characters. Schoenberg's *Erwartung* (*Expectation*) was a monodrama from 1909 from a text by Marie Pappenheim, who was the physician-cum-poet cousin of Bertha Pappenheim, the famous "Anno O" who was one of the principal subjects of *Studies on Hysteria*. The plot of *Erwartung* features great repression—a woman, who we soon learn has murdered a lover, stumbles across his body in the forest and thinks it's a tree-trunk. She has repressed the deed. We hear all the hallmarks of hysterical symptoms. Her music is highly atonal and *athematic* (there are supposedly no melodies or themes in it), which make it sound ultra-chaotic even to modern ears. *Studies on Hysteria* was also massively influential to Richard Strauss, via his librettist-collaborator Hugo von Hofmannsthal, who made his *Elektra* into a Freudian hysteric, who famously lives in the shadows, spits and bites people, and finally dances herself to death after flinging back her head and arms like a maenad ("zurückgeworfen wie eine Mänade") and dancing herself through hysteria into death. Of course, Strauss didn't have to get the diagnosis exactly right—Elektra did not repress anything at all. Her trauma is the death of her father, and that is hardly repressed; it is, by contrast, the only thing she actually focuses on. She lives only for revenge. There is clearly an artistic fascination here with the lone, female hysteric, without the fundamental Freudian insight of the condition. And hysteria isn't really a recognized condition today—we know so much more about

---

[24] Friedrich Nietzsche, *The Case of Wagner*, trans. Walter Kaufmann (New York: Vintage, 1967), 166.

the various symptoms and psychological grounding—but the basic Freudian insight is not really challenged. Hysteria itself has become a chimera.

And most pop songs claiming to be about hysteria aren't. Consider Muse's "Hysteria" (*Absolution*, 2003) in which a character signals musical aggression and frustration, trying to "break out." While heavy rock riffs and a wild guitar solo summons up its dark side, the music video shows a man in his cell in a mental hospital smashing his furniture. The man has been obsessively watching videos of a woman he admires, getting more and more angry and jealous as the song progresses. His outburst is neurotic frustration and despair—nothing has been repressed in the past—he is attempting to deal with his trauma consciously. And the tradition of misdiagnosing hysteria in pop music culture goes back at least to Def Leppard (*Hysteria*, 1987), whose love ballad "Hysteria" gives the mild and simple pop chorus (with that lovely, clean, reverberating guitar sound):

> Oh, I get hysterical, hysteria
> Oh can you feel it, do you believe it?
> It's such a magical mysteria.

All the singer means, as the pleasant musical cushioned bedding shows, is a general sense of Cole Porter's "You do something to me / something that simply mystifies me." This isn't even neurosis; it's just a straightforward love song.

Just Kiddin's "hysteria" (*Hysteria*, 2018) gets somewhere closer. Perhaps the female voice itself takes us nearer, portraying a woman struggling because a lover has started to control her thoughts (perhaps through gaslighting her into believing she is "hysterical" when in reality she isn't):

> You've been running around in circles in my mind and it's changing me, and I've been letting you control what's deep inside, and it ain't like me

But even here, the fact that the sufferer is perfectly conscious of the obsessive thinking shows that we are talking about more neurotic behavior. In terms of the music, the word hysteria is followed at the end of the chorus by a moment of silence; we don't have the outbursts of the Muse song, nor do we have any sense of the unconscious bypassing the conscious censor and controlling the whole dialogue.

Finnish singer Anna Abreu's electro synth-pop anthem "Hysteria" (*Rush*, 2011) defines hysteria in her lyrics as a "crazy love emotion," where two lovers push their love to its physical limits. From the dirty bass and 1980s retro-synths and sexy vocalizing, we get the impression that the "hysteria" here is basically just sex.

These are all portrayals of something other than hysteria, although this is scarcely surprising since hysteria, by its own nature, generally doesn't recognize itself as such. True examples of hysteria are difficult to find, because when someone tells us that they have a trauma, they are de facto not repressing it. But there are still many places where we can find it at work.

The key distinction we make here is that hysteria is a symptom of something else, not an end in and of itself. The manifestations of hysteria, variously in physical symptoms, vocal tics, unsupported beliefs, and parapraxes (unintended actions), are the mechanism by which an underlying trauma speaks to the world. That is to say: hysteria speaks by every possible means but speech. Or perhaps, more properly, hysteria speaks but never articulates itself through speech. This theme will be returned to in the next chapter when we consider Lacan's "Four Discourses."

## Patrick Wolf, "Childcatcher"

If we want to find a pop song whose source is a past trauma that plays itself out with physical symptoms in the present, we may have to dig quite deep to find something more traumatic than Patrick Wolf's account of a pedophilic experience in "The Childcatcher" (*Lycanthropy*, 2003). Wolf played on his name throughout this period, giving us images of werewolves and lycanthropy. He often uses this to represent the unconscious forces that the conscious mind tries to repress. Think of any werewolf in popular fiction—the man (or woman?) who lives by day, often doesn't realize what s/he does at night, and if they do, they usually want to stop it but can't. The werewolf is in many ways the uncontrollable "Jekyll and Hyde" scenario, which Stephenson published only a few years before Freud's theories of the unconscious id, ego, and superego. Herman Hesse's *Steppenwolf* (1927) comes closer to Freud; the character in this novel is split between his refined and sophisticated existence, on the one hand, and his unchecked animal aggression and homelessness, on the other. Patrick Wolf's songs generally are subject to sudden breaks in almost all parameters of the music, and they cannily depict the massive material impingement of a chaotic, repressed underworld and a regular upper world—a form of hysteria breathing through as a musical symptom. "The Childcatcher" is no exception.

On the surface, "The Childcatcher" may seem like a poor example of hysteria. Like Elektra—the character-narrator (the child or adult remembering childhood) is dealing with the trauma by remembering its details in all of their graphically explicit horror. However, there are musical indications flying at us from all sides that the trauma has been *and still is being* repressed to some degree, and that the symptoms of hysteria have been and are still erupting through the surface.

Our graph of the song (see Example 2.3) shows the passage of time from left to right (rendered as hypermetric units: each being essentially a four-measure phrase) and instrumentation from top to bottom. The shapes in the body of the graph simply show what sounds are present at any given moment. The wavy lines show Wolf's movement between different voice types, and filled squares depict intensity (volume or sometimes rhythmic density), with gradients representing an increase or decrease. The graph can't represent every nuance, but it can at least help us zoom in on areas of interest.

Let's take the big snapshot first. The song has a bassoon bass almost throughout, which binds the song's sections together. There is a basic verse-chorus structure, with the verse recounting the tale of horror, and the chorus singing "You better run, run, run as fast as you can, but you can't run, run from the childcatcher's hands." The choruses happen at hypermeasures 4–5 and 8–9, so you can see how there is a growing intensity across this montage-like pattern. But, as intensity grows, things start to

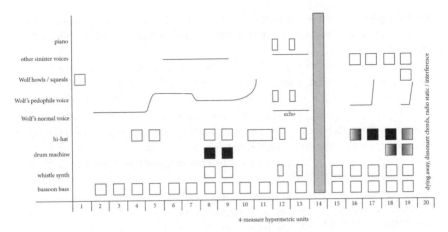

**Example 2.3** Graphical representation of Patrick Wolf's "Childcatcher."

break down. Between hypermeasures 12–13 we hear two-measure units of a childish, synthesized penny whistle noise, alternating with heavy drums in quick succession, but at hypermeasure 14, there is a total breakdown of flow. The drums stutter, the singer stammers, the volume keeps running wild. This is the real moment of breakthrough of symptoms, when the regularity of the four-measure phrase gets completely shattered. The music after hypermeasure 15 starts to slowly rebuild and regroup, trying to cover over these horrific cracks with each instrument adding to a slowly building ostinato layer, before the song ends in a complete full musico-psychological breakdown, with the sounds of fading voices, dying chords, radio-static and white noise, all constantly interrupting each other suddenly—a human, repression machine is breaking down.

The distorting interruptions to the musical flows, the bursting cracks and fissures in the surface represent physical breakthroughs of the unconscious, what Freud might call "the return of the repressed." The philosopher Theodor Adorno had a word for this in the music of Mahler, "*Durchbruch*"—breakthrough.[25] Remember that Freud's hysteria "converted" trauma that had not been laid to rest into physical symptoms. These musical eruptions or breakthroughs are those physical symptoms. The symptoms are physical here in the sense that the instruments themselves are suffering while the singer narrates, but the physicality is doubly felt in Wolf's control of his voices. He gives us (i) the voice of the (former) child—his own voice, (ii) the voice of the pedophile—a gruff, low, aggressive tone, (iii) howls and squeals, and (iv) the backing vocals that seem to be driving him on his journey, but can also be the disembodied, ghostly voices of the past. In the graph, we've shown these four voices and used lines to show Wolf's journey through them. It seems as though the general narrative is that these unconscious voices are something outside of his own constitutive ego, which

---

[25] Theodor Adorno, *Mahler: A Musical Physiognomy*, trans. Edmund Jephcott (Chicago: University of Chicago Press, 1992), 5.

are driving him toward physicality, taking him through the trauma that he can't speak himself—he can only mimic the pedophile's voice—toward the brutal physicality of the wolf's howl.

Even in Wolf's masterful control of voices, we find subtle attempts to keep repression alive, which just stimulate more and more symptoms. Wolf sings about repression in hypermeasure 16, after the main breakdown, where he tries to "pull himself together" musically, with the solid harnessing of the instrumental forces into a strong, driving, controlled, rhythmic, goal-oriented state of togetherness. He sings: "This is the age of constipation; this is the age of martyrdom." "Constipation" here—hardly an example of scatological humor—represents the classic Freudian anal retention, the refusal to let bad things out. "Martyrdom" represents the pre-#MeToo era of suffering in silence and "chalking it up to experience"; in a word, repression. But as we move further away from the trauma, with all this talk of a stiff upper lip, we come closest to it. We've already heard Wolf's inability to finish some sentences ("you can't run, run, you can't ..."). Wolf begins whispering in the pedophile's voice: "I think you even enjoyed it; I think I even saw you come." The word "come" is a half-spoken, embarrassed noise that turns into a harsh squeal—it becomes a word that he can't actually *say*, and instead, *it says him*—it becomes a physical symptom and shows us that, for all this song is a huge #MeToo statement (at least within the protagonists' world), the process of repression and its transformation into hysteria are still at work. The graph shows that there are two striking, compact transitions from singing to squealing in this last section of the song, rapidly retracing the steps that the much longer first section had more thoroughly and more subtly trodden. What we find in the song's overall trajectory, then, is that there is an even more polarized stalemate between the conscious attempt to deal with the trauma and the entrenched repressive mechanisms that convert it into symptoms.

We may think of Wolf's "wolfings out" not as an expression of raw id, nor even as a celebration of controlling the wolf inside of us (see the movie *Teen Wolf*); the wolf here is hysteria, not the id.

But what we've really done here kind of puts the cart before the horse. We're looking at the diagnosis that's already there. Wolf is only *partly* repressing in this song, which is more a form of "talking cure" in itself. Most hysteria, at least in Freudian tradition, requires a psychoanalyst to speak through the fractured subject and discover the hidden trauma, deal with it, and hope that the symptoms stop. However, there are certainly songs with more successful repressions, to the extent that we see their workings but not their traumatic source, which remains deeply hidden.

## St. Vincent, "The Apocalypse Song"

"The Apocalypse Song" comes from Annie Clark's (St. Vincent's) debut album *Marry Me* (2007). Although the title of the album is a reference to a running gag on *Arrested Development*, it might well remind us that one of the "symptoms" of hysteria in nineteenth-century women was not getting married! The song begins with power and inexorability. In fact it begins with the famous drum rhythm from Ravel's *Bolero*, also featured in My Chemical Romance's "Black Parade," Muse's "The Globalist," and Suede's

"Still Life," and is a symbol of control and the power to bring listeners to a shattering climax. From this indicator, it seems as if the song is going to build in one direction, and from the title, we might imagine this to be the apocalypse. However, although the singer's position is typically vague, it seems as though Clark is diagnosing the "other" in a relationship as an hysteric—someone who is afraid of getting close to someone else (Clark begs, "give me little death," that is, an orgasm). This "other," however, seems to be choosing to give his/herself to religious zealotry (figured as "hysteria"). The first part of the song flows as a fairly straightforward verse-chorus cycle, in which the verses describe the other person's problems in a vague way, while the chorus is much fuller and marks a quirkily seductive attempt to insult the hysterical partner into moving on from their unknown repressed trauma—"I guess you are afraid of what everyone is made of." From then on, we are subject to musically hysterical breakthroughs:

*First insult: Religious repression*
At 1:20 Clark sings in a mock religious aside (a kind of bridge section), "all of your praying amounts to just one breath / Please keep your victory, but give me little death," and we hear her delicately reverberated vocals sending mock prayers to heaven. She seems to be trying to strip away the other's religious attempts to paper over their trauma in order to allow them a truer fulfillment, which the anthemic chorus offers. The strings have been fervently playing clipped, staccato notes, with suppressed dynamics, but now give us the full swirl of post-repressive enjoyment. Religious repression turns into religious hysteria at the end of the song.

*First mock-hysterical outbreak:* 2:15. We hear our musical interruption, initiated by the kind of stomps and claps that Queen enjoy in "We will rock you," but in the background an organ (a religious symbol) struggles to break through, and the angelic chords of "Time" (as if time is running out) become sexualised through chromatic dissonance. Rhythmically, we get the communal aggression of Queen's rhythm, whose togetherness gradually gives way to asynchronicity and disaggregation. Is this the repression of the church, the repression of the individual who uses the church to furiously keep their trauma locked away, or the attempt of the singer to break through the other's repression?

*Healing/seducing chorus:* The chorus bursts back in at 2:37. She is trying to coax him/her out of a repressive, hysterical state with seducing chromatic harmonies and religious "plagal" cadences, but these latter are transformed into the seductive "minor version" of the "subdominant" chord.

*Second mock-hysterical outbreak/religious repression insult:* 3:15. The chorus disintegrates orchestrally, like the famous moment of the Beatles' "A day in the life" with a stuttering repeat of "what everyone is made of," as if we are somehow breaking the fourth wall and listening to a record stuck in a groove. The "Queen" drum-stomps and hand claps return, but now in full synchronicity, while Clark sings "So take to the streets with your Apocalypse refrain" and the organ plays seamlessly, now hushed and united with strings. It seems as though the repression has won out. The sufferer will not pass through it, and is hysterically shouting about the end of the world in the streets.

*Final sting:* 3:32. The multi-layered vocals disappear as Clark sings, "Your devotion has the look of a lunatic's gaze." This insult is delivered by her lone, unaccompanied voice, making this a last ditch plea from the heart—no longer from society but from the singer (at least the protagonist) personally. She, in turn, returns the gaze of the apocalyptic hysteric with pity and pleading. But neither work. The trauma remains repressed.

## A Cure? Alanis Morissette, "Thank U"

Unlike several other psychological conditions that Freud, and later Lacan, thought could not be cured completely, hysteria can be treated by undergoing psychoanalytic treatment to bring traumas into conscious light. Alanis Morissette, in "Thank U" (*Supposed Former Infatuation Junkie*, 1998), sheds off the yoke of masculine psychological framing even in the title of her album, but she also does so in the song. The music video, too, casts Morissette as visually looking like a Freudian hysteric, walking the streets naked, though this image is also twinned with the image of her new spiritual awakening and purity after her trip to India. Morissette described herself as drowning in work, and she desperately wanted to come up for air.

The verses describe symptoms after the opening synth-pop lullaby-like world is evoked. She describes being on antibiotics, overeating, masochism, chasing after fame, bottled-up grief, blaming other people. The storing up of grief and shelving of traumas seems to be self-diagnosed as the root cause of her burnout. When she starts to "let go," "jump off," "unabashedly bawl [her] eyes out," "grieving it all one at a time," we realize what the music has been telling us all along, with its gentle, warm yet affirmative power—that she is better. In the life-affirming chorus, she says "Thank you" to both her unnamed trauma ("the terror") and the place of her awakening ("India"). Unlike the St. Vincent and Patrick Wolf, there are no interruptions, distortions, musical unconscious breakthroughs of repressed torture—we have a plain and simple vision of a human post-catharsis, post-repressive state.

It is worth noting that we are not just cartographers of the unconscious but devotees of its importance. We want to hear the unconscious sing! Listening to "Thank U" and its late nineties/Gap advert/neo-spiritualist/No Logo/soft-critique-of-capitalism-without-follow-through worldview, a listener has to wonder if this destination is a good end point for Alanis. One of the things that we'll keep coming back to in this book is the idea that these formations of the unconscious aren't objects blocking the formation of an otherwise pure self; they are the self; you are the interplay of id and ego, and a little repression—let us be clear, not trauma but repression—isn't such a bad thing. One lesson of psychoanalysis is this: you aren't there in this higher system that Freud calls consciousness; "you" are the whole system of the psyche and its effects. If we listen to the end of "Thank U," where a scream replaces the pop-psychobabble of the lyrics, we can perhaps sense an aporia that has grown in the place where Alanis's old "bad" desires were installed. It's a kind of indeterminate mix of yeses and nos that suggest there is—at best—an ambivalence about the transformation Alanis has made. We'll pick this up again in the next chapter when we look at Lacan's **Four Discourses**.

## Psychosis

Neurosis does not disavow the reality, it only ignores it; psychosis disavows it and tries to replace it.[26]

### "Psychotic Reaction," Count Five

Songs claiming to be about psychosis often aren't. Consider first "Psychotic Reaction" by Count Five (1966). The group describes feelings of general depression from unrequited love—"Can't get your love; can't get affection." The songwriter fully accepts this reality, where, as Freud says in a different case, "the psychotic reaction would have disavowed reality."[27] The whole song rehearses the Rolling Stones' "I can't get no satisfaction" of the previous year, even with similar grungy guitar rock accompaniment pattern. Perhaps the only way for Count Five to outdo the Stones was to go further into mental anguish and declare themselves psychotic. The band shout, "Uh oh little girl. Psychotic reaction. And it sounds like this," before playing in double time, more percussively with effects such as muted strumming and caterwauling with mouth organ and guitars. This is all very improvisatory, but it is a slightly aggressive outburst rather than anything like true psychosis, which, for Freud, begins similarly to mourning where a subject withdraws investment from objects in the world, and the libido turns in on itself and, crucially, delusions arise. This delusional state then replaces the subject's reality with a new reality. Psychotic language (as we will discuss shortly) was itself a subject of Freudian fascination, particularly for Lacan, whose PhD thesis was on this topic. Freud believed that the psychotic's incoherent language could be understood just as dreams revealed key meanings. For Lacan, the psychotic condition was also about a failure to accept the "name of the father"—or, put more simply, the law. The psychotic does not set about to break the law; the psychotic does not accept the law—he/she *disavows* it. In this sense, then the alternate reality stirred up by Count Five's "outburst" could not really be called psychotic as it works well within the parameters of the norms of 1960s rock-and-roll. Even if the "rock out" sections represent a different form of reality to the words described in the narrative of general teenage dejection, they are not presenting a

---

[26] Sigmund Freud, "The Loss of Reality in Neurosis and Psychosis," in *The Standard Edition of the Complete Psychological Works of Sigmund Freud*, vol. XIX, trans. James Strachey (London: The Hogarth Press, [1924] 1961), 185.
[27] Ibid., 184.

new reality that substitutes on a permanent basis for the real reality; they are just giving us an insight into how they feel.

## "4.48 Psychosis," Tindersticks

Playwright Sarah Kane's last play, *4.48 Psychosis* (2000), depicts a state of clinical depression, which she had herself suffered. The play utilizes the literary technique of schizophasia or "word salad"—the confusing and often unintelligible speech common in schizophrenia, which is an underlying condition that psychotic states are sometimes caused by. The British group Tindersticks wrote a song of the same name on their album *Waiting for the Moon* (2003), and they come closer, certainly, than Count Five in conveying the psychotic experience. However, there is a crucial difference in the way that psychosis is dispersed between the singer and the musical "voices."

Consider first "Expressionism" in art, music, and literature. One facet of Expressionism was the idea of casting interior mental intensity outside—we might say projecting internal trouble outward. Note how in Munch's famous "The Scream," which adorns (albeit defaced) the cover of this book, the person in the center is painted a ghostly white, and outside is a world of screaming color clashes. Is the person screaming? Or are they trying to cover their ears from the sounds of the scream outside? Or are they listening to music? To the psychotic, there may be no obvious difference.

And so it is with this musical portrayal of psychosis—where the instruments in the ensemble are giving a more accurate portrayal of a person in the grip of psychosis than the person singing. Singer Stuart Staples begins counting down from a hundred in irregular intervals, mimicking a person unable to pass the "serial sevens" test, often used to determine the mental function of a patient. The voice used to "sing" the song is only spoken, and spoken in a very-matter-of-fact cold and clinically detached tone, very low and hard to hear in the audio field—it projects a kind of "out of body" experience—a common symptom of psychosis. "And there is my body dancing on glass."

The words often speak straightforwardly about a kind of paranoia—one of the common symptoms:

> The television talks full of eyes—the spirits of sight, and now I am so afraid, I'm seeing things, I'm hearing things, I don't know who I am.

These are declarations of paranoia, however, rather than the schizophasic language that we might expect and which saturate Kane's play. While we don't really find a lyrical analog to this type of psychotic language in the song, we do hear it musically. The words are recited over an unduly loud, distorted, low guitar riff, which begins as a simple oom-oom-cha pattern (think Jimmy Hendrix's "Foxy Lady" rhythm, but without any of the real harmonic interest or bite of his chords) and is played gently but overdriven with fuzz. This is low-level guitar noodling without any sense of direction. Layers build up, but we hardly feel as though there is an end in sight. This is a classic "wall" of psychotic

**Example 2.4** Edvard Munch, "The Scream" (1893).

fog, through which we are struggling to see the world as it is. The music is an outside representation of the internal chaos, just like the psychotic scream of Munch.

It would not be true to say there is no telos here—no aim nor goal. Certainly, there isn't really anything that could suddenly make the singer feel well again, but as he begins to sing of 4.48 approaching "the happy hour" (actually 3:20 in the song), the guitar wall starts to turn toward a major key, and an organ starts to replace some of the noise indicating a kind of temporary release from the psychosis, a clearing of the fog, reminding us that psychosis can occur in waves or "episodes." Staples describes it as a "clarity visit" when the alarm clock goes off at 4.48. There are also indications that the root cause is "love":

> I would rather have lost my legs, pulled out my teeth, gouged my eyes, than lost my love.

We can't equate love to desire, but it's worth comparing this 2003 song briefly with one of the songs from the Tindersticks' first album from 1993. The slow, scraping, squeaking guitar sounds are reminiscent of songs from their first album such as "Whiskey and Water," which portrayed a sordid world of libido-driven haze. There Stapes also recited words amid similarly distorted, smoky guitar fog, but here, the words are pure libidinal drive:

> Softly nudge toward her, gently put inside her, and that other life just seems so ugly to me now

But he begins singing in the chorus—quite a catchy tune:

> So tell me how it feels; it feels so good.

This depicts the sexual act and the naughty talk during it. It gives a sense of musical release, though the libido keeps returning in a verse-chorus cycle. In "4:48 Psychosis," however, the libido does seem to be depicted, musically at least, as the root cause of the malady, but there is no structural break into song, no catharsis, satisfaction, euphoria, rather just a slow and subtle turn toward a temporarily more positive state—a calming of the psychosis, a rare moment of near clarity—a "visit."

## Dory Previn, "Mr Whisper"

The opposite side of the coin is explored by Dory Previn, poet, songwriter, married to conductor André Previn. In the 1970s she was dealing with the big topics in her songs: "With My Daddy in the Attic" deals with Stockholm syndrome and incest. Her song "Mr Whisper" begins as a country blues, regular song, with four square beats to the bar—catchy and quirky and light-humored. But, as it unfolds, the lyrics start to become deeper and darker in tone as we realize that there are sinister things beneath the calm and light facade. She sings of an imaginary friend who keeps her feeling sane, and this works to create a veneer of musical normality. However, beneath these blues riffs and laid-back lap-steel slides, we begin to hear of a loss of control. Mr. Whisper is no childlike imaginary friend, but a voice in her head that takes over her:

> I think I can control him, But instead Mister Whisper takes control, guides my heart and rides my soul the minute that he steps inside my head.

All this over the jolly blues singing. We then learn of electroshock therapy:

> Just when I am sure he'll stay, they shoot me with a bolt or two, they try to drive my mister friend away.

There are occasional reverb effects that project the voice into a kind of "out of body" experience, like that described by the Tindersticks, but we soon move toward an utter ramble and stream of consciousness. Part of this stream of words is like a psychoanalytic "free association" session:

> I lost my blue buttons he sent me on my birthday, but my blue buttons came loose ... loose ... Lucy Brown ... Lucy in the sky ... Luce ... Lucent ... Lucid ... Lucidity ... Lucifer ... Light ... Hang luce ... Stay loose.

As the veneer of musical normality shatters, we hear a range of whispering voices and radio static in the distance, asynchronous and chaotic. Mr. Whisper himself seems to multiply, and by the time the song fades out, there are three other voices. The poem, utterly chilling, then ends. Exploring the opposite trajectory to Tindersticks, we have now slipped from a relatively stable state into full psychosis.

### Early vs. Late Radiohead and the Sound of Psychosis

There are two ways of viewing the transition that Radiohead made between 1997's *OK Computer* and 2000's *Kid A*. For some it represents a band at the apex of their powers abandoning the thing that made them great, while for others it represents moving from the high of the former album to the even greater heights of the second. We write this book ourselves divided between these two perspectives! But rather than delving into those aesthetic judgments, we will use this final section to try and explain why Radiohead may have made this change. In turn, that discussion will be useful in making the larger point we have considered in this section about how hard it is to see neurosis or psychosis in popular music.

Psychosis and paranoia are related conditions. Indeed, paranoia is a subtype of psychosis, characterized by the full intellectualization of the objects of paranoia into a coherent worldview. In the case of a full psychotic episode, the patient is unlikely to be able to come up with an explanation of their beliefs that makes sense as a coherent whole. However, in paranoia, the elements that derive from the paranoiac psychosis are so coherent with a conceivable world that there would be no obvious schizzes or disjunctions in the narrative. An easy example is, of course, conspiratorial thinking. There are many conspiracy theories that have no basis in reality at all, yet they still attract adherents because they are, at some level, explanationally "complete"; from a distance, they are a coherent and seamless worldview. On a personal level, to be paranoid is like having one's own personal conspiracy theory, in which the perceived workings of the world differ from reality.

Conversely, we can imagine as fully psychotic someone who sees entities that aren't there. When trying to explain these entities to another person, there would be a similar effect to someone explaining the plot of a film with a nonhuman agent as if it happened: imagine *ET, Short Circuit, Gremlins*, or *Teenwolf* being explained by someone as if the story happened to them. Indeed, a wider point can be made here, which is that the medium through which neurosis or psychosis is perhaps best demonstrated is visual as well as auditory.

One way of understanding the motivation for the switch in style between the two Radiohead records is the attempt they made to make music that sounded like, or somehow represented, paranoia and psychosis. *OK Computer* is an album that touches on themes such as paranoid delusions of power, execution, or trauma; on abrupt changes of mood; and on moving between fixations and images that intrude. External entities like the state, aliens, artificial intelligence appear, manipulating the subject and threatening it from the periphery of thought. Yet, while thematically, this all points to the creation of a work that gives us a glimpse into paranoia and psychosis; sonically, the album never really gets close to that goal.

Consider the most famous song on *OK Computer*, "Paranoid Android," a song we'll analyze more fully in Chapter 5. Despite all the schizzes and contortions between its constituent parts, "Paranoid Android" is a largely seamless whole to the listener and fits entirely within the conventions of indie music of the late noughties. The overall musical impression of the album seems to offer a relief from psychosis, as at the end of "Karma Police," which celebrates its passing, "phew, for a minute there, I lost myself," or the entirety of "No Surprises" and its calming sound at the end of the record.

We can posit that the struggle to create more accurately the sound of psychosis and nonintegration led to the sharp disjunction between *OK Computer* and *Kid A*, the latter in moving beyond the stylistic conventions of indie rock and incorporating artifacts from modernist electroacoustic composition and *musique concrète*. These new tricks allowed Radiohead to create soundscapes of parts that can't be integrated, such as the brass midway through "The National Anthem." These sections remain distinct and, therefore, sound eerie, strange, and compel us to do the work of integration ourselves through careful listening. In contrast to the common model of the "reckless" psychotic, sufferers of the condition are often engaged in a struggle to carefully protect themselves against such ingresses of irreality, and perhaps this feeling is captured by the act of considered listening. Similarly, the lyrical content of the record is much more partial, with repetitions used to emphasize fixations on concepts. We hear much more about events and actions, rather than emotions, as if the focus is on getting the listener to understand the phenomenological feeling of experiencing the vignettes being presented. The language reads like an after-report of psychotic hallucination at times: "There are two colors in my head / There are two colors in my head," or "This is really happening."

This brings us nicely back to the disjunction between *OK Computer* and *Kid A* and a wider point about music. While *Kid A* can be said to be a much better attempt to get across psychosis in musical form, that form is still not one that is particularly apt to the task. Music is an artform about listening and integrating, and the experience of listening to music is seldom horrific or disturbing in the same way that, for example, watching a horror film can be (that said, we haven't begun our analysis of Cannibal Corpse yet). So, although there might be better presentation of psychosis in *Kid A*, the main effect of this on the listener is a demand to listen to the more complicated textures of the music.

# 3

# Bright Eyes (and Friends), and The Antlers Meet Jacques Lacan

As surely as night follows day, Lacan follows Freud in our account of twentieth-century psychoanalysis. By the time Lacan began his work, a number of reactions to Freudianism had played themselves out in developments in psychology, spiritualism, feminism, child development, philosophy, and other avenues of research. Many of Lacan's own additions to Freudianism are inspired by structural linguistics and a line of post-Hegelian philosophy concerned with alterity (otherness). One of the many things that make Lacan's work so interesting is his insistence that he was not improving Freudianism, but returning to its true essence. This is a fairly controversial way to describe Lacan's project, because there are some points at which there seems to be a very big departure from traditional Freudianism.

Much of Lacan's return to Freud can be explained by two influences noted above—linguistics and Hegelian philosophy. One of Lacan's central claims is that the unconscious is structured like a language, which means that the unconscious follows the rules of a language. Without diving too deeply into structural linguistics, we can say that there are two axes along which language is constructed. The first, which Lacan calls **metaphor**, tracks the way in which words substitute for another. If we take "the CAT sat on the mat" as an example, the term CAT could be replaced by DOG, HORSE, and so on, but also by LETTER or CHILD. The exact terms that can be linked this way depend on the construction of the individual's unconscious. Each subject's history is one in which the links between these terms has been forged by their experiences. Someone who was scratched by a cat might link CAT to "OW" or FEAR. Someone who had a cat might link it to CHILDHOOD or WILBUR (if the cat was so called). Obviously, there is quite a distance between these two destinations! The other axis is **metonymy**, which dictates the way in which the sentence is constructed: "the → cat → sat → on → the → mat." These two axes are sometimes linked in music to chord *substitution* (like those "tritone subs" we find in Jazz, where the chord called "G7" can be metaphorically related to "D♭7") and *progression* (where G7 is followed by C).[1] Lacan likens this latter, metonymy, to "desire," saying categorically that "desire is a

---

[1] For a fuller exploration of metonymy / metaphor in this context see: Kenneth Smith, *Desire in Chromatic Harmony* (New York: Oxford University Press, 2020).

metonymy"—we want G7 to move to C; we want "sat on the ..." to move to "mat."[2] But let's park these two axes for a moment and think about the other big Lacanian inspiration, alterity.

Alterity became a central concept in philosophy with Hegel's "master–slave dialectic" (this will become important when we look into masochism in Chapter 7). In the master–slave dialectic, Hegel shows that identity is not constructed individually, but interpersonally. Rather than a master simply being a master and a slave a slave, the master can only become a master when recognized as such by the slave. Yet, in this act of recognition, the slave can be seen to hold true power. The master is only a master and relies on the slave for his/her full identity. The slave, on the other hand, entering into productive relations with the world via labor, is capable of constructing an identity of her/his own without the master. This thought was taken up by phenomenologists, who used it to emphasize that our world is not constructed individually, but requires the presence of another.

In both of these aspects described above, we can contrast Lacanianism with Freudianism. In the latter, the unconscious works within and for the subject, and all otherness—everything external to the subject—is just data to be processed by the unconscious mechanisms. The Freudian unconscious is working for itself; the driving agent is the libido and its operation is solipsistic. This is no longer tenable in the Lacanian system where the unconscious is trying to achieve recognition from another and is directing its productive forces to ask not only "what am I" but, more pertinently, "what am I to you?"

This question of "what am I (to you)?" is further complicated by the new status of the unconscious as being structured like a language. There are really two languages in play here. One is the language of my own unconscious, and how the metaphorical and metonymic structures within it are connected. The second is the language in general, the language of the Other (sometimes called the big-Other), which represents not what an individual unconsciously produces, but how that production is likely to be interpreted by another who speaks that language. To put it simply, we each have our own private language, which we have to use to communicate with the other who speaks the general language. Because they don't identically match up, communication isn't possible. The section below looks at this issue of the difference primarily between the "symbolic," "imaginary," and "real" orders, between what we want to communicate, and the tools we have to communicate it. Whew, that was a lot of theory! Let's listen to some music.

## "Fevers and Mirrors": Real, Symbolic, Imaginary

Of Bright Eyes' second album, *Fevers and Mirrors* (2000), Conor Oberst, singer-songwriter, explains:

> The fever is basically whatever ails you or oppresses you ... in my case it's my neurosis, my depression. The mirror is, as you might have guessed, self-examination or reflection in whatever form. This could be vanity or self-loathing.[3]

---

[2] Jacques Lacan, *Écrits*, trans. Bruce Fink (London: W. W. Norton, [1966] 2006), 439.
[3] Taken from a mock interview (actually given by Todd Fink, impersonating Oberst) held on the album itself.

Several of the images that pass through this album are fully Lacanian in character and can help us explore some of Lacan's most basic insights, before we move deeper into his more complex view of the unconscious.

## The Mirror Stage and the Real, Symbolic, and Imaginary

Taking Oberst's obsession with mirrors, we can first draw parallels with Lacan's famed concept of the "**mirror stage**." Lacan wanted to understand how humans come to form a sense of self, and he theorized about the moment we accept an identity. A baby (around six months according to Lacan) encounters its mirror image and recognizes itself. From that moment it forms a mental image of itself, an image that Lacan called the "**ideal-ego**." Sylvia Plath, a poet with a sense of tragic depression to rival Oberst's, wrote in her poem "Mirrors": "I am silver and exact. I have no preconceptions." This may be true, but as Lacan takes pains to show, this is misleading, because, while a mirror may be exact, our own perception is faulty, and because the whole drama is processed mentally, requiring our brains to synthesize the images, we can say that this experience is **Imaginary**. So, rather than "recognizing" ourselves in the mirror, Lacan calls this a "misrecognition." And from here on, our lives irreversibly enter an Imaginary dimension. This Imaginary realm pollutes us forever, meaning that we cannot forget the ideal-ego that has been formed. We are forever forbidden from a deep state that Lacan calls **the Real**—perhaps a version of Kant's "noumenon"—the "thing in itself" that we are alienated from. Throughout adulthood, this gap between the Real as Lacan calls it and the Imaginary is continually reinforced. And here lies the crux, which Oberst describes eloquently. In the song "A Scale, A Mirror, and Those Indifferent Clocks," Oberst talks of this moment as a disease in the making, through one of the most musically declamatory moments in the album, punctuated by regular triple-meter beats, as though he is reading a manifesto: "Now I know a disease that these doctors can't treat, you contract it the day you accept all you see is a mirror and a mirror is all it can be—a reflection of something we're missing." The crucial moment is the acceptance that the mirror reflects something missing; it covers over a fundamental gap—a **lack**. And this lack is, in essence, the Real, the thing we can never fully know. The scansion of these lyrics within the melody is also crucial, because there are no cadences, no chances to breathe in this long melodic rant. It is as if the false reality is covering up the musical reality beneath that is not allowed to break through the surface. At least not yet.

But in Lacanian theory, the mirror stage doesn't quite stop there. The child then looks to the adult world to have its ideal-ego symbolically validated—"is this really me daddy?" And this validation comes from a place that Lacan calls the **Symbolic**, which is near synonymous with concepts such as Law, the Father's name, and even Language (soon we will call this the **ego-ideal**). The album opens and closes with the sounds of a father teaching a child to read, framing the album with the moment when a person is undergoing initiation into the Symbolic realm. But Lacan calls the adoption of language a "defiling" moment; it pollutes us, sullies us forever. Language acts in a similar way to the ideal-ego that we inhabit, because, once we encounter language, we essentially *live* in it, we rely on it to communicate (even to ourselves). But, as we all know, language, like the mirror, is always inaccurate and cannot communicate our true meanings. Oberst's next line, in his litany of alienation, is "And language just happened, it was never planned, and it's inadequate to describe where I am." Essentially then, the Real is impossible to accurately imagine, and the Imaginary (how we *think* we feel, for example) is impossible to be fully articulated in language (the Symbolic). And the "loss" at every stage of this communication chain comes to embody the "lack" at the heart of human life, at least for Lacan. Bright Eyes fill this gap in the song with wonderful images (Imaginary) and a poetic list of words (Symbolic); after the words have failed—the barrage of complaints that the fever-ridden brain fires out in quick succession is replaced with a lovely, lilting flute melody that seems to be an attempt to flood the gap with pure music that tries to communicate in a clearer way (though still with interference) than words can.

Ironically, however, Oberst then holds his mock interview as part of the same track. This was actually given by Todd Fink, impersonating Oberst, discussing his fake childhood traumas, depression, neuroses, attention-seeking ("I hate it when people look at me") using dark humor to obfuscate an honest discussion, almost as an exaggerated demonstration of the futility of communication within language. Failing, he turns instead to music, and the rest of the album unfolds.

## Harouki Zombi: "*Objet petit a*"

Orenda Fink, member of Azure Ray, had collaborated with Oberst in Bright Eyes off and on throughout the late 1990s and early 2000s. In 2012 she teamed up with Of Montreal's Nina Barnes. As a duo, calling themselves Harouki Zombi, they dressed as geishas and adopted imagery from Haitian Voodoo, putting on party spectacles of dancing and music. Their main release was the single "*Objet petit a*," a bemusing title to many, but, to others, a reference to a crucial concept in the Lacanian worldview. While the song does allow us an insight into the concept of the *objet a* and serves in many ways as a useful illustration, it also can invite us to consider other Lacanian concepts that spiral outwards from this.

### *Objet petit a*

The "*a*" is one of Lacan's "**mathemes**," his algebraic way of communicating his concepts and their relations, so often used in his seminars. The *a* basically stands for *autre* ("other"), and its lower case indicates that the "other" operates in the Imaginary realm. (Remember the big-Other is found in the Symbolic world.) This is what the "*objet petit a*" meant to Lacan in the 1950s, but in the 1970s, he realized that our desires are drawn toward the Imaginary other, and he therefore redefined the term to mean "object-cause," representing both the Imaginary object of our desires and their very cause. He also thought of it as being connected to the Real, which we cannot know and therefore imagine—thus, "*objet petit a*" is also an Imaginary attempt to cover up the gap we perceive between ourselves and the Real. Lacan finds the "*objet petit a*" in the leftover surplus that remains when we have tried (and failed) to imagine or articulate the Real. Thus "*a*" serves as a meeting point for various Lacanian psychological processes, which is why it is so crucial to his view of the unconscious. When discussing the music of Robert Schumann, Žižek tries to encapsulate some of these entwined aspects by saying:

> Objet petit a is the unfathomable X, the mysterious *je ne sais quoi* which is to be found nowhere in positive reality, yet whose presence or absence causes this positive reality to appear "entirely different."[4]

Focusing on Schumann's songs, Žižek explores the "inner voice" that occurs in the liminal boundary between the piano melody and the vocal melody.

> With Schumann, the privileged link between melody and voice is broken: it is no longer possible to reconstruct the full melody from the solo vocal line, since the melody, as it were, promenades itself between vocal and piano lines—there is no single line, neither vocal nor piano, in which the melody is "played out in full." It is as if the melody's proper place is on some elusive, intangible third level which merely echoes in both of the levels that the listener actually hears, vocal and piano.[5]

Žižek thus locates the melody as "*a*"—an Imaginary *sense* of melody that we invent ourselves as listeners to fill the gaps between the different "voices" in the music. This is something that we often find in pop music too and is something explored by Harouki Zombi.

The opening lyrics are breathily sung/spoken: "I heard what you said; I heard how you said it; he heard what I said; I heard how he said it." This shows us that, during an act of communication, two key parameters for identifying meaning have been received—the *what* and the *how*. It reminds us that there is a gap, an *objet petit a*, between (i) what we say and (ii) how we say something. And this information, for us listeners, is not forthcoming. When the chorus arrives, we hear the two voices surround us with overlapping melodies—one simply singing "*objet petit a*" above, while the other follows with more French text "*Je crie ton nom*" ("I scream your name") to the extent that neither—and paradoxically both—are properly the melody. Rather, the Imaginary melody itself—the object *a*—is constructed by listeners in their attempt to fill the gap between the voices.

Matters are further elaborated in the accompanying music video; remember that Harouki Zombi were almost primarily visual artists. Here we see a naked female body, seemingly a zombie, remaining mute, but occasionally mouthing the words of the song, almost in time. This creates the sense that the voice is either internal—instead the character's head—or else external—the character is also listening. The voice becomes the object *a* in this sense also. Given that the lines are "I scream your name," and

---

[4] Slavoj Žižek, *The Plague of Fantasies* (London: Verso, 1997), 263.
[5] Ibid., 253.

yet we don't hear a scream, we might remember Munch's *The Scream*, where we are famously unaware whether the scream is inside the person's head or outside (are their hands trying to block it out?). Žižek asks, "Is not the 'inner voice' as the paradox of a voice which cannot be materialized thus an exemplary case of the Lacanian *objet petit a*?"[6] In discussions of the *objet petit a* in pop culture, commentators often evoke the famous scene in David Lynch's *Mulholland Drive*, where a singer collapses and her voice (also in French, as a version of Orbison's "Crying") continues to sound.[7] When the singer collapses, the sound source is revealed as a sham, and the whole fantasy at that moment in the film collapses—the onlookers have realized there is a gap between the Imaginary and the Real, and that they were filling it with an "a."

**The Gaze as Object "a"**

Sticking with Harouki Zombi, we also *see*, as well as hear, various expressions of this same object *a* at work, and just as in Lynch's film, the "*a*" is shown to be a fantasy—the work of the Imaginary. As the chorus nears, the Zombi-singer asks us to look at her ("open your eyes") and immediately removes a blanket like a curtain, to reveal her naked body. This, in effect, unveils the object of desire, but then goes on to show us that this is a fantasy. She proceeds to eroticize her body by drawing lipstick on herself, though she does this by tracing a line from her neck to her naval—reminding us of an autopsy room—the body is a dead thing. But, and here is the crux, she is still alive in some strange sense, as a zombie.

From the beginning of the video that accompanies this song, we can see that the eye, gazing at us, plays a complex role. The zombie lady keeps almost looking at us directly, but always furtively, turning away from us time and again as if she cannot bear to meet our gaze. It is tempting, though often misleading, to follow the film theorist Laura Mulvey into regarding this female on-screen feeling "objectified" by our masculine **gaze**. Mulvey coined the term "male gaze" and attempted to use Lacanian theory as a "political weapon" to show us how filmmakers and viewers should stop objectifying the female forms on screen by gazing at them. And she's right; they *should*.[8] Mulvey used Hitchcock's *Vertigo* to expose this, the film beginning with a giant eye that looks at us. But here is the problem with Mulvey's account of Lacan. This eye is gazing at *us*, not the other way around. For Lacan, the gaze is not something that we do—we *look* at things, *view* them, or *watch* them. The gaze is a mysterious something that we imagine to be watching *us*, reducing us to objects. The gaze is also not just a phenomenon of vision. Lacan took the idea from Sartre, who felt the power of the gaze as a noise one hears while looking through a keyhole—reducing one to shame, making one feel gazed at. Sartre thought he was a subject, but the gaze now paralyzes, *objectifies him*.

---

[6] Ibid., 262–3.
[7] See, for example, Todd McGowan, "Lost on Mulholland Drive: Navigating David Lynch's Panegyric to Hollywood," *Cinema Journal* 43, no. 2 (Winter 2004): 67–89; Allister Mactaggart, " 'Silencio': Hearing Loss in David Lynch's *Mulholland Drive*," *Journal of Aesthetics & Culture* 6, no. 1 (2014): 1–11.
[8] Laura Mulvey, "Visual Pleasure and Narrative Cinema," *Screen* 16, no. 3 (1975): 6–18.

Now, for certain, the female figure here seems to be uncomfortable with being looked at by us, and she may well be feeling the power of the gaze coming from us in her own subjectivity (the characters on screen can, of course, feel the gaze too, just like we can). But look closely at the video behind the woman. After about thirty seconds of Harouki Zombi's video, the amorphous mass of crumpled paper and blackness in the deep background that bleeds into the zombie's raven-black hair morph into an eye. We can just about make out the occasional blink of thick black lashes and a glistening black pupil. This is a gaze on a grander scale; it makes us *as well as her* feel objectified; we are being watched. This perhaps comes closer to Lacan's idea of the gaze than Mulvey's politicized notion (however much we applaud the notion from a gender political standpoint—that is, we *should* stop making films that parade women around to be looked at by an assumed male audience). This shows that the power of the gaze is something bigger, reducing us viewers to shame—we are the ones watching a woman undressing; the power comes from the screen, from the women who put this video together; we are the ones who should be ashamed and turning our eyes away. The act of removing the blanket (accompanied by the words "open your eyes") posits her impossibly autopsied body as the eye, looking at us. Nowhere is this clearer than when the camera focuses on her breasts, which in a sense fulfill the same role as the "eyes" gazing at us, asserting their power while we feel powerless.

And what is the gaze really? The gaze is something that works in our Imaginary realms; we get a glimpse of something that reminds us of the Real, and our fantasies flood the gap between this and our imagination. The gaze is, essentially, the *objet petit a*, with which, in a sense, it is near synonymous. But remember also that the gaze is musical. In *Mulholland Drive*, referred to earlier, the moment of realization that the singer's voice is living on despite her collapse, which comes as a shock to the viewers (the two women watching the drama), who both feel the gaze—they realize they are being duped; someone is gazing at them from behind the curtain (so to speak). And the same logic pertains here. The high, breathy "*objet petit a*" comes from another place to the "I scream your name" beneath. In the final chorus, the "*objet petit a*" is notable for its absence, too. It is removed, at least for a while, but its power still permeates. In fact, high synthesized noises adopt the same pitches as the voice and take us back to our starting point, where we recall Žižek discussing the unbridgeable gap between Schumann's piano melodies and the singers of his songs, a gap that we fill with phantasy. And this phantasy is the *objet petit a*, which gazes at us throughout this song.

### The Zone between Two Deaths

A novel aspect of this song and the duo's aesthetic disposition more generally is the role of the undead in this gaze. This isn't just anything gazing at us—this is the dead, living. Lacan gave us some tantalizing ways of thinking about life and death, or more so the ways that the liminal boundary between them fascinates us. He looks at the ancient Greek plays concerning Antigone and Elektra and attributes much of the "sex appeal" of those characters to the fact that they are stuck in a place between two deaths.

In his *Ethics of Psychoanalysis*, Lacan posits that some characters can die in real life (a Real death), but return to pay a debt or exact vengeance (a Symbolic death; think of Hamlet's father, for example). Other characters can die to all intents and purposes, choosing to live a reclusive half-life where they are "dead to the world" (Symbolic death), but not yet actually dead (Real death). There are different aspects to this "zone between two deaths" (a term that was raised during a question-and-answer session after one of Lacan's seminars). One of these aspects is their fascination. Characters in this zone are among the most interesting—they are lifeless but also deathless—like the giant eye looking at us. Another aspect is the sense of focus. Lacan claims that this is a realm where desire is reduced to a simpler monodirectional drive. Think of zombies in Scooby-doo—there are no complex dialectical tricks being played, the monsters just come straight after Scooby and Shaggy. So it is with many songs about zombies. Have a listen to Ryan Gosling's album *Dead Man's Bones*, which features many songs about this theme, perhaps most famously with the choir of school children singing "My body's a zombie for you," each thud on the beat sounding like one of the zombie's lurching feet. In other words, my body wants you, and it won't be distracted or diverted. Chilling.

And perhaps the eroticism of these few Harouki Zombi songs is found in the play between both aspects of this zone between two deaths. We find the physical entrainment of the body and its mechanical insistence on obtaining the object of pure drive most clearly in the "Swamp Theme," a dance beat, with lyrics like "We'll make your body move," that speaks of physical control and complete captivation, not worlds away from Gosling's "My body's a zombie for you." Similarly, in Harouki Zombi's "Soldier's Gun," we find images of women in convulsions and fits, perhaps ecstatic spiritual states, but also regurgitating black sludge, emphasizing the nonalluring, dark, physical aspects of zombie life. However, even here, we have lyrics like "I'm more than a Soldier's Gun, but you can load me if it's just for fun." (Perhaps the regurgitation is symbolic of excessive gun powder—with obvious *entendre*?) Lyrics like these indicate the more seductive aspects of these characters of bleak beauty, like Antigone or Elektra, who live in the zone between two deaths. The living-dead body carving itself up for postmortem in "*Objet petit a*" does so with lipstick; the lips also kissing the screen; the frequent clips of Geishas, the orgasmic breathing in all of the songs, that seem to come from nowhere—all of this speaks of eroticized death. The songs certainly exist in a kind of undead limbo. Firstly, each song in itself ends without any teleological structure; they start in a place, undertake no particular journey, and arrive at a similar place to the start; little vignettes. Secondly, in the artists' careers, too, this project was one that was destined to be a limbo moment—a brief experiment, part of neither's main career trajectory.

If we return to Bright Eyes themselves, we can find a slightly less phantasmagoric version of the beauty lying between two deaths. In a bonus track on some editions of *Fevers and Mirrors*, there is a lesser-known Bright Eyes song, "Jetsabel Removes the Undesirables," a song that references Edgar Allen Poe's poem "Annabel Lee," and Oberst peppers words and phrases from the poem throughout his own text. These quotations are paying Poe his due, given that he foreshadowed the band's name in the poem, "Annabel Lee":

> And the stars never rise, but I feel the *bright eyes*
> Of the beautiful Annabel Lee.

In the poem, Annabel Lee is entombed in a sepulcher by the sea, while her lover lies with her, night after night. Her death is Real, but she is Symbolically undead, because she is named, kept alive in memory, refused rest; the lover, however, is Symbolically dead (dead to the world) but alive in the Real. The poem carries on Poe's own deep concern for this topic, as Poe claimed (very much *of his time*) that "the death of a *beautiful woman* is, unquestionably, the *most* poetical topic in the world." However, Oberst inverts the position of Annabel Lee to make himself, the half-dead/dying/dead one—who imagines the moments of death as well as the post-death entombment— "if you want, maybe drop by sometime put some flowers on my grave so that I will look beautiful in my silent sepulcher." In this regard, the song is perhaps more akin to Poe's "For Annie" in which the main character conquers the "fever called living," and we witness the end of his life, while he remembers the sparkling (bright?) eyes of his lover. "Jetsabel," fittingly, is generally a funeral dirge with simple, plodding, minor key alternations of chords, with a couple of more tortured departures that seem, in the final moments of the song, to represent the transition from life to living between two deaths. The recording of the verses is beset with an unusual, haunting distortion of the recorded voice at the close of each stanza on phrases such as "Cracks and lines on my face" or "They will never haunt me again." The significance of this is not made clear until the final lines, when the distorted, ghostly sound takes over—"Haunted by the ghosts of those bright eyes." Oberst is crossing over, not into death but into a state between his Real death and his Symbolic death—he wants to be kept alive through memory and haunting. Ironically, of course, the inverse is true at a broader level, because Oberst is, at the time of writing at least, alive, enacting a kind of Symbolic death. Either way, it is in this zone of fascination in which they *become* the gaze—the bright eyes—that the music and its singer place themselves.

## The Graph of Desire

> Now everything's imaginary, especially what you love ... When I hear beautiful music, it's always from another time. (Bright Eyes, "Lime Tree")

One of the things that annoys many about psychoanalysis is the double bind by which the theory is either correct and agreed with by the subject, or correct but so hurtful to the subject that it must be disagreed with. In this latter instance, it is repressed. The early works of Bright Eyes elicited similarly strong responses from listeners. There were those who thought songwriter Conor Oberst was a precocious genius, and others who had a visceral dislike of his music. We are in the former camp. In his early Bright Eyes albums, Oberst seems to have achieved something rather impressive, which is to have intuited much of Lacanian psychoanalysis, and expressed it in song. In this section we're going to unpack what is going on in some of his early works, matching them to

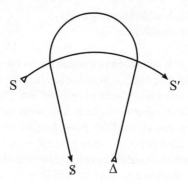

**Example 3.1** Lacan's Graph of Desire, Level I.

the aspect of Lacanian theory known as the **graph of desire**. As with much of Lacan's work, this is all about *self* and *other*, although here we find many resting points on the paths between this binary.

### Level I. "No Lies, Just Love"—The Subject Splits

The first stage of Lacan's graph of desire (Example 3.1) traces some of the concepts we have visited already, particularly the mirror stage. This level represents a primal moment in our lives, early on, when our very subjectivity is formed. The delta symbol in the bottom right represents the subject's primal **need**—pure, bodily, natural instinct. The loop shape that passes around the graph ends on a symbol that indicates a "**split subject**" ($). This "splitting" occurs because the Real of the subject's need passes through the line that goes from left to right, from S to S'. This S stands for "**signifier**," and thus the line is a chain of signifiers (think of a string of words maybe, or a series of nonverbal communications). Well language, as discussed above apropos of *Fevers and Mirrors*, is "inadequate to describe where I am," according to Oberst. The subject thus becomes split by his/her encounter with language, which, for Lacan, forever pollutes us.

A song that embodies this in a rather neat example, though rather reductive, comes from the final verse of "No Lies, Just Love," one of Bright Eyes' earlier songs from *Oh Holy Fools* (2001). After taking us through a general mood of near-suicidal self-reflection, the protagonist decides to give himself "a few more days" and focus on thoughts of his unborn nephew, for whom he writes this song. The song, as a means of musical as well as linguistic communication—a **signifying chain**—is to form a brutal accession into the cold world ("I wrote that this for a baby who is yet to be born"). Remember that the baby in the womb is purely Real; it has not encountered the Symbolic world, and therefore its only driving force is pure need. Oberst's song subsides in intensity to an almost unaccompanied semi-spoken calm before the storm, representing perhaps a lullaby, or at least a moment of hushed communication to the unborn infant.

I hope that womb's not too warm, 'cause it's cold out here and it'll be quite a shock to breathe this air, to discover loss.

The cold air, of course, represents life outside of the plenitude of the womb, in which all need was satisfied. The reference to the discovery of "loss" that will leave a permanent mark on the child registers beautifully the encounter with the transformation into a split subject. In this case, the signifying chain isn't referred to as "language," but eye communication that could betray "lies" (which signification always is, ultimately), but Oberst imagines love gushing out of them:

So I'd like to make some changes before you arrive, so when your new eyes meet mine they won't see no lies, just love.

The music now erupts in a wall of sound, with blazing trumpet solos, all instruments capturing a womblike profusion of pure excess, as if cushioning an unborn child. Bear in mind that the song has up to this point been filled with images of Oberst wanting to reverse this flow—move back from being a "split subject" (this "fucking wreck") toward something purer ("like snow; like gold"). But this, for Obert as for all of us, and as shown in Lacan's graph, is impossible. The journey is one-way. The subject is polluted by its encounter with the signifying chain, symbolically registered in the song as the cold world (of lies) outside.

## Level II. Ideal-Ego to Ego-Ideal

The second level of the graph (Example 3.2) looks much more complex (and it is), but only one or two significant aspects need to be discussed here. Firstly, the signifying chain is now more intricate, although it is the same in essence. The "signifier" now passes the "**signification of the Other**" ($s(A)$) and then the **Other** itself ($A$), finally passing on to an enunciation of signification (voice). Essentially, nothing has changed here between the arrows of the two diagrams. The Other, remember, does not represent another person, or people, but the very Symbolic realm of communication itself. The "signification of the Other" indicates its language or signifying system. This holds a special place in the diagram and is called the "*points de capiton*" or "quilting point," but more of this later. The crucial step that we would like to talk about is that the $S$ (the split subject) now appears in the bottom right, replacing "need"; this is because the first level of graph has turned the human into a split subject forever, so the continued encounters with the signifying chain now produce a different set of results. The main takeaway point from this level of the graph is the passage between what Lacan calls the "ideal-ego" ($i(a)$) and the "ego-ideal" ($I(A)$). Note that these are algebraically given the same symbol, but the latter is in capitals. This is because the first is Imaginary, the second is Symbolic, although both happen in the psyche of the individual.

The ideal-ego is the image that is formed after the mirror stage—the Imaginary version of ourselves that we operate with. The ideal-ego is necessary in the schema because we need some impulse or entity that reacts to the splitting of the subject not as

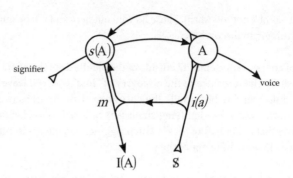

**Example 3.2** Lacan's Graph of Desire, Level II.

a fait accompli but as a situation that needs to be integrated. The initial movement in this graph comes from the reality of the subject to the intention legislated by the ideal-ego who tries to rectify this split. (An alternate discussion of the psyche's response to the split subject can be seen in the next section on Lacan's four discourses.) After the full immersion in the signifying chain, in which the Other and the Other's signifying world-order are encountered and accepted, we then start to see ourselves from the perspective of the Other, the "ego-ideal." Thus, we acquire a Symbolic sense of self—we imagine seeing ourselves as the Other sees us. And this, as you can imagine, is where psychological problems are going to start brewing.

For Bright Eyes, let's start with the song "Something Vague" from *Fevers and Mirrors*. It begins with a recognition that subjective (Imaginary) perception is disconnected with reality: "Now and again, it seems worse than it is, but mostly the view is accurate." Mirroring with the song's general concern for vagueness, and the blind search for our sense of self ("ideal-ego"), Oberst distracts himself and focuses on how he wants the Other to see him: "I'm standing on air with nothing holding me, and I hang like a star, fucking glow in the dark for all those starving eyes to see, like the ones we wished on." As he becomes a "star" (doubtless in multiple senses), the music bursts into one of those wonderful sudden influxes of climactic Bright Eyes music—all instruments playing full-throttle. This is pure ego-ideal (viewed from the perspective of the Other), and it represents an escape from the troubles of struggling to define an ideal-ego amid all this vagueness and lack of meaning. And there continues to be a tug of war throughout Bright Eyes' oeuvre.

Throughout *Lifted* (2002), Oberst wrestles with his "ideal-ego" and "ego-ideal" and demonstrates the feeling that his music and emotionally driven persona are "an act," played out for the benefit of the Other. From the first song on the album, "Method Acting," through to "False Advertising," we find the same concern. In "False Advertising," Oberst sings of how he (his persona? the protagonist in the song?) is nothing but a puppet. As the song begins, he sings unaccompanied, "on a string" twice, to a rising bare four-note interval (C♯-F♯), to enact the puppet-master animating the puppet. And this puppet for the Other, with the power of the Symbolic Order working through him, pours his heart out on stage, "with my sorrow well-rehearsed." Through these songs, he confronts the huge gap between his own sense of self (Imaginary) and the sense of self that he has come to (Symbolically) occupy the eyes of the Other, going so far as to cynically demand "so give me all your pity (and your money)." While Oberst sings to his audience, and to us, the crowd of singers behind him in the record (and on stage in live performances) sing "we used to think that sound was something pure." And this seems to be the rub of the matter, an idea, stretching back to his earlier music, as we'll now explore, that sound or music should be something pure and somehow Real, and that everything else is just ideal-ego or ego-ideal.

In the earlier "Going for Gold" from *O Holy Fools* (2001), Oberst seems to be paraphrasing Robert Burns's famous line "O wad some Power the giftie gie us *To see oursels as ithers see us!*"—"If I could talk to myself like I was someone else, then maybe I would take your advice, and I wouldn't act like such an asshole all the time." Oberst sings of a competition, which he will undoubtedly win, to become "the Champion of Idiots." He sings of people consumed in a film, imagining themselves as a hero, before returning to mundane existence. He imagines them then listening to folksingers, playwrights, and poets, all "dispensing their wisdom."

> They will detail their pain in some standard refrain; they will recite their sadness like it's some kind of contest.

The melodies lilt and descend like drooping sighs. So far, the tone of the song has been quite despondent and dispassionate; the cynicism has been directed toward the Other and the whole process of ego formation. The music then changes and breaks its repeated chord progression cycle as he reaches toward something different. He continues the theme of the contest:

> Well, if it is, I think I am winning it, all beaming with confidence as I make my final lap.

The song now develops a new theme in closing, describing a "kid" who sits on the bus with her walkman, and another who cries when practicing the violin because of the purity of the sounds. This leads to his final summation "now to me, everything else, it just sounds like a lie." And then the real music starts—ironically, not a violin, but a lilting (though anthemic) flute melody.

Essentially, then, Oberst is realizing and despairing of the vacuity of the game of playing the ego out in the Other's world—the "ego-ideal." He longs for the more interior world of the walkman and the private music practice, a world in which music is purer, outside of the Symbolically driven music industry, the world of the ego-ideal. But whether music can be this pure, this Real, is another question, answered partly by the chorus of "False Advertising"—the unison chant of "we *used to* think that sound was something pure." For Lacan, the Real ("something pure") is forever barred from us, registered by the fact that on the second stage of the Graph of Desire, the subject is already split, and its halves can never be joined again.

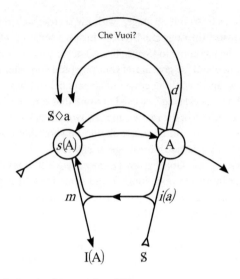

**Example 3.3** Lacan's Graph of Desire, Level III.

### Level III. "Nothing Gets Crossed Out"—What Do They Want from Me?

The next stage of the graph (Example 3.3) extends above it like a giant question mark, and this visual likeness is no coincidence. The subject's journey has functioned as a neat, self-contained unit thus far. However, a small piece of energy now escapes the circuit—the lines stretching above the A, which loop around to the left, represent this excess or remainder of what cannot be symbolized in the whole system described above. This "d" thus stands for "desire," and it is expressed in the form of a question: **Che Vuoi?**—"What do you (the Other) want from me?" This, Lacan argues, is the fundamental question we ask ourselves unconsciously and is the single greatest cause of human anxiety and neurosis. From a baby's perspective, this is inscribed in Lacan's version of the Oedipus complex in which a baby wants to be the "be all and end all" to the mother—*it wants to be what the mother wants*. And this is compounded when we meet the Symbolic order and have to deal with more complex relationships. In each case, we make phantasies ( $S \lozenge a$ ) that attempt in vain to answer this question.

One of Bright Eyes' most anxiety-ridden songs is "Nothing Gets Crossed Out" from *Lifted, or the Story Is in the Soil, Keep Your Ear to the Ground* (2002). This has all the hallmarks of a depressed, anxious subject. Oberst describes this from the outset:

> The future has got me worried, such awful thoughts, my head's a carousel of pictures, the spinning never stops.

To go with this literary image, the music keeps circling through the verses, overlapping phrases without Oberst catching a breath, as if one image instantly gives birth to the next without respite. There are no melodic answer phrases ("consequent" phrases), just musical question marks ("antecedent" phrases). And these musical questions are all the same—what do they want from me?

As we move deeper into the cause of the singer's *ennui*, we find images of failed attempts to work out what other people want from him. We first have the pathetic school boy trying to squeeze affection from a girl ("I started carrying her books"), and this leads to "doing lots of drugs," all in an attempt to "follow the leader." The next line—"I almost forgot who I was, but came to my senses"—is filled with pathos, not only because he has forgotten who he is in the attempt to please the Other, but also because this image of himself (who he *is*) is constructed by his encounters with the other. When he regains his composure ("I'm trying to be assertive and making plans"), he shows that, deep down, he is still trying to work out what the Other wants from him ("I want to rise to the occasion and meet all their demands"). This mention of "demand" is intriguing as it raises an interesting point. The Other does constantly make demands on us, and we might imagine that we could fulfill these. Your record label demands a new song by Christmas; you produce a new song by Christmas. Bloomsbury are getting in our grill to finish this book; job done.[9] However, the point is that the subject realizes unconsciously that the stated demands are not really desires—when someone asks him to carry books or do drugs, he can fulfill that—but he can't know what is *really* wanted of him. And this is the crux. Oberst describes working on the album and comparing it to Tim Kasher's *Black Out* (also 2002), once again measuring himself against other people's work—using it as a stick to beat himself. He also articulates the problem faced by many artists, in what to do in one's next album that can live up to the hype or the expectations from fans—more of the same, something different? It's impossible to predict what fans want—you can only tell afterward what they didn't want.

The song ends unhappily with the protagonist lying down, waiting to be lifted up. And this comes as an appeal to the Other. This is a person broken by the inability to meet the Other's demands, yet the true failure is the consistent reliance on the Other in the first place. And that is a problem that most of us can relate to.

### Level IV. "The Road to Joy"—Jouissance, Failure, Drive

The fourth stage of the graph of desire (Example 3.4) cuts another line through the whole system. This line, dividing the question mark described above, is, contrary to the title of the previous song discussed, a huge "crossing out." It tells us that **jouissance** is impossible to articulate. Three new terms need noting (plus "**castration**," which in this case basically just means impossibility and inability). "Jouissance" is much stronger than pleasure; it is pure enjoyment ("Joy") but experienced as pain. It is something that is Real and, therefore, can't be symbolized. In this upper chain, jouissance confronts a particular moment—a mark or **signifier of the lack in the Other**—a moment when we unconsciously realize that the Other is just as "split" as we are. We encounter a pure failure on the Other's part, and this comes with a certain shock. Jouissance is now

---

[9] This is a humorous counterfactual. We delivered the book on time, and Bloomsbury have been wonderful to work with from start to finish.

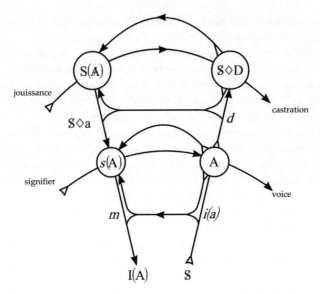

**Example 3.4** Lacan's Graph of Desire, Level IV.

tainted and can't be symbolized or communicated through signification, and all that remains of it are small pockets that become fixed to parts of the body or ideas and are known as "**drives**" ($ \$ \Diamond D $), which will occupy us in Chapter 6.

The Bright Eyes' song that perhaps symbolizes the impossible path *of* Joy (or rather *jouissance*) is "The Road to Joy" from *I'm Wide Awake It's Morning* (2005). This track, the last on the album, is the fullest in terms of its orchestration and is notable for a total breakdown of musical communication. At the climax of the song, Oberst shouts "let's fuck it up boys, make some noise," and the following is a huge deluge of instrumental blasts from trumpets, guitars, strings, drums, all playing out of time with each other in a huge burst of blissful but dissonant and jarring chaos. If anything, this is a representation of (the impossible to represent) *jouissance*—pure physical enjoyment, alien to the symbolic, social order, registered as quite a traumatic, painful moment. As the song gets back into gear, the crucial aspect is that fragments of this musical chaos—the trumpet motifs, the wild organ, the manic drums—all start to coalesce before fragmenting again, now semi-rhythmically. It is as if this brief moment of social cohesion has broken the *jouissance* into small pockets of localized energy, now circulating as drives, now flying off in all directions.

Another aspect of this breakdown of jouissance is that its breakdown is shown lyrically to be a mark of failure—the S($\bcancel{A}$). Oberst categorizes the Other here, as history, and also as our inability to learn from it:

> So I hope I don't sound too ungrateful for what history gave modern man: a telephone to talk to strangers, machine guns and a camera lens. So when you're

asked to fight a war that's over nothing, it's best to join the side that's gonna win, and no one knows how all of this got started but we're gonna make them certain how it's gonna end.

This then refers to the disillusionment with the war, which at that time was happening in Iraq. The war had been a subtheme of the album, and now this explosion of *jouissance* is also rendered as the horrifically violent sounds of war, ironically cast as joy, Oberst adopting the ironic position of the Other. Just before the ultimate chaos, he metaphorically registers this in his own world as his own failure as a singer:

Well I could have been a famous singer if I had someone else's voice, but failure's always sounded better so fuck it up boys, make some noise.

This may be his own Imaginary failure (his voice), but it represents a personalized version of humanity's failure—war and its supposed necessity. Thus, war becomes a magnificent symbol of failure in the signifying discourse of the Other.[10]

## Four Discourses

The Antlers' (2009) album *Hospice* is going to be our jumping-off point for an exploration of Lacan's "Four Discourses," which marks his attempt to capture the pitfalls and pathologies that bedevil any attempt at communication.[11] The problem, as in so many of the cases we have hitherto considered, is entrenched in the divided structure of the psyche, between the conscious and unconscious parts. As we just saw, Lacan has a special "matheme" to show the problems of the subject split between its "true" unconscious desires and their conscious manifestations, the $\frac{S}{}$. As explained above, the capital S stands for "subject." By dividing it with a bar, Lacan represents the two domains that psychoanalysis claims that any subject encompasses—the conscious and the unconscious. We could imagine a machine that can perfectly process the symbols it encounters wouldn't have such an issue. It would be a whole subject "S,"

---

[10] Another angle into *jouissance* can be seen in The Naked and Famous track "Girls Like You." The song's refrain "Don't you know people write songs about girls like you?" is supposed to be an angry rebuke to a self-centered, dismissive person. However, after listening to the song, it is clearly not just that. The verses start gradually building up, through various recriminations about the "girl's" conduct, toward the rebuke in the chorus. But this isn't a building of anger or bile; it is rather a building toward climax, toward enjoyment—a tension and an anticipation, as the tempo accelerates and the instruments start to harmonize. By the time we reach the second "Don't you know people write songs about girls like you?" it's clear that, despite the pain ostensibly caused by the girl, this is still really a moment of celebration. Here we have one aspect of Lacanian jouissance, an excess of promised desire so impossible and intense that it becomes the same as pain, the pain of its absence and the pain of its presence. Later in the song, the description of "beautiful pain," directed at the "girl," seems to be really one that is sent to the author, whose *jouissance* is so totally captured by the image of this girl. "What if you couldn't feel beautiful pain" ... what would happen if this *jouissance* wasn't available?

[11] These discourses are the central concern of Jacques Lacan, *Seminar XVII: The Other Side of Psychoanalysis*, ed. Jacques-Alain Miller, trans. Russell Grigg (New York: W. W. Norton, 2007).

where the meaning was unified. But things for us humans are not that simple. For the human, according to Lacan, "a signifier represents a sign for another signifier."[12] Let's rephrase that in a simplified way and focus on how that might be rendered as a statement about our discourses, that is, the language we use: "A word represents a notion to another word." Now the traditional way of thinking about what a word represents is that "a word represents a notion." That's how it would work for our machine, above. Whatever you mean to say, you simply say. For Lacan though, there is never just a word for a human subject. Words are always addressed outside ourselves, to another subject. So a word is always sent to try and communicate some notion to something else. This something else is the other, a big-Other or a little other, we don't mind right now; all that matters is that every letter has a destination, and the contents of the letter must be in accordance with what the other waiting at the destination expects from us.

A woman walks into a room ... no, this isn't the setup of a joke. Imagine what you may say to the woman as she walks in. It is hard, because, as a reader, the question you would always want an answer to, in response to the question we have just asked, is "who is this woman?" Let's say you are at work in an office, laboring over a spreadsheet in one window while watching a baseball game (or the test cricket for our UK friends) ball by ball in a side window. If the woman is your sports-obsessed friend, you may say "another Yankees/England collapse"; if she is the CEO, you probably wouldn't be so bold and may express a blandishment about the company. If it is your line manager, you would probably say something about your progress on the spreadsheet—uninteresting to your coworker, inappropriate for your CEO. Still, so far this is fairly simple—the right message gets sent in each case. The problem Lacan poses is further complicated by the issues we have with interpreting what the other wants and misunderstanding our tools to communicate to that other. At this point in our book, we can clearly say: a conversation is never between two full subjects. There are always other entities in the mix, whether they be individual unconsciousness or collective ones.

The four discourses discussed below were introduced by Lacan in *Seminar XVII, The Other Side of Psychoanalysis*. Just as his contemporaries Deleuze and Guattari were writing their own attack on the centrality of the Oedipus complex to the practice of psychoanalysis (*Anti-Oedipus*), Lacan was grappling with the same problem. Lacan's solution was—as with most of his work—nuanced and complicated, but a few key characteristics can be identified. Firstly, we have moved beyond the Freudian language of Oedipus, of fathers, mothers, and so on, and into Lacan's less-libidinized, "matheme-atical" language. Furthermore, the Oedipal figures have also been displaced from their central roles in psychoanalytic practice. We have mathemes and discourses representing the subject, the analyst the other, the complex, but the sexualized libido instilled by the Oedipus complex is no longer the driving force behind the productions of the unconscious. Instead it is language, and the relationship of any subject to the

---

[12] Jacques Lacan, *Seminar XI: The Four Fundamental Concepts of Psychoanalysis*, trans. Jacques-Alain Miller (London: Vintage, [1964] 1998), 207.

other, the big-Other, and their own unconscious complexes, that dictates these four general patterns of how a discourse will proceed.

The four discourses are one of the psychoanalytic tools that are apt for an analysis of the everyday. We can see discourses everywhere, and they always fit into the patterns of Lacan's four discourses. So far our illustrations of psychoanalytic concepts have involved quite specific examples in which one can see, beneath the musical presentation, a glimpse of an unconscious. We hope that in this section we offer a more universal tool for understanding popular music and, as such, have therefore devoted quite a long section to it.

## Traversing the Four Discourses

The first thing to think about with our discourses is how we go around them. In Example 3.5, we find three arrows and three blockages. Of immediate importance are the three arrows. In each discourse we move from the bottom left position to the bottom right position, in the shape of a clockwise arch. And as we make this traversal, we move around blockages until we meet the final, unpassable void "//" that prevents the circuit from being completed. The first blockage, the horizontal line between the positions in the bottom left and top left, represents the move from unconscious to conscious and the difficulty of choosing a signifier that can represent the unconscious. The path along the top, though not showing a blockage, is called "impossibility" by Lacan, so we can definitely say there is a difficulty there! This is the moment of communication where an agent sends a message to another from our own language (unconscious) to their language (unconscious). We already have a concept for the issue of moving from one language to another—translation. And even if two subjects share the same mother tongue, Lacan tells us that their individual unconsciousness are unlikely to have chained together the signifiers and the concepts in these languages in the same way. Think about Barcelona. You may well like the idea of Barcelona—the football, the architecture, the beaches, and so on. But another person may darkly remember Freddie Mercury and Montserrat Caballé singing about it and may be experiencing intense emotional anguish about the experience.[13] So if you ask someone, "shall we go to Barcelona?" trying to propose an exciting trip, you may well be triggering some unknown horrors in the other person that they had repressed since October 26, 1987. A further slippage occurs when the other produces meaning from the agent's discourse, moving downward into the corner. And, finally, we have the impossible gap at the bottom of the diagram, //, which separates the product of the discourse from the true intention that initiated it.

There are four distinct positions in the discourses. The bottom left position (see Example 3.6) represents **truth**, the originary content that the discourse tries to communicate. This truth lies beneath the **agent**, which tries to enunciate (or otherwise

---

[13] As a personal aside, Stephen has threatened to have this song played at Kenneth's funeral as his purported "last wish." In the unlikely event that Stephen does indeed outlive Kenneth, I (Kenneth) wish to make it a matter of public record that I have no such wish.

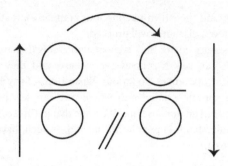

**Example 3.5** The space in which Lacan expresses the four discourses.

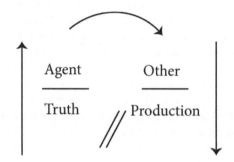

**Example 3.6** The space in which Lacan expresses the four discourses.

pass over) this truth to the **Other**, to whom it is addressed. This passage between the three initial terms results in a **production**, some interpretation or understanding of meaning—or, in many uses of the discourses, the failure to produce meaning. Communication runs around Lacan's space in a clockwise direction.

The discourses in Examples 3.7–3.11 are populated by four "mathemes," which variously occupy the different nodes on the diagram, rotating in a carousel. We have already encountered $\$$, the mark of the split subject, divided between its conscious and unconscious, and between the imaginary order—what it wants to be—and the symbolic order.

Next we have S1, the **master signifier**. The master signifier wants to be understood by all other signifiers in one way, hence its mastery. The master signifier dreams of being immune to slippages of meaning, able to transcend any individual unconscious, universal to all.

S2 is knowledge or the **big Other**. It is the mechanism by which a signifier is understood out there in the world. When Lacan says that "a signifier represents a sign for another signifier," S2 is the process of that second signifier interpreting the first signifier and understanding it as a sign (knowledge).

Finally we have the *objet petit a*, which we have already met. In the discourses, it variously stands for lost enjoyment or escaped meaning.

## The Discourse of the Master

After that dense exegesis, without any musical examples, let's jump into The Antlers' *Hospice* and discuss the four specific discourses. Through the arc of the album, *Hospice* tells us a number of intertwined stories. The two main ones are about an abusive relationship breaking up and of a hospital worker falling in love with a terminally ill patient. There are a few smaller narratives tied in, including an abiding homage to Sylvia Plath, but they are less important for our analysis than the main two. Thinking back to Freud, we can differentiate them in terms of the manifest and latent content of the song. The latent content—what is really being sung about—is a story of an abusive relationship. And while this sometimes comes out as a straight-up narrative, it is more often disguised by falling back to a second register, of the relationship between the dying patient and the hospital orderly. In this analysis, we are going to be looking at *Hospice* as a story of an abusive relationship, and how the relationship between the two protagonists is understood, over time, by the "author" of the album.

In the discourse of the master, the master wants to be master. What would this mastery involve? One way of thinking about it is that the master is understood as master by all others. In Lacanian terms, that signifier has one meaning for all other signifiers. In ordinary language, the master is whatever s/he says s/he is. Now, this sounds quite simple on the surface, but on reflection, we might unpick some of the difficulties of such a thing. The problem is that there are two entities here, the master and the other the master is addressing. The master ostensibly has control over their own domain, and they can claim to interpret the signifier in whatever way they wish. But the other is outside of the master's power. It is really difficult to create a signifier that cannot be misinterpreted by another. If we think about musical history, even the most consensual statements can still be the subject of disagreement. Some people don't like The Beatles; some people don't think Beyonce is fabulous; some people don't cry in Beethoven concerts, even when safely ensconced in the company of strangers. If the master is trying to send over some fact about themselves, again, we can see how this is undermined. Even monarchs, tyrants, and tech-company CEOs struggle to be seen in only one way to all of their subjects. Indeed, though totalitarian projects tend to spend much of their time engaging in propaganda to try and establish one fixed way of interpreting certain signifiers, this attempt always fails and dissent is always present.

The master narrative that we see at the beginning of *Hospice* is something like an attempt at communicating fidelity and love. The narrator (the agent) needs to explain the impossibility of addressing his girlfriend (the other) in such a way that his words and actions are registered in the way he intends them. The intention is a kind of completeness, a totalization of the romantic relationship—in the common parlance—love or true love. The first track, "Prologue," is purely musical, without lyrics, but already we can tell that a key theme will be communication. A beautiful, mournful melody descends but is often obscured by the "interference" from sounds of wind, soft whitenoise, and radio static. The opening of the second song continues in this vein with the profound "hum" and "noise" that trail the entire album. "Kettering" introduces the soft voice that brings a crucial line of direct attempt to communicate, which softly sings: "I wish that I had known in that first minute we met, the unpayable debt that I owed you." Again the crystal-clear production lays bare the imperfection of the communicating vessel for the message; the singer's voice is recorded so perfectly that our attention is drawn to the myriad extra sounds produced by his vocal apparatus—from the diaphragm to the lips. The sound isn't coming from a magical acousmatic space; it's coming from a faltering homo sapien. How can we recapitulate this opening line in terms of the master discourse? Perhaps we might risk a paraphrase:

> I wish I had known when we met, that I could never provide (pay) what you expected from me (the debt); I wish that I had known that I couldn't communicate that I loved you; I wish that I had known that I couldn't give you what you wanted.

It is quite a heavy first line to drop. Indeed, it is so heavy that the song's register changes to the metaphor of the patient and the orderly. The next song—"Sylvia," also beset with interference and the infernal hum of electric wires struggling to let a message pass through—returns to this original impossibility at the onset of the song: (another paraphrase of ours) "Sorry, I don't know what I said but you're crying now again and that only makes it worse. Let me do my job." Again, we can see the failings inherent in the master discourse. The impossibility of totalizing communication to the Other, the impossibility of sending a signifier across that will represent the sign the agent hopes it will. "I don't know what I said"; I don't know where this slippage happened. "But you're crying again"; but it has happened, and something other than what was intended has been produced—*the objet petit a*. "Let me do my job"; let me fulfill this master position, not to be your master but to give you what you demand, what you really want. We hear the same thing at the end of the song—the disappointment at the failure of the signifier, the narrator's struggle for mastery and despair at the failure it always produces. Soft words act as a postlude to the song and follow its climax. The choruses are the most anthemic in the album, summoning up all of the hope, despair, and triumph of the situation, leading after the second chorus to the resounding trumpet solo. But all of this overwhelming activity is frustrated by the commensurate increase in the amount of distortion that almost covers up the jubilant expression of *jouissance*. The more the music tries to communicate pure expression, the more the forces of impossibility prevent it. Once the track dies down, the singer admits that he is "scared to speak" and only talks when the patient is sleeping: "That's when I tell you everything." Note the follow-up line: "I imagine that somehow you're going to hear me."

If the master discourse is impossible to complete, because of these slippages and breaks in meaning as we move in the arc from bottom left to bottom right of the matrix, why do we even bother? Lacan's answer is that the line at the bottom of the discourse: $ // a$ is impossible to traverse in reality—hence the gap "//", but can be traversed in **phantasy**. Hence the formulation for phantasy in Lacan's works is $ \Diamond a$: the split subject "$" fantasizes that it can have some sort of relationship "$\Diamond$" to the object "$a$," its desire. What is this relationship of the mark $\Diamond$, known as the punch or lozenge? Lacan tells us it is both greater than ">" and lesser than "<", and also a "∧" and a "∨." Here Lacan is telling us something about desire: that we can have a number

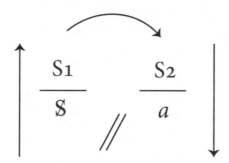

**Example 3.7** The discourse of the master.

of different relations to objects of desire. We can renounce them; we can want them in conjunction with other things; we can want them on their own; we can want to destroy them or just imagine that we can have them. In "Sylvia" and at the beginning of *Hospice*, we hear that the fantasy is coming up with a solution to the problem inherent in the master discourse, that this loop of communication could be closed, and that Sylvia would "hear" the narrator.

Moments in which this phantasy becomes real don't crop up too often in *Hospice*. We hear a little glimpse in "Bear," one of the more accessible and self-contained songs on the album, when the singer shares hopes of playing charades in Chelsea, drinking champagne (despite doctors' orders), and being "blind and dumb until we fall asleep." However, the general direction of *Hospice* leads toward collapse and the end of the relationship, as symbolized in the end of the narrative by the death of the patient. The failure of the master discourse, the failure to obtain mastery, can lead to two other pathological modes of discourse being used: the discourse of the hysteric and the discourse of the analyst.

### The Discourse of the Hysteric

Here's another moment in psychoanalysis with an unfortunately gendered name and an (all too) neat response to it from Lacan. The discourse of the hysteric is not limited to women. True, Lacan says that all women are hysterics, but only insofar as they are all humans; men and women are both hysterics; this is our "default" mode of discourse.

In the bottom left of Example 3.8 we have $a$ in the position of truth. The unattainable thing, the unfulfilled desire. And truth, lying as it does in the lower half of the image, is in the position of the unconscious. Above this we have $\$$, the split subject, in the position of the agent. This left side is really the key to the hysterical discourse. The thing that is desired, or the true topic of conversation, is unconscious and thus cannot be articulated. The thing that speaks for it is the split subject—and in this case, the conscious part of the split subject. As such, when the bar is crossed between the truth and the agent, there is a significant slippage of meaning. To put it another way: what the agent speaks is not the truth. Here we can go back to Freud's latent/manifest

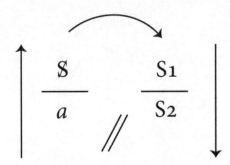

**Example 3.8** The discourse of the hysteric.

distinction. The manifest content of the hysteric discourse is not the same as the latent content. This raises a few issues. Not least of them is that the discourse is very unlikely to work when the wrong thing is being asked of the other. The true desire is not being spoken, but a false one.

On the right-hand side, we have S1, the master in the position of Other, and we have S2, knowledge in the position of the product. The most important element on this side is that the master is being addressed. The hysteric's discourse is ambivalent toward the master. The hysteric needs the master to send their demands to, to be their addressee. But the hysteric also wants to overthrow the master(s), constantly finding them inadequate. The reasons for this inadequacy should be apparent; the hysteric speaks to the master about the wrong thing, so the "knowledge" produced is always negative, knowledge of another failed attempt. This knowledge becomes the hysteric's knowledge of their history, of all of their failures.

To understand the hysteric's discourse, we really have to understand the difference between that which wants to be expressed by $a$ and that of which $\$$ can speak. Here, $a$ is trying to express the hysteric's symptom. In this instance, the symptom is the truth of the hysteric's condition, the "real" thing in the unconscious that is trying to be enunciated. Unfortunately, the hysteric as subject— $\$$ —is unable to speak of this true symptom, so they have to speak of a second, false symptom. Again, the manifest/latent distinction is important here. Let's think about an example: the hypochondriac goes into the doctor's surgery again. They have been googling their aches and pains, and google has suggested it may be something serious. The hypochondriac's accounts of their pains and worries is true for them as a subject. But why do they keep returning to the doctor so consistently? The real symptom that motivates this could be very different: a fear of mortality, a demand for contact with the other, the doctor as a replacement father/mother. All of these true symptoms are unlike the actual thing the complaint refers to. So even if the doctor can assure the patient that they do not have a terminal illness (this time), the wound that is then closed is not the real wound, and the problem will persist. No wonder that the hysteric wants to decry the master and cry to the master in equal measure.

In *Hospice* we clearly see a hysterical position being *attributed* to Sylvia by the narrator. Is this true, or is it a projection on behalf of the narrator? We can never know the truth of that, but let's take the narrative as we find it in the songs and look for the hysterical discourse. A good place to start is to pick up the thread of "Sylvia," where we move on from the fragile precision of "Kettering" to a building plea addressed to the eponymous Sylvia, with the constant hum of distortion described above, providing a constant indicator that the message is going awry:

> Sylvia, get your head out of the covers, let me take your temperature; you can throw the thermometer right back at me if that's what you want to do, okay?
> ...
> Sorry, I want us to ally, but you swing on little knives; they're only sharp on one side.

In this last line we can see a particular asymmetry in the relationship between the two protagonists. While the narrator is trying to be the master, this mastery is being rejected by Sylvia.

We learn more in "Atrophy." The singer's opening melodic line is repeated four times, each accompanying a different image of the same thing: how the protagonist is following orders. The Other has been living "in front of [her] skull," "making orders," making rules and impossible injunctions. Each line descends like a great sigh above sparse, lifeless piano chords as if there is no energy left in the instrumentalists to support these melodic sighs in the musical human that enunciates them. A hi-hat enters to gently drive the song forward, but it gives a militaristic, march-like topic that reenforces the straitjacket of rules. At 1:40 there is one of those beautiful key changes that lift us into another realm, a heavenly phantasy, without lyrics, as if this is the real message that the hysteric-singer is unable to enunciate, even to herself. The second verse adds more intensity, becoming more classically Freudian with explicit "threats of castration" when calls go unanswered. "In your dreams I'm a criminal, horrible, sleeping around while you're awake, I'm impossible, constantly letting you down." At 4:05 there is a breakthrough of pure electronic whitenoise and interference. The music-only "chorus" has built to a climactic point where we might normally expect a huge "terminal climax" to intrude upon the song and take us to some form of anthemic resolution. But, instead, we hear pure *noise* that changes and subsides over several minutes, seemingly dissolving into the rapidly repeated sound of a chinking glass. This sounds like a reverse process of Trevor Wishart's "Imago" (2002), which was constructed from manipulations to the sound of the chinking of two whiskey glasses. In any case, these real musical sounds are the hysterical outburst—the return of the real—when the message to the master has failed.

Sylvia's hysterical story is considered further in "Two," and we gain a glimpse into her own understanding of her symptoms: childhood illness ("Then they stuck you in machines, you came so close to dying") and issues with an abusive father:

> Your daddy was an asshole and he fucked you up
> Built the gears in your head, now he greases them up

And no one paid attention when you just stopped eating
"Eighty-seven pounds!" and this all bears repeating

There's also the failed marriage, although who it was that dreamt up this symbolic solution to a real problem isn't clear: "Two ways to tell the story, no one worries; Two silver rings on our fingers in a hurry."

What can we make of all of this in terms of the hysteric's discourse? Well, if we put Sylvia in the position of the hysteric for now, we can see it might go something like this. In the bottom left (truth), we have whatever is the real problem with Sylvia [a]. It could be the issues with her father, or childhood illness—it isn't clear how much she is aware of the real meanings of these dreams she has. Above this we have the agent $, who addresses the Other. This is the angry Sylvia, of "Sylvia" or "Atrophy," shouting at the narrator about her illness, his infidelity, how he disappoints her. This is addressed to the narrator, who is in the position of the other, acting as master [S1]. But the hysteric is out to destroy the master, not to accept him. All the master produces is knowledge [S2], but in a negative sense. Knowledge of how things go wrong, how nothing is actually capable of curing the true symptoms—the marriage that did not work to stop fear of infidelity, the child who was aborted to avoid the protagonists' own adulthood, the promises of cures that did not come, the anesthetizing trips to the Chelsea hotel that only delay the inevitable flights. So the product, all of these failed attempts, is never the thing that can truly speak to what is missing. From the album's content, we can only conjecture at what that might have been. In our chapters on Freud, we said that psychoanalysis put a huge emphasis on famility and "daddy issues." Perhaps that obvious reading is a good one here. Musically, this aggression toward the abuser (other, qua "Master") involves lyrical recriminations (google the lyrics and you'll find a list of recriminations). Repetition of the melody is paramount in this song. The texture changes throughout, but the melody is repeated *ad nauseum*. And it's a very similar melody (see Example 3.9) to the one used by Bright Eyes in their early song about desire and control, "A Perfect Sonnet" (2003). We'll study repetition a lot more in Chapter 5, but for now this species of repetition is all about gaining (or taking) control and mastery.

A crucial line in the text that joins forces with this musical repetition is the line "this all bears repeating," as if the patient is fending off the all-too-easy psychoanalytic explanation that the patient is in the grip of a repetition compulsion (more in Chapter 5). This is all about turning on the master and taking control.

The harmony that supports the endless melodic loop is simple and memorable. So memorable in fact that when the bass drops out or the chords are distorted, the ear can make adjustments and fill in the gaps. The music can be disjointed in real life, but we perceive it as whole. In a way this is also a hysteric's problem. In Bright Eyes, however, when the Real breaks through—it breaks through as a lush phantasy of wholeness—remember those songs where a flute takes over after the words have failed to communicate. In The Antlers, by contrast, the equivalent moment in "Two" yields an eerie, ghostly, echo of the Real. Even in this litany of complaints against the master,

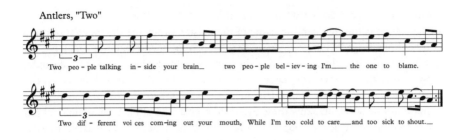

**Example 3.9** Comparison of the melodies of The Antlers' "Two" and Bright Eyes' "A Perfect Sonnet."

and his unreasonable demands, there is a failure to communicate the *a* that lies in the bottom corner of the graph. And it's a musical as well as textural *a*.

## The Discourse of the University

The hysteric wants but rejects the master. The master discourse shows how the position of mastery is empty. Both of these discourses can be classified as being skeptical toward the possibility of mastery. Conversely, the university discourse tries to reify the power of the master. The agent of the discourse is knowledge, which is supported by mastery. In other words, for the university, the master is never in question. The master simply is, and the role of the university is to transmit the knowledge that the master has guaranteed to be truth. Things that aren't universities can speak in the university discourse. What characterizes it is a sense of certainty, inflexibility, and the belief that the answer to a question has always been preordained. There are a number of institutions and bureaucracies in contemporary society that can be argued to function under this principle, whether they be the police, the press, government agencies, or charities. Mastery in these instances can be an ideology or just a set of rules. The certainty that the master gives the agents of the "university" allows them to take whatever actions they believe that master would ordain in the knowledge that they are the "right" types of discourse.

In the university discourse, S1—the master signifier—moves to the position of Truth. This master provides the truth underpinning wider knowledge (S2) in the position of the agent. So, what's going on in the left side of this discourse? Well, what we have here is the signifier, the name of the master, providing the foundation for a body of knowledge. Where can we see this happening in contemporary society? The obvious answer is in the institution of the university. In Stephen's subject, philosophy, they do this all the time. The name of the master such as Lacan or Kant is used to justify the body of knowledge, which our institution uses to speak to the other. We're doing it in this book, invoking these two dead men as the ultimate guarantors of our interpretations of a slew of pop songs they would have never heard. These masters provide a kind of backstop or guarantor to the knowledge that we speak to the other using. In the university discourse, this other is *a*. In the other three discourses, *a* has been a kind of lack or absence. Here, it works no differently. The question posed by *a*, which the university responds to, regards the body of knowledge that the university holds. Something has been seen as missing, or not fully explained. Now, the failure implicit in this discourse is that the university, rather than investigating the phenomenon *a*, will overwrite this moment of newness or difference by simply returning to its old master discourse. In other words, university-like institutions are bureaucratic, unchanging, monolithic bodies through which a predetermined discourse is continuously reproduced. They often work in service of a certain type of mastery, but can be agents of power themselves. This is the joy of the bureaucrat painstakingly applying all the rules, or the police, the laws. This suspicion of technocracy was by no means one created by Lacan and has long been in circulation in proverbs such as "Generals are always prepared to fight the last war." The meaning of this proverb is that the generals never let doctrine have a genuine dialogical encounter with truth. Lacan's argument was that modern societies are increasingly falling under the discourse of the university.

University discourse may be one of the hardest things to see in the album *Hospice*. However, it is something that we often find as a trope in other works of popular culture that encounter the question of love. Anything that attempts to systematize, or that gives you a list of rules or methods or procedures, can be considered a form of the university discourse. Think *Men Are from Mars, Women Are from Venus*. How many days should you wait to text someone back? There is always one character in any romcom who pops up with a set rule—usually the over-cocky best friend saying "four

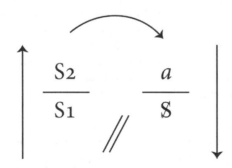

**Example 3.10** The discourse of the university.

days." The joke is, of course, that there is often no universal pattern that works in every case, and the application of the rule always leads to misunderstandings and failures; yet again, something essential is lost in the discourse. Some of the things that look most like university discourses to us now are those involving gender and more segmented or rigid gender roles. There's an extent to which this happens in *Hospice*. One way in which this happens can be seen in the setup of the album itself: the narrator's role as a hospice worker indicates a certain paternalistic relationship to the cancer patient, and there are a number of references to a responsibility of the male narrator to save the patient/partner from her situation.

We might also find the university discourse directly in the music. Notwithstanding the open/free sense in which an endless amount of "hospital time" structures many of the songs, with their free-floating forms, like clouds passing us by at different speeds, for some tracks The Antlers still have the fundamentally anthemic chorus-verse structure underpinning them. Think of the "uplifting" chorus of Sylvia, for example (and the trumpet solo in the classic "middle 8"), where the masculinized drums and slash guitar announce the start of a radically different mode of communication, very different to the fragmentary utterances of the "verses"; we now have a "holistic" chorus—what Drew Nobile might call a "telos" chorus, which marks a sense of arrival at a musical celebration of security, assurance, and comfort in the old order.[14] The chorus acts as the ultimate guarantor of meaningful musical communication; we can subvert it for much of the album, but it's still there and makes some of the most memorable tracks.

## The Discourse of the Analyst

The transition between the university discourse and the analyst's discourse that will characterize the narrator's journey in *Hospice* is hinted at in "Kettering":

> You made me sleep and uneven, and I didn't believe them
>     When they told me that there was no saving you.

At the onset of the album, the narrator is in the position of the nurse and the dutiful boyfriend. In the first of these roles, he is told by the doctors that the patient is going to die, but resolves to continue nevertheless. Here, at the metaphorical level, the relationship, which is the true "hospice," is at the same level as the nursing relationship. The narrator is sure what processes, policies, and treatments he needs to turn to to ensure that he can fulfill the roles expected from him. We hear about these stratagems in more detail in "Atrophy," whose mechanical treatment regime is described musically in the intensely claustrophobic melodic pattern, which essentially repeats the same melodic fragment:

> That ring on my finger, I'm bound to your bedside, your eulogy singer
>     I'd happily take all those bullets inside you and put them inside of myself

---

[14] Drew Nobile, *Form as Harmony in Rock Music* (New York: Oxford University Press, 2020), 86.

This is the kind of attitude we discussed in the university discourse section: taking a quotidian notion of what is required of oneself and then trying to do that. You marry to reduce the anxiety of uncertainty. You are selfless and therefore gain trust.

An interruption to the narrative flow of the album comes with the song "Thirteen"—a fragmented, largely instrumental track that closes with the distant, plaintive feminine voice crying "pull me out from under the house" (a reference to Plath's first suicide attempt), which is a crucial cry for psychological help. This is a clear demand that the carer needs to respond to. The shift from this attitude of the narrator (or observer) is brought about with the onset of the next song, "Two." Again, the doctors come and tell the narrator that his situation is hopeless: "A doctor came to tell me, 'Enough is enough.'" But, instead of trying to act into his role and prove the doctors wrong at this point, there is a subtle change in the narrator's mood. Consider the artful ambiguity in the next line, by placing the line break after "wanted."

> He told me something that I didn't know that I wanted:
> To hear that there was nothing that I could do to save you

Did the narrator not want to hear it or did the narrator not know that he wanted to hear it? Regardless, this moment seems to be the crucial moment in the narrative arc of the album. From this point, the narrator, and his understanding of what happened to the patient and the other party in the relationship, becomes properly psychoanalytic. From here, the carer no longer simply plays the part that he thinks society has awarded him, the dutiful nurse or the loyal partner. His journey to get there is through an understanding of the position of the other, the patient. Once he accepts things are terminal, he acquires a renewed compassion for the patient. The "refrain" that she is said to sing sets up her actions and contextualizes them: childhood illness, abusive parenting, a struggle of an extended duration. With each verse from this point onward, there is an increased sense of warmth in the growing instrumentation, and a purely instrumental section at 1:56 offers us some of the richest, most empathetic and reflective piano figurations—full chords wrapping a comfort blanket around the listener. Yet, this happens above bell-tone-like pitches that are articulated individually but reverberate to offer an echo—as if this is a "split" sound—a divided subject. The second and third verses of next song, "Two," could be spoken by either party. Instead of thinking about how happiness could be recovered, we hear why happiness is impossible. "Two half families tearing at you"; "Two people talking inside your brain / Two people believing that I'm the one to blame." The constant reinforcement of this "two" naturally registers the psychoanalyst's acknowledgment that the subject is divided ( $ )—"two people talking inside your brain ... two voices coming outside your mouth." We should recall that these two people (perhaps more properly, agencies) form the speaking subject and the unconscious that is actually speaking of its symptoms. In "Two" the problems of the relationship are historicized, which is crucial to the psychoanalytic process, and the narrator seems to move to an understanding that all desire is created in the subject, is synthetic, and aims at things that are unattainable. In doing so, he becomes an "analyst."

In the discourse of the analyst, the speaking agent is $a$, supported by Knowledge [S2] in the truth position. This means that the analyst knows the essential absence of jouissance and its impossibility. So while all of the other discourses are, to some extent, chasing the [$a$], be that desire, knowledge, or certainty, the analyst is aware of the impossibility of this quest. Because [$a$] this knowledge is in the position of the agent, the agent of the discourse will always be aware that totalization or closure isn't possible. The trajectory of the album *Hospice* is a slow progression to the understanding that even approaching this $a$ is ephemeral. In the first half we see a whole slew of strategies that try and eliminate the split subject and grab the $a$, like Wile E. Coyote and his ACME-supplied equipment, trying to construct an assemblage that can grab the roadrunner. The narrator however transcends the brute repetition of the unfortunate canine and, under the weight of his trauma, is finally pushed to acknowledge that the process is impossible. This is not without cost, as we shall show in our analysis of the penultimate track "Wake" in Chapter 5.

Perhaps, even more importantly, the other that the analyst speaks to is known as being a split subject ("two"), so the product of the discourse at the lower right part of the diagram, S1, is now the symptom; the $a$ of the hysteric discourse is here named by the analyst. In "Two" we hear about Oedipal problems ("Daddy was an asshole, he fucked you up"), physical problems ("eighty-seven pounds!"), and trauma ("a new dream, more like a nightmare"). The narrator, in analyzing the relationship in the final half of the record, gains both an understanding of how the patient's symptoms formed (and what they are) and an understanding that there is no "other" enjoying. Both contribute to an understanding of the situation that is more developed than the conception of duty that drives the first half of the album. To make this a bit more concrete, when she won't trust him, this is the acting-out of the wound caused by the father's betrayal. When she can't enjoy the stable domesticity that he tries to create, this is an echo of the fear of disaster caused by childhood illness. We can now begin to understand her position more sympathetically, because the things we mistakenly attributed to the patient as a whole subject we now attribute to the part, the unconscious part of the "two." It isn't her speaking, it is it.

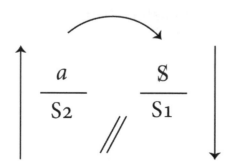

**Example 3.11** The discourse of the analyst.

To understand that the other's speech is coming from the unconscious is to be aware that such speech has a complicated origin—certainly more complicated than our commonsensical intuition that the other is in control of their speech. As we learned in the discourse of the hysteric, it was essentially the symptom that was speaking and being spoken about. In "Two" the narrator is beginning to understand this. The formulas he tried to use at the outset of the album were always going to fail; it isn't just him who is the problem. Instead, it is the whole system. Being human means that you aren't set up to achieve perfect communication; you will always find that language and discourse are failing you. That allows us to understand ourselves better, as the subject always split between conscious and unconscious, always looking for a unity and an enjoyment that is ephemeral. A second observation for the analyst is that the other is also in this position. They are not enjoying; in fact, they are just like you are, struggling, buffeted by forces beyond their subjective understanding.

These two pieces of analytic knowledge allow the analyst to escape some of the problems of the other discourses, but in turn bring about their own problems. The animating struggle for the *objet petit a*, the thing that puts the unconscious into play as a dynamic system, the thing that drives us on; the analyst knows that this doesn't really exist. That is a dangerous kind of knowledge. In many situations, the act of pursuing some *a* that we think will make us happy *is* the very thing that brings happiness. Not all of the functions of the unconscious are bad, though psychoanalysis does focus on the various failure modes (named conditions and illnesses) that these processes can lead to. But sometimes a touch of repression or a quest for the *a* can be a good thing; the unconscious can protect us from things we don't want to know and motivate us to act. In "Bear" we can hear the narrator engage in a kind of wistful reminiscence of a time that had some truly horrible memories, but also some moments of happiness: "We'll pay charades up in the Chelsea / Drink Champagne." It is clear that there is both a pain and an enjoyment in the memories of these times.

"Wake" isn't so much a forgiveness of the patient, but of the narrator forgiving his earlier self for being stuck in the other discourses. The protagonist now opens himself to society, addressing those outside of the hospice setting, with a church organ soon becoming part of the song, and the constant male-voice choir "humming" to offer us a clear sense of facing society once again after the patient's death. He denies his earlier role—pick up her clothes? "that job's not mine." In the final moments there is a ghostly synthesized echo of the cry from "thirteen"—"pull me out"—a reminder that the appeal to the analysts' discourse offered the one hope of the album, so that the album has an afterlife.

The analysts' discourse is shed in the final song—the "Epilogue," which is a "nightmare" from the now-fired orderly, recalling the screaming and cursing of his departed loved one. The nightmare is a depiction without any analytical discourse from any other—it therefore becomes his own plea to the analyst: here's my dream, help me. The album's musical parting shot is to interrupt itself with a melodic but distorted guitar riff that then fades into oblivion; it marks though the inception of some new possibility, a way out of the fabula of the album. Perhaps the album's last word after the journey through discourses is to ask us to assume the role of analyst.

One downside of the analytic position is the possession by the analyst of this knowledge that *a* is unattainable, the realization of which can also come with consequences. Our readings of the psyche so far have discussed the motivating power of desire; we started off talking about how wonderful the "wanting of wanting" is, and how it can have a certain charm. The analyst, viewing this process from without, can lose some of that charm, and there is a danger with analytic approaches that become cynical or cruel in the way that they decode the desire of others and coolly pursue their own desires. We might think of the "character" played by Bill Murray in his great films of the 1980s and 1990s. How about John Winger in *Stripes* (Columbia Pictures, 1981): Life in the city is a bad joke, joining the army is joke, basic training is a joke, all the other cadets are a joke, passing training is a joke, military discipline a very bad joke, invading Czechoslovakia a joke. How about *Ghostbusters*' (Columbia Pictures, 1984) Peter Venkman? In *Ghostbusters*, being an academic is a joke, being a Ghostbuster is a joke, meeting the mayor is a joke (a great joke about their nemesis Walter Peck having "no dick"). Encountering and "busting" ghosts, a joke. It is not so bad for Bill, but the question we can always ask is to what extent is this character facilitating the enjoyment of others? In music, we might wonder the same about Frank Zappa and his sardonic humor outlined in Chapter 2. Zappa, in many ways, is giving us the analysts' discourse there—he knows about everyone's sex lives and knows what makes them all tick—but what he does with that knowledge may cause us to think a little deeper about the ethics of assuming an analytical position.

## The Last Word Goes to Alanis

Let's revisit Alanis Morissette in the final section of the chapter. The album *Jagged Little Pill* (1995) certainly has some aspects of the discourse of the hysteric in its most famous moments. Particularly in "You Oughta Know" we have a song trying to establish what one's relations was/is to another. Indeed, much of *Jagged Little Pill* follows something of the discourse of the hysteric or the discourse of the master. The preponderance of the words "I" and "you" is noticeable. Generally in this "I-you"-ing, Alanis is either trying to establish which predicates she can and can't attach to herself, or what her relationship is to the various addresses of the songs. There are a number of songs that were huge hits following Alanis's breakout that operated in a similar space: Jewel's "Foolish Games" (*Pieces of You*, 1997) or Natalie Ibruglia's "Torn" (*Left of the Middle*, 1997) have a similar position.

Morissette's follow-up to *Jagged Little Pill—Supposed Former Infatuation Junkie* (*SFIJ*) (1998)—reconsiders the subjects of *Jagged Little Pill* in a very different discourse. Morissette has a kind of distance, as discussed earlier, in songs like "Thank U" from the raw emotion of the events discussed. The point here is a quick and simple one, which is that *SFIJ* shows the two possible responses to the various failures entailed by being in the discourse of master or of the hysteric. A song like "Thank U" goes back to a sort of university discourse truism: "How about me enjoying the moment for once" rather than a genuine analytical moment that understands the situation as it was. However, there are moments like this on the record, such as "Unsent," in which we see Alanis treat the other in every discourse as a subject of their own, with desires (and therefore an unconscious) of their own. It is, in our opinion, a much more effective song for that. In being more effective, it illustrates a point that Lacan was always very keen to make, which was that the act of analysis has to be specific, unique, and jump off from its own starting position each time; that is, the starting position dictated by the individual subjects within that act of analysis. There is no external solution or application of wisdom that simply works in every case. Instead, every case must be explored in terms of its uniqueness, not its ubiquity.

Part 2

# Adventures in Popular Music and Psychoanalysis

# 4

# Phallocentrism, Sexuation, and the Chora: From Lacan to Kristeva; Gaga to Björk

## Lacan and Sexuation

**"Was will das Weib?"**

Freud famously asked, "Was will das Weib?"[1] ("What does a woman want?") The lines sum up a whole epoch of men thinking about men and, even more problematic, men thinking about women. And Lacan's recorded spoken words lay him even more open to charges of masculinism:

> In all the time people have been begging them, begging them on their hands and knees—I spoke last time of women psychoanalysts—to try to tell us, not a word! We've never been able to get anything out of them. So we call this *jouissance* by whatever name we can come up with, "vaginal," and speak of the posterior pole of the uterine orifice and other such "cunt-torsions"—that's the word for it![2]

However, despite his diatribes, Lacan's work does, it must be admitted, recalibrate gender differences in the psyche in more profoundly subtle ways than did Freud. This is not to say that they are unproblematic in the twenty-first century, but they are certainly more nuanced and lead more fluidly to the modern world where gender identification is ever more recognized as a matter of choice (whether these choices are consciously or unconsciously made).

In the 1960s and 1970s, Lacan seemed to derive a perverse pleasure from taunting the women's liberation movement. He would sometimes boast of how, after they had initially been incensed by one of his slogans, they would come to realize that he was actually working in their favor, thus winning them over to his cause by showing them that he was already part of theirs. There was certainly an amalgam of phallocentrism

---

[1] Ernest Jones, *The Life and Work of Sigmund Freud*, vol. II (New York: Basic Books, 1961), 421.
[2] Jacques Lacan, *Seminar XX: Encore. On Feminine Sexuality: The Limits of Love and Knowledge*, ed. Jacques-Alain Miller, trans. Bruce Fink (New York: W. W. Norton, 1998), 75.

and egocentrism in his seminars, in which he time and again offers us aphorisms designed to sound provocatively sexist—and may well *be* sexist, but never in the way his soundbytes might at first suggest. Thus is his statement in "God and the Jouissance of the Woman" from *Seminar XX: Encore*: "Woman can only be written with a bar through it. There's no such thing as woman."[3] After recoiling in horror, it's worth unpacking what he means by this and giving him some of the benefit of the doubt, at least for a while. When Lacan refers to "~~Woman~~" or "~~the~~ woman" with those strikethroughs, he means something at once both general and profound. First the more general aspect.

## ~~The~~ Woman

If we revisit some of Bright Eyes' Saddle Creek friends, we find on the joint album *Oh Holy Fools: The Music of Son, Ambulance & Bright Eyes* (2001) a pair of sequential songs: "Katie Come True" by Son, Ambulance, and "Kathy with a K's Song" by Bright Eyes. "Katie Come True" is a simple ballad concerning a man watching a film and desperately wanting the actress to become a reality for him—"Will you step into the light from the screen?" Music acts as a kind of mediator between the singer and the nonexistent woman (~~woman~~)—"The fabric of your invisible body is being sewn with music." The music that the singer refers to (and participates in) will become crucial in a moment, but for now, let's note the perfectly gendered stereotype of a man watching a woman in a movie and fantasizing that she could be real—a full exemplification of what Mulvey was complaining about in Hitchcock's *Vertigo* and most of Hollywood cinema. The music builds in intensity as new instruments are interposed. When he tries to "make out [her] shape," the piano plays a wonderfully rhapsodic descending triplet figure that pulls against the duple meter and helps us imagine the act of drawing lines around an amorphous object. The song's structure is certainly end-weighted, as the singer's obsession becomes more and more intense—louder, higher, fuller in texture, more bellowy—before dissolving into wordless high yelps. There is deep delusion and denial here—"Everyone else just lies to me; they say you're a dream"—but frustration keeps breaking through and triumphs in the end to show us that the man is suffering from his denial of reality in the name of a fantasy of "~~Woman~~. Lacan thinks of this as a masculinist imagination of women, a falling in love with "the idea," rather than the real person: "But what he approaches is the cause of his desire that I have designated as object *a*"—a purely Imaginary experience. Lacan cryptically says, "To make love, as the expression indicates, is poetry."[4] Again, though, this is all written from the phallocentric—and we might add heteronormative—perspective. Lacan writes, "Woman is a signifier. With it I symbolize the signifier whose place it is indispensable to mark—that place cannot be left empty."[5] Could women or, indeed, other men not write "~~Man~~" or "~~the~~ man?" This is where things get more complex and actually much more profound in Lacan's worldview.

[3] Ibid., 72.
[4] Ibid., 72.
[5] Ibid., 73.

The principal thread of Lacan's contemplation of the nonexistence of ~~Woman~~ ties in with his fundamental contention that "there is no such thing as a sexual relationship"— one of his recurrent slogans. We might well ponder the related question of whether there is a possibility of true love in the complement to Son, Ambulance's song—the following (and final) song on *O Holy Fools*, which directly comments on the previous track: "Love is real, it is not just in novels or the movies." As if to recall Lacan's idea that making love is making poetry, Oberst describes, "And I will be there with this pen in my hand / To record all the while." As in the previous song, however, this is a man protesting too much—his growing anger and aggression show that either he believes his version of love excruciatingly deeply in the face of what the rest of the world believes (or knows), or he is slipping into delusion. The final moment is infused with unreality, when he cries over and over again, "I can hear it now" (referring to her song), reminding us of Isolde as she imagines Tristan ascending to heaven ("can't you see … can't you hear … ?"). The song's three Oedipal chords—the famous "three-chord trick" of the primary chords in A major—start to leave their orbit and rise up onto different plateaus, as if something is being transfigured, or perhaps someone is imagining life outside of "the law," a life where love is possible. The singer seizes love in his words, but marks it musically as a fantasy. But to understand fully how this fantasy refers back to "~~the~~ woman," we need first to explore Lacan's views on gender or, as he calls it, sexuation.

## Choosing Sexuated Logic

Lacan has a very precise reason for claiming that love (and a sexual relationship) is basically impossible. He claims that there is a fundamental asymmetry and incompatibility between the sexes in a (normative in the 1970s) binary notion of gender. He calls this entire infrastructure of differences "sexuation" because it is a process of divergence that can be chosen or adopted rather than simply inherited biologically. Views on gender and how we identify with it have developed much further than Lacan would have imagined, and it is important to consider Lacan's two categories without the stereotyped associations of 1973, but for the purposes of elucidation here, we will retain them, though we will reverse them at times as we progress and advise readers to approach them with caution and to acknowledge that their openness to adoption from any biological position, as we will see, is part of the Lacanian worldview.

Lacan believed that when we choose gender ("One ultimately situates oneself there by choice"),[6] we are choosing a way of structuring our lives around *jouissance* in a particular way: we follow two very different logics. These logics are structured around what he thought of as the "phallic function," which he associates with the law, language, and the Symbolic realm. (As you can see, this is why we think of him as "phallocentric"—even women's desire is explained in relation to the masculine Symbolic world.)

---

[6] Ibid., 69.

In Lacan's version of sexuated desire, men are in complete submission to the phallic function; they are utterly subject to the law, to language, to reason and the limits of the "rational," all socially proscribed. However, from inside their cage of phallic discourse, men harbor a secret fantasy of an exception—there is someone (another man) who escapes the rule of the law. This imagined man is often referred to as Freud's "Primordial Father" from his essay "Totem and Taboo." In the mythology of this essay, a group of sons are jealous of the father who escapes the law and enjoys all of the women. The sons bound together and kill him, but then become so full of remorse and guilt that they can no longer bring themselves to enjoy life. Lacan's male logic is similar to this story; the imagined exception to the rule of the law keeps the other men in a state of envy, guilt, and, worst of all, impotence, leaving them incapable of fully approaching *jouissance*. We might think of Lou Bega's fairly appalling "Mambo No. 5" as the exemplification of the imagined exception—the guy who gets to enjoy all the girls: "A little bit of Monica in my life / A little bit of Erica by my side / A little bit of Rita is all I need / A little bit of Tina is what I see." Lou Bega here plays the fantasy role of the "exception." The fact that this guy is completely unreal and, doubtless, highly unsatisfied with his lifestyle should be fairly obvious (imagine having to listen to that awful trumpet riff all day!), but the fallacy runs much deeper than that; it is based on an idea that full satisfaction is out there as a possibility somewhere, lying just outside of social law. What drives male desire, for Lacan, is the envy of this exception and the phantasmatic illusion that it would be possible to achieve satisfaction. This phallocentric version of desire goes back to Schopenhauer's *Will*, and it's the model we find in Wagner's *Tristan*, where the thought of an impossible union drives the lovers through a fantasy of possibility. *Tristan* is weird because it's so symmetrical—both lovers share this same "masculine" version of desire. It is this model of desire that Conor Oberst tries to break through with his unreal insistence that "love is real."

In Lacan's vision of female desire, there is greater preparedness to speculate than Freud, but only just. And he still allows for a certain unknown "mystical" aspect to seep into his model—remember that Freud called women's sexual lives "a dark continent."[7] In Lacan's logic, women's desire is not completely subject to the phallus; woman is "not-whole":

There's no such thing as Woman because, in her essence—I've already risked using that term, so why should I think twice about using it again?—she is not-whole.[8]

Remember Lacan's irritating tactic of baiting women with a derogatory soundbyte? His attempt to placate comes when he explains that this is a good thing; remember the phallus—including law, language, reason, and society—are artificial, manmade (literally) constructions that Lacan says women aren't wholly invested in. In fact he qualifies that further—"She is there in full (*a' plein*). But there is something more (*en*

---

[7] Sigmund Freud, "Inhibitions, Symptoms and Anxiety," in *The Standard Edition of the Complete Psychological Works of Sigmund Freud*, vol. XX, trans. James Strachey (London: The Hogarth Press, [1926] 1959), 212.
[8] Lacan, *Seminar XX*, 72–3.

*plus)*"—and calls women's *jouissance* a "jouissance beyond the phallus."⁹ "Being not-whole, she has a supplementary jouissance compared to what the phallic function designates by way of jouissance." In a way, this is less sexist, because it recalibrates what was once thought of as a lack in women as a positive. However, of course, this new positivity is all still framed by using the male as yardstick against which to measure the female. For a fuller discussion of Lacan's phallocentrism, we will have to wait a little while longer, but suffice to note here that Lacan is careful to say "supplementary" here, not "complementary." And this is his fundamental point, that these two very different structures of desire are incompatible. There is a further qualifier in Lacan though, when he claims that, unlike men's logic, where there is an imagined exception to the rule, there is no imagined exception to the women's logic; in feminine sexuation everyone is a little bit exceptional. This is what we wish to illustrate now, but as we do so, we'll try and empty out some of these overloaded gendered pigeonholes and flip things around a little. And this is partly how Lacan wanted it.

Degendering the role of these kinds of logic, we might contrast the male artist Jay-Z's "Girls, Girls, Girls" as a model of feminine logic, against female artist Charli XCX's "Boys" and her own masculine desire. Žižek prepares the way for this by degendering the topic of feminine sexuation (where everyone, without exception, is assumed to be a little bit exceptional):

> Recall the standard male seducer's list of female conquests: each is "an exception," each was seduced for a particular *je ne sais quoi*, and the series is precisely the series of these exceptional figures.¹⁰

For an illustration of this feminine logic in its application to a "series," we might go further (if we can stand it) in the direction of "Mambo 5" and consider Jay-Z's "Girls, Girls, Girls" (*Blueprint*, 2001). To mock 1970s slow-dance strings, a sample of "There's Nothing in This World That Can Stop Me from Loving You" by Tom Brock is heard while Jay-Z recounts a list of girls, recalling a personal remembrance of each. Although each "remembrance" exemplifies the rapper's quite-staggering racial stereotypes, there is a specific and unique fascination that each person exerts, beginning with the Spanish "chica" that "don't like me to roam / So she call me cabron plus marricon / Said she likes to cook rice so she likes me home," ending with "I got this ho that after twelve million sold / Mami's a narcoleptic, always sleepin' on Hov.'" Each girl is exceptional. An irony of this song is that the sampled female backing vocalist is alone and wordless, as if she lies outside of language and the law, but represents all of the women; perhaps she is the fascinatingly feminine "not all"—the mysterious *something* that escapes phallic law for each individual. A nod to the masculine logic, however, comes from Jay-Z's peers—the various guest male rappers utter "girls, girls, girls" in rough out-of-tune voices as if they are all watching (and probably drooling) from the sidelines, jealously watching the imagined "exception" (Freud's primeval father) get all of the girls.

---

⁹ Ibid., 74.
¹⁰ Slavoj Žižek, *Interrogating the Real: Selected Writings* (New York: Continuum, 2005), 294–5.

The opposite of this situation is Charli XCX's "Boys." It's an almost precise corollary on the surface because Charli sings of how she can't stop "thinking about boys":

> I need that bad boy to do me right on a Friday
> And I need that good one to wake me up on a Sunday
> That one from work can come over on Monday night
> I want 'em all.

The thing that's different here from Jay-Z is that none of these boys is special in any way; they are all placeholders; none of them escapes his role as a notch in the bedpost (in fact they are not even *that*)—nameless, faceless, characterless boys. (True, we might argue that Jay-Z's girls are just appallingly racist stereotypes, but at least he describes other aspects and actions that make them feel like real people.) However—and this is the true masculine logic—Charli XCX does refer to, or directly address, the exception to the rule—her "darling"—as the song reaches its close, and the gentle poppy refrain of "Boys" almost disappears into the ether (the drums and bass drop out; synthesized pings [the sound of crossing off a "to do" list?] and the word "boys" remain). The musical form also marks this "darling" as exceptional. The song has a very gentle, nonteleological feel; it ambles along in a very uncomplicated way when singing about "boys," until we reach the rupture, the "darling" section—the music then becomes equally remarkable—she sings higher; we have a change of harmonic direction; there are more vocal effects—multiple voices, vocal cracks as she switches between registers, giving us a clearer demonstration of raw (real) emotion. The reverb almost makes it all sound like a thing of the past, this coupled with the weakening of the boys' role in the trimmed-back orchestration. Thus, Charli XCX passes these juvenile-bagatelles off as a necessary diversion, but they are unexceptional; the real exception is her "darling" who escapes the whole series of lovers. And thus, by Lacan's lights, Charli XCX occupies a masculine position, whose one big exception contrasts Jay-Z's feminine position, which finds something exceptional about each lover in his equally sordid series.

Let's take a pause here and recall what we're doing in this book. Our objective has been to use psychoanalysis to provide a reading of various artworks from (largely) late nineties and noughties pop and rock music. And in the process, we have been trying to offer our own definitions and readings of some key concepts from Freudian and Lacanian psychoanalysis. As we said in the Introduction, this is not a psychoanalysis of the authors of the songs we are writing about. Psychoanalysis takes time and care, and a three-minute pop song isn't enough to provide a definitive analysis of the subject(s) who wrote it. But musical commentary isn't ever really definitive; it is just a way of trying to understand something that we share with others. The great philosopher Kant said that this act of being impelled to share what it is about a work of art that we are attracted to, and the impossibility of this task as the work of art always escapes such a totalizing definition, is what makes something a work of art, rather than just a thing that we find pleasant. We have taken that pause here, though such a reflection would always be helpful when going through these musical texts, because this is a point where we can redo some of the analysis above, adding in the additional source—the videos that accompany the songs. With this extra bit of evidence, we can come up with very different interpretive frameworks, which do not necessarily negate the others, but provide a different conception of the desires and drives we may be able to sense under the surface of the songs.

Let's start with Jay-Z. Listening to "Girls Girls Girls," we are struck by the reductive nature of the stereotyping in the various characterizations of each girl, where each appears to a greater or larger extent as instantiations of a trope. This factors into a reading of the song as an expression of the worst kind of male desire, where each woman's individuality is effaced by the stereotype, broken down into a series of partial objects rather than understood as a whole, and where counting one's "score" matters more than anything else. We open with Jay in an elevator, putting up a front: gesticulating, smirking, "of course I love all of y'all." But the doors of the elevator open and we're in a 1990s Gap advert, where the titular girls gently sway in their Khakis. The "girls, girls girls" chant that sounds somewhat sinister on record is now fronted by a dazed Biz Markie (the "Clown Prince of hip hop"). Verse 1 begins, and we see Jay in a series of domestic vignettes where he is being dressed down by each of the girls (Carmen Electra's passively pouting cameo as the "French Chick," being the one exception). Jay looks entirely out of place in each girl's milieu; her friends and family look at him as one might look at a man who has not only just arrived in an elevator but also dropped a malodorous fart in it.

As the second verse progresses, Jay becomes increasingly irrelevant, fading into the background of the "Model" and sitting as a passenger who doesn't get any particularly special treatment (a single pillow!) from the "Stewardess." By the third verse, where the characters are seemingly compressed to limit the damage to Jay's ego, things seem to have escalated to the point of embarrassment. "Paranoid," "Hypochondriac," and "Narcoleptic" are largely disinterested in him. The "Chinese Chick" just wants his masters to bootleg. Jay is now Rodney Dangerfield whose catchphrase "I don't get no respect" would apply here appositely. He falls into resigned anger at this situation with the "African chick" and regresses back to puerile humor with the "Narcoleptic." By the end, the video has effectively deconstructed the hypermasculine "Hova" (J-Hova = God) and reduced him to the status of an average Joe trying to navigate the world in such a way as to keep his ego intact.

Here we are back to some of the Lacanian concepts we thought about in Chapter 3, namely the Imaginary-Symbolic-Real, the ego ideal, and the other. Is this song about gendered, sexual desire, or desire in general? In the recorded version we can easily read it as being about the former, but in the video version, we see this added element wherein Jay's others act as real people, not two-line caricatures. In seeing this, we realize the song can be read in a different way to a story of ownership of women, to one of serial rejection by them. And there is even a further level to this analysis when we consider whether the rapper even wants to be Jay-Z, or is simply forced to do so to please the big Other who expects this kind of performance from him. Literally undressing himself as he leaves, shaking off the Jay-Z personality, he walks out as friendly old Shawn Carter.

How about Charli in the "Boys" video? As this video is directed and produced by Charli XCX, we can hope that it aligned fairly closely with her artistic intentions. Oh, where to start. *SO* many boys. What we see here is somewhat of an inversion of the previous position we were in, listening to the song. Charli's desire here is very specific insofar as all boys—and we see so many—are adored in their singularity. In the video, there is no essential boy presented as the prime boy, merely an unending stream of boys, sometimes recurring. The video is wholly written in desire, which nicely underlines the following point. Modern pop music in the form of video is one of the best vessels to explore desire and, as such, is an excellent way for generations of pop stars to explore all kinds of desires, genders, and sexualities and reveal them to society. The advent of MTV in the 1980s allowed a proliferation of sexualities to be presented to the public, and, beyond psychoanalysis, we can see the effects of this exposure in the rewiring of society to a much more accepting position of different manifestations of desire.

## Symmetry/Asymmetry: A Word with Hailee Steinfeld and Lady Gaga

The fundamental point of Lacan's sexuation is the incompatibility and asymmetry of these two ways of structuring jouissance. Žižek retells a cautionary tale of Sarte and de Beauvoir's famed "open marriage":

> It is clear, from reading their letters, that their "pact" was effectively asymmetrical and did not work, causing de Beauvoir many traumas. She expected that, although Sartre had a series of other lovers, she was nonetheless the exception, the one true love connection, while to Sartre, it was not that she was just one in the series but that she was precisely one of the exceptions—his series was a series of women, each of whom was "something exceptional" to him.[11]

Sure, there are millions of reasons why relationships break down, and we are not marriage guidance counselors (nor was Lacan!), but Lacan's point is that even when relationships seem to work well, there is a fundamental impossibility because the two structures of desire work differently. Before we get onto this, a little speculation. Lacan does not really assess the dangers of both people sharing utterly symmetrical (i.e., both masculine, or both feminine) logics. Diplomatically put, he was "of his time" in terms of assuming a heteronormative relationship—even if the + and − attractions were based on his logic of sexuation rather than any biological notions of gender (i.e., a heterosexually identifying pair could easily be "homosexually" (to use the term of Freudian/Lacanian clinical parlance) sexuated). Remember, we are never discussing actual "homosexual" relations here, nor are we discussing actual gender identifications. We can only speak in these Lacanian terms of the logics of sexuation that Lacan gendered in his own idiosyncratic way (and which would probably survive better ungendered). It is not really tackled in Lacan about what goes wrong when symmetry is present (+ and +, or − and −). We'll pick up this thread in Chapter 8, but for now, let's hit "Rock Bottom." This is a song from Hailee Steinfeld's 2015 album *Haiz* and might give us a clue to the +/+ or −/− problem, though we would not wish

[11] Ibid., 314.

to speculate too wildly about what Lacan might have thought. In this song, a couple move in perfect sympathy:

> You hate me now and I feel the same way
> You love me now and I feel the same way
> We scream and we shout and make up the same day

As in their utterly symmetrical relationship, the accompanying video swings between poles of love and hate as the couple fall out and make up on a permanent basis. The symmetry is palpable. During the first verse and chorus, the childish simplicity of the identical nature of their desires is reduced to its most rudimentary object in the video: sweets, specifically a 100-g box of "Sour Patch" (not even the adult's watermelon flavor, but the "kids" variety!). *She* has the sweets; they argue because *he* wants the sweets; later on they feed each other the sweets and they are happy. The imagery is as trite as that. However, the worrying thing about this relationship is that she wants it to descend further: if asymmetry doesn't work, symmetry is even more flawed: "We're on the good side of rock bottom and I hope we keep falling." As they go to a nightclub, she responds to the smiles of the rapper (DNCE) and jumps on stage to join him in an ecstatic chorus while her partner leaves dejected. In the taxi home, the couple break up and then all-too-predictably kiss in the rain. The drama is structurally the same as Oscar Wilde's "A Florentine Tragedy," in which a boring, bourgeois couple use a third person to inject a dose of asymmetry to the relationship, which then renews their ardor for each other, though they just collapse back into new symmetries. Finally seeing something new in each other, after murdering the third party, Wilde's play ends:

> **BIANCA:** Why Did you not tell me you were so strong?
> **SIMONE:** Why Did you not tell me you were beautiful?

It's probably safe to say that if a relationship is so predictably symmetrical that it needs a third person for each party to notice something new about each other, it is probably still doomed. Anyway, this chapter is not about relationship counseling, so let's go back to the hardly healthier relationships of Lady Gaga's "Bad Romance." Did we tell you that's where we're going?

"Bad Romance" from *The Fame Monster* (2009) sits uncomfortably for many reasons. For one thing there is disjunction between the song (the music) and its famous video by Francis Lawrence, despite the fact that Lady Gaga always conceives her videos and songs together as one artistic conception. The music seems to be about a person addicted to bad romances, masochistically relishing the grizzly aspects ("I want your love and your lover's revenge"). Sure, this is not exactly a psychologically healthy state of affairs, but the video sets a scenario of human trafficking in which Gaga is taken from a bathhouse and dances in front of buyers, lap-dancing on the guy in the center, who immediately outbids the other men and buys her at the erotic climax of the song. In the final *coup de grace*, Gaga blows up her buyer in bed. Pop videos generally add a specific scenario to a more generally ambiguous song plot, but the idea of a difficult

**Example 4.1** The girls in "Bad Romance."

romance story is hardly compatible with human trafficking. How does it square? The video was the most watched on YouTube for a while (until Justin Bieber's "Baby" came along) and is a hard-hitting comment on the illegal sex industry. How then can we even begin to tackle this hyper-real disjunction with Lacan's accounts of "normal" (which means "neurotic" for Lacan) desires and relationships. Firstly, we're going to set aside the appalling scenario that is *really* taking place (the sex slavery) and take a look from a cold, formal perspective at the ways the two groups (coinciding with male and female groups in this video) perform their hyperstereotyped logics of sexuation. Secondly, we'll refer back to our deconstruction of the "male gaze," which, remember, was a (laudably productive) misreading of Lacan. Through both approaches, we'll explore the musical twists and turns that take us on a journey through the harrowing narrative.

Let's forget for a moment the big "master signifier" (the one signifier that acts as linchpin for all other signifiers)—the click of the button when Gaga is sold—and dissect, from a purely formal perspective, the different logics of serialization (qua sexuation) that we see on display. Imagine for a moment that this is not a harrowing tale of human cruelty, but the opening scene of "Grease." This is no straightforward disavowal of the horror, but an examination of the fundamental scenario that the horror feeds off. For the men watching the dancers, there is an "exception" logic at work. Gaga heads up the dancing women; she is always dressed differently and appears to enjoy herself (forget, for a moment, that we have already seen tears in her eyes in private). The men here see her, thus, as the exception to these other identical/faceless dancers, as shown in Example 4.1.

By contrast, as they appear to the women dancers, the men are all unique (within the relatively broad parameters of what we might call "a motley crew"); we have a range of outfits, tattoos, wolf-masks, golden jaw braces, and so on. We assume that their desires are all basically the same though—to outbid each other and buy Gaga.

# Phallocentrism, Sexuation, and the Chora

**Example 4.2** The boys in "Bad Romance."

The male fantasy here is that the female "object of desire" has the same logic as them—each imagines that she wants *him* as an exception. Of course, this is pure fantasy—in reality, the poor woman doesn't want any of them, and probably doesn't want any of them equally, *without exception*. But the men assume that their exceptional logic is true of the "other," and this is where things are doomed. When she picks out the main brute (probably because he just happens to be seated in the center of the gathering), he emerges to the others as the fantasy exception—the mythical father of Freud's *Totem and Taboo*, the one who enjoys without limit all of the women. Doubtless, if Gaga didn't explode him in the final scene, the other men would club together and murder him out of collective jealousy (and then feel too guilty to touch Gaga anyway). Noticeably, it is only when she plays out the game of picking him as her male exception by lap-dancing on him and when he decides to "pick" her in turn that the computer screens read that Lady Gaga is "sold."

Let's now start to pick apart some of this by (i) listening to the music and (ii) thinking more about the "gaze" relationship. Remember from Chapter 3 that the Lacanian gaze is not about a bunch of men gazing at a woman and objectifying her (though this is what is generally meant by the term "male gaze" from film theory). The gaze itself is a mysterious source of power emanating from the object we are watching—a kind of hidden subjectivity behind the thing we are looking at. By contrast, the gaze reduces the watcher to a passive, powerless object. The power in this video-tale is clearly on Lady's Gaga's side as proven when she exacts revenge by blowing up her captor. (Of course, the real tragedy is that this is not often reflected in real life; think of the millions of women and men, boys and girls sold into slavery across the world, who can't seize power as Gaga does in the final moments.) A tough pill to swallow for a musician is also that the song is framed by an electronic version of Bach's *Fugue* No. 24 BWV 869, a musical symbol of the patriarchy that Gaga plays her part in symbolically blowing up. As Nancy Bauer claims:

> The man who drools at women's body parts is punished, but then again so is everyone else in the place. And if this man can be said to drool, then we need a new word for what the camera is doing to Gaga's and Beyoncé's bodies for upwards of 10 minutes.[12]

In Bauer's spirit, let's recalibrate our camera lenses, but also our stereo equipment before listening to the song again.

## The Sexuated Acoustic Gaze

The song refers to the gaze, not just in the obvious dimension of the video but also in the music itself. Let's consider some key moments and see (or rather hear) how they play into the drama. David Bard-Schwarz, discussing Schubert's song "Ihr Bild," likened the repeated pitch to a gaze that represents a person's image in a picture gazing at the beholder.[13] The music theorist Heinrich Schenker also claimed that repetition in this song has the effect of "staring" at us—a gaze by any other name.[14] We hear a regular off-beat synthesized stab in the second verse of "Bad Romance" and, for a short while, it's not clear why. A few seconds later we hear (and see, if we're watching) the references to Hitchcock's great "gaze" trilogy of films—*Rear Window* (1954), *Vertigo* (1958), *Psycho* (1960). "I want your Psycho, your Vertigo shtick / Want you in my Rear Window, baby, you're sick," sings Gaga. The musical stabbing naturally represents both the sexualized violence of *Psycho*, famously encapsulated by composer Bernard Herrmann's shrieking violins, and the eyes that are such a key part of this scene, which exert uncanny "gaze" power (Example 4.3). *Vertigo*, a reference that Gaga explores later, was the film that Mulvey's "male gaze" was based on, while *Rear Window* speaks for itself via a temporarily wheelchair-bound journalist who is fascinated with what he sees when he watches out of his back window; when the gaze turns back on him, he is powerless.

The gaze is primarily about imagined or perceived power relations. Even when we feel powerful or in control, there is another power gazing at us that at times reminds us that we are neither powerful nor in control. Many of the problems with assessing where power lies arise because we assume the gaze to be at fixed locations, when, of course, it is always at a higher level than we imagine. Here is one way (of many ways)

---

[12] Nancy Bauer, *How To Do Things with Pornography* (Cambridge, MA: Harvard University Press, 2015), 13.
[13] David Bard-Schwarz, *Listening Awry: Music and Alterity in German Culture* (Minneapolis: University of Minnesota Press, 2006), 27–57.
[14] "Repeating that tone in a slow tempo, after a rest no less, amounts to a staring at it, as it were, and while we do this ourselves we feel ourselves miraculously transported." Heinrich Schenker, "Schubert's 'Ihr Bild' (Heine)," in *Der Tonwille: Pamphlets in Witness of the Immutable Laws of Music*, vol. 1 (issues 1–5), ed. William Drabkin (Oxford: Oxford University Press, [1921] 2004), 41.

**Example 4.3** The eye from Hitchcock's *Psycho*.

of conceiving the gaze relations in this song, concerning Gaga as singer (not as slave in the narrative of the video):

**Gaze Level 1**: Lady Gaga is the object because men are looking at her.
**Gaze Level 2**: Lady Gaga is the subject, fascinating (active verb), doing what she wants, reducing the watching men to drooling idiots (objects).
**Gaze Level 3**: Lady Gaga is the object because, in order to objectify the men, she needs to play the game established by them as subjects.
**Gaze Level 4**: Lady Gaga is the subject because she is making new rules and the men simply have to follow them. (By the way, she's making a fortune.)
**Gaze Level 5**: Lady Gaga is the object because the viewers could choose not to watch.
**Gaze Level 6**: Lady Gaga is the subject because she chooses this career and could leave it anytime she wants.
**Gaze Level 7+**: Infinite regress … ultimately the power of the gaze is nowhere; we imagine it.

Perhaps the truly disturbing nature of the video is that it invalidates some of these normative gaze relationships (qua power relations) in the Hegelian spirit of the master–slave dialectic we discussed earlier—sex slaves are genuinely powerless and have no (or little) control over their situation, and few are able to seize power as Gaga does in conquering their captor. This disturbance to the usual debates about empowerment/disempowerment of sexualization of female artists is perhaps the true gaze of the whole drama—the nagging sense of reality that forces us to reevaluate our whole psychological constitution of perceived power relations.

What, then, is Gaga's endgame? Empowerment in a form of self-subjectification. But it is an empowerment driven by the feminine logic of sexuation, rather than the masculine. She is not saying "look at me; I'm an exception to the rule"; rather, she says (and in her own words):

> When I say to you, there is nobody like me, and there never was, that is a statement I want every woman to feel and make about themselves.[15]

This is, in a nutshell, the logic of Lacan's feminine sexuation: everyone (without exception) is special in a unique way. This is the opposite of what many who look at

---

[15] Cited in Bauer, *How To Do Things with Pornography*, 13 (originally from the *Los Angeles Times*).

and listen to her with masculine logic might assume—that Gaga has the "X-factor." The masculine logic is after all what frames the film *A Star Is Born* (2018), with the film's constant insistence from her husband (of course) Jack (played by Bradley Cooper) that everyone has talents, but a rare few possess the exceptional ability of having "something to say." In fact, the way she is foregrounded in the now ubiquitous song "Shallow" is that the male frames her (singing the first verse); she mimics (second verse) and then jumps into the deep end to find her own voice—she becomes the exception to phallic law. But perhaps the film and the song are not so male-oriented as all that. Remember that Gaga is portrayed throughout as extremely vivid and down-to-earth, unexceptional in almost every way. Even in the man's world, she is standing up for Lacan's feminine logic. And let's be honest: the feminine logic that Lacan gave us is less morally questionable than the masculine, which is ruled by jealousy of the exception to the law and the desire to *be* the impossible exception—the richest, the most successful, the most desired.[16] There is a stupidity to masculine logic; a kind of rat race, we are fully immersed in the Symbolic order, jealous of an imagined man who isn't. The feminine logic is more liberating, less illusory, and more in line with liberal values. The problem is, of course, that you can't expect everyone to possess it—there will always be an unbridgeable chasm between the two very different logics. We might term this the *Gaga Paradox*—she wants to be seen as exceptional in the same way that everyone is exceptional, but for many, she is just the exception in saying that.

And when we pick at a thread in one logic, there is always a knot that we have to untangle with the other. Think of Gaga's "Born This Way," which we will later consider when we explore another concept—"the abject." The song is ostensibly an anthem for Lacan's feminine logic—we are all equal and unique. Gaga's "Born This Way Foundation," devoted to young people's mental health, is testament to Gaga's commitment to this logic. Viewers of the video, however, are all being gazed at throughout. The opening music is a sample of the music from *Vertigo*. One half of this book's writing team has written extensively about this music and how it "gazes" at us.[17] Suffice to say here that it's a symmetrical opening motif (even if you don't read music, just look at the symmetrical wave patterns in Example 4.4) that outlines a mysterious chord (an arpeggiated augmented triad), which always has a weird effect in music, because normal tonal language is asymmetrical—it's all driven toward a center-point, "the tonic." The chord in this example, though, is a symmetrical chord—kind of tonal but kind of nontonal. And even in this symmetry, there are little asymmetries peaking out at us (if you do read music, look at some of the fine details in Example 4.4). It's a motif very much part of *Vertigo*'s obsession with the gaze and the eye that gazes at us. As it's used in the film, an actress's eyes fill the screen in the opening titles, but the

---

[16] At the time of writing, Donald Trump is still insisting he has won the 2020 US election; at the time of editing, British prime minister Boris Johnson is today feigning an apology for a culture of Covid-lockdown parties in 10 Downing Street.

[17] Kenneth Smith, "Vertigo's Musical Gaze: Neo-Riemannian Symmetries and Spirals," *Music Analysis* 37, no. 1 (2018): 68–102.

**Example 4.4** Opening music from *Vertigo*, by Bernard Hermann.

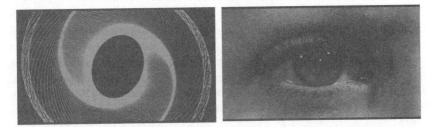

**Example 4.5** *Vertigo*'s gazing eye.

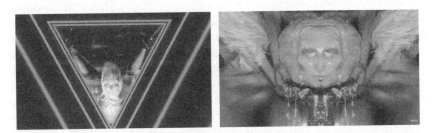

**Example 4.6** Lady Gaga's gazing vagina.

camera soon disappears into the pupil and we see a world of spirals, patterns, and shapes while the music spins its web (Example 4.5). And the gaze keeps us feeling "uncanny"—strange, unsure of what is going on. As we'll tackle soon, the video displays many vaginal images of birthing of strange objects, as if the vagina itself is the eye that is gazing at us (Example 4.6), often doubled on the screen like two eyes. For us, though, the gaze in the music is matched by the strangeness of some of the words that just don't quite fit. Gaga's lyrics make a distinction between "him" (presumably just a guy) and "H.I.M" (something behind the guy?) spelling the letters out in her narrative. Who is he? God? A pimp? Either way, he is marked out as the exception, and this exception is mysterious, H.E becomes a gaze that we can't quite square with the narrative.

Thought about this way, we might come around to the view that the gaze is what rules male desire (at least in Lacan's sexuation), and the point of female desire is that there is already a little bit of the gaze in all of us, which we have to accept as part of our subjectivity.

## Have Your Phallus and Eat It?

There is something ridiculous about the phrase "you can't have your cake and eat it." By "having," presumably we mean "keeping," but "having cake" is all about eating it, surely? That aside, there are certainly situations where the logic of sexuation is dysfunctional because a person tries to cater for both types of logic. We referred in Chapter 1 to Prince and his live performance of "While My Guitar Gently Weeps," but perhaps we can see at work the twin structures of sexuated logic tearing each other apart. In many ways, the "super group" is always already a problem. Imagine a choir of Pavarottis. In a performance with Prince, Tom Petty, Steve Winwood, Jeff Lynne, and Dhani Harrison, the idea is supposed to be that everyone is equally exceptional—feminine logic—and this is inscribed in the entire format (Example 4.7). But Prince, being Prince, has to be more exceptional than the other exceptions, stealing the show and undermining the entire collective group ethos. In many ways, the point of George Harrison as a guitarist was that he was extremely talented and versatile, but you didn't need to be reminded of his talent at every opportunity.

In fact, Prince, who often toyed with androgynous imagery, plays with this double logic all the time anyway. Say you're a rockstar and you want to be the star of the show. Get a pretty average band to back you; that way you'll stand out as a real exception. If you want to *really* be a rockstar, get a phenomenal band of unique personalities and make sure you *still* stand out. Think of the phenomenal musicians Prince shared a stage with as his backing bands—Maceo Parker, Sheila E, Doctor Fink, to name a few. Each is already an exception in her/his own right (masculine logic), but together they are *all* exceptional (feminine logic). But note how Prince outshines them all (while obviously giving them full respect as musicians in their own right) by putting himself as the linchpin—the "phallic" or "master" signifier. When the band leaves you (or you leave them), the logic divides—the feminine logic goes with the band (literally "The Band" if you're Dylan), the masculine logic goes with the "solo" act. That is usually the only way these incompatible logics can function in the long run.

Another example, this time from a female artist, could be Joni Mitchell. While considering her own position in the various groups she has performed in, we can find the conflation of masculine and feminine logic in her songs themselves. Take, for example, "Coyote," itself a song performed in one of the greatest tribute gigs of all time—the 1976 "Winterland" gig that was Scorcese's *The Last Waltz*, now with Dylan's former "The Band." Scorcse directs here so that the camera is mostly on Joni with a rather lackluster Robbie Robertson (The Band's non-lead singer) lurking in the background, seemingly desperate to take the guitar solo. His presence becomes the dreaded "Coyote"—the predatory male who seems to be hounding the protagonist in the song.

**Example 4.7** Prince (in a red hat), Tom Petty, Steve Winwood, Jeff Lynne performing "While My Guitar Gently Weeps" at the 2004 Hall-of-Fame inductions.

**Example 4.8** Joni Mitchell in Scorcese's "The Last Waltz," 1976, with Robbie Robertson lurking in the shadows.

The song, as it appears on *Hejira*, has a similarly "feminine" lineup of males with something exceptional about each—virtuoso bassist Jaco Pastorius, Bobbye Hall on percussion. Mitchell always hired and worked with guys with serious chops, who were top of their game, real "A-list" jazz players like Pastorius, Herbie Hancock, Wayne Shorter, and Charles Mingus. They are all exceptional, but Mitchell is the real exception in the lineup. The "Coyote" song itself has this logic too—each verse describes the flirtations with the coyote—a guy (purported by some to represent Sam Shepard) who seems to represent the predatory men who follow her throughout life, from town to town, always ready to pick her up. But throughout this ballad, she flirts with the various forms of the coyote, always giving every stanza a stiflingly atmospheric groove until she, as a refrain, bursts out onto the freeway at the end of each verse, musically (with a change release of tonal and instrumental energy) as well as lyrically. She makes herself the Coyote's exception—the one that escapes him, the one that lives outside of his law, the one with the power, the one that turns his gaze back on him. But she also escapes him in a more profound sense because she is also expressing an attitude of indifference; he isn't being labeled as a predatory pervert appearing in the car park; he is not about to be reported to the police; she entertains him briefly and then wanders off. This makes herself, ironically, more appealing to him, to the extent that he pursues and pursues, obsessed by her uniqueness. He wants her as an exception; she doesn't want him because he is *un*exceptional. Their letters have crossed in the post.

## Julia Kristeva and Björk: Post-Lacanian Critique from the (M)other

Listen to Björk's "Mouth's Cradle" from her 2004 album *Medúlla* (2004). You will hear a new world of vocal noises featuring beatboxers, Inuit throat singers, not to mention Björk's own highly idiosyncratic and versatile palette of vocal techniques. If we had to say what the song was "about," we would probably reference, say, a mother and a baby, but there is no real narrative thread to hang onto.[18] This is a tableau, but not a static one. The song is bursting at the seams and threatens to be torn apart and the pieces flung in different directions. On this album, Björk wanted "to leave out civilization, to rewind to before it all happened,"[19] and there are plenty of these rewinding noises, vocal samples creating strained loops that make us feel disoriented yet surrounded by maternal voices. Running beneath the psychology of this song is the classic Freudian uterine fantasy—the impossible return to the womb-like state of plenitude that we all deeply want, but radically fear. But the world Björk paints is perhaps more complex than this, and it provides an ideal opportunity to focus on the role of the maternal bond in the developing psyche. It also gives us a chance to recast some of the Freudian-Lacanian insights into the psyche in a less phallocentric light.

Lacan's, and Freud's before him, inability to account for women in their masculine view of the psyche (in which women were a speculative "other") was answered by a prominent former student of post-structuralist Roland Barthes'—the Bulgarian theorist Julia Kristeva. Although she has often been ambivalent about her relationship with feminism, she set out to reframe Lacan's discourse as an empowering theory of the psyche, which placed the experience of women at the center. Given that so much of Freud and Lacan's work centered on the early psychological development of

---

[18] For a political analysis of this song's perceived collective meaning across the artist's fanbase, see Shana Goldin-Perschbacher, "Icelandic Nationalism, Difference Feminism, and Björk's Maternal Aesthetic," *Women and Music: A Journal of Gender and Culture* 18 (2014): 48–81.
[19] Cited in ibid., 61.

a child, and particularly its relationship to the mother, she gave the debate a much-needed reorientation to focus around that maternal aspect of the bond. As a post-structuralist, she took a different view of the human subject too, which she describes always as a "subject in process" or "on trial"—the subject is always tentatively placed, it is ever-changing, always subject to radical reconfiguration—certainly not as fixed or formulated as Freud's or Lacan's subjects.

Kristeva's maternal version of the psyche drew from Plato's notion of the "chora," a maternal place, a receptacle, which a child is born out of and carries with them through life and which exerts a profound influence. This is perhaps the biggest insight, that we carry this maternal space around with us, and it lurks beneath our existence in "real life." Our word "lurk" here might sound menacing and sinister, and in many ways, it is the ideal word to describe what's going on, because there is both a horror and fascination with this chora, which both draws us in and pushes us away. It is also this chora where music and poetry reside.

As Kristeva defines the **chora** in *Revolution in Poetic Language* (1974), it is "a non-expressive totality formed by drives and their stases in a motility that is full of movement as it is regulated."[20] To understand what she means, we need to take in a couple of relatively standard terms, which she used slightly idiosyncratically. The chora is the realm of what she terms "the **semiotic**," which is our pre–mirror-stage state, the realm of sensation, drives, emotion, the sounds and impressions of words, rather than their any form of meaning. It was regarded as musical, poetic, feminine. In opposition to this comes "the symbolic," which we come to inhabit after the mirror stage—the words of fixed meanings and identities associated with patriarchy and masculinized law. Kristeva claims that when we pass through the mirror stage, we start to "**abject**" the mother, radically distance ourselves from her, and we also abject ourselves from the chora. To see this abjection, we might reconsider Lady Gaga's "Born This way." As mentioned, the "gazing" eye becomes the "gazing" vagina. Hitchcock's *Vertigo* spirals, although with the same music, are now triangles—and the impossible, mythical unicorn stands briefly in the center. *Vertigo* music plays throughout the opening "Manifesto of Mother Monster," during which the mother monster is birthed. The details here are very graphic and require a rather strong stomach. The vagina is the site of both eroticism in Gaga's later dancing and horror in these opening moments. The feelings of horror are part and parcel of our abjection of the maternal body[21]—the thing we once clung to for dear life now becomes a thing of horror; it represents what we cast aside in order to enter society. The layers of music that build up in this song even show us this process of abjection. Traumatic electronic sounds "birth" the song proper after the *Vertigo* introductory section. As Gaga begins singing about how "My mama told me when I was young / We are all born superstars" (note the affirming feminine logic of sexuation—we're all unique, without exception), the music nurtures us with cradling string accompaniment. The groove is polluted by broken techno sounds as

---

[20] Julia Kristeva, *Revolution in Poetic Language* (New York: Columbia University Press, [1974] 1984), 25.
[21] Julia Kristeva, *Powers of Horror: An Essay on Abjection*, trans. Leon S. Roudiez (New York: Columbia University Press, 1982).

she reaches adolescence: "She rolled my hair and put my lipstick on / In the glass of her boudoir." The next stage is almost full maturity, hence the drum machine that kicks in as she sings of self-acceptance of life beyond the mirror stage: "'There's nothin' wrong with lovin' who you are, She said, 'cause He made you perfect, babe'" (note again the references to "He" [masculine logic] and the uniqueness of the individual [feminine logic]). The chorus remains in full swing, without any references to these early traumatic sounds. In the video too, there are no signs of the abject maternal body. Until the second verse. Here, we return to those disturbing, dirty, fuzzy samples that are visually accompanied by Gaga and others now painted as skeletons in the Mexican "Día de los Muertos" tradition. This atmosphere of horror is certainly a form of gaze, but it reminds us of the death that awaits us as well as the horror of the trauma of birth that preceded us. While, sure, the corpses here are clearly symbols, they are indexes of abjection, where in real life a real corpse would immediately shock us. As Kristeva claims:

> The corpse ... does not signify death. In the presence of signified death—a flat encephalograph, for instance—I would understand, react or accept. No, as in true theatre, without makeup or masks, refuse and corpses show me what I permanently thrust aside in order to live.[22]

Toward the end of the track, the euphoria begins to subside as textural layers of the dance beats drop out to leave the acapella anthem (with hand-clapping), while the semi-naked figures writhe around in black and cream fluid. After this image and its return to the abjected maternal state from which we entered the world, we have a short section of synthesized F♯ triads, alternating major and minor. They are so low in the mix that we get the impression that they have always been lurking beneath the surface—drowned out. They present a kind of ungendered image perhaps, reminding of the nineteenth-century associations between major/minor and masculine/feminine, as if the raised major third was the "+" symbol and the descending minor third the "−" symbol. Perhaps this oscillation is the harmonic equivalent to the as-yet-ungendered baby, or perhaps the bisexual construction that Gaga promotes.

But the point of this undifferentiated musical state is that it was there throughout the song; the chora similarly follows us along throughout our lives, and we do crazy things like watching gory horror films, because we are fascinated with the material state of reality and sensation before we had to thrust these things aside in order to keep our fragile senses of identity, which we can't shed at any price. In fact the semiotic chora underpins our whole psychical constitution, and yet it fascinates us. Imagine a person peeking through a gap between their fingers at a gory film.

Björk's "Mouth's Cradle" engages with this chora in umpteen different ways and gives a different view of the psyche than we might receive from Freud or Lacan, or even Lady G. One thing that becomes clear in both the song and the psychoanalysis is the role the maternal voice plays. It is what Michel Chion calls, following Pierre Schaeffer,

[22] Ibid., 3.

the "acousmatic"—the sounds we hear (as for babies in the womb) without the source being seen.[23] And this mother's voice is generally portrayed as singing lullabies to a child—"rock-a-by-baby," and so on. These lullabies are supposed to lull a child to sleep, their soothing voices reminding them of the protected state they are from. They are an escape from the outside differentiated world. Björk recognizes the need to keep this world away: "I need a shelter to build an altar away / From all Osamas and Bushes." But think of Brahms' famous lullaby: "Morgen früh, wenn Gott will, Wirst du wieder geweckt" (You'll wake again *if God wishes*). There is always an element of fear to these lullabies—"When the bough breaks, the baby will fall."[24] Doubtless, these lines are lost on presymbolic babies, living in the semiotic rather than the symbolic realm, and the desired soporific effect will be achieved regardless. What Björk does, though, is remind us that there is a dangerous and sexual element in this whole maternal matrix, as we will see.

Björk plays on the undifferentiated sounds of the maternal chora—the myriad voices, the blurring of inside and outside. Many of the noises recorded are of a choir played backward (a little like the voices of *Twin Peaks*), giving the impression of "rewinding" that Björk spoke about, and giving a sense that we are back in a place where time doesn't just run forward or a place before even time existed. Björk also makes the music sound like it is being played underwater at times, and there is often a feeling that the sound samples are manipulations of a bottle glugging. But the point of Björk's song that chimes with Kristeva is that this is a place that lasts forever—"There is yet another one / That follows me wherever I go / And supports me." This chora can be accessed at any time, but we tend not to be able to face the experience—we both want it and fear it, but it is always with us. It is part of the repressed unconscious—this unconscious, for Kristeva, can only be reached through the jouissance of horror or sex (*la petite mort*).

And here is another aspect that Björk draws out—the link between sex and maternity. Are the sounds that open the album and permeate the song the panting, the pushing, and the groaning of a woman preparing to give birth, or the sounds of amorous activity? Are the teeth that act as "ladders" to the "mouth's cradle" an act of fellatio or the act of breastfeeding—or both? This ambiguity between the two is part of the focus on the "drives" in the chora—the chora is where the drives belong, each drive with its own clear path toward satisfaction (though Lacan always writes "satisfaction" in scare quotes, because satisfaction is impossible, or, rather, a drive is only "satisfied" when it continues to circle its object *a*). Björk sings of "The simplicity of the ghost-like beast / The purity of what it wants and where it goes." Again, this "beast" that knows what it wants and where it goes could refer to the penis finding its target, or the mother's nipple finding its home in the baby's mouth, or the drive finding its aim. The fact that Björk's musical utterance is here followed by silence can imply many

---

[23] Michel Chion, *The Voice in Cinema*, trans. Claudia Gorbman (New York: Columbia University Press, 1999), 18.
[24] For a consideration of the role of the maternal voice, in relation to this lullaby, see Karen Bottge, "Brahms's 'Wiegenlied' and the Maternal Voice," *19th-Century Music* 28, no. 3 (2005): 185–213.

things, but, perhaps, it's the lack of any dialectic of desire—there is nothing more to be said; the drive wants what it wants. Then silence. Or, rather, then more drive.

The song reminds us that a prominent feature of Björk's distinctive voice is her play of horror and beauty. After three minutes into the recording, the issue of horror as a co-component of the sexual aspect becomes increasingly clear. The contrapuntal voices become increasingly dissonant and suffused with menacing sound effects. The sinister choral voices include very high women's and low men's voices, sounding like a black mass, mixed with the sound of backward recordings (like *The Exorcist*). On the line "mouth's cradle," we also hear the uncanny sounds of a mechanized voice, which, combined with the image of teeth (the boundary between the inner and the outer world) as a kind of "vagina dentata," offers castration.[25]

An aspect of the chora that Björk sums up well here is the plurality of the drives. In the final minute of the song, there are acoustic hands pulling the subject in all directions at once—a thousand noises vying for attention, and we cannot drown them out. While, yes, each of the drives has a clear goal—the oral drive wants to suck; the anal drive wants to shit—drives are always "partial" and are, at first, part of an uncoordinated whole. In later life, the drives, even for Freud, become coordinated by the primacy of the genital drive. But infants are initially autoerotic—they take pleasure from their surroundings without seeking it. Their drives reach out in all directions, craving not only to be satisfied but also to be ordered.

As you can see, what Kristeva added here was a strong sense of the maternal in her vision of the formation of the (remember: temporary) human subject; what she subtracted was the near-exclusive focus on male development—here the baby, whatever gender, is subject to the same processes. Remember that Freud developed the Oedipus complex but didn't know what to do for women—an inverted Oedipus complex? Jung developed the "Electra complex," but it was never really taken as seriously as Freud's. In some ways, Lacan circumvents the problem by twisting the Oedipus complex anyway and making it non-gender-specific. Kristeva, however, goes perhaps the furthest and tries to strip the whole discourse of its phallocentrism while still preserving the intensely gendered difference of the then normative parental roles.

---

[25] The myth of the vagina that contains teeth crops up in psychoanalytic horror fantasy scenarios from time to time and threatens castration to anyone who wants to penetrate.

# 5

# The Death Drive and Unconscious Production

## The Freudian Death Drive

> If we are to take it as a truth that knows no exception that everything living dies for *internal* reasons—becomes inorganic once again—then we shall be compelled to say that *"the aim of all life is death"* and, looking backwards, that *"inanimate things existed before living ones."*[1]

Reading this in isolation, we might form the impression that the famous "death drive" (or death "instinct") is the tendency of a life-form to seek its own extinction. Post-Freudians called this instinct "Thanatos," the Greek personification of death, which opposes "Eros," the god of life and love. But the passage above comes from Freud's "Beyond the Pleasure Principle" (1920), following one of the most brutally honest openings to any chapter:

> What follows is speculation, often far-fetched speculation, which the reader will consider or dismiss according to his individual predilection. It is further an attempt to follow out an idea consistently, out of curiosity to see where it will lead.[2]

And, as we will see, there is much more to the drive than a straightforward one-way ticket to death. The concept was acknowledged and rejected roughly in equal measure by the psychoanalytical community, and the death drive had a life of its own. Freud himself became more and more fixated on it, and when he came to write *Civilization and Its Discontents* in 1930, he was firmly sold on the idea. However, the concept has a fascinating lineage and finds numerous expressions in the art world. Indeed, for some, it acts as a kind of driving force for artworks themselves. We'll survey some of the vicissitudes of this so-called death drive and see how its changing nuances can be seen in a variety of guises in popular music.

---

[1] Sigmund Freud, "Beyond the Pleasure Principle," in *The Standard Edition of the Complete Psychological Works of Sigmund Freud*, vol. XVIII, trans. James Strachey (London: The Hogarth Press, [1920] 1955), 38.
[2] Ibid., 24.

### Belle and Sebastian, "I Fought in a War"

First, Freud. Working from the basis that most of us operate with pleasure as our goal—the so-called pleasure principle—Freud struggled to understand species of repetition that did not aim for pleasure. He observed this in patients returning from the Great War, suffering "war neurosis," whose nightmares were filled with returns to the trauma:

> Now dreams occurring in traumatic neuroses have the characteristic of repeatedly bringing the patient back into the situation of his accident, a situation from which he wakes up in another fright. This astonishes people far too little. They think the fact that the traumatic experience is constantly forcing itself upon the patient even in his sleep is a proof of the strength of that experience: the patient is, as one might say, fixated to his trauma.[3]

Taking an example from Scottish band Belle and Sebastian, we might listen to "I Fought in a War" (*Fold Your Hands Child You Walk Like a Peasant*, 2000). This song is structured around repetition. A simple verse-refrain pattern loops around, each cycle beginning with the phrase "I fought in a war." Remembering the horrors of a war itself, each verse takes us back to the primary trauma. The first verse, for example, "I left my friends behind me to go looking for the enemy, and it wasn't very long before I would stand with another boy in front of me and a corpse that just fell into me, with the bullets flying round." Note how the song is generally a past-tense experience, but it moves freely between the past and an active present, making us feel the strength of the psychological imprint.

But "repetition compulsion," as Freud was to call it, was not just there to destroy the healthy psyche of the individual (though it may well have achieved that). The sufferer uses repetition to continually search around the site of the trauma to find positive new slants on their experience, to find some kind of escape route, or, indeed, to *master* the trauma. Thus, each verse is in a dark minor key, and its chord progressions have the grim predictability of fate, always returning to the chord center—their dark trauma. But each refrain looks for hope in a memory outside of the trauma and thinks of the girl back home making a necklace out of shells for her returning lover. And with this image the refrain moves to a major key briefly, offering a glimmer of light before the trauma takes hold again, and we sink back into the inescapable minor key.

The childlike innocence of Belle and Sebastian's music—singers with soft voices, gentle instrumental performances, and so on—may help us reflect on another horn of Freud's dilemma with the life "beyond the pleasure principle." He had observed in small children the tendency to play a game that he called "Fort da."

> This good little boy, however, had an occasional disturbing habit of taking any small objects he could get hold of and throwing them away from him into a corner,

---

[3] Ibid., 13.

under the bed, and so on, so that hunting for his toys and picking them up was often quite a business. As he did this he gave vent to a loud, long-drawn-out "0-0-0-0" accompanied by an expression of interest and satisfaction. His mother and the writer of the present account were agreed in thinking that this was not a mere interjection but represented the German word "fort" ["gone"]. I eventually realized that it was a game and that the only use he made of any of his toys was to play "gone" with them.[4]

Freud's explanation was that the child was suspending his pleasure to create a fulfillment when the mother returned:

How then does his repetition of this distressing experience as a game fit in with the pleasure principle? It may perhaps be said in reply that her departure had to be enacted as a necessary preliminary to her joyful return, and that it was in the latter that lay the true purpose of the game.[5]

The child was essentially teaching itself about control, mastery, and risk. Again, we find the compulsion to repeat unpleasurable things has a positive endpoint. And the same is true of Belle and Sebastian's "I fought in a war." While the verse-refrain cycle repeats itself on loop (see Example 5.1), the song intensifies with each repetition, adding additional instrumentation that exemplifies the slow mastery of the topic. This builds up to the moment when, in the midst of minor-key despair, the singer declares, "I can't see hope, I can't see light," when the Morricone-style fate-driven electric guitar blasts out its trill-like figures that symbolize the Spaghetti Western cowboys looking death in the face for the final shootout. We've already heard the Mexican-sounding trumpet solo in the instrumental section, telling us that the character is wrestling with his inescapable destiny.

Perhaps the most significant thing about this whole musical attempt to master trauma through repetition is the final "cadence," which would normally end either in a minor key to indicate a note of sombre fatality (with the tense chord B7 moving ineluctably to E minor) or in a major optimistic key (with a tense D7 chord moving to rest on a G chord). Yet, the song does neither; it ends abruptly on both B7 and then D, indicating that the future resolution of the trauma, be it on a projected E minor or G major, is uncertain. The drama is inconclusive, leading us to wonder whether these cycles of repetition are going to spin on endlessly in some unsung version of the song. Another musical mystery is the placing of the singer's voice, which becomes ever more overtaken with reverberative effects, culminating in a kind of double-tracked reverberation in the soundscape, as if the singer is becoming increasingly distanced from the scene he is describing. Has he died already? This would add additional to the final refrain where the "boy" the girl is waiting for becomes a "man" the girl is waiting for. Perhaps, though, a clue to a more psychological barrier to the romantic

---

[4] Ibid., 14–15.
[5] Ibid., 15–16.

146                    *Listening to the Unconscious*

| Verse 1 | Fragile male vocal with weak guitar in story-telling fashion.<br>E minor key |
| --- | --- |
| Refrain 1 | Marginally higher melody and stronger vocal; fully strummed guitar.<br>G major key |
| Verse 2 | Bass enters; jangling guitar arpeggios; drums enter; reverberation effects on singer's voice indicates distance.<br>E minor key |
| Refrain 2 | Sweeping strings enter with heavier drums.<br>G major key. |
| Instrumental | 'Spaghetti Western' trumpet solo.<br>E minor key. |
| Verse 3 | Trumpet disappears, replaced by solo electric 'Spaghetti Western' clean guitar counterpoint.<br>E minor key. |
| Refrain 3 | More reverb and delay on vocals.<br>G major key. |
| Instrumental | Trumpet reappears.<br>Ends on B7 to D 'half cadence'. |

**Example 5.1** Cumulative buildup of instrumental layerings of "I Fought in a War."

dream of heroic return lies in the cheerless reflection that "the sickness there ahead of me went beyond the bedsit infamy of the decade gone before." He is now forever psychologically separated from the things he loved, condemned to repeat his trauma eternally.

### Lady Gaga, "Replay"

The limbo in which Belle and Sebastian's war veteran finds himself trapped is then entered by Lady Gaga, whose "Replay" (*Chromatica*, 2020) begins "Am I still alive?" In fact these lines are sung with extremely distant reverb, Gaga only very slowly coming into coherence. We learn that the singer is probably coming around from being unconscious after a major trauma. We don't know the details—something to do with a former lover and a gun, and a question mark over "who pulled the trigger." Despite the highly produced dance beat, there are plenty of psychological similarities to Belle and Sebastian. The gloomy minor key throughout, along with the antique-sounding modal melody, evokes somewhere strange, distant, and dark, possibly even the site of trauma in the unconscious memory. The victim is struggling with repetition, singing over and over "the scars on my mind are on replay." That this whole song represents the forces of Thanatos, whether Lady G intended it or not, can be heard even before she begins to sing. The first thing we hear is a kind of synthesized postmodern incarnation of the string tremolos that usher in the Valkyries from Wagner's famous "Ride of the

**Example 5.2** Wagner, opening tremolandi from *Ride of the Valkyries*, resembling the synthesized tremolo that begins Gaga's "Replay" (2020).

Valkyries" (Example 5.2), made most famous in popular culture through *Apocalypse Now*'s Robert Duvall, whose helicopter, "Death from Above," acts as the Valkyrie in Norse Mythology who selected those who were to die in battle.

However, this song represents subtly different psychological effects to those explored by Belle and Sebastian, because repression is now involved, and offers us new twists to the "inhuman" nature of the death drive that will become significant as we proceed. The patient is struggling with repetition not only in its traumatic aspects that we might liken to Freud's war veterans but also with its game-like structure of mastery over a situation. Gaga sings:

> Every single day, yeah, I dig a grave, then I sit inside it wondering if I'll behave. It's a game I play and I hate to say, you're the worst thing and the best thing that's happened to me.

But another difference with "I fought in a war" is that Gaga now spares us (and possibly spares herself) the grisly details. There is an attempt at repression that keeps bursting through as symptoms, leading us to suspect that there is a strong component of hysteria here, rather than a more straightforward "trauma neurosis," which Freud believed could resemble hysteria in its symptoms: "The symptomatic picture presented by traumatic neurosis approaches that of hysteria in the wealth of its similar motor symptoms."[6] Gaga also refers back to the antiquated idea of the wild, hysterical woman scratching her nails into the dirt. She is consciously trying not to repress; she is trying to remember, to avoid hysteria. But she fails.

Freud's discussion of the "motor" symptoms might also remind us that his imagery was highly mechanized and hydraulic. What we find in Gaga's song is that the human-machine seems to be breaking down. When the questioning voice materializes out of the opening reverb, there is nonetheless a light vocoder effect on it. The constant repetitions of syllables and phrases act as symptoms of the breakdown of bodily machinic function: "The scars on my mind are on replay, r-replay." The constant, rapid fading in and out of volume in the accompanying instruments is another technique

---

[6] Ibid., 12.

for creating a collage of technological breakdowns and reboots. This technological malfunction might also point the way to later thinkers who interpret the death drive as a radically nonhuman element of the psyche.

Like Freud, whose death drive was purely speculative in that early essay, "Beyond the Pleasure Principle," and who began by musing on something he couldn't explain, so Gaga confesses to not understanding: "Psychologically, it's something that I can't explain … Does it matter? Does it matter? Damage is done Does it matter? Does it matter?" But notice the different voices that sing these lines—different Lady Gagas seem to be singing from different locations in the sound field: the repressive sensor telling us to, essentially, "forget it" ("Does it matter?"), trying to console the ego that injures itself by trying to uncover its repressed trauma through repetition and bring it into the light of day ("scratch my nails into the dirt to pull me out okay"). What a reminder of the positive goal of the death drive (however unachievable it often is).

As we will see, the death drive is fundamentally the most nonhuman element of the human psyche. Stephen described this once, claiming:

> Death drive is the ultimate avatar of the non-human instinct underneath the subject: it is variously conceived as a compulsion to repeat, ruin, suffer, return to a state of nothingness, breakdown and to revisit trauma. It is also Janus-faced, being described as both the motor of creation and destruction in the psyche. What death drive is not however is, as in its most facile reading, a simple desire for what consciousness would conceive of as "death."[7]

However, as we read in Freud and later writers, Thanatos gets blamed for everything that goes wrong, or that we can't understand about the psyche—he becomes a "catch all" for anything that does not go as predicted, or is not ostensibly predicated on the pleasure principle. As Jean Hyppolite comments at the end of one of Lacan's seminars on the topic:

> It is an extraordinary enigma, the return to matter, and a bit vague in my opinion. One has the impression that one is in the presence of a series of enigmas, and the very name he gives them, *death instinct*, is itself a leap in relation to the phenomena accounted for, an enormous leap.[8]

However speculative Freud was about the concept of the death drive, Thanatos enjoyed a life of his own after Freud, and we need to consider the changing role of the phenomenon through the twentieth century. First stop, Lacan.

---

[7] Stephen Overy, "The Genealogy of Nick Land's Anti-anthropocentric Philosophy: A Psychoanalytic Conception of Machinic Desire" (PhD diss., Newcastle University, 2015), 95.

[8] Jacques Lacan, *The Seminars of Jacques Lacan, Book II: The Ego in Freud's Theory and in the Technique of Psychoanalysis 1954–1955*, ed. Jacques-Alain Miller, trans. Sylvana Tomaselli (New York: W. W. Norton, 1988), 66–7.

## The Symbolic Death Drive, Entropy, and Ground Zero

Lacan's second seminar, "The Ego in Freud's Theory and in the Technique of Psychoanalysis" (1954–5), deals extensively with Freud's "Beyond the Pleasure Principle" and the nature of the death drive. The seminar was lively that year, with extensive discussions of Freud's most nebulous concept. And Lacan grappled with this idea for years, changing its shape as his mature ideas began to form. We will deal here with four particular twists that Lacan gave the death drive, through two songs, both appropriately titled "Mr Self Destruct," neither of which, despite their titles, fall into the obvious Freudian pitfall of presenting the death drive as a simple return to a state of nonbeing. Our four Lacanian refinements will be embodied in these songs, before we listen to a more subtly synthetic song from Amy Winehouse that encapsulates all four. In a nutshell, these changes to the death drive are as follows:

1. The death drive, in line with the then emerging discipline of information theory, can be identified with "entropy."
2. Lacan regards every drive as a death drive, each pursuing *jouissance*, which is an intense pleasure experienced as pain.
3. The death drive isn't biological; it belongs, together with other drives, in the Symbolic realm.
4. The death drive doesn't just aim to destroy but wishes to repeatedly rebuild.

### Nine Inch Nails, "Mr. Self Destruct" (*Downward Spiral*, 1994)

The song opens with aggression. Are these the sounds of gunshots or basketball? As the bangs increase, we know that some kind of violence is about to be unleashed; we just don't know in what form it will take place. Even by Nine Inch Nails' standards, the musical crash comes when the wall of distorted, ear-splitting, cacophonous percussion enters. Above this wall of noise, if we can make out the whispers, we hear a voice talking to us, saying "I am the voice inside your head." Each line that the inner voice delivers to us is responded to with the words "and I control you."

Guitars soon burst in, and we reach some semblance of heavily distorted metal normality. We might think of these explosive sounds as some kind of raw, uncontaminated id (like we found in Pearl Jam in Chapter 1). They may well represent that, but listen to the voices above (if you can hear them). The voices claim to be "religion's message," "denial, guilt and fear," "prayers of the naive," "the lie that you believe." These are all highly Symbolic positions in the sense in which Lacan means the term—they are social products, redolent of the law, language, and the "Big Other." These messages are controlling the human subject and driving it on a path of self-destruction, declaring "I am the exit."

Lacan stripped Freud's psyche of much of its mechanistic imagery (though, as we will soon learn, he was also fascinated by cybernetics). In doing so, he showed his dedication to a belief that most of our mental work was produced socially as we learnt in Chapter 3. The drives, he thought, were not raw and free-willing; they were tainted by language and order. Indeed, around the time of his *Seminar XI*, he began to think of all drives as being located in the Symbolic Order, rather than being tied to biological matter. The drives at some stages in Lacan's thought were operating in the Imaginary realm, but they were never Real. The death drive too is, therefore, Symbolic, nonbiological. Like any other drive, it is shaped by the demands of Big Other. The death drive thus fundamentally pertains to our social relations/interactions with the laws, rules, regulations, norms, customs, language. And this is what Nine Inch Nails show us with their aggressive "Mr Self Destruct"; the drive to disconnect is coming from outside, from Symbolic forces that push the subject toward destruction.

For Lacan, the death drive was also Symbolic because it also lies beyond the pleasure principle:

> [The Symbolic order] tends beyond the pleasure principle, beyond the limits of life, and that is why Freud identifies it with the death instinct ... And the death instinct is only the mask of the symbolic order, in so far—this is what Freud writes—as it is dumb, that is to say in so far as it hasn't been realised.[9]

That is clearly the case for Mr. Self Destruct, although, as we will see now, it takes him on the path of pleasure, albeit a path that runs parallel to the path of pain.

In classic Nine Inch Nails style, a radical cut (1:47) is made through the caterwauling texture to reveal a soft acoustic guitar and gentle whisper, which lasts for almost a minute. The whisper now focuses on the more personal, masochistic drives: "I am the needle in your vein; I am the high you can't sustain." Three things need to be said of this minute-long interior section of the song.

Firstly, this image of drug abuse shows that the drive is now acting in one sense for the pleasure principle (short-term high) while working beyond the pleasure principle in the long term (the come-down/the dependence/addiction, etc.). This brings us to the Lacanian idea that the drive wants to pursue its own extinction through *jouissance*— extreme physical pleasure but experienced as pain. Because each drive seeks its own extinction, for Lacan, every drive is a death drive. Even when the drive *seems* to be working for the pleasure principle, in reality it isn't.

Secondly, these drives are multiple; there is no "single" death drive here; they are all pursuing the same goal, removal of themselves because their presence is not pleasurable. The "pusher," the "whore," the "bullet," the "need you have for more," and all pseudonyms given by Nine Inch Nails for the same phenomenon. We might remember that Freud's original essay used the plural form "Triebe" rather than "Trieb."

Thirdly, this interior space carved out by the Nails—with the lone acoustic guitar and whispers about drug-taking—does not stay intimate and antisocial for long, and we are cast back out into the Big Other to reconfront the Symbolic texture of the death drive: "I am the truth from which you run" and a host of further rounds of "I am [insert

[9] Ibid, 326.

aspect of the Symbolic order here]." It reminds us, perhaps, that inside the drugtaker's insular den, the Symbolic can never be kept at bay and the death drives are always Symbolic, however much, in quiet moments, we might feel them to be Real.

## Soft Cell's "Mr Self Destruct"

We've written about the ludicrously overblown type of display of hedonistic pleasure and destruction in Bruce Springsteen's "Born to Run" that makes such a public spectacle of itself. We can't (at least *we* can't) listen to that song without imagining gasping crowds cheering the hero on his path to self-destruction. The same is true of an alternative "Mr Self Destruct" song by Soft Cell (*The Last Night in Sodom*, 1984). This song also highlights the narcissistic aspects of the death drive—a kind of public (social) performance, played out for the Big Other to watch and approve of. The rock n' roll 1950s aesthetic summons up all of the images of motorbikers and American diners and swooning dancers. But Soft Cell do more than reinforce this Symbolic aspect of the death drive; they focus on the repetitive nature of it, and its desire to not only destroy but also create.

In *Seminar VII*, "The Ethics of Psychoanalysis" (1959–60), Lacan claims:

> Freud's thought in this matter requires that what is involved be articulated as a destruction drive, given that it challenges everything that exists. But it is also a will to create from zero, a will to begin again.[10]

A refrain from the narcissistic persona in "Mr Self Destruct" that punctuates the song and serves as its outro are the lines: "Building your life up and smashing it down." In this final section, the images of building and smashing on-repeat are musically compromised by the fact that the music offers a single (i.e., not repeated) wave of construction and destruction. During the construction phase of what Brad Osborn would call a "terminal climax,"[11] layers of brass are added and additional vocals build toward a shattering moment when the whole edifice crumbles about our ears. What the words offer, but the musical form withholds, is the repetitive nature of this whole process. "Mr Self Destruct" is playing the same game of mastery that Freud's friend's child was playing—"Fort da"—not only destroying but also creating, as Lacan would put it, *ex nihilo*: from, or out of, nothing. All that remains at the end of Soft Cell's cataclysm is the brief sound of an old TV, highlighting again that this is a Symbolic spectacle, performed for the specular enjoyment of the Symbolic Big Other.

Another aspect of this pleasure in destruction and rebuilding is that rebuilding is a way of mastering "entropy." "Entropy" is a term used in information theory that was borrowed from Ludwig Boltzmann, from thermodynamics.[12] Entropy can

---

[10] Jacques Lacan, *The Seminars of Jacques Lacan, Book VII: The Ethics of Psychoanalysis 1959–60*, ed. Jacque-Alain Miller, trans. Dennis Porter (New York: W. W. Norton, 1992), 212.
[11] Osborn, "Subverting the Verse—Chorus Paradigm."
[12] Claude Shannon, "A Mathematical Theory of Communication," *Bell System Technical Journal* 27 (July 1948): 379–423; (October 1948): 623–56.

mean different things in these contexts; in Boltzmann, which was nearer Freud, it was related to thermodynamics and represented the dispersal of energy as the temperature of a system changed. Energy is never destroyed, but it gets dispersed so chaotically that it can't be harnessed anymore. The Second Law of Thermodynamics states that entropy always increases within a closed system. In information theory, Claude Shannon was attempting to work out how much "information" was lost in telephone wires, but his formulae are now used to calculate degrees of disorder or randomness. Lacan was drawn to this idea, particularly the idea that entropy was irreversible, and likened the Freudian death drive to entropy in *Seminars II* and *VII*.[13]

Yet, what the child is doing in "Fort da," and what Soft Cell's "Mr Self Destruct" is doing, is attempting to master and control this tendency toward dissolution and destruction by rebuilding. We might think of Marcel Duchamp's "The Bride Stripped Bare by Her Bachelors, Even (The Large Glass)," which was broken in 1927 and which Duchamp attempted to repair with wire. And Lacan, in thinking that every drive moves in a loop shape around its object (as we'll explore more in the next chapter), also suggests that this is happening in our psyche; we run in the direction of entropy, helping it along its way, and then try to rebuild afterward. Perhaps the musical message of "Mr Self Destruct" as the broken TV makes its noises is that entropy *is* irreversible, however much we try to rebuild; we can never regain what was lost. This comes through the lyrics too, much earlier, but narcissistic Mr. Self Destruct, nonetheless, thinks he can rebuild. The music tells us otherwise.

> You couldn't escape from this fact of life
> That existing makes you a mess
> That every decision or feeling or reason
> Causes some sort of mental distress

What we can build, though, is something different.

## Amy Winehouse, "Back to Black": 4 Lacanian Aspects

Amy Winehouse's song "Back to Black" (*Back to Black*, 2006) offers an opportunity to see both the Freudian death drive and its Lacanian reincarnation in action. The song, supposedly inspired by Winehouse's doomed relationship to Blake Fielder-Civil, who briefly left her for an old flame, describes a person struggling with the need to simultaneously cling to trauma and let go of it. The double-edged Freudian sword of the repetition compulsion is clearly there in the looping chorus, with its chilling line "I died 100 times." But we can take each of the four Lacanian tropes outlined above and see this same death drive in its multivalent action, each focusing on what "blackness"

---

[13] Lacan, *The Ego in Freud's Theory and in the Technique of Psychoanalysis*, 114; Lacan, *The Ethics of Psychoanalysis*, 211.

means in the song: we might talk of the Symbolic Black, the Ex Nihilo Black, Black Jouissance, and Black Entropy.

## The Symbolic Black

The song, in both text and music, is an attempt to say "goodbye." The line "we only said 'goodbye' with words" indicates that there needs to be a deeper level of severance—a deeper destruction of the relationship, and the song now attempts to a musical farewell. The music video features a funeral assembly with members of a marching band— New Orleans jazz funeral style—lumbering up to give the former lover a good send-off.[14] Black imagery is everywhere: black jazz traditions, black clothes for mourners, black-and-white film footage. This is a death drive being played out by the Symbolic Order. In real life, the lover is going back to "*her*," but in the fantasy space, he is being symbolically laid to rest in his own black hole. We have all the musical hallmarks, too, of a musical Symbolic life—the gospel choir, the piano octaves like tolling bells, the syncopated beat that summons up shuffling marching musicians, the motown groove in its minor key—these provide all the gravitas needed to put us at a funeral scene even without seeing the video.

Blackness itself is a huge symbol, full of drives that pull our interpretations in different directions, but on what level is the drive to return here (we've been here before) symbolic, played out in the realm of the Big Other? "Black," in Winehouse's song, is often thought to be the run to the bottom of despair, drink, and drugs. It can also be part of Winehouse's famed Symbolic return as an artist to black music of bygone eras—Motown, jazz, R & B. As a young white woman, her somewhat carefree attitude to cultural appropriation in her music, and her 2008 incident (in which she was filmed drunkenly singing racist slurs), might lead us to interpret this as a return to black lovers, or even self-identification as black, given her performance style. As Daphne Brooks, professor of English and African American studies, claimed at the time:

> Well beyond merely singing, as a white woman, about her desire for black men, Winehouse, in what is perhaps her real innovation, has created a record about a white woman wanting to be a black man—and an imaginary one at that, stitched together from hip-hop and bebop and juke-joint mythologies.[15]

However we conceive it, blackness for her is a form of silence on one level. She sometimes struggles to really say the word. At the end of the first chorus, she leaves us hanging on "back to ..." and eventually completes with "... us," implying that there are more rounds of self-destructive repetition to be played out. But this blackness is not a one-way passage; it is a place to return to forever ...

---

[14] A "tenor horn" player is featured in the video, nodding rather to the brass band tradition. One of the present authors plays the tenor horn, but to no great acclaim.
[15] Daphne A. Brooks, "Amy Winehouse and the (Black) Art of Appropriation," *The Nation*, September 10, 2008. www.thenation.com/article/archive/amy-winehouse-and-black-art-appropriation/.

## Black Entropy

Black, for Winehouse, certainly represents a form of entropy, a drive to disorganize, to disengage, to disconnect. Again, though, we find a paradox in that the drive is Symbolic and social. The farewell rite celebrated in the song (and not just in the video, which is the icing on the funeral cake) is essentially acting as the Symbolic that behaves as the motor for repetition, but this Symbolic act brings people together briefly in the utmost form of ritual organization. Visually there is a dress code, a march, a burial; musically there is an unassailable groove and cyclical chord progression that drives the repetition in the most organized way. But the death drive aims not only to repeat but also to push through repetition before returning to it. We'll learn in Chapter 6 that Lacan's diagram of the drive is loop-shaped; it makes an attempt to leave its orbit of the imaginary *a* at the center, but always returns to it. As soon as the funeral music is over, the crowds disperse, disaggregate, and quite possibly never meet up again. The fantasy of the death drive, however, is that reassembling from an entropic state is possible. (Indeed, one of the tragedies of funerals is that the same elements are never repeated exactly—there is usually at least one member of the family missing when they next assemble.) This drive to disorganize, along with the fantasy that reorganization is possible, is entropy in its fullest. As we will discover when we consider our next Lacanian property of the death drive, in Winehouse's song, each entropic moment does, however, yield a new type of organization; something emerges from the ashes.

## The Ex Nihilo Black

One of the classic sections of this song is the breakdown at the work's core, when, after another failure to verbally produce the word "black," we are met with deafening silence. Out of this silence we hear the same drum beat that kickstarts "Be My Baby" (1963) by the Ronettes, one of the many African American "girl groups" of the 1960s that were so influential to Winehouse. (The drum beat also kickstarts Scorsese's film *Mean Streets* [1973], which summons up another world, closer perhaps to that inhabited by Winehouse herself.) Winehouse then begins vocalizing around the word "black," over and over, building up to a climax of the word itself, while we are wafted by a wall of strings and a gospel choir. Is this about starting to rebuild life from out of the black hole? Is it the drive to create again *ex nihilo*? Sure, but with the expectation that it will be destroyed again. As she's already told us: "I died 100 times." Repetition may draw us down to the dark center, and repetition might equally draw us out again into creation, but it is always to be destroyed all over again. This endless loop might not pertain to the final moments of the song, however, where "black" leads not to an attempt to rebuild but rather to a somber, final minor chord. But we might allow the Symbolic cycling movement of repetition within the song to move us outside of it and consider that Winehouse went on to marry Blake Fielder-Civil one year later and repeat and repeat the path to self-destruction until her own tragic death from alcohol poisoning in 2011.

## Black *Jouissance*

The subject of Chapter 4—Lacan's theories of sexuation—could be perhaps revisited here in terms of drugs. Remember that Lacan claimed that there was a gendered difference (whose gendered nature we don't have to adhere to) in the ways male and female desire is typically structured around *jouissance*. The male way, fueled by jealousy of an *other* who could access *jouissance* directly, was to seek *jouissance* in some place outside of his limits (remember that the male is completely governed by the Symbolic Order). The female way was fueled by acceptance that there was a more subtle level of *jouissance* already within her (she was not completely in the Symbolic and had access to a more direct *Jouissance* in the Real). On the one hand, it would be embarrassingly trite to reduce these complex structures to the drugs—he loves "blow" (the stimulant used to help escape the law of the Big Other through euphoria), and she loves "puff" (the interior, mellower relaxant)—but the point is that these two different drugs are symbolizing two different ways of structuring the death drive that pushes toward *jouissance* that lies at their core. And these two different paths, as Lacan predicted, lead to the point of incompatibility where "there is no sexual relationship." These drives are all leading to the deeply physical *jouissance* but have different structural relationships to it that make the lovers incompatible.

## Machinic Desire and the Death Drive in Grandaddy and Radiohead

So Freud articulated his theory of the unconscious using the imagery of hydraulics—the fluid libido was channeled, dammed, rerouted, overflowing, drained. Lacan, as we showed in Chapter 3, added a sharp linguistic edge to his theory of the unconscious—"The unconscious is structured like a language." The narrative then usually runs that Deleuze and Guattari, in their devastating critique of the Freudian-Lacanian tradition, then recalibrated the human-machine into what they called "desire machines" that "work only when they break down, and by continually breaking down."[16] Their claim was that Oedipus (or, rather, Freud and Lacan via Oedipus and his triangle of "daddy, mommy, me") had wired up us artificially and that psychoanalysis as practiced by their schools keeps the Oedipal system working, and *not working*. As The Antlers sang in their song "Two":

> Daddy was an asshole, he fucked you up / Built the gears in your head, now he greases them up.

Deleuze and Guattari might also substitute "Daddy" here for "Freud" or "Lacan." But it would be wrong to think that Lacan had no interest in machines, and, particularly in

---

[16] Gilles Deleuze and Felix Guattari, *Anti-Oedipus*, trans. Robert Hurley, Mark Seem, and Helen R. Lane (Minneapolis: University of Minnesota Press, 1972] 1983), 8.

his early seminar of 1954–5, where he muses repeatedly on the death drive, the human psyche still had a mechanistic way of functioning and breaking down. Lacan's *Seminar II* is sometimes called his "Cybernetic Seminar." Lacan had been heavily influenced, albeit quite temporarily, in the emerging metadiscipline of "cybernetics" that was coming out of a series of conferences in MIT, spearheaded by Norbert Wiener, whose 1948 book *Cybernetics: Or Control and Communication in the Animal and the Machine* was making waves in the United States and beyond. As the early cyberneticians defined the term, it was taken from the Greek κυβερνητική (*kybernētikḗ*), which tends to mean "steersmanship," which primarily concerned the role of feedback loops. If we are steering a ship and a wind comes from the East, the helmsman would steer eastward to counteract the force—this is called "negative feedback" and is concerned with regulation. If we were to steer to the West, the bow would doubtlessly chase its own stern resulting in a catastrophe—this is called "positive feedback." We find this in Aristotle's view of music in Greek Tragedy, which Lacan also describes.

> In Book VII [of The Politics] his [Aristotle's] subject is catharsis in connection with music … In this text catharsis has to do with the calming effect associated with a certain kind of music, from which Aristotle doesn't expect a given ethical effect, nor even a practical effect, but one that is related to excitement. The music concerned is the most disturbing kind, the kind that turned their stomachs over, that made them forget themselves, in the same way that hot jazz (le hot) or rock 'n' roll does for us. It was the kind of music that in classical antiquity gave rise to the question of whether or not it should be prohibited.[17]

The idea here is that, rather than the general view of how we should use calming music to gently escort our wound-up emotions to a state of placidity, we should engage in wild, reckless music that pushes us to breaking point and leads us over the precipice into catharsis. You can see how either way of using music to deal with emotional (libidinal) problems involves a certain mechanistic attitude. Music and the mind are considered two cause–effect systems that can connect to each other and produce certain predictable effects. For many years, of course, mental health institutions treated patients in a mechanistic way; the use of electroshock therapy or frontal lobotomy was relatively common. (Interestingly, for all of this, early cyberneticians, including Wiener, stood firmly against this practice.) Early cybernetics included key figures such as Ross Ashby, a practicing psychiatrist; but even Wiener made the psyche a part of his cybernetic worldview, claiming that psychodynamics could exemplify cybernetic theory, but it should be "rewritten in the language of information, communication and feedback."[18] Lacan followed this challenge and did indeed take much from cybernetics as he showed us in his *Seminar II*. He explicitly explored the distinctions between humans and machines in the role of thinking:

---

[17] Lacan, *The Ethics of Psychoanalysis*, 245.
[18] Steve Heims, *The Cybernetics Group* (Cambridge, MA: MIT Press, 1991), 126.

We are very well aware that this machine doesn't think. We made the machine, and it thinks what it has been told to think. But if the machine doesn't think, it is obvious that we don't think either when we are performing an operation. We follow the very same procedures as the machine.[19]

And it is to the connections between human thinking and machine thinking, a common concern in art and certainly in popular music, that we now turn. This strongly pertains to the death drive for two reasons. Firstly, the death drive essentially represents the most radically antihuman, antianthropomorphic part of the psyche; and secondly, the death drive is, as we described, a kind of catch-all term for the machine not working as we expect. This is why androids are rarely described in music as actually working! Another critic of Lacan's was Jean-Francois Lyotard, who mused further on the death drive, adopting the position that it represents a kind of breakdown in the psychic system, wherein a drive fails to attain its goal by being broken off, collapsing in on itself, or reverting back to an earlier state. As Lyotard claims in his *Libidinal Economy*:

> The death instinct is simply the idea (as opposed to the concept) that the machine for collecting and draining energy is not a well regulated mechanical device. In this regard Freud points to the repetition of acts, situations, discourses or gestures (nightmares, repetition of failure) that cannot be fulfilments of desire (of "pleasures") in the equivocal sense of the term (the first theory of desire), but that, on the contrary, are associated with the most extreme suffering, the grinding of the psychical apparatus, and the "subject's" scream.[20]

Deleuze, too, believed that the breaking-down of the drive (which he called "desire-machine") was inscribed in its very functioning:

> Desiring-machines, on the contrary, continually break-down as they run, and in fact only run when they are not functioning properly: the product is always an offshoot of production, implanting itself upon it like a graft, and at the same time the parts of the machine are the fuel that makes it run.[21]

It is a great shame that death drive was called "death drive," a name that, in ordinary parlance, is likely to summon up notions of a journey to the most dreaded of existential events. We hate death and spend a lot of time imagining it and fearing it. We hate what it takes from us. We hear of it and we think of sadness and loss rather than the key elements behind the death drive, which are repetition and accident. In our text thus far, we have successfully repressed any base urges we might have to swear (though we have quoted many obscene songs), but in colloquial language, a better name for the "death drive" would be the "fuck-up tendency." Things repeat, and they repeat imperfectly.

---

[19] Lacan, *The Ego in Freud's Theory and in the Technique of Psychoanalysis*, 304.
[20] Jean-Francois Lyotard, *Libidinal Economy*, trans. Iain Hamilton-Grant (London: Athlone, 1993), 13.
[21] Deleuze and Guattari, *Anti-Oedipus*, 31.

And it gets worse. The things that tend to repeat are the big things. In a footnote in Chapter 1 we talked about the different forms of libido. The things that tend to be repeated are those that have huge amounts of these types of libidinal energy attached to them. What is going to push its way out of the id? A thing with a little pressure building up, or a thing with lots? Clearly the latter. This helps explain why we tend to repeat the best and worst things that happen to us.

The second function here, beyond the fact of repetition, is the failure of repetition. When things repeat, they don't always repeat perfectly. The psyche, in reacting to the pressure attached to these things, finds that it is increasingly necessary to drain the energies building up. As Freud assures us, the unconscious doesn't think; so how can we expect it to come up with a plan? Instead, it experiments and often comes up with strange, compromise formations that make little sense.

An excellent example is found by returning to The Antlers' song "Wake" in which the narrator, now free of the patient/partner who is respectively dead/separated, begins to relive the trauma of the relationship. In Chapter 3 we discussed the various accounts of pain and also flashes of pleasure (such as "Bear") in *Hospice*. These formations stay in the unconscious; as we keep repeating, no drive ever dies there, it just gets built over. Back at home, the narrator finds that the weakening of censorship in sleep allows the episode to repeat in various forms. The situation is complicated and makes little sense:

> I am falling from the ceiling into bed beside you … dreams still follow storylines like fictions … now it's not a cancer ward, we're sleeping in the morgue … men and women blue and white … heavy shovels holding earth, you're being buried to your neck

Time doesn't exist here. "I don't work there in the hospital; they had to let me go." All we have are the constituent parts of the story, mashed together and then smashed apart, before being configured into some kind of horrific image that reactivates all of the affect attached to the original situation. Does the narrator want this, or does he not want it? The answer is both; there is an ambiguity conveyed by the song, a joy in return and a despair at the return and the recurrence of the "weight" he is placed under. We are all slaves to the historical construction of our unconscious, though ego defines what is us to some extent, so does id and its reservoir of former loves and hates, fears, and joys.

Another example of the death drive compelling us to strange action is found in Current Joys' "A Different Age" (*A Different Age*, 2018). The whole song operates under very distinct repetition, plodding along in alternation between its two sections. Nick Rattingen does not seem to particularly like the song: "[a] joke, and the melody I wrote, wrong." It isn't pleasurable for him; he seems to be beyond the pleasure principle here. The words he shouts are angry, but not particularly interesting. He is out of time, he is out of place in the city, but both notions seem to have a significant quantity of libido attached to them. As notions of being outside and the desire to be inside (an artist) collide in the song, we find that something genuinely interesting emerges from the repetition. The instrumental section at the end, though glacially slow, retains a bizarre sense of motion and anger powered by undead libido.

Here we come to the final point about the death drive, which is that it is needed by the psyche to ensure that we are not, as we discuss below, simply reduced to the status of closed cybernetic systems, trapped in a repetitive loop forever. The death drive, in having the capacity to do something weird, unplanned, and irrational, allows us to do something new and different. It allows us to break out of behaviors. Yes, many of the constructs that it makes are simply failures and rapidly abandoned, but, occasionally, they lead to genuinely new things.

## The Year 2000 and the *Software Slump*

If Radiohead's 1997 *OK Computer* represented premillennium tension, Grandaddy's 2000 *Software Slump* represented a certain cusp-of-millennium ennui. The album is full of references to a mechanized human existence, full of clunky and disappointing AI agencies, broken wiring, malfunctioning systems, failing communication. The functioning of the psyche has a strong role to play in this rather neutropian (one could hardly say utopian or dystopian) dream of the emerging future. The fictitious group within the album's narrative world create a humanoid named Jed, who is a recurring figure across several Grandaddy songs, two from the album ("Jed the Humanoid" and "Jed's Other Poem"), an earlier song from an EP in 1999 ("Jeddy 3"), and a later incarnation of Jed's alcoholic son, Jeddy 4 ("Jed the 4th"). The character's various iterations paint a fascinating picture of the mechanisms of the psyche not only in themselves but also in their relationships to the humans around them. Singer Jason Lytle confessed that

> I used Jed as my therapy vehicle, I guess ... I was attempting to approach the subject of drinking, and possibly the fact that you may perhaps drink a little bit too much ... Humor has always been way up there at the top of my list of dealing with anything that could be considered serious. Sometimes you don't wanna be smacked in the face with certain bits of reality like that.[22]

And this use of Jed as Lytle's therapy is also partly representative of how Jed is deployed within the songs themselves.

## "Jeddy 3's Poem"

The first song or "poem" of Jed may perhaps be simpler than his later iterations and serves as an excellent introduction to both the character of Jed and the relationship with his humans. Like Lacan says, if the computer doesn't think, then it's clear that

---

[22] Alex Wisgard, "'I Think My Brain Is Working on Another Level ...'—Grandaddy's Jason Lytle revisits The Sophtware Slump," *The Line of Best Fit*, August 31, 2011. www.thelineofbestfit.com/featu res/interviews/i-think-my-brain-is-working-on-another-level-grandaddys-jason-lytle-revisits-the-sophtware-slump-67011.

160    *Listening to the Unconscious*

| Part 1            | Part 2             |
|-------------------|--------------------|
| Machine voice     | Human voice        |
| Human instrument  | Machine instrument |

Example 5.3 The structure of "Jeddy 3" human vs. machine; instrument vs. voice binaries.

Example 5.4 The opening of "Jeddy 3"—computerized melody and improvised piano chords.

we don't think either. The song has two parts, which are perhaps best described by a simple grid in Example 5.3.

The relationship between the human and the machine is instantly fascinating in this song. The piano accompanies Jeddy 3's stilted one-syllable-per-second expression as he relates his simple poem (see Example 5.4).

If you listen to the song, you'll find that in this first section, the machine narrates this melody with pitched "singing." The melody itself is quite simple, but some very subtle touches demonstrate the humans' link with their machine. There is a piano accompaniment—fully improvised. If you've ever accompanied a bad singer while you've played piano, or even guitar, you'll know the feeling of this; the pianist is trying to follow the slightly unpredictable singer as best as s/he can and to guess what keys s/he is going to modulate through. The human pianist here is fully equipped to improvise around the machine, always playing the chords just a little moment after the melody notes are sung as if s/he needs to hear the direction the machine is going in and synchronize as best as s/he can. Sometimes the machine throws them curve balls, and they have to slowly adjust. So, for example, when the machine sings a $g\sharp$ pitch at the end of the first line, this takes the piano into a new direction, and you'll hear the piano trying to help steer the machine back to something more normal with its G chord at the beginning of the next line. This happens a couple of times. Incidentally, there are machines that have been taught to improvise—George Lewis's famous *Voyager* software in the 1980s—but in this relationship with Jeddy 3, the humans are having to adjust to the machine's way of thinking. But listen to what Jed is singing—a harrowing attempt to keep the world outside (perhaps to be alone and insular, eschewing the pianist trying to accompany him?) and leave him alone with his alcohol. Grandaddy

**Example 5.5** The "Jed Theme."

have created a humanoid, and the first thing he does is break down in the same way that we humans break down. We could discuss Nietzsche and his Übermensch of the future and the more modern idea that technology and AI are going to become this same Promethean figure, but this is clearly not it—the machine is immediately anthropomorphized; it sees the world from a human point of view and breaks down like a human does. As Lacan predicted, it is "thinking" the way it is programmed to think—like a human death drive—to fail and fall apart continually.

The relationship between the human and the machine is not simply the one-way passage of the human adjusting to the machine's way of thinking, even in the musical fabric. In the second half of the song, the roles are reversed, when we hear a synthesizer—a machine—badly replicating the lush orchestral strings that we associate with deep emotion. Above this, Lytle sings his very human reflection on the creation of the machine "Jeddy 3 is what we first called him, then it was Jed"—a melodic hook that will feature in all future songs about Jed (see Example 5.5). The interesting aspect here, however, is that the final letter "d" gets stuck and we hear a constant "dddddd" playing across the soundscape, implying that this "human" voice may have been mechanized all along, again breaking down like a machine is destined to do. Hopefully you can hear how the band is starting to use Jed to think through the relations between the human psyche and machine operations, and these develop across the songs. There is also a double-form of death drive here. The human wants to die into the machine; the machine wants to die into the human. Both keep the other alive as a compromise.

### "Jed the Humanoid"

This song gives an account of Jeddy 3 from the cradle to the grave. Sung as a tragic lament—a ballad, in fact—each repeated phrase of the Jed theme from above outlines the story how Jed was created from scrap parts in the kitchen and eventually became lonely, starved of attention, and found the liquor cabinet, drinking himself to death. Lytle's pitches are always repeated with distorted echo and interference as if Jed is communicating from somewhere behind the wiring. The ghost in the shell can also be heard in the plodding sub-bass that reminds us of the metrically regular, stilted machine melody of "Jeddy 3." The repeated phrases of this ballad structure (identical musical verses, repeated to accompany the metrically identical text) also serve a kind of mechanistic role, as if lament, loss, and despair are caught up in a repetition compulsion—they are all processes that are doomed to repeat on life's great conveyor belt. Or, perhaps, it is as if the mind is stuck in its groove, like the breaking-down machine. Another chapter in this tale is that Grandaddy *use* Jed like a machine, and this is ultimately what kills him; his tragedy is that he feels like a human being and therefore feels used. They used him to "compile [their] thoughts" and "solve lots of problems"—"We learned so much from him." They have been using the computer to program their own thinking, to improve their lives, and have borrowed its compiling mechanisms. Remember Lacan—if the computer isn't thinking, then we aren't thinking either. The tragedy of the machine is the tragedy of the human, and vice versa.

### "Jed's Other Poem ('Beautiful Ground')"

Referring back to Jed's first poem, this song begins with an unaccompanied human voice, singing what sounds like a very wayward melody but is, in fact, the "Jed Theme," before giving us Jed's final thoughts on life. Critic Dorian Lynskey called this one "the saddest robot song ever written,"[23] and he is probably right.

Like a handful of emotionally intense robot songs (and other far-out songs like "Bohemian Rhapsody" or "Space Oddity"), this one strings together elements that form a very distinctly disjointed narrative. Think of Radiohead's "Paranoid Android," for example, with those three different types of music—the tense opening of "please could you stop the noise, I'm trying to get some rest"; the edgy anger of "ambition makes you look pretty ugly"; the gentle prayer of "rain down"—and the final aggressive guitar pyrotechnics. In *Software Slump* we begin the album with a tripartite structure in "He's Simple, He's Dumb, He's the Pilot," which draws doubtlessly on Bowie's "Space Oddity." But "Jed's Other Poem" is perhaps more fascinating in its tripartite structural consistency (inconsistency), as shown in Example 5.6.

The extent to which the human and the machine have merged here—or at least the extent to which their lives and stories have intertwined—is marked as a difficulty in discerning whose voice is speaking or singing at any given moment. This is a posthumous poem, and it seems as though the narrator, who opens with the bald "Jed theme," now sorrowfully offers us something like the equivalent of Baroque "recitative"—the rather wayward melodies that would always introduce the narrative that sets the scene for the subsequent song ("aria") in Baroque opera. In the bard tradition, this is something akin to the "gather 'round folks and listen to my tale." The ballad that then follows is the poem itself. Over a mock-tragic, synthesized alternation of heavy chords, "fat" bass and "dirty" drums, and a sound like a swinging metal gate, the tale unfolds with the line, "You said I'd wake up dead drunk, alone in the park. I called you a liar, but how right you were." The interesting aspect here is that it seems that the humans had predicted Jed's entire downfall, the extent to which he would

---

[23] Dorian Lynskey, "Readers Recommend: Songs about Sci-Fi and Space," *The Guardian*, January 27, 2006. www.theguardian.com/arts/filmandmusic/story/0,,1695555,00.html.

| Part 1 | Part 2 | Part 3 |
|---|---|---|
| • Narrator<br>• "Jed Theme"<br>• Unaccompanied<br>• Digital noises of technology dying | • Jed's poem<br>• New melodic cycle<br>• Mock tragic synthesized Baroque<br>• Swinging gate noises | • Narrator's / Jed's reflection?<br>• Ghost voice<br>• Real harp accompaniment<br>• Sounds of nature<br>• Ends in machine breakdown noises |

**Example 5.6** Structure of "Jed's Other Poem ('Beautiful Ground')."

become human and break down as a human. We learn so much more about Jed's human emotions here. He declares: "I try to sing it funny like Beck, it's bringing me down." Jed has been trying to mimic human behavior for aesthetic purposes, which perhaps is one of the most defining, mechanistic aspects of human behavior as we learned when thinking about Lacan's mirror. Again the repeated musical cycles speak of mechanistic actions—life on a treadmill—but this eventually gives way to a different vision. Jed is jaded, tired of repetition, and wants to move on. And where does he move to? Of course, he sinks. Through a denial of the life-drive (eros) inherent in the melody (the struggle for melody to rise upward out of its repeated pattern and reach a climax), the words speak of the beauty he finds in giving in—the title of the poem is uttered—"Beautiful Ground" with a melodic sigh. This is perhaps the classic "death drive"—the need to dissolve materially and create poetry in one single stroke. And this from a machine.

The final part of this triptych song is the most ambiguous and, perhaps, cuts closest to the bone. Over a beautiful, angelic harp, we hear the disembodied, ethereal voice of either Jed or the human, who sings a sinister: "Test tones, and failed clones, and odd parts made you." One of the unsettling aspects is that we don't know if this is the human addressing Jed, reminding him of his origins—in which case, why? And why does this message seem to come from above—from Robot heaven where Wall-E doubtlessly plays the harp? Perhaps, it is rather the voice of Jed telling the humans that they are also constructed of junk machine parts. This may explain the unusual emphasis on the final word, "odd parts made *you*" (with a musical unanswered question in the melody), as if the machine is reminding us that we are more like him in origin than we think.

## "Jed the 4th"

This song, written over sixteen years after the first three songs, gives us a brief and humorous glimpse of Jed's son—Jeddy 4, who is now living a life of his own, outside of the group's control. They were Jed's family, but they are now barely acquaintances of his progeny—"He don't come around anymore." However, Jed 4 is "in Betty Ford" (presumably the drug rehabilitation clinic, rather than conducting an extramarital affair with the wife of Gerald Ford). The message here—"like father like son"—picks up on the final line of "Beautiful Ground"—"odd parts made *you*." Jed 4 was born just like a human; and just like a human, he has inherited the human propensity to repeat its mistakes and aim for the bottom. There are comic touches in this song when the singer's natural human voice gets hijacked by robot sounds that distort his pitch. This gives the impression that just as the Jed-bots become more and more human, the creators become more and more hijacked by machinic behavior.

## A Moral?

Is there a moral to the tale(s) of Jed the humanoid-cum-poet-cum-alcoholic? We might well reflect on how he fulfills those four Lacanian properties of the death drive, but also consider what else he brings to the table. Jed wants to create *ex nihilo*, and Grandaddy themselves keep creating from every destruction of Jed. Jed pursues painful *jouissance* through alcohol and poetry, which also take an entropic hold on him. As a program machine, his linguistic operators are Symbolic, programmed, and operational in the Big Other. But—and we might learn this from Lyotard as well as Freud, for whom the death drive was a placeholder term for whatever was not working toward the pleasure principle—the death drive is also a fault in the system. As Stephen claimed elsewhere:

> What is called the death drive or the beyond of the pleasure principle is in fact evidence of the failings of the psychic system to work efficiently and always properly provide the pre-conscious-consciousness system with not only the tools to complete its goals, but even an understanding of what these goals might be.[24]

But these breakdowns in the psychic system make for great art.

As we said in the section on repetition, the death drive is a powerful force—so powerful that it can prevent the actualization of things that have enough force attached to them to cause serious symptoms, as in hysteria. The death drive, and its ability to make these forces recur in parallel, means that these forces can create formations that surprise us. We can imagine Jason Lytle cooking away with premillennium tension, fearing the digitization of society and fearing his own alcoholism. He is particularly unable to voice the latter, but when all three are firing at once and demanding that they be processed by the unconscious, the compromise formation, "I'll make the computer a drunk," is beautifully effective. The point here is that readings of the unconscious typically focus on a drive, a desire, an object, and object *a*. The unconscious is thereby treated as a serial system, whereas, in reality, it is massively parallel, all drives are always active, and all have various levels of investment. One way of thinking about the death drive is as the unintended (and how could anything be intended, since the unconscious doesn't think) consequences of the drives' simultaneity. As Freud says in section 5 of

---

[24] Overy, "The Genealogy of Nick Land's Anti-anthropocentric Philosophy," 104.

"The Unconscious," they don't compromise with each other, but they all demand, and a solution has to be enacted even if it can't have the rationality of compromise guiding it. In fact, so much the better for that. Rational thought is overrated.

### "Paranoid Android" (*OK Computer*, 1997)

Just like things often end badly for humans, things never end well for androids. In the final moments of *Blade Runner* (1982), Rutger Hauer's replicant, Roy, offers us his "tears in the rain" speech as he himself produces tears (improbable for a "replicant" we imagine) before ending his life. Douglas Adams's original "paranoid android," Marvin, lives in boredom and misery because he is undervalued. In Radiohead's "Paranoid Android," however, it's not the paranoid android him/herself who suffers at the hands of the machinic death drive, but the song itself. The song was never intended to be a serious study of paranoia as a psychological condition. There were walls of humor surrounding the entire song's creation. The song was originally a twelve-minute prog-rock epic that left the band falling about with laughter; the stimulus was, apparently, an "inhuman" woman that Thom Yorke met in a bar. The video by Magnus Carlsson reused characters from the animated TV series *Robin* into a darkly comic "Day in the Life"–style video of Robin's bizarre exploits. While we can't imagine that the song has all of the consistency of a Freudian or Lacanian psychoanalytic experience, the whole psychoanalytic conceit is that works of art represent much more than their intentions, revealing things that the artist was unaware of; the truth comes to the surface in spite of the artist sometimes. In any case, humor often disguises the truth by putting it into plain sight. We therefore look at "Paranoid Android" not as a study of paranoia but as a study of the death drive, as a study in how to simultaneously create and destroy.

Tim Footman declares that "six-and-a half minute, three-part epics about neurotic robots were not the sort of thing they were supposed to do, and they knew it."[25] The follow-up album to *The Bends* had to be different. The song "Lift" was not included on the album, despite being breathtakingly beautiful, because it was too near the consistency of their previous successes. The band is noted for constantly reinventing themselves when they are in a strong position, rather than sticking to a formula until it stops working (probably one of the reasons why they are one of the only bands to come out of Britain in the 1990s and still remain highly productive and acclaimed). The drive to keep recreating from the remnants of destruction, however, is also part and parcel of the same fundamental urge. Remember how the defining moment of "Creep" is really the violence of the distorted guitar that tears through the entire fabric of the song. This happens, too, with *OK Computer* (1997) as an album concept, but is also at work within its songs themselves, perhaps most obviously "Paranoid Android." Each of the song's three sections (four if you include the outro, which draws from the second section) drives toward a self-annihilating act that allows a new song to emerge. Commentators have always made glib comments about "Paranoid Android" being like

---

[25] Tim Footman, *Radiohead: Welcome to the Machine OK Computer and the Death of the Classic Album* (Surrey: Chrome Dreams, 2007), 50.

three songs in one, but these are not three totally different songs; firstly, they are not complete in any way, they are fragments; secondly, they have common threads. They may seem to be completely different, but they are three phoenixes, each rising from the ashes of its successor. Each creates *ex nihilo* from the same elements. Some fairly light music analysis can help us see this, and perhaps even hear it anew.

The musical analytical framework below was inspired by Stravinsky's *Symphonies of Winds* funnily enough. In 1962, Edward T. Cone attempted to show how the stylistic thread that joined the parts of Stravinsky's career together was a way of handling blocks of seemingly disparate musical material. On the surface, there were violent interruptions from contrasting material that destroyed any semblance of musical logic. But somehow the radically different blocks of music did seem to cohere. By zooming in on their similarities, Cone produced diagrams that showed coherent strands weaving between the different strata of Stravinsky's new "montage" form of composition. Kenneth has extended this to analyze the radical disjunctures that seemed to break apart Modest Mouse's songs, theorizing what that unconscious thread of consistency that we can feel actually is at any given moment.[26] It teases out the connective tissue. Were these connective tissues planned? Of course, but probably not consciously. Musicians like Radiohead jam and experiment; musical ideas shape themselves through the musicians, sometimes in a great battle of wills.

Example 5.7 is not as analytically intense as Cohn's or Kenneth's previous work, but it has the same fundamental features. The three different "songs" are located on three separate strata: song 1, song 2, song 3. These blocks of material are placed along the temporal axis of the graph, and their properties are written in bulleted lists inside. Dotted lines show the connective tissue that binds the material as one seemingly unique block (a song within a song) is replaced by another. You will notice that song 2 has two iterations. The notation below may be useful, but is not essential to follow. It basically indicates that a significant thread that unites every section of the song (until its own purposeful destruction in the final section) is the undulation of a single interval (two notes, one higher than the other) that separates three notes (think of the sound an ambulance makes, or the central section of "Somewhere over the Rainbow").

### Song 1, "Please Could You Stop the Noise ..."

The song begins with undulating "thirds" in at least three layers (shown in Example 5.7); they create a bedrock of what would normally be a purely consonant, reassuring interval. However, each line of thirds stutters its way through rhythmically, giving the impression of fragility, nervousness—everything *should* be well, but it isn't. Even here, then, we can see that there is a rhythmic drive to break up the peace of the harmonic stability. And we find this in other parameters of song 1. Beneath the high "What's that?" sustained note, we hear more sinister thirds in an edgier guitar, full of reverb and seemingly far away, with a computerized voice repeating "I may be paranoid but

---

[26] See Kenneth Smith, "Formal Negativities, Breakthroughs, Ruptures and Continuities in the Music of Modest Mouse."

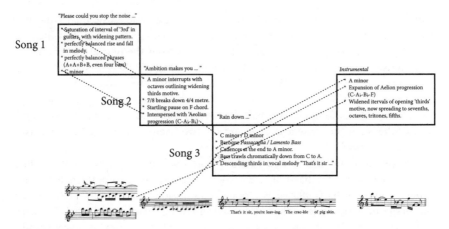

**Example 5.7** Formal diagram of "Paranoid Android" showing interconnective song units.

I am not Android." This is a doubly ironic sentence because paranoia usually doesn't recognize itself as such, and neither does androidcy; so the subject's mechanized voice shows that it has fallen into its own trap. More persistently though, it shows a great confusion over what to believe. And these machine voices are not the organic "unborn chicken voices" described in the text, but the world of the Big Other, repeating itself and creating unanswerable questions in the subject.

Listen to the melody rise in slow steps to a gentle peak and then fall back to its origin. It creates a perfectly balanced and ordered undulating motion. If we call this part of the melody "A," then we have a classic A+A+B+B phrase structure, with the B being the high, reflective, questioning "what's that?" lyric. This wonderfully tight-knit structure is repeated before it is interrupted by song 2. These moments of perfection, riddled with insecurities, are never allowed to rest. The death drive always needs to destroy and rebuild.

### Song 2, "Ambition Makes You Look Pretty Ugly ..."

When song 2 intervenes, it is not really an invasion of new material; rather, it seems to grow out of a latent thought in song 1. There is a carefully shaped segue, and the delicate octaves in the acoustic guitar now sound bare against the erstwhile lulling of thirds. These guitar octaves outline a musical motif that acts as a template for much bigger things in the song. The basic pitch rises from A, up to C, and then down again but further to A♭. Let's call this the "A-C-A♭ figure," which becomes sung to the words "ambition makes you look pretty ugly" (or, if you're a self-consciously ambitious person who can't handle the sentiment of this statement, you could also pin your motif to the words "kickin' screamin' Gucci little piggy"). It's a kind of distortion of the undulation of thirds that we got so used to in the first part. The A♭ acts as a kind of destabilizing, disruptive force, but one that takes us on to new adventures. In fact, throughout the song, there will be a kind of struggle going on between two keys—A minor and C minor. ("Hang on!" the music theory devotee will say "what of the G minor key signature in your examples above." To which we would respond that the key signature here, taken from the official guitar player's sheet music, doesn't seem to reflect the sense of home key the various parts of the song move between. It's not "wrong," because G minor does crop up a lot; it's just not entirely "right.") The key struggle actually seems to be a modern incarnation of what Robert Bailey found in Wagner's *Tristan and Isolde*—a "double tonic complex," actually between the same axis of A and C—two "homes" portrayed at once, two centers of gravity.[27]

We can hear in this section of the metasong, how the heavy guitar riffing (which soon forms the basis of Greenwood's firework display) outlines the chord progression C-A♭-B♭-C, played as a looped progression. Music theory nerds (which one of the authors of this book identifies as) will recognize the classic rock "Aeolian" progression—a kind of heavy-rock substitution for the C-F-G-C primary chords, so named for its likeness to certain aspects of one of the old church modes—the "Aeolian" (play an A on the piano and then go up on the white keys to play a scale; it'll sound quite "old-worldly"). The point here, though, is that the initial jump from C-A♭, now at chord level, comes from the melodic A-C-A♭ motive. It seems as though the patterns at the lowest level (pitches) are being telescoped onto the next level up (chords), and we might also say approaching the next level—keys—because this section is broadly in A minor while the song opened in C minor. A♭ here is being a disruptive element that threatens to rock the boat a little too much. You see how everything connects?

The harmony isn't the only seemingly disruptive force though. The meter is subject to changes when the comfortable 4/4 becomes 7/8. This creates the effect of skipping an eighth note every now and again. It makes it sound as though the CD is skipping. The message is suffering interference; the machine is breaking down.

Instrumentation (think of when the "Creep"-style distorted guitar "invades") is a massive consideration, but our contention is that the subtlety of the harmonic underpinning creates a connective tissue that the surface of shifting instrumentation doesn't quite obliterate—at least not yet. It helps us determine whether these interruptions are coming from outside or from an inside projected outside (the paranoid schizophrenic's conundrum)—a self-destruction. This is all shown, partly by the harmonic grounding, to be an interior dialogue. And the gesture accompanies lyrics that confuse the addresser with the addressee: "You don't remember my name; I guess he does." These lines may remind us of the Lacanian *Che Vuoi*—the question of the neurotic—"What does the Big Other want from me?" This demonstrates a Lacanian rather than Freudian death drive wedged firmly in the Symbolic rather than the biological.

Song 2 ends on pregnant pause—an F major triad, as other instruments recede and space clears for perhaps the emotional core of the song.

---

[27] See Bailey, *Richard Wagner, Prelude and Transfiguration from "Tristan and Isolde."*

### Song 3 (3'37"), "Rain Down ..."

This section, as Dai Griffiths remarks, "depicts rain of biblical proportion."[28] Song 3 summons up the aesthetics of the Baroque era, with its passacaglia—a dance of variations over a "ground bass"—a repeated chord pattern that served as a basis for the variations above. Listen to the classic *Canon* in D by Pachelbel, and you'll get the drift. The "rain down" section also combines another Baroque tradition of the "bass lament." A classic here is Dido's aria, "When I Am Laid in Earth" from Purcell's *Dido and Aeneas*. This is a specific form of ground bass, where the bass descends chromatically (to the interval of a fourth) and always accompanies the act of mourning, lamenting, or general sorrow. In classic Passacaglia fashion, the layers build and build toward a climax, at which point Yorke sings those alternating third undulations that lie at the heart of the whole work—"That's it sir, you're leaving; the crackle of pigskin," each grammatical unit articulating the symmetrical rise and fall of a third (see Example 5.7).

More specifically though, the section plays around an opening descent from C down to A, filling the third chromatically as it passes. However, it stops before arriving at the A♭ that disrupted the previous section and then skips to other chords to end the loop after zooming in on this initial A-C axis. The repetitive motion of this whole "ground bass," though, is positive, surely. It builds and builds into a perfectly constructed edifice. It also builds a religious belief in the power of the Symbolic—it is essentially a prayer to escape a world of Gucci, Yuppies, Networking (we could surely add our own list of modern horrors). Remember Rutger Hauer crying in the rain—here we add the other "human" element that escapes machine logic—religion, prayer, and worship of a Big Other. Footman describes Yorke here as "a little like a secular preacher fronting a gospel choir, the effect heightened by the drawled 'God loves his children.'"[29] And it is this last line that accompanies the moment when this "prayer" runs out of steam or, maybe, runs out of hope. It undoes itself; it breaks down. The final "yeah" that Yorke sings is full of biting ("yeah, right!") sarcasm, indicating an acceptance of hopelessness that brings the prayer down to a hollow "Amen" or, as Leonard Cohen would describe it, "a cold and broken Hallelujah." It is then a form of repeated death in the Symbolic. And thus ends this third song within a song. Full of repetition, building toward hope and collapse (repeat), the dissolution of modern life into entropy described in the lyrics that try and escape the tightly knit musical construction beneath, the Symbolic Big Other that drives the repetition, the musical drive toward *jouissance* in this most climactic, bitter-sweet moment in the song—these things all attest to the death drive. But we must also remember that addition by Lyotard and Deleuze—that this is all part and parcel of the machine breaking down, the faults in the system. The whole "paranoid" aesthetic of the song, the fragility that time and again capsizes into destruction, shows that things are not working as they should.

---

[28] Dai Griffiths, *OK Computer, 33 ⅓* (New York: Continuum), 53.
[29] "Radiohead Album by Album," *Steve Hoffman Music Forum*. https://forums.stevehoffman.tv/threads/radiohead-album-by-album.976042/page-19.

### Return of Song 2 as Instrumental Destructive Force

The wordless song 2 reprise is the ultimate destructive force in the song. It returns violently and gives the impression that song 3 was happening in some kind of parallel universe or an interior world. Maybe, these heavy guitars and their constant riffing over the "Aeolian" progression represent some kind of raw id—improvised immediate expression. But the fact is that the linchpin is the "Aelion" progression (now extended to include an extra chord [F]), which is, in effect, just as much a "Symbolic" rotary chord structure as the "ground bass" in song 2, just uploaded now to the more volatile environment of guitar caterwauling. Another thing that stands out here are the distortions (or Symbolic destructions) of the thirds that saturate the first version of song 2, now creating angular melodic jumps—worthy of Schoenberg or Webern—that represent clear attempts to attack the fragile stability of the song's very foundations. And this is successful, bringing the "song" to a seemingly premature close (notwithstanding its overall length, the final moments are as interruptive as the section itself).

## AI in Pop? Music the New Humor?

This constant process of death and renewal within a single pop song flouts all expectations of a pop song's structure. The cycles of formal units offered in Drew Nobile's recent book, *Harmony as Form in Rock Music*, nearly go out of the window with a song like "Paranoid Android."[30] In many ways, what Radiohead are staging—in the guise of AI that masks their own intentions—is the death of the pop song. They had already proclaimed it dead in 1993 with "Pop Is Dead" (*Pablo Honey*), although this ironically perfect pop song in which pop is only Symbolically killed needed a couple of follow-up albums later to actually kill it in the Real (remember our Lacanian discussion about the "zone between two deaths"?). As noted, though, these "deaths to self" are not actual deaths, but can mark the ultimate sense of rejuvenation, revitalization, reinvigoration, and reinvention that bands like Radiohead pull off all the time. And this happens under the banner of the death drive. Think, by contrast, of the Rolling Stones, R.E.M, U2. Great bands, to be sure, but perhaps they are so invested in their survival (their life-drive) that they don't self-destruct enough.

It's worth a final consideration of the role of AI agencies in popular music. Grandaddy and Radiohead seem to be suggesting its use as a tool for "compiling our thoughts"—as an inhuman avatar for the human to consider its position. Can it be said to represent the death drive that is the radically antihuman part of the self? Well, perhaps not entirely. Remember that in both Grandaddy and Radiohead, and almost every deployment of an android since *Blade Runner*, there is an attempt to show their uniquely human attributes—CP30's campness or Marvin's depression. The message then, apart from a fascination with the difference between humans and androids, is the Lacanian one—if the computer isn't thinking, then we aren't thinking either. In

---

[30] Nobile, *Form as Harmony in Rock*.

turning robots into humans, thus anthropomorphizing, we're actually secretly turning humans into robots in a way that would perhaps be traumatic to confront head on through an act of sacrifice of our human nature (think of Robocop perhaps, the deanthropomorphized being). What this projection accomplishes, though, masks the antianthropomorphic death drive, the desire to die to the self Symbolically and renew (on repeat) in the Big Other.

Perhaps these mechanical figures also point to a need, analogous to humor, to say the unsayable, to behave mechanically, inhumanly, which we can't do in real life. As we saw, when we discussed the role of the unconscious in the telling of jokes, music can also have an analogous role in this. Perhaps, then, the musical death drive and the death-to-the self that we find in musical projections of AI have a particularly special resonance. We project ourselves again and again, on repeat, into Symbolic worlds that we create and destroy over and over. Perhaps, music itself is the death drive par excellence.

# 6

# "Do You Want To Be the Ebb of This Great Tide?": Lacan, Freud, Nietzsche, Deleuze, and "Joy in Repetition": Prince and LCD Soundsystem

### Joy in Repetition, from Prince to Pharrell Williams

The chorus of Pharrell Williams's 2013 hit "Happy" (from *Despicable Me 2*) repeats a circular chord progression that exemplifies a continuous yet complete satisfaction loop. A variant of the classical set progression known to us theory-heads as "augmented sixth" → dominant → tonic progression from the eighteenth century, this chord progression begins on a dissonant and heavily extended D♭ chord (with ♯11 and ♮7) that drives downward to a "dominant" chord in its minor form (C minor⁷) and then onto the "tonic" of F major. The progression embodies a narrative that positions us first at a quirky place away from home (chord ♭VI, with an "augmented sixth"), turns us toward home (chord V, the dominant), and finally takes us home (chord I, the tonic). This song is one expression of pure joy, happiness, and optimism, but it repeats just like most other pop songs. It's fair to say that the song is a good one for producing "ear worms" so it repeats in the mind long after the four-minute-six-second confines of the track itself. We might think that this pure joyous experience puts paid to the dark Freudian "repetition compulsion" that became synonymous with the "death-drive." When we explore repetition in Freud, we tend to look always *beyond* the pleasure principle, but remember that this was a form of repetition that bucked the more normative trend of repeating positive experiences simply because they produce pleasure. More is written about repetition as a problematic breakdown in the psyche than the more obvious form of repetition that works *for* the pleasure principle rather than against it. It is therefore worth our while going back to the pleasure principle and rekindling some of the spark of joy in repetition, though, as we will see, the joy *within* the pleasure principle may be no less complex than the form of repetition that lay beyond it.

Prince's "Joy in Repetition" (*Graffiti Bridge*, 1990) uses the same chord progression as the chorus for "Happy," but uses it absolutely exclusively (Williams's song has a "verse-chorus" structure with much more variety). Prince's entire song riffs over the same three-chord cycle with slight variations: $D\flat^9 \to Cm^9 \to Fm^7$.[1] This is the main repeated element of the song, which undergoes various changes of state or transformation. In 2011, one fan on *prince.org* pondered:

> I'd like to know what he was reading at the time, because the idea and especially the title of the song ("joy in repetition") seem to reflect several central psychoanalytic ideas. I doubt Prince was really gettin' his Freud on at the time, but perhaps he was into something else that employed those thoughts.[2]

For all the focus on repetition, we do not experience the typical cycle of repeated formal units in the song. It doesn't quite use a verse-chorus structure, because there is no real repeat. The song does have what Nobile calls a "cycle" of formal units, but it only goes once around the circuit. Here is a formal overview.

| | |
|---|---|
| 0:00 | Introduction |
| 0.15 | Three verses |
| 2:00 | Bridge? |
| 2:23 | Chorus |
| 3:00 | Guitar solo/audio collage |

The verses don't interchange with choruses; they repeat in themselves until they have to slip out of their circuit into something new—a chorus that, itself, is never repeated. However, the narrative described in the text shows us that the song's story will repeat endlessly throughout human history. Repetition comes through lyrically on different levels, working up to the musical level of chord progressions as if it is repeating in different spheres of existence, like a fractal. Let's look at some of the aspects.

A man walks into a bar (no joke) and watches a woman performing a song that has been sung many times over the months (repetition 1). She keeps repeating the same two words over and over (repetition 2) without us ever finding out what the words are. The man is so full of desire and tension that he eventually jumps on stage and takes her out the back, where the drops of rain punctuate the repeated words (repetition 2.1). They share physical contact that they want to prolong as eternal repetition (repetition 3). This repetition is prolonged musically (repetition 3.1). The verse's foundational chord progression slips into the entire bridge and chorus, and a growing sense of developmental variation is felt above the progression. The chord progression forms a loop in which each chord "discharges" (Daniel Harrison's word for the release of

---

[1] The $D\flat 9$ chord uses a major seventh rather than the normally implied minor seventh.
[2] "What Is 'Joy in Repetition' About?" *Prince.Org*, May 22, 2011 (novabrkr). https://prince.org/msg/7/359343.

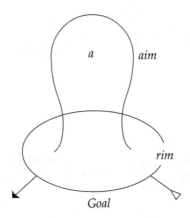

**Example 6.1** Lacan's model of the drive circuit.

tension that occurs when chords resolve into each other.[3] A spark of joy is released with every progression. When the guitar improvises or solos toward the end of the track, it uses a typical minor "pentatonic" blues on F (a common blues improvisation scale), with an Aeolian frame and blue notes on the occasional C♭ (to make it sexier!). This is pure elaboration within the productive space demarcated by the chord repetition. And this repetition is not necessarily repeating in the hope of gaining joy, but is rather the joy itself. To really comprehend this, an appeal to Lacan can help.

Lacan's "Deconstruction of the Drive," as articulated in *Seminar XI*,[4] breaks down the idea that the drive aims at satisfaction. He notes that Freud writes "satisfaction" in inverted commas, because it is never really possible.[5] Lacan believes that the drive aims not to *hit* or *obtain* the mysterious object "*a*" (the fantasy of the other) but to loop around it and return to its circuit. The erogenous "rim" of the circuit (see Example 6.1) is the location of the drive, which "aims" (in the way that an archer would aim) only to make a loop shape around the *a* and return to its ultimate goal, which is continued, repeated circulation. And this repetitious circulation is where the drive's pleasure comes into force—it is not end-orientated (teleological) but continual.

And it is the repeated loop around the "*a*" that Prince summons up perfectly. Thinking back to "Happy," Pharrell Williams is portraying something more like an unsustainable moment of pleasure and hoping to prolong it, which he can achieve for only a short time. Prince perhaps more realistically encapsulates the moment of generally aiming for something pleasurable, but always secretly aiming to circulate this certain pleasurable something without ever hoping to actually attain it. Note how his repeated chord progression aims toward F minor, but when it arrives, it contains the

---

[3] Daniel Harrison, *Harmonic Function in Chromatic Music: A Renewed Dualist Theory and an Account of Its Precedents* (Chicago: University of Chicago Press, 1994).
[4] Jacques Lacan, "The Deconstruction of the Drive!" in *Seminar XI: The Four Fundamental Concepts of Psychoanalysis*, trans. Jacques-Alain Miller (London: Vintage, [1964] 1998), 161 73.
[5] Ibid., 165.

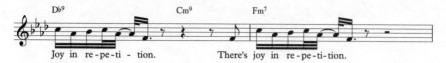

**Example 6.2** Prince, "Joy in Repetition," chorus riff.

**Example 6.3** Prince, "Joy in Repetition," final moments.

seventh, meaning that, if this were classical grammar, it would need to resolve further (to B♭, for example), as shown in Example 6.2.

Another aspect of the Lacanian drive pertinent to this track (and many others, perhaps even all of popular music) is the linguistic nature of the drive. Freud had conceived drives as hydraulically motivated, as we explored in our first chapter. Freud also used two separate terms "Instinkt" (simple biological imperatives) and "Trieb" (drives that are generally associated with parts of the body that are socially determined). The two became conflated in early translations of Freud, where we sometimes read of the "death instinct," which is better rendered as "death-drive." When Lacan revisited the drive, he showed it to be linguistically ordered rather than purely mechanical. Deleuze was to later revise this further, but, for Lacan, the original biological stimulus of the drive is forever changed when the subject encounters language. And this linguistic element permeates the Prince track under inspection. Note how the most sexual part of the song is the final guitar-based improvisation, where the voice delivers repeated words or phrases as punctuation marks. The verses had delivered the story almost like an operatic "recitative" with heavily syllabic metric regularity, almost spoken. Just listen to Prince sing "Up on the mic repeating two words, over and over again was this woman he had never noticed before he lost himself in the articulated manner in which she said them." By the end of the song, Prince is vocalizing the word "joy" with the same scales playing on the guitar (see Example 6.3). This is pure circulation of the object *a*—the mask of *jouissance*.

It's also worth remembering, however, that even in this "joy" of repetition, the death drives lurk, reminding us that Lacan thought that every drive was a death drive because each ultimately, on a deeper level than the circuit, seeks its own extinction. The singer is singing "Soul Psychodelicide"—Soul Psychedelic Suicide? The minor key of the piece also shows us that this joyous, erotic encounter is also dangerous and dark.

## Freud, Nietzsche, and the "Eternal Recurrence"

Freud owed a great debt to philosophy, though it wasn't always acknowledged and a chain of palpable influence is hard to determine. So many philosophical ideas, such as Schopenhauer's "Will," which was such a clear forerunner for Freud's "drive" or "libido," were ubiquitous as influences in *fin de siècle* Vienna. You didn't have to read Schopenhauer to hear about him; you could go to the opera and see some Wagner or Strauss, or you could pop into the Secession Building and see some of Gustav Klimt's paintings. If you wanted to find an artistic forerunner to the Freudian stream of consciousness, look no further than Arthur Schnitzler's *Traumnovelle* (*Dream Story*), 1926. Freud wrote to Schnitzler:

> I have gained the impression that you have learned through intuition—although actually as a result of sensitive introspection—everything that I have had to unearth by laborious work on other persons.[6]

And Friedrich Nietzsche was even more ubiquitous than Schopenhauer in Viennese society. How much of his dichotomy between Apollo and Dionysius survives in the Freudian antagonism between Eros and Thanatos, or between the id and the superego? Even where influences were not direct, they were hovering in the air.[7]

It's clear that Nietzsche in his own way formulated something of the Freudian unconscious, which is the primary concern of our present book. In *Beyond Good and Evil*, he claimed:

> I shall never tire of emphasizing a small terse fact, which these superstitious minds hate to concede—namely, that a thought comes when "it" wishes, and not when "I" wish, so that it is a falsification of the facts of the case to say that the subject "I" is the condition of the predicate "think." It thinks; but that this "it" is precisely the famous old "ego" is, to put it mildly, only a supposition, an assertion, and assuredly not an "immediate certainty." After all, one has even gone too far with this "it thinks"—even the "it" contains an interpretation of the process, and does not belong to the process itself.[8]

---

[6] Sigmund Freud's letter to Arthur Schnitzler, May 8, 1906, Syndics of Cambridge University Library, MS.Schnitzler.B31.

[7] Some of the more recent considerations of Nietzsche's influence on Freud, particularly in relation to repetition, include Eva Cybulska, "Nietzsche's Eternal Return: Unriddling the Vision, a Psychodynamic Approach," *Indo-Pacific Journal of Phenomenology* 13 (May 2013): 1–13; Pokeung Wu, "The Idea of Repetition in Marx, Nietzsche and Freud, and Problems of Modernity," MA diss. (UC San Diego, 2010); Mathias Risse, "A Freudian Look at What Nietzsche Took To Be His Biggest Insight," in *Nietzsche on Freedom and Autonomy*, ed. Ken Gemes and Simon May (Oxford: Oxford University Press, 2009), 223–45.

[8] Friedrich Nietzsche, *Beyond Good and Evil: Prelude to a Philosophy of the Future*, trans. Walter Kaufmann (New York: Vintage Books, 1966), 24 (aphorism 17).

Remember, too, that Idealist philosopher Friedrich Schelling (1775–1854) wrote extensively about the unconscious in nature, particularly in relation to art and the creation of artworks, claiming: "The I [*ich*: ego] is conscious according to the production, unconscious with regard to the product."[9] In other words, artists work consciously to create, but *what* they create is largely a matter of the unconscious. In many ways this is the premise of our own book; it doesn't matter whether any of the popular musicians carefully studied their Freud in college, or whether they are shooting from the hip. Artworks, as we know, mean infinitely more than their artists intend.

One of the fascinating lingering questions about Nietzsche and Freud concerns the concept of repetition. In these lines from Freud's *Beyond the Pleasure Principle*, Freud talks of *die ewige Wiederkehr des Gleichen* (the eternal recurrence of the same), which was one of Nietzsche's central—if rather obscurely presented—doctrines.

> This "perpetual recurrence of the same thing" [*die ewige Wiederkehr des Gleichen*] causes us no astonishment when it relates to *active* behaviour on the part of the person concerned and when we can discern in him the essential character—trait which always remains the same and which is compelled to find expression in a repetition of the same experiences.[10]

And yet perhaps, as we will see, the crucial element that Freud adds to the "repetition compulsion" is fundamentally different to Nietzsche's. For Freud, repetition marked a malfunction in the workings of the unconscious that caused endless pain—the "death drive." For Nietzsche the "eternal return" or "eternal recurrence," as it is sometimes translated, seems to mean something altogether more positive and life-affirming. But what Nietzsche actually meant by the eternal return differs depending on who you ask. We'll therefore unpack the concept, before giving you our reading of it, and then demonstrate how LCD Soundsystem employ a subtly different model of repetition to Freud's "beyond" the pleasure principle, one more commensurate with the pleasure principle itself and more in keeping with what we might call the Nietzschean model of repetition. And to help us, we'll need to appeal to some readings of Nietzsche from one of the biggest critics of psychoanalysis, Gilles Deleuze, who we will meet again in Chapter 7, though in that chapter we will be appealing to the more psychoanalytically invested, rather than critical, writings of Deleuze.

## Eternal Recurrence, Occurring for the First Time

Nietzsche describes the eternal return (or eternal "occurrence," "repetition"—*ewige Wiederkunft*) as his "abyssal thought"; by this he means it was something that pulled

---

[9] K. F. A. Schelling (ed.), *Friedrich Wilhelm Joseph Schelling's Sämmtliche Werke*, vol. I (Stuttgart: Cotta, 1856–61), 613.
[10] Sigmund Freud, "Beyond the Pleasure Principle," in *The Standard Edition of the Complete Psychological Works of Sigmund Freud*, vol. XVIII, trans. James Strachey (London: The Hogarth Press, [1920] 1955), 22.

him into the extent that he couldn't escape from it. The genesis of the idea makes for a good story:

> Now I shall relate the history of Zarathustra. The fundamental conception of this work, the idea of the eternal recurrence, this highest formula of affirmation that is at all attainable, belongs in August 1881: it was penned on a sheet with the notation underneath, "6000 feet beyond man and time." That day I was walking through the woods along the lake of Silvaplana; at a powerful pyramidal rock not far from Surlei I stopped. It was then that this idea came to me.[11]

Nietzsche is walking around Lake Silvaplana and then, suddenly, something occurs to him. (A thought comes to him from somewhere; remember our definition of neurosis?) What if everything that happens will happen again? What if every event is destined to return, over and over and over again. Boom! But why does this thought get him trapped in the abyss? Well, for one thing, it's hard to figure out what it all means. If everything recurs, what are the consequences? Nietzsche sits down and ponders, staying there for some time, mind racing; no easy answer comes to him. He knows it is a huge thought, but how to explain it, how to work through it?

Frustratingly, Nietzsche never really gives us an answer. At least, not a coherent one. Some scholars think that his final project in progress when he was struck ill and became unable to continue working would have been to write a metaphysics that encompassed concepts like eternal recurrence and will to power. Because that didn't happen, we instead have a few scattered fragments around his works in which he writes about these concepts. They contain all sorts of ambiguities and contrasts and, as a result, are hard to integrate into one single model of understanding. We'll consider three versions of eternal recurrence here.

The first we shall call the psychological reading. The quote we want to consider is a long one, below. The key headline is the nature of the question, it being a hypothetical "what if?" and then the test for that thought experiment—"would you do this or this?"

> The heaviest weight.—What if some day or night a demon were to steal into your loneliest loneliness and say to you: "This life as you now live it and have lived it you will have to live once again and innumerable times again; and there will be nothing new in it, but every pain and every joy and every thought and sigh and everything unspeakably small or great in your life must return to you, all in the same succession and sequence—even this spider and this moonlight between the trees, and even this moment and I myself. The eternal hourglass of existence is turned over again and again, and you with it, speck of dust!" Would you not throw yourself down and gnash your teeth and curse the demon who spoke thus? Or have you once experienced a tremendous moment when you

---

[11] Friedrich Nietzsche, "Why I Write Such Good Books," in *On the Genealogy of Morals* and *Ecce Homo*, trans. Walter Kaufman (New York: Vintage, 1989), 195.

would have answered him: "You are a god, and never have I heard anything more divine." If this thought gained power over you, as you are it would transform and possibly crush you; the question in each and every thing, "Do you want this again and innumerable times again?" would lie on your actions as the heaviest weight! Or how well disposed would you have to become to yourself and to life to long for nothing more fervently than for this ultimate eternal confirmation and seal?[12]

Here Nietzsche is asking us how we would react if we were told that the world would eternally recur, positing two potential responses. We can curse and wail in woe ("Oh God, not this again"), or we can delight in it ("Yes! Okay!"). What Nietzsche is asking us is, essentially, "If we had to live our lives over again, would we be proud of our actions?" Would we love each and every last thing we did, so its repetition through all eternity was a joy to us? Or would we curse, would we decry our own actions, and wish we had done otherwise regarding so many of our decisions? All those days you didn't turn up for work, skipped school, had an extra serving of dessert, gave up too easily, gave in too quickly; they will all happen again.

By posing this question, Nietzsche is upping the stakes entailed by our everyday decisions. Next time we think, "I'll stay in bed today" might we not think, "but would I be happy for this action to reverberate thorough eternity?" and upon realizing that this isn't just one aberration, once, as a little exception we allow ourselves, but that it would be an aberration marked in fate forever, we should just get up and attack the day. This tends to be the most popular contemporary reading of eternal recurrence. It fits within the tradition of reading Nietzsche as an (anti-)moral philosopher, concerned with values. While it is a neat reading, we must ask, does this really have sufficient weight to be the thought that drags one into the abyss?

Our next reading, the grand metaphysical reading, has that weight. In it, we read eternal recurrence as a metaphysical claim about the fate of the universe. Once the universe is over, it starts again, and then again, and then again. So all history repeats serially, over and over and over. Here is Nietzsche's best description of it:

> Whoever thou mayest be, beloved stranger, whom I meet here for the first time, avail thyself of this happy hour and of the stillness around us, and above us, and let me tell thee something of the thought which has suddenly risen before me like a star which would fain shed down its rays upon thee and every one, as befits the nature of light.
>
> —Fellow man! Your whole life, like a sandglass, will always be reversed and will ever run out again—a long minute of time will elapse until all those conditions out of which you were evolved return in the wheel of the cosmic process. And then you

---

[12] Friedrich Nietzsche, *The Gay Science*, trans. J. Nauckhoff (Cambridge: Cambridge University Press, 2001), §341.

will find every pain and every pleasure, every friend and every enemy, every hope and every error, every blade of grass and every ray of sunshine once more, and the whole fabric of things which make up your life. This ring in which you are but a grain will glitter afresh forever. And in every one of these cycles of human life there will be one hour where, for the first time one man, and then many, will perceive the mighty thought of the eternal recurrence of all things:—and for mankind this is always the hour of Noon.[13]

Here we are told that everything you see around you, don't worry, it will come again. It is hard to know what to make of this. Claiming that this manner of repetition occurs forms a very metaphysical proposition. It is something that is absolutely impossible to verify. Still, it is the kind of thing you could easily contemplate for an hour next to a rock, as Nietzsche did.

One explanation for why Nietzsche may have written this form of recurrence is that it is an antireligious interpretation of existence. In some religions, people tend to view the world and human lives as things that happen only once, before we are judged. Live, be good, and then go to heaven. By stating that everything recurs, Nietzsche upends this, and rather than things being singular, they simply continue on, over and over. We have to ask again: Is this thought truly the one that Nietzsche would get stuck on as his highest formula of affirmation?

There were many great readers of Nietzsche in postwar French philosophy (George Bataille, Pierre Klossowski, for example), but we're going to concentrate on Gilles Deleuze for the remainder of this chapter. Deleuze took the idea that Nietzsche was a metaphysical philosopher very seriously. Instead of identifying him as a critical figure, the antimoralist we spoke of earlier, Deleuze sees Nietzsche as possessing a coherent and brilliant response to Kantian philosophy. In *Nietzsche and Philosophy* (1983), Deleuze takes three elements of Nietzsche's thought—elements that Nietzsche himself claimed to be core concepts—and combines them into a single, coherent ontology (a theory about what there is). These form a triangle of eternal recurrence, will to power, and the overman, which are crucial to the vision of joy in repetition that we propose in this chapter.

## The Second Occurrence of Eternal Recurrence in the Work of Deleuze

Of the three Nietzschean concepts he deployed, Deleuze is faithful to two, but the third is somewhat twisted to fit with his vision. Will to power, in Nietzsche's writings, can be read as a kind of basic ontological unit, the primary thing that everything else is derived from:

---

[13] Friedrich Nietzsche, "Notes on the Eternal Recurrence," in *Oscar Levy Edition of Nietzsche's Complete Works*, vol. 16 (Edinburgh: T. N. Foulis, 1909–13), 249–50., xx–xx

This world is the Will to Power—and nothing else! And even ye yourselves are this will to power—and nothing besides![14]

For Deleuze, will to power takes two forms. In the first aspect, it is the interplay of all of the forces that make up our world. These forces are all positive; they all want to become something; they all want to enact some kind of change in the world. The second aspect of will to power is as a mechanism for deciding, when various forces come together, which one prevails and what the outcome is. So will to power is both the demand for and resolution of all change. Deleuze's word for this constant flow of change is one of *becoming*. Deleuze, following other thinkers of affirmation such as Heraclitus and Spinoza, reads the Nietzschean world as always in a process of *becoming*, rather than one of *being*. If we see the world in terms of becoming, we are aware that stability and consistency are illusions, masking the real nature of things. That "mask" would be the notion that everything is in a state of being; that things simply are what they appear to us as. So becoming is associated with flows, processes, and change, and being is associated with a more static view of a world composed of fixed identities. The more we think about what our world must be—the more we philosophize—the more we are dragged toward the former. Conversely, the more we remain rooted in the world of common sense, and the heuristics and shortcuts that exist to give us an actionable perception of the world, the more we stay in being. That might sound complicated, but the point really isn't. If you were aware that everything was slowly changing, and nothing is now what it was minutes before, the world would be a disorienting place. Instead, we have an illusion of permanence, so when you return to a thing that has changed, the default is to still see it as what it was before. This is what Heraclitus meant when he said we could never step in the same river twice.

By thinking about the world in terms of will to power, we can totally change our understanding of the world. It is a powerful tool that allows us to analyze the dynamics of how things come about at the most macro (nations, history) or the most micro (atoms and molecules) levels. Any given situation is simply an interplay of productive forces, and the stronger ones enact change. One brilliant aspect of this is that it allows us to think about force genealogically. At any point in history, there have been dominant forces in the will to power, but there have also been other forces present that were not making themselves known. Who is the best band in history? Many would say The Beatles, maybe some would say Radiohead. But how many other bands could there have been if the right four people connected in the right way and unleashed their productive capability? In all of history, the real best bands form a small subset of the total bands that were theoretically possible. Similarly, how many other creative and brilliant processes of becoming have been prevented from manifesting in history? An obvious example is the historical subjection of women, limiting their capacities as positive forces in many situations and, therefore, blocking their will to power.

---

[14] Friedrich Nietzsche, *The Will to Power*, vol. 2, bks. III & IV, ed. Oscar Levy, trans. A. Ludovici (Edinburgh: Foulis, 1913), 431–2.

That blocking of will to power may be a cause for regret. But Deleuze's bending of eternal recurrence allows him to set up a resolution to that. While Nietzsche said that repetition is repetition of the same, Deleuze says that repetition is repetition of difference. Difference, for Deleuze, is a bit of a tricky thing to get your head around. We generally think of difference in terms of preexisting identity. Things exist, we note their properties, and then note how they are different. For Deleuze, however, difference is not secondary like this, but primary. Difference is the genetic condition for production, for will to power to work. Change flows across differences. Deleuze gives the example of the difference between the cloud and the ground. In the space between a charged cloud and the earth, there is a potential for the production of lightning. And this kind of difference presumes no identity of things to be different. It is just the grounding where production can happen.

So the return of difference is the return of production/becoming/will to power. Whatever forces were repressed or kept down today will surely reoccur tomorrow and try to manifest themselves as those enacted by will to power again. We can only repress and refuse and suppress and maintain a status quo for so long, before change enacts itself, and these forces make themselves known.

This change over time—moving toward an uncertain point, which we'll call "teleonomy"—is how Deleuze reads the overhuman in Nietzsche's work. When Nietzsche urges us to become the overhuman, his description of what it would be like to be the overhuman is strangely lacking. There is no figure there for us to find. That is because we don't know what the end point is! We are on a road of becoming with no clear end point in sight.

What we can see much more clearly than the end is the force of resentment, the "last men," who are terrified of the capability of the will to power, to will change, and who try to deploy a whole range of tools in service of the status quo and the suppression of difference. The world of becoming keeps progressing according to will to power—of which we are just one manifestation. It is important we get past readings of will to power as "will=demand" for "power=domination" that proliferated due to Nietzsche's sister and executor being an ardent Nazi. Will to power is the complex network of forces that is everything that exists, and Nietzsche has a positive message about it:

> The play of forces and force-waves, at the same time one and many, agglomerating here and diminishing there, a sea of forces storming and raging in itself, for ever changing, for ever rolling back over in calculable ages to recurrence, with an ebb and flow of its forms, producing the most complicated things out of the most simple structures; producing the most ardent, most savage, and most contradictory things out of the quietest, most rigid, and most frozen material, and then returning from multifariousness to uniformity, from the play of contradictions back into the delight of consonance, saying yea unto itself, even in this homogeneity of its courses and ages; for ever blessing itself as something which recurs for all eternity,—a becoming which knows not satiety, or disgust, or weariness.[15]

[15] Ibid.

Our mission as potential overhumans is to enter this flow state of becoming and to work with it, like Ogmios going about his *Zen Motoring*.[16] Imagine the hubris of a last man, who looks at himself and says: I am the end of history, nothing can come after me, nothing can come that will be better than me. What would Jeddy 4 make of such cruel claims? No, as Nietzsche says:

> All beings so far have created something beyond themselves. Do you want to be the ebb of that great tide, and revert back to the beast rather than overcome mankind? What is the ape to a man? A laughing-stock, a thing of shame. And just so shall a man be to the [Overhuman]: a laughing-stock, a thing of shame. You have evolved from worm to man, but much within you is still worm. Once you were apes, yet even now man is more of an ape than any of the apes.[17]

## LCD Soundsystem's "All My Friends"

For the entirety of "All my friends" that piano part rides along, throbbing restlessly. The feat here is that it's ultimately unchanging, and yet both the foundation for the entire song and the catalyst that keeps pushing it to higher places. As "All my friends" progresses, more and more elements enter the fray. Here's another synth melody, another guitar part, a slight uptick in the intensity of Murphy's vocals, all staking on top of each other in a wave that's perpetually cresting ... You can drown in it, if you want.[18]

What characteristics would a music that represented Nietzschean recurrence have? Here we list what we consider to be the twofold properties: (i) The music must express joy. Nietzsche is, above all, affirmative. His is not the repetition of the Freudian death drive, which relives a history of mental traumas in the vain hope of a cure. The music must accept change; it must not try to intervene against production on behalf of an anthropic idea of organization. It must not be organized by the "outside," but it must absorb the changes wrought through connections it makes with the outside. The "acceptance" and the "yes" that Nietzsche tries to elicit from us are interlinked with repetition. This is not just a "yes," but a repeated "yes." Lyotard's *Libidinal Economy* understands this and closes with the words "Yes, Yes, Yes, Yes." (ii) There must be an absence of teleology; *teleonomy* must organize the material. While teleology has an end in view attributed to an agent and believes that processes move toward that specific end, teleonomy is more open, describing systems that are moving somewhere, but with no obvious agency guiding them, progressing via feedback, trial and error, experiment, and failure. If teleology exists in the Lacanian imaginary, teleonomy is in the real. If a piece of music has these properties and does so within a framework of some sort of

---

[16] *Zen Motoring* (BBC3, January 16, 2022), written by Ivan Battaliero-Owen.
[17] Friedrich Nietzsche, *Thus Spoke Zarathustra*, ed. R. Pippin, trans. A. del Caro (Cambridge: Cambridge University Press, 2006).
[18] Ryan Leas, *LCD Soundsystem's Sound of Silver, 33 ⅓* (New York: Bloomsbury, 2016), 103–4.

**Example 6.4** Continual piano riff in "All My Friends."

repetition, then we may find it to be illustrative of the interpretation of the Nietzschean "eternal return" at stake in this discussion.

One may well think automatically of particular examples from various repertoires, but the one that struck us as exemplary in this regard is "All My Friends" from *Sound of Silver* (LCD Soundsystem, 2007). This was voted as Pitchfork Media's #1 song of 2007, and although Nietzsche's "abyssal thought" concept does not feature in Pitchfork's ranking matrix, the song is all more enriched by exemplifying it. The song accepts repetition; it builds on it and does not shy away from the repetitive conditions of productive "difference" described by the singer.

The lyrics describe the band themselves making yet another record, with yet another tour, but repetition is heard most immediately in the piano/keyboard's permanent riff, which is a live recording rather than a sample; its rhythmic imperfections, its unstable, wavering touch and tone are joyfully accepted and, in fact, mimicked by the other instruments and repeated time and again (actions reverberating through time). This pivotal riff (see Example 6.4), emphasizing the octave pitch *a*, does not stop until the song is over after about seven minutes. However, this repetitive element per se is almost beside the point (most pop songs have a riff); this is not, in itself, eternal recurrence—it's just a commonplace little metaphor for it. What is important are the ways that this riff spirals outward teleonomically, not teleologically, to joyfully create the song that unfolds. We hear this in at least two forms: (i) joy and (ii) teleonomy. Ryan Leas gets into the spirit of this dichotomy when he explores the complete album *Sound of Silver*, claiming: "Any of these songs could be the devil-may-care character in the corner of the party. Any of them could be the collective euphoria."[19] These songs summon up Nietzschean *amor fati*. Specifically in the song "All My Friends," however: "Its universal and crushing truth is that it's never coming back quite the same way, but its universal and reassuring triumph is that … you might just discover a new definition of home for where you are right now."[20]

### Joy and Teleonomy

While joy is a subjective emotion that will strike all listeners differently, the song is clearly in the major mode throughout, using only two alternating major chords (I and

---

[19] Ibid., 28–9.
[20] Ibid., 54.

IV), meaning that the harmonic tension in the song's tonality is minimal; we don't crave any form of harmonic resolution. The joy expressed needs to be the celebration of the freedom that repetition brings; thus, the dance-floor element with the sixteen-beat rhythm that soon enters in the drums showcases repetition as a liberation rather than a cage. The drummer builds his rhythm from nothing and is free to produce drum-fills every four bars, each drum-fill different to the last and, unusually for a drummer, each one more understated than the last, almost as if the drum-fill itself had been a protest against repetition (Oedipus putting on the brakes), but comes to realize the futility of it. "Would you be the ebb of that great tide?"

The lyrics grow to a joyful moment that affirms negative experiences as positive, claiming that the singer's "stupid decisions" in life would not be changed: "I wouldn't change one stupid decision." This is a sentiment of "no regrets!" The song is an obvious affirmation of "going with the flow" of repetition. Not trying to change the past. Even if we bought in to our first definition of Nietzsche's eternal recurrence—the morality thought experiment of our "psychological" reading—this would pass the test.

The song follows no teleology whatsoever in neither the lyrical content nor its musical sense of momentum. A graph of the whole track is given as Example 6.5, which shows four-measure hypermeasures as circles, each shaded to reflect volume and intensity. The form of the song develops in a particular direction, yes, but it is designed to give us the illusion that the music is freely forming itself in front of our ears. It is clear, however, that—like Ravel's *Bolero*—the song grows in intensity and scope from one state to another (a difference in that Deleuzian sense that yields a productive space in-between two entities). This happens because the small micro repetitions spin outward. These micro repetitions (of what Middleton, following Phil Tagg, calls "musemes") create miniature cybernetic feedback loops.[21] Listen to the subtle ways that the drums and bass enter in measures 19–20. The players enter very tentatively and try out little expansions of the central pitch, exploring the territory that each inhabits, slowly pushing its boundaries to create a riff of its own. We've used light-gray shading to capture at least something of the lightness of touch in these instruments; dark gray represents the full-throttle high intensity, which comes later. The drums emphasize the beat, of course, but slowly build up in intensity to the sixteenth-note pattern, somewhere between measures 19–27, so subtly that we can't discern the exact point at which the four beats per measure of the drum-kit first become filled with microbeats. The bass, too, plays a few $a$'s and $d$'s here and there exploring teleonomically to drive change outward. The drum rhythm adopts the same little sixteenth-note quirky beat-skip of the piano and absorbs it so that the piano doesn't have it anymore and just plays four to the floor. This is all teleonomy; the music has no clear aim; it needs only to try to carve a path forward without any thought or expectation of where it will arrive.

There is no "outside"-directed formal organization here, and the pop song has none of the standard formal refrain tropes except perhaps the opening phrase "and so it starts" or "that's how it starts," each showing a new cycle of repetition (marked with an "X" in Example 6.5). A "middle eight" or "breakdown" section is notably absent

---

[21] Philip Tagg, *Music's Meanings: A Modern Musicology for Non-musos* (New York: MMMSP, 2013).

*Do You Want To Be the Ebb of This Great Tide?* 187

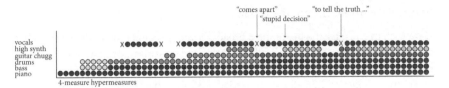

**Example 6.5** Hypermetric structure of "All My Friends."

(the singer describes how, in his words, "it comes apart, like it does in bad films," but the music doesn't fall into this same trap). The song is internally self-organizing; it manages its own process of change. The song *becomes* only because its instruments explore outward from its central piano cell. When the guitar enters, for example, it trails the piano's central pitch, while the upper sawtooth synth merely trails the vocal melody. This sawtooth moves an octave higher at one point and swoops down to its "leading note" (the note in the scale that needs to rise to arrive at "home," in this case g♯) and back upward to exhibit its self-encompassing and self-fulfilling nature. Structurally, this happens in the classic "guitar solo" slot, but, in fact, the guitar duet (with the high, sawtooth synthesizer) that fills this space scarcely demonstrates a precomposed solo from the guitar; *Total Guitar* magazine may one day notate it, but we doubt that many guitarists will aspire to perform it with the same enthusiasm that they might greet the tablature for the "Bohemian Rhapsody" solo. Both instruments form a productive contrapuntal relationship and bounce ideas off each other, developing (different) materials that explore the outer limits of the repetitive groove pattern.

To close the song, the final sentence is open-ended: "If I could see all my friends tonight." Then what? The conditional tense opens up a space, but we have to fill in the main clause ourselves. There is no cadence to close the song; it just stops. Looking through this analysis, we can see a damming-up of repetitive flow toward the end; all instruments are represented with dark gray on the diagram, and the lyrics begin to ramble a tightly knit, quick-fire chain of consciousness. Ryan Leas, observing the band's "last" performance in 2011 (before reuniting), commented:

"I remember the way his body thrashed between singing 'To tell the truth' and 'This will be the last time.' Was that subconscious in revolt?"[22]

And the song stops, casually and without ceremony, with an ending that becomes a cry that production is stopping both in the internal world of the song, and also in the band's career. The friends that the singer asks for, are not names called from a nostalgic position—a dead repetition; the friends represent differences, elements in a network with productive spaces in-between. The singer is trying to locate his connections, and is willing to accept whatever he finds.

[22] Leas, *LCD Soundsystem's Sound of Silver*, 2.

## Bigger Repetition: Alternative Versions

If we wish to consider the matter on a broader level, we could look to the band's other versions of the song. The song's official music video brings nothing new, except to reinforce the aspect of minimalism[23] within the song: one could film the official music video on a budget of $20; all that is needed is $5 for a bucket of water and $15 for a pair of step-ladders (have a look on YouTube and you'll see what we mean). But several live versions exist, including a "London Session" CD from 2010, the comparison with which proves rewarding. Without wishing to play "spot the difference," several of the differences recorded in this case comment on the flow of repetition as the song enters a new and different productive space and performs a new level of repetition within it. The drum-kit starts off here and is much louder, making itself (rather than the piano) the center of attention. Its acceleration toward the dense sixteen-beat pattern is much clearer, and its improvisatory nature is foregrounded. And improvisation is the key to Eugene Holland's vision of Deleuzian *Difference and Repetition*,[24] and while we may disagree with his interpretation of what difference means in this context, it is interesting that he valorizes jazz improvisation as the ultimate form of repeating with difference. It becomes clear that the song's melody is just one set of crystallized variants of a few pitches that are improvised afresh in live performances. A melodic highpoint is constructed when the singer reaches upward to word-paint the line "if the sun comes up, if the sun comes up," a high point that was never there in the recorded track. The singer also keeps the melody buoyant on some occasions, where it normally descends ("when the motor kicks in"); he adds a melismatic variant on the line "when we're running out of the dru-u-ugs," and he stays on the same c♯ pitch against the change from an A chord to D, leaving an unresolved dissonance (the only one in the song) for the key line, "I wouldn't trade one stupid decision another five years of life." (Notice that the swooping sawtooth followed suit, playing g♯s against the prevalent a.) Question: Is dissonance in this context an attempt to slam the Oedipal brakes on—a protest against repetition? Dissonance is teleological; it needs resolution; it looks to the future. Perhaps a way out of this paradox would be to claim that the singer is declaring his clear acceptance of fate and, in so doing, leaving the unresolved pitch behind without trying to re-Oedipalize it (resolve it), as Freud might have done were he a composer of electronic indie tunes. These four examples of difference are all "obvious" word-painting examples that mimic the text, where the official recording resists such obvious interaction with "outside" musical codes (and perhaps we might say clichés), but now, in the heat of the live moment, the singer goes further and opens himself up to such calls from the outside to "intensify" positive emotional affect in the inside, demonstrating the act of accepting repetition.

---

[23] Singer James Murphy was influenced by New York minimalism, as shown in his "Hello Steve Reich" mix of Bowie's "Love Is Lost" (*The Next Day*, 2013).

[24] Eugene Holland, "Jazz Improvisation: Music of the People-to-Come," in *Deleuze, Guattari and the Production of the New*, ed. Simon O'Sullivan and Stephen Zepke (Continuum: New York, 2008), 196–205.

In essence, the difference between the types of repetition in the "death-drive" in Chapter 5 and "joyful" repetition found in the play of Deleuzian difference in Chapter 6 is that one is psychologically healthier. But it's not as simple as thinking that the first repeats bad experiences, the second repeats good ones. There were two different models of repetition posited here, one a psychoanalytic model of repetition that happens inside the subject. There are things that are laid down in the id, drives, clusters of libido around concepts, or, in Lacanian terms, chained concepts. Due to the ways in which the psyche functions, these formations, once laid down, have a tendency to repeat. Sometimes in pleasurable ways, sometimes in unpleasant ways, and sometimes just strangely. This isn't necessarily good or bad, it is just "us," how we humans are wired. The second type of repetition is a repetition in being-in-general, not just in us. In *Nietzsche and Philosophy*, but also in the later text *Anti-Oedipus*, Deleuze does something incredibly interesting with psychoanalytic thought, which is to pull it out of its confines as a tool for describing what happens within the subject and to ask us if we cannot understand the *whole* of existence in terms of psychoanalytic concepts. Is not the whole of becoming proceeding like a drive? Is the human tendency to repeat not part of nature? Can we not collapse ourselves into nature? Hence the idea of desiring machines not being part of a subject, but the very substrate from which everything derives. This is a complicated theory to whizz through so quickly, so we'll stop there. One commonality between these two readings is a need for openness; both death-drive and eternal recurrence provide rewards to those who can be open and experimental and can cause stasis in those who would be the "ebb of the great tide."

One aim of this book is to offer the reader newer ways of thinking through old issues, and repetition in music is certainly as old as the hills. We can't offer a history of the topic in this book, but perhaps we can stimulate our readers to think about this Nietzschean-Deleuzian perspective in some aspects of repetitious music as a supplement to the existing literature on this topic, such as Elizabeth Margulis's seminal book *On Repetition: How Music Plays the Mind*.[25] Thus, we invite you to think of how you play with repetition in your own musical experiences. You might think of repetition in musical form, for example. Even simple verse-chorus structures—in which organized units alternate and project a narrative—could embody some of this Nietzschean repetition, though this kind of alternation may be more characteristic of a Hegelian "dialectic," selective and synthesizing rather than accepting and affirming. The trance-like effects of minimalist music might alternatively bring us closer to the affirmative feeling of riding the waves of repetition, especially in pieces such as Terry Riley's *In C*, which allows individuals to negotiate their relations with the surrounding players and explore the Nietzschean-Deleuzian space of "difference," twisting the repetition in unseen directions while remaining broadly faithful to its own impulses. Minimalism also aims for repetition as a mind–body event, however, and its transcendent aesthetic may arguably hinder a Nietzschean quest to take hold of the world and cry

---

[25] See Elizabeth Hellmuth Margulis, *On Repeat: How Music Plays the Mind* (New York: Oxford University Press, 2014). Margulis explores some of the more Freudian aspects, incorporating Deleuzian insights from Rahn, considering a "tendency toward repetition in music to represent some sort of unified psychological principle" (78).

"yes"(?). You might think of William Basinski's ambient *The Disintegration Loops*, where we witness the slow disintegration of repeated tape loops—an ode to decay and entropy. There is an "acceptance" of change here, but this would surely be the opposite of Nietzsche's project; there is no teleonomy, no dynamism, no joy—perhaps Nietzsche might call this "sick music" (as he had called Wagner in a different context). You might think of Groove—which incites us to dance, aiming at a libidinal intensification as something we "get into"—we have to accept. Possibly though, groove's tight control is a problem—the controlling DJ in most electronic dance music essentially asks the dancing or listening subjects to adhere to an inflexible groove, despite aiming to dissolve them into a productive film. We might hear Heaven 17 cry "[We don't need this] fascist groove thang" (1981). However you feel about these types of music, and whatever music you listen to, there will always be repetition in music, but will it be eternal?

# 7

# S & M and Pop Perversion

## Perverse Structures?

**Billie Eilish versus The Manic Street Preachers**

In the Lacanian worldview there are conditions that assume a certain frightening aspect because the sufferer doesn't necessarily recognize they even have a problem. Such is the lot of the pervert. The word has a highly sexualized ring to it; we may be forgiven for automatically associating the term pervert with "peeping Toms," men stealing underwear from washing lines in the middle of the night, men in public parks wearing trench coats or suspiciously baggy trousers. Popular pictures of the pervert pervade in the psyche, but often have little to do with the psychical reality of the perverse patient. We also need to consider the role of perversion as a problematically male problem (if, perhaps, hysteria was regarded as the female problem). We certainly can't filter out the sexual component of the pervert altogether, but there is much more complexity in the pervert's condition than a simple "overenthusiasm" (shall we say?) for matters sexual. It's also hard to diagnose perversion, as Arlene Richards, one of the few psychoanalysts who studied perversion in women, reports. Patients don't arrive at the doctors' surgery to report "I think I'm a pervert" in the way they might begin a session by reporting well-known tropes of other conditions—depression, anxiety, suicidal ideation, and so on. Because part of **perversion** involves not believing that there is a problem (and, as we'll see, the pervert believes that s/he is part of the *solution* to other peoples' problems), symptoms are often not disclosed, or those symptoms presented are often assumed to be part of other conditions.

Freud allowed himself to be fairly straightforward about perversion, at one point defining it as essentially something that "differs from the normal."[1] He claimed that babies are *polymorphously perverse*, meaning that they can take pleasure from all the zones of their bodies—everything is potentially erogenous. In normal development, these erogenous zones fall under the control of the genital drive, but the mature pervert prolongs the child's earlier state of hypersensitivity to all things erogenous. For Freud, civilization represses the polymorphously perverted parts of the child as it becomes

---

[1] Sigmund Freud, *The Standard Edition of the Complete Psychological Works of Sigmund Freud*, vol. XV, trans. James Strachey (London: Hogarth, 1963), 208.

an adult in a similar way that, for Foucault, social norms would eventually become mutually defined against perversions.

Lacan took a very different course in his studies on perversion, arguing that perversion was a psychical "structure," dependent on neither perverse acts nor Foucauldian social definition. For Lacan, as expressed in *Seminar XI*, acts that we normally consider perverse often aren't formally perverse; they may not be entirely *healthy*, but they still lie outside the purview of perversion. By contrast, seemingly innocuous, common behaviors suddenly take on a more sinister, perverse role from a Lacanian point of view. For instance, the final line in the "Lord's Prayer" is, for Lacan, "the recognition of the absolute authority of the desire of the Other, that Thy will be done!"[2] For him, this becomes a sort of formula for perversion. Let's see why.

Perhaps Lacan's fundamental criterion of perversion is that the pervert knows what the Other wants. Remember that the "normal" (qua neurotic) question—"What does the Other want from me?"—is the core question around which the majority of us unconsciously structure our psyches. For Lacan, the pervert knows (or rather *believes* s/he knows) the answer to this question. A normal person uses phantasy to answer this question, and in Lacan's world, the formula for perversion is the inversion of his formula for fantasy ($ \$ \lozenge a $ = phantasy; $ a \lozenge \$ $ = perversion). The neurotic's phantasy is thus the opposite of the pervert's "knowledge," and this polarity has several implications.

Firstly, the pervert believes that they are not acting out their own will, but they are acting out the will of the big Other. Lacan explores the writings of the Marquis de Sade, who we will soon examine for ourselves. As Lacan says: "It is this which befalls the executioner in sadistic experience, when, at its most extreme, his presence is reduced to being no more than its instrument."[3] As we'll find in the ultraperverse sadistic language of certain "death metal" tracks, there is a sense that the actions described are being carried out at the behest of God, or some other Symbolic presence. Thus Lacan's formula of "Thy will be done!" For many, this is perhaps the most surprising Lacanian insight because we normally associate a sadistic pervert with ultimate selfishness, choosing their own satisfaction over the well-being of other people.

Secondly, and perhaps more narcissistically in a colloquial sense, the pervert believes themselves to be the object of the other's drive. Remember that the object of the drive, for Lacan, is the phantasy object called "*a*"; thus, the pervert believes that s/he is this same object *a*—they are what their victims want. It's worth exploring the reasons for this delusion. In a basic Lacanian Oedipal upbringing, a child wants to be the phallus for its mother—in other words, it wants to be the thing that fills the symbolic gap in the mother's psyche; it wants to be the "be all and end all" to the mother. However, the pervert does not even believe that the mother lacks anything because s/he completes the mother in any case. Thus, the pervert does not accept castration either in the mother or in him/herself. The pervert never feels powerless, never lacks control, never lacks anything, and doesn't perceive a lack in the other. The

---

[2] Jacques Lacan, *Seminar XI: The Four Fundamental Concepts of Psychoanalysis*, trans. Jacques-Alain Miller (London: Vintage, 1998), 254.
[3] Jacques Lacan, "Kant with Sade," trans. James Swenson, *October* 51 ([1963] 1989): 61.

pervert believes him/herself to be this phallus and is never disabused of this notion. Often a weak father figure is blamed for this. Because the pervert does not accept punishment, nor do they accept that there is even a possibility of them being wrong, the pervert can hardly ever be treated psychoanalytically. In the main, Lacan gave up treating perverts as a fruitless labor.

There are other dimensions to perversion, and we will find particular nuances within the two categories of perversion that we will soon explore—masochism and sadism—but for now, we offer a rather general but hard-hitting example of perversion from the Manic Street Preachers. In honor of popular musicologist and theorist Stan Hawkins, Kenneth has written a chapter on Britpop band Pulp, subtitled "Perversion in Pornosonic Pop," which explored every stage of Pulp's career, particularly focusing on the band's musical exploration of perverse topics that often center around the figure of Jarvis Cocker, referred to by one reviewer as "Britain's thinking pervert."[4] Cocker's personas stage dramas that show that he believes himself to be always the object of the other's drive. It's rarely the phrase "I want you," but far more often "you want me" that runs his scripts. General narcissism, and an attitude of "you want me," is inherent to so much popular music, and these can be just hallmarks of the whole pop economy. But Cocker goes beyond the norm, as does another British band from the same era. Let's take the Manics' early song "You Love Us" (*Generation Terrorists*, 1992).

## The Manics

The chorus of the song simply repeats the lyric "You Love Us," each word delivered on the first beat of the measure, almost unpitched in its slow shouted delivery—as if the Manics are saying "read my lips." *We are the objects of desire that you want.* The chord progression beneath this anthemic chorus is all "backward." G→ D→ C→ G moves backward around the three primary chord functions, which might, at least in classical chord grammar, normally rotate Tonic (G) → Subdominant (C) → Dominant (D) → Tonic (G), where each chord *wants* to go to the next along a path of well-worn harmonic desire. Here, however, we move Tonic ← Dominant ← Subdominant ← Tonic, where each chord kind of wants to go back to the previous one! We are essentially going anticlockwise instead of clockwise; we're going up the down escalator. Sure, this explanation is an oversimplification of chord syntax in pop and in no way would wish to suggest that simply going backward around the cycle of fifths was inherently perverse; plenty of passages in pop do this—not least the end of just about every blues track (the "twelve-bar blues" in C finishes G-F-C).[5] But have a listen and see if you agree with us that this extended passage sounds a little like we are swimming upstream. Besides, the lyrics orientate us too – "you love us" is all backwards. In the closing line of Bowie's chorus of "Changes" as he sings about turning back the clock, we have a long line of such backward chord movement—as though Bowie has pressed rewind on the

---

[4] Smith, "Pulp: A Paradigm for Perversion in Pornosonic Pop."
[5] More recent theory suggests that the F here is a "softener" to the dominant function at the end of the twelve-bar blues. See, for example, Nobile, *Form as Harmony in Rock*, 33.

entire song up until this point. In classical chord syntax, this pattern would at one time have been regarded as "weak" or somehow "wrong." The Subdominant to Tonic motion was always redolent of religious satisfaction as a "plagal cadence," a big "Amen," an agreement to ignore our deeper instincts and look to the cross. While the effect here in the Manics is not exactly religious, it does bring about a kind of collective sense of self-satisfied rejection of a normative desiring path. Not "we love you," but "you love us."

While the refrain "You Love Us!" is perhaps the most structurally clear perverted aspect of the song from this Lacanian perspective, there are many other perverse acts here, which all feed into the same Lacanian structural narrative. One key aspect of the song is the image the group are promoting to (or against) the media; their message is essentially "everyone else is fake; we are for real." Indeed, the line "our voices are for real" will remind many of what is perhaps the Manics' most famous moment when, on May 15, 1991, lyricist and rhythm guitarist Richie Edwards took out a knife and carved the words "4 Real" into his arm to prove to Steve Lamacq that they were not "four hero-worshiping kids trying to replicate our favorite bands."[6] A more subtle image of their authenticity (qua realness) is the giant picture of a fingerprint as a stage backdrop in the video—but perhaps public self-harm is more attention-grabbing. The Manics begin the song declaring that "we are not your sinners"; they show no recognition of castration; they see themselves as genuine and, therefore, beyond the law. Their "realness" makes them pure. This is another mark of the pervert, as we will see.

As with many Manics' songs of that era in the early 1990s, there are plenty of shock references. Given that the band were heavily influenced by the poetry of Sylvia Plath, some of the holocaust references that strike us as an ultra-pretentious link back to Plath's poem "Daddy," among others. Plath likens "Daddy" to a Nazi, her being "a bit of a Jew." The Manics' line "You love us like a holocaust" comes from this tradition and bears a trace of Plath's equally perverse:

> Every woman adores a Fascist,
> The boot in the face, the brute
> Brute heart of a brute like you.

This may sound masochistic, and it is, but it is possibly matched by the almost sadistic images of Richey stroking himself while balancing a portable TV that is screening the explosion of Hiroshima on his open-zipped crotch. This is all part of the perverse enjoyment of lack of castration. Along with images from the verses, of throwing acid into our faces (or the Mona Lisa's face—qua mother of the art world—in some versions) or poisoning our water with strychnine, these are not only perverse but also sadistic, as we will see. A paraphrase of the whole song might be: "I'm your torturer; and you love me."

The music video accompanying the song certainly has features that are designed to shock, not least the image of Richey and Nicky Wire covered like Siamese twins in a huge shirt that says "suicide babies" while they feed each other oysters (possibly

---

[6] "17 Stitches for Manic Richie," *NME* (May 25, 1991).

the most yonic of all seafoods; there is no need for a phallus here because, perversely, there is no lack). But many of these images are not structurally perverse: the hands massaging Wire's back that make a vaginal shape; Wire's sucking of a lollipop—these are not the perverse aspects. The perversion of the video comes from images of the band sexually massaging huge printouts of their own images (they are the objects *a*; they don't *lack* anything); the perversion comes from their alignment of their gaze with ours; the perversion comes from the final crowd stage invasion (screaming perhaps "the band are our objects *a*"). Perhaps more subtly than all of these in the video are the occasional subliminal images of inspirational thinkers and figureheads such as Nietzsche, Malcolm X, Chairman Mao, Lenin, and others. Mathijs Peters reminds us:

> The cover of their 1991 single "You Love Us" … presents a collage of pictures taken from both "high" and "low" culture, presenting the band's inspirations as a postmodern collection of fragmented ideas and creations that, again, all revolve around alienation, subversion and resistance. It shows pictures of Robert Johnson, Karl Marx, Bob Marley, Marilyn Monroe, Aleister Crowley, Robert DeNiro in *Taxi Driver*, Beatrice Dalle in Beineix' 1986 film *Betty Blue* (the band was briefly named "Betty Blue" in the beginning of their career), The Clash and more.[7]

Why is this perverse? Because the band, as in many of their songs, believe in themselves to be the instruments for revolutionary (mostly socialist) figures who are their Big Others. We might fast-forward to "Revol" from *The Holy Bible* (remember the pervert's formula: Thy Will de Done!), when each line of the verses dismisses another world leader; the first verse deals chronologically with the Russians (Lenin, Stalin, Khrushchev, Brezhnev, Gorbachev, Yeltsin); the next globalizes the list (Napoleon, Chamberlain, Trotsky, Che Guevara, Pol Pot, Farrakhan). The song even has a one-phrase chorus like "You Love Us" above the same self-satisfied G←D←C chord progression (give or take a couple of chromatic slides): "REVOL, Lebensraum, Kulturkampf, raus, raus, fila, fila." The same tearing-down of idols occurs on "Faster" from the same album: "I am stronger than Mensa, Miller and Mailer/I spat out Plath and Pinter." Yet the group, while tearing down their idols, are constantly filtering influence or even direct quotation from these figureheads through their music. The single "The Masses against the Classes" began with the voice of Chomsky. As Wire says candidly in an interview with Dorian Lynskey: "We've always been honest that the things we're trying to pass on are better than what we can do as a band."[8] In this way, they see themselves as conduits for the voice of the big Other—"Thy will be done!" Perverts.

Hopefully we've now shown you how, under Lacanian logic, some acts that seem perfectly benign—an inversion of "we love you" into "you love us," can signify a perverse structure. And the opposite is true—seemingly perverse acts can often have no basis

---

[7] Mathijs Peters, *Popular Music, Critique and Manic Street Preachers* (Switzerland: Palgrave Macmillan, 2020), 159.
[8] Interview with Dorian Lynskey, "The Manic Street Preachers: 'I'll Always Hate the Tory Party. But Now I Hate Labour, Too,'" *New Statesman* (July 8, 2014). www.newstatesman.com/culture/2014/07/manic-street-preachers-i-ll-always-hate-tory-party-now-i-hate-labour-too.

in perversion as a clinical structure. To foreground our discussion of masochism as a category of perversion, we might take the difficult topic of self-harm. Richie's "4 Real" is not, as it is sometimes plausibly described, a display of masochism. Perhaps one of their saddest songs opens with the line "Scratch my leg with a rusty nail. Sadly it heals." Edwards confesses:

> When I cut myself I feel so much better. All the things that might have been annoying me suddenly seem so trivial because I'm concentrating on the pain.[9]

Their song "Roses in the Hospital" (another Plath inspiration) describes stubbing cigarettes out on his arm "to let pain out." Self-harm is certainly different to masochism, where the masochist coerces another into hurting him/her for sexual pleasure. As succinctly described on any lifeline website for self-harmers, this practice tends to be viewed as a way of converting emotional pain into physical pain, which can be more concretely felt and dealt with. This may not be healthy behavior, but it is not perverse.

At the moment we are writing this, this manuscript is about 70,000 words long, and we think we have done a very good job thus far of mixing our voices in the text seamlessly, thanks to Google Docs. However, at this moment, Stephen is going to offer some personal reminiscences on the Manics. (Kenneth wrote much of this section to this point and will pick up his pen again in a moment to consider Billie Eilish). After all, if one can't be allowed a little narcissism under one's own name, how can one enjoy it?

Ken: Over to you Steve.
Steve: [*Uncorks a Vina Tondonia Blanco, slowly pours a glass,*] Thanks Ken.

Whenever I reflect on my musical tastes as a teenager—something I occasionally consider when I make a nostalgic YouTube playlist or, indeed, when writing this book—I wonder why I used to like the Manic Street Preachers so much, yet cannot bear them now (indeed for the last fifteen years). As we noted at the beginning of the chapter, the end of the psyche's development, for Freud, is the exit from the Oedipus complex into a domain where the polymorphous perversions of the infant have been corralled into narrow pens of heteronormativity.[10] This is effected by the creation of an ego, a sense of self that can be capable of loving the required things. And, as we learnt in the sections on narcissism, these investments take two forms, anaclitic (external) and ego (internal) investments. If this ego creation doesn't happen correctly, the vicissitudes of these frustrated drives can turn toward perversions. As Freud tells us in *Drives and Their Vicissitudes*, it can be just as efficacious to hate something as it is to love it. I wonder if the first three Manic Street Preachers albums are a form of the musicalization of this attempted process of self-becoming. In them, there are

---

[9] "Manic Street Preachers: Richey Edwards," *BBC Wales* (December 2, 2008). www.bbc.co.uk/wales/music/sites/manic-street-preachers/pages/richey.shtml.
[10] This provides the grounds of Deleuze and Guattari's attack on Freudianism in *Anti-Oedipus*.

many songs that try and define the self in opposition to others (often the capitalist "other"), and then another smaller set that empathizes with the others of the other: the excluded ("Little Baby Nothing," "Yes," "La Tristesse Durera"), and then far fewer again that manage to posit a positive conception of the self. And those that do, like "You Love Us" or "Faster," find nothing there, where that self should be.

What is the song "You Love Us" about? What kind of account does it give of why we should have these loving desires? Upon listening, we find "You Love Us" as a placeholder, an empty shell waiting for a reason. But in lieu of presenting that reason, it comes out as an empty assertion. What we have is a kind of ersatz perversion, a prefabricated perversion that says: you want me—why, well, because I am looking like Guns and Roses and/or a reader of books and/or against the system. The relationship of the teenage listener to the Manics is mirrored by the relationship of the Manics to their own icons. When we ask them to help build us, they, in turn, look toward the icons of 1980s rock and mid-twentieth-century politics to fill in their own selves. This aggressive, perverse iconography is like catnip to a teenager—and there, perhaps, the pervert finds a receptive audience—but when looking back on these songs, I can't help feeling that my contemporary opinion is probably closer to what my father's would have been then—"What is this?"[11]

Richey, in an early interview, said: "As Camus said, if God does not exist I am God—and that's what we try to do, we try to create ourselves. Y'know, be in a band. Y'know go down to London and try and do something." Camus's existentialist viewpoint isn't a million miles away from Lacan's idea of the analyst in the discourse of the analyst. In realizing that *a* doesn't exist, we can return to a healthier pursuit of our desires, understanding what we desire and why we want it, but still being open to the possibility of enjoying it. For the existentialists, too, we make a choice to be who we are. But this choice is hard. To be in a band and go to London isn't enough to create an ego. The Manics' solution to this problem—to present an ego when there was none—was to become perverts or to mimic perversion.

The apogee of the early Manics' attempt to construct a positive articulation of the ego is perhaps "Faster," which is full of declarative "I am" statements. Yet, again, what is really there? There are positives that are so vacuous as to be meaningless: I am architect, pioneer, purity. Then the negatives: "idiot drug hive, the virgin, tattered and the torn," perhaps a bit more personal, but still rather general. Singer James Dean Bradfield describes this voice in "Faster" as "a cold, disembodied voice" and one he struggled to put appropriate music to.[12] In these years, the band had a clear aesthetic and followed a kind of *via negativa*, a means of defining themselves as what they were not. Bradfield again: "It is much easier to be in a band when you are younger and when you have got the ability to wear certain clothes and not feel like a dick ... you're not just standing behind the music, but behind an image too."[13] But there are performers who have a

---

[11] Kenneth vividly remembers a conversation at the Overy family dinner table on October 7, 1996, when Overy's parents threatened, "I'm sorry Stephen, but if you're going to see the Manic Street Preachers tonight, you're going to have to eat some more potatoes."

[12] Mike Connolly, *Manic Street Preachers: From There to Here* (BBC2, September 23, 1998).

[13] Ibid.

similarly strong aesthetic and manage to convey more of their ego in a song than the Manics did in their first three albums. Think of Lana Del Rey's "Video Games," a text that is full of desires that are a positive choice, a text in which Lana owns her desires not as a pervert but as a person(a). So it goes with many of the songwriters we have discussed to this point: from Phoebe Bridgers to Pavement, something is presented as a conception of the self and its desires (in a straightforward way by the first, less so by the second), giving something that we can grasp.

Perhaps the clearest example of the projection of perversion by the early Manics is found in comparison to their own later work. Sean Moore says in the documentary *From Here to There* that "through *The Holy Bible* we [isolated and alienated] ourselves, whereas [with *Everything Must Go*] we felt like we were being embraced by people."[14] The content of their work at the time of *Everything Must Go* is markedly different from *The Holy Bible*. Let's consider the B side of "Design for Life," "Mr Carbohydrate." It is positively jolly in comparison with the Manics' previous songs. In this rather cheerful song, we hear about Nicky Wire—formerly an alienated and vicious "suicide baby"—present himself as a Welsh bloke with a love of cricket and snacks. There's definitely a sense of development of a sense of self and the abandonment of the previous perverted disposition. "Mr Carbohydrate" is a "take me or leave me" kind of guy. Nicky Wire confirmed this reading in a contemporary interview: "For the first time I'm completely comfortable and at ease in where I grew up and what it means and how it formed me. I'm twenty-nine now and I have reached a bit of maturity, because when you're young you react against it."[15] Music has a strange relation to the unconscious. It can certainly give "us" what we want, but not always what we might need.

## *Billie Eilish*

Billie Eilish's hit "Bury a Friend" is often described in extremely dark psychological terms. Carmen Chu, for example, writing in *The Gavel*, calls this "an exploration into nihilism and sadism"; "Looking deeper, this fabrication of the mind reflects the masochistic and the sadistic."[16] And yet, the more obvious problem with this song is the theme of suicide; the line "I want to end me" seems to cut sharply through the threadbare musical texture and stops it in its tracks. The textural hook in the very first line of the vocals, which has an emaciated form of the vibe from The Doors' "People Are Strange," is initiated by a sinister voice in the night. The call of "Billie" comes from the top bunk of two bunk beds, before Billie responds with the bouncy but sinister hook: "What do you want from me?" This question—a direct Lacanian "*Que vuoi?*"—is all we need to hear to know that Eilish's persona in the song is neurotic and nonperverse.

---

[14] Ibid.
[15] Ibid.
[16] Carmen Chu, "Emo-Pop Princess Billie Eilish Wants You To Be Terrified," *Gavel* (February 23, 2019). https://bcgavel.com/2019/02/23/emo-pop-princess-billie-eilish-wants-you-to-be-terrified/.

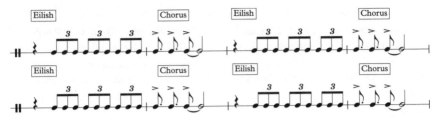

Example 7.1  Billie Eilish, "Bury a Friend," rhythm from 2:08.

The song is itself a play of voices of the Other's gaze. The audio collage of sinister noises, as well as the horror music tropes that lurk beneath, contributes to the profound effect of marking the gaze of the Other watching us in the night. The pervert would assume the position of this very gaze and believe him/herself to *be* the gazing subject, but here Eilish's position is normative. Eilish's musical tone is pure but always fragile with minimal accompaniment—there is no backbeat, no filler layer that would flesh out chord progressions. Rather, there is just a complete array of ultraprecise, mostly acapella voices that surround her, each corresponding to the images we see in the video of medical professionals sticking dozens of needles into her back, or dozens of hands grabbing her from all sides. These voices with their associated imagery are all the demands of the other, which Eilish answers with true Lacanian phantasy. This phantasy may involve aspects of horror films (most specifically "The Ring"), which is why so many find this song perverse, but, in reality, at least in the formal Lacanian sense, it is normal.

At around 2:08 into the song, we arrive at what we might call the "middle eight (a)," which consists of four rhythmically quirky iterations of an interrupted phrase, rendered in Example 7.1. There is patter here between Eilish and the external voices, who behave like the four fates in Gluck's opera *Orfeo*, each crying "No, No, No, No!" She establishes a smooth triple time/triplet flow, but it is always interrupted by the voices of the Other(s) who bring their hammers down in full harmony to stop her flow. She is not able to please them, or even know what they want.

The second "middle eight (b)" equally has a fourfold iteration of a phrase, but this one grows in intensity. This time it is not the fates who say "No, no, no, no," it is Eilish who repeats in their place, "I can't say no." She is unable to withstand the demands of the Other.

Normal too is the so-called sadistic masochistic imagery, which comes from the lines about stapling one's lip to the floor, or burying a friend. But note how, once uttered, these words are responded with a quirky, vocally harmonized (qua superego) "urggh" from the voices, as if this is causing displeasure. It's not what they want; a pervert wouldn't admit this threat of castration. There is no masochism or sadism here. There is, however, the big danger—suicide. The song's most chilling silences are those that follow the repeated line, "I wanna end me." Suicide is tragic, utterly tragic. But not perverse. Even if we took perversion as simply the act of contravening the natural law, Lacan quite provocatively calls suicide (if it is resolute and determined rather than impulsive) "the only completely successful act," because the conscious mind is enacting the unconscious will of the death-drive.[17] Suicide, as a constant theme of the early Manics ("Spectators of Suicide"; "Suicide Is Painless"), is normally associated with depression or melancholy, neither of which are perverse conditions. Remember that a perverse person does not believe him/herself to have a problem; they are the solution to everyone else's problem. And, perhaps, this serves as a poignant reminder for why, for Lacan, perverts could not normally benefit from therapy.

But what if these voices that surround Eilish's head are coming from within. Think of Munch's "Scream." It seems, from Eilish's own admission, that they are. She claims that the song is written

> from the perspective of the monster under my bed. If you put yourself in that Mindset, what is this creature doing or feeling? I also confess that I'm this monster, because I'm my own worst enemy. I might be the monster under your bed too.[18]

This position and its sinister afterthought does not change the fundamentally neurotic economy. The voice in the head here is still phantasy, which is still neurotic and nonperverse. All of the Other's demands upon us—even if they really are there—are always being synthesized in the Imaginary phantasmatic realm. These voices are all imagined, or at least our experience of them is always imaginary. Thus, from whatever angle we take this from, although Eilish is made (making herself) to look ultraperverse here, her fundamental constitution seems to be just neurotic.

## Female Perversion?

Because castration was such a male-dominated concept, by refusing to accept castration, the pervert was always considered male. What had been labeled "castration fear" in the prior literature was really about men's fear of losing potency, of experiencing pain and/ or of loss. But these things are not necessarily exclusive to men, as Arlene Richards, among the first to rigorously redefine the female implications of perversion, pointed out. In her pioneering article, "A Fresh Look at Perversion" (2003), she describes her work with three patients who, were they male, would have been quickly classified as perverse but, on account of their gender, notwithstanding the identical symptoms, could not traditionally be classified as such.[19] Richards dismisses the prevailing idea that perversion is about *literal* castration, which traditionally only explained why men

---

[17] Jacques Lacan, *Television: A Challenge to the Psychoanalytic Establishment*, ed. Joan Copjec, trans. Denis Hollier, Rosalind Krauss, and Annette Michelson (New York: Norton, [1973] 1990), 66–7.
[18] Clifford Stumme, "What Does 'Bury a Friend' by Billie Eilish Mean?" *The Pop Song Professor* (February 20, 2019). www.popsongprofessor.com/blog/2019/2/20/what-does-bury-a-friend-by-billie-eilish-mean-lyrics.
[19] Arlene Kramer Richards, "A Fresh Look at Perversion," *Journal of the American Psychoanalytic Association* 51, no. 4 (December 2003): 1199–218.

can be perverse. Castration is now shown to correspond in women to the fear of loss of genital pleasure, fear of genital pain, and fear of loss of reproductive function. This more open definition of castration broadens the field of perversion while allowing us to keep an eye on the gendered differences. Rather than focusing on part of the genitals of one sex, Richards makes it clear how "castration fear" and perversion can apply to both sexes.[20]

> By bringing the aggressive and envious feeling of the infant to the fore, the Kleinians add another important dimension. By integrating these dimensions, we can rid ourselves of the false dichotomy between perversions in men and identical symptoms in women that cannot be thought of as perversions as long as we use the narrow definition of perversion as a response to fear of castration by penile ablation.[21]

Thus, "castration" (or rather the disavowal of it) is still a root cause, but is not exclusively phallic. For most of Richards's analysis, however, perversion appears to be "like-for-like" for men and women, but Richards goes further in locating a certain perversion that can form in the mother–baby relationship. She reminds us further that Freud, in *The Economic Problem of Masochism* (1924), believed that masochism was primarily female as a preparatory self-defense against the pain of childbirth.[22] But beyond birth, Richards refers back to Estela Welldon's definition of perversion as "perverse mothering":

> The mother is caught in a world where she is powerless except for her power over her child. Isolated, neglected, and disempowered by being denied the opportunity to earn money, she has no other object than the baby for either her lust or her aggression. This leads her to use her child to meet her sexual needs and satisfy her aggressive impulses. Welldon defines this as perversion. According to her, perversion is a syndrome in which the sufferer feels compelled to substitute some aggressive action for genital satisfaction.[23]

Richards claims that, following this, the mother mistreats the child as a way of mistreating herself. "When she beats her child, it is as much a masochistic self-injury as it is a sadistic attack."[24]

Now for some music. We might consider Eminem's "My Mom" (*Relapse*, 2009), which blames his abusive upbringing to his perversely abusive mother, Debbie Nelson-Mathers. After the release of this song, and others, Nelson-Mathers attempted to

---

[20] Ibid., 1210–11.
[21] Ibid., 1213.
[22] Sigmund Freud, "The Economic Problem of Masochism," in *The Standard Edition of the Complete Psychological Works of Sigmund Freud*, vol. XIX, trans. James Strachey (London: Hogarth, [1924] 1961), 157–72.
[23] Richards, "A Fresh Look at Perversion," 1212.
[24] Ibid., 1214.

sue her son, unsuccessfully, for $10 million. We profess no investment (or interest) in the truth of the relationship between the rapper and his mother, but we can find maternal perversion—albeit described by the son and denied by the mother—formally registered in the song itself and some of its related public discourse.

It is clear from listening to both sides argue publicly over the years that we can't build psychologically on these fragmentary, poetic, and doubtlessly embellished accounts. But, whatever the truth, in the perversions described in the song "My Mom," we find the "mom" protagonist poisoning the son with prescription drugs—principally valium. The whole rap becomes focused on the maternal "mm" sound as a kind of mock-mantra, repeated *ad nauseum(mm)*. This, as well as the reverb that the vocals fade into at the final moments, helps create a sense of distance between the then and now. The mood of the song has the same jazz-funk funereal vibe as Winehouse's "Back to Black"—with heavy, bouncing bass, minor key, and brassy punctuations. Eminem, always obsessed with the letter "m" (for mother? For "Marshall Mathers"?), highlights it throughout, peppering the chorus with internal assonance such as "I aM what I aM," "valiuM," and so on. As the song develops, the voice becomes increasingly verbally intense as insults from mother to son pour forth, depicting the abusive home scenes.

We might remember Welldon's claim that a mother's abuse of a child occurs in situations when she has no form of control and no ability to work. Inviting now "the real Debbie Mathers" to "please stand up," it's clear that this was her own position; she was unable to work to support the family, who consequently relied on state support. Equally, in the perverse situation, abuse is usually an altered form of genital satisfaction—in this case, getting high through drugs. By bringing the child forcibly into the drug relationship, this is a form of sublimated sexual abuse. (Again, though, remember that we are analyzing Mathers's public narrative, not making an assessment of the "truth.")

Note also Richards's remarks that the mother is inflicting pain on herself masochistically, rather than being sadistic toward the child. Throughout the mother/Mathers relationship, Debbie assured us that everything that happened to the child happened to the mother, and vice versa, like-for-like. She took drugs; he took drugs; he earned millions; she wanted ten of them; he wrote a song about her; she wrote one about him, as we will see. Once the accusations of abuse came forth via music, the response had to come through music. "Dear Marshall" was recorded as an "open letter" from Debbie by rap group ID-X on their album *Set the Record Straight* (2000). ID-X adopt a similar vibe—slow, measured, Bondesque guitar tones, minor key gravitas, jazz inflections, piano with delay/reverb that invites us back into the past. Of course, she reads her letter rather than raps, apologizing "before God" but, nonetheless, blaming Eminem. She also adopts the classic pervert's position of speaking for the big maternal Other—in this case, "lots of mothers"—the (M)Other. But the "like-for-like" aspect of the mother and son's masochistic bond is what really stands out; both mother and child have to suffer together. Thus, as Richards indicated, mother–child abuse is not simple sadism, but has a masochistic component. And it is to the sadomasochistic experience (if it exists) that we must now turn.

## S & M: Same Perversion?

There are probably as many species of perversion as there are perverts, and this chapter could become a book in itself. But two very particular types of perversion occupied Freud and Lacan greatly and, in turn, influenced Gilles Deleuze's *Présentation de Sacher-Masoch* (1967). This book, in full psychoanalytic vein—published five years before his more famed diatribe against the psychoanalytic clinic in his collaborative work with Felix Guattari, *L'Anti-Œdipe* (1972)—thoroughly revisits the questions of sadism and masochism, noting the fundamental premise that both conditions were formulated from studies of literary works, and that we need to return to this literature when we wish to learn more. In 1893, when Krafft-Ebing looked for the full catalog of symptoms, he opened texts by the Marquis de Sade and Sacher-Masoch. Deleuze reopens and reads their books closer than his predecessors did. Still writing in a Freudian-Lacanian vein, Deleuze reveals much more of what the source texts tell us about these two very distinct conditions.

Deleuze's fundamental aim is to disentangle the two perversions, which both Krafft-Ebing and Freud conflated into a single sadomasochistic entity. On the surface, sadism, if defined as gaining pleasure from inflicting pain, would seem to be a perfect complement to masochism, if defined as taking pleasure in receiving pain. Taken at face value, we might simply pair each pervert up with a counterpart like yin and yang. However, as Deleuze points out, it is far from this simple. In over a dozen ways, Deleuze shows how the goals of the masochist cannot be fulfilled by a sadist, nor vice versa. To give a very simple illustration of one major incompatibility: the sadist needs his/her victims to dislike their torture; the masochist, as lover of receiving torture, would, therefore, make the sadist recoil in horror. Both the masochist and the sadist need to be in ultimate control over the other, which renders them incompatible.

Freud had originally argued that sadism was primary (i.e., came first) and masochism was merely a "turning-around" of the drive on itself. Lacan later suggested the opposite: masochism was primary, but sadism arose as a result of the subject's rejection of the idea of harming him/herself. While accepting that there is often an element of S in M, and M in S, there is no formal combination of both as "S&M" for Deleuze: "Sadomasochism is one of these misbegotten names, a semiological howler."[25] Indeed, Deleuze unearthed a contradiction in Freud's logic in that Freud had always maintained that a drive cannot transform into another drive, so there is no such thing as a sadistic drive turning into a masochistic drive. Deleuze believes that there *is* sometimes a passage from sadism to masochism, but both remain distinct. He claims this single potential passageway is a kind of reboot—a process of "desexualization" and "resexualization." This new sexualization needs to be grounded in new erogeneity (which was alienated from the sadist), and the sadism must be "projected." Deleuze calls this whole process "defusion" of the instincts into a different amalgam of Eros and Thanatos.

---

[25] Gilles Deleuze, *Sacher-Masoch: An Interpretation* (London: Faber, 1971), 115.

But sadomasochism is often exploited in art because few of the characters who discuss or portray the phenomenon are as wholly invested in sadism as de Sade was, or in masochism as Masoch was. And we need to disentangle them carefully and remain open to learning more about the twin structures of sadism and masochism in the artworks (songs) we will study. We will perhaps even learn more about their authors (though not necessarily in the ways they intend) in the process.

Before considering the vast differences between the two perversions, Deleuze can help us dispel a couple of myths. Firstly, he radically claims that sadism/masochism are not some additional aspects of the death-drive that lie "Beyond the Pleasure Principle"; Deleuze says that there is no "beyond" this principle, rather there are just "some rather strange complications in the workings of pleasure."[26] Both sadistic and masochistic pains are still performed for the benefit of the big Other, though Deleuze cites Nietzsche rather than Lacan: "If pain and suffering have any meaning it must be that they are enjoyable to someone."[27] Deleuze says that if the pervert implies that the gods delight in it, this is psychotic. But Deleuze also radically disconnects the element of pain; at least he disconnects pain as the ultimate goal of both conditions: "In sadism, no less than in masochism, there is no direct relation to pain: pain should be regarded as an *effect* only."[28] What is then special about each condition? Deleuze's entire book tries to unpick this, and, though he offers a numerical list of differences in the final summary pages in his book,[29] holistic reading of the whole tome allows us to pinpoint several more. Table 7.1 summarizes Deleuze's formal incompatibilities between S and M as nos. 1–11, with our own additions (all from Deleuze's wider text) alphabetically listed. The full list is presented for reference, but we will zoom into the most significant aspects as we explore the two perversions in practice through our own examination of artworks.

In order to disentangle these two terms, we will take examples of what we believe to be exemplary masochism and sadism in turn. We will then explore some examples that represent the confused and contentious nature of the passages between them. We first tackle "pure masochism" and then "pure sadism."

## Pure Masochism

### Tom Lehrer, "The Masochism Tango"

As shown above, a vital aspect of masochism is humor (category *n* in our list). The masochist uses the downward force of humor against him/herself as further debasement, showing him/herself that the fundamental scenario s/he is part of is ridiculous; it is a way of self-shaming. It is no small irony, then, that one of the

---

[26] Ibid., 97.
[27] Ibid., 103.
[28] Ibid., 105.
[29] Ibid., 115.

Table 7.1 Deleuze's differences between S and M

| | Sadism | Masochism |
|---|---|---|
| 1 | Specular-demonstrative | Dialectical-imaginative |
| 2 | Driven by pure, universal negativity; articulated through repetition and multiplication | Operates with disavowal and suspension |
| 3 | Quantitative reiteration, acceleration | Qualitative suspense, frozen |
| 4 | There is masochism specific to the sadist | There is sadism specific to the masochist |
| 5 | Negates mother; inflates father | Disavows mother; abolishes father |
| 6 | No phantasy. Pure action. Fetishism is employed sometimes, but divested of its fundamental disavowal | Fetish and phantasy. Imagination. Fetishistic disavowal (fetishist disavows the mother's lack of penis; substitutes with an object) |
| 7 | No aestheticism | Aestheticism |
| 8 | Institutional | Contractual |
| 9 | Superego and identification. "His ego only exists in the external world"[a] | Ego and idealization. No superego. Masochist manipulates woman into this role |
| 10 | Different forms of desexualization/resexualization | |
| 11 | Apathy | Coldness |
| a | Torturer is powerful, in control, but enacts the will of the big Other | Torturer feels uncomfortable and weak; enacts the will of the little other |
| b | Imperatives and obscene descriptions serve a higher function of demonstration | Imperatives and nonobscene descriptions serve a higher function of a mythical and dialectical order. Frozen descriptions |
| c | Nonconsensual | Consensual |
| d | Higher function needs pleasing; higher form of violence enacted on lower level | Higher function needs educating |
| e | Pornographic language is demonstrative, instituting | Pornographic language is dialectical, mythical, persuasive |
| f | Language is beyond censorship | Language passes censors |
| g | Speculative way of apprehending the death drive | Imaginary, dialectical, mythical way of apprehending the death-drive |
| h | Father punishes his family by persuading daughter to torture the mother. "Alliance of father and daughter" | Mother punishes the father via the son. "Alliance between son and oral mother"[b] |
| i | The Symbolic Order and Law are paternal | The Symbolic Order and Law are maternal |
| j | Abolishes law | Maintains law with contract. Temporarily gives law to mother |
| k | Androgynous. The boy plays the role of the girl in projection to the father[c] | Hermaphroditic. Mother has phallus; so does the son |
| l | Infinite. Never ends. Repeated | Finite. Third person initiates the rebirth of the victim as a new man. Father returns as hallucination |
| m | Believes in reality even when s/he is dreaming | Believes in the dream even when s/he is in reality |

(continued)

Table 7.1 Deleuze's differences between S and M (continued)

| | Sadism | Masochism |
|---|---|---|
| n | Irony elevates and overreaches the law, finding loopholes, appealing to a higher principle of nature | Humor descends, follows the law (punishes) but shows the law to be stupid |
| o | Wants perfection and universalism (cf. Kant's "categorical imperative") | Wants to alleviate guilt; makes sexual pleasure possible again |
| p | Thanatos, under Eros, is turned outwards | Thanatos remains as a residue and bound by the organism |

[a] Deleuze, *Sacher-Masoch*, 107.
[b] Ibid., 59.
[c] Ibid., 60.

most accurate portrayals of the masochistic spirit should come from musical comedian Tom Lehrer in his "The Masochism Tango" (*An Evening Wasted with Tom Lehrer*, 1959). The dance genre chosen for this parody is a clear symbol of sexual domination itself; the tango was the most heterosexual of the dances in which the male lead jerks and whirls the female around the dancefloor, who herself also tries to dominate. Lehrer opens with one common rhythm that is often used in tango, but more often associated with rhumba (see Example 7.2), and quickly moves toward the more classic tango rhythm with strident quarter-notes—a strict 4/4 with the last beat emphasized as a sliding "up-beat" to the next measure (see Example 7.3) as if the male is really forcing authority on the female, taking the ground out from under her feet. The irony here is, of course, a mock role reversal—the female in the masochistic situation (at least in the heteronormative scenario) is supposed to be the in-control torturer—the dominatrix. Or is she? Remember that the masochist in all of Sacher-Masoch's writing is the male "victim" who is always actually in charge; the female "torturer" (who is really the victim in another sense) is being temporarily granted power, but the driving force is still the male, pushing upwards from his supine position beneath stilettos. In this way, Lehrer has the masochistic domination relation neatly summed up musically. This is also reinforced by the fact that all of the lyrics stem from the male who demands to be treated badly, expressing delight at the very thought of the violence inflicted upon him. We have no sense that the female torturer is enjoying the scenario; there is no evidence of a sadism that would indicate that Lehrer had confused the situation with the sadomasochistic nonentity. All of the instructions are coming from the "victim" as meta-instructions: essentially, "tell me to do this."

Much of the humor is lyrical. It's difficult to hear the words "blacken my eye, set fire to my tie" without laughing, but, as always in well-crafted musical humor, the lyrics work in tandem with the musical surface. If you're writing a tango song, you can flip a coin to decide whether it's going to be in G minor or D minor. This one is in D minor and is a straight-up tango although the dramatic pauses and ad hoc interjections add comic touches. But if we added "serious" lyrics to this music, it would be passable as a genuine tango, without being an overt parody. And this is part of the point—in the

Example 7.2  Tango rhythm 1: "Rhumba."

Example 7.3  Tango rhythm proper.

masochist's scenario, humor is used as part of the cure, used to help the sufferer realize the stupidity of her/his genuinely dark lusts.

The particularly genuine aspect of this experience is the deployment of phantasy. We learn from Deleuze that the masochist is sustained by this phantasy, reveling fully in its power.

> He [the masochist] does not believe in negating or destroying the world, nor in idealizing it: what he does is disavow and thus suspend it, in order to secure an ideal which is itself suspended in phantasy.[30]

S/he has to believe that the situation is phantasmatic, even when it isn't. When faced with the situation being a reality, the masochist would experience pain in all the wrong ways. We find such a dramatic moment in the song when Lehrer entreats his beloved, claiming that his heart is in his hand. The music abruptly stops, and Lehrer utters a revolted "ugh" sound (see Example 7.4), as if he has suddenly seen through the romantic cliché and summoned up the literal meaning. His whole phantasy world has been glimpsed in its reality, and it thereby elicits horror. Of course, the moment immediately passes and the merciless tango rhythm picks up the pieces and puts us on the masochistic conveyor belt once again.

[30] Ibid., 30.

**Example 7.4** "Eugh!"

A crucial aspect of masochistic phantasy is the fetish. The masochist refuses to accept that the mother is lacking; s/he refuses to see the female as a castrated male. This is called "fetishist disavowal." The fetishist clings to objects that represent this "phallus"—we'll learn a little more about this in the next chapter, but it is sufficient for the moment to note that the masochist requires fetishes, all serving as symbols of the mother's abundance—her lack of lack. Lehrer's text confesses that every time he hears drums, he has a Pavlovian response of feeling pain; the distinctive rumba rhythm, which mimics drums, serves as a kind of phantasy version of the percussion section that structures the masochistic/tango experience, all fully imaginary. Earlier he had described how "you caught my nose in your left castanet," and we know that the pain is also adopting a rhythmical character. But this rhythm produces an atmosphere of suspense, not one of accumulated energy; the strong tango rhythms here are all about a fixed temporal frame, which is highly characteristic of the masochistic experience—the genuine masochist's contracts always specify a fixed amount of time in which the experience is to be conducted.

After the fetishistic drums that substitute phantasmatically for pain, next comes the image of the rose between the woman's teeth, which the character envies. This envy is fueled partly on account of the pain the rose inflicts, and partly as a fetish—a phallic symbol of the mother's nonlack.

A crucial aspect of the masochistic experience is the coldness of the torturer. Remember that the masochistic torturer can't be a sadist; firstly, the sadist would have to be in control and so would the masochist; secondly, the masochist can't stomach the thought that the torturer is enjoying her/himself, nor can the sadist suffer the victim to enjoy being tortured. The masochist needs the whole scenario to be cold. Deleuze subtitled his account of Masoch "Coldness and Cruelty." As we consider Marvin Gaye's venture into masochism in due course, we'll think more precisely about what this coldness means, but suffice to say that the whole masochistic scene is described as "frozen," for two reasons. Firstly, it is frozen in time. Time has to appear to stand still. Secondly, it is frozen because the torturer is to gain no real pleasure from the experience; s/he must be indiscriminate, cold, disimpassioned, deliberate. Lehrer's song is frozen in both of these ways. He describes how his torturer's heart is as hard as stone "or mahogany." As we will

**Example 7.5** Final measures of "The Masochism Tango" by Tom Lehrer.

see, this image of hardened natural elements is particularly apposite in masochism as nature plays a vital role. The clinical regularity of the musical tango is highly conducive to this chilling coldness; the almost absurdly comical strength of every beat of the stark 4/4 quarter-notes (all are equally strong, as if fighting against the natural inclination to make beat 1 strongest, followed by 3 and then 2 and 4) emphasizes only the last note like a whip cracking down to punctuate the proceedings. Each beat is a cruel and exacting stroke of musical time with no sense of forward momentum; it is static time, which adds suspense as it mercilessly refuses to budge. Funnily enough, the end of the experience is also musically suspended as Lehrer sings the final line. Note in the excerpt from the score in Example 7.5 how the word "masochism" is suspended out across as 2/4 bar, as if Lehrer can't quite bring the situation to an end, although he knows that he has to; his contract is up, his hour with the dominatrix is over, and she has to get back to her normal family life, or at least dance with her next partner. The unassailable rhythm finally ceases as both chromaticism and a 2/4 meter drag the song to its end.

### "Masochistic Beauty"

Marvin Gaye's rather bizarrely conceived song "Masochistic Beauty" (released posthumously in 1985) might seem, at first listen, to be uttered from the perspective of a sadist. This might follow some of Gaye's confessions about his love of the Marquis de Sade:

> "In my adult life," he said, "the Marquis would become a fascinating character of evil. I identified with his wicked ways. He had a power to raise the blood pressure. He fulfilled fantasies. As prince of darkness, he wasn't afraid of the hot stuff. There were days—nights, weeks, months—when, I, too, played the role. But God had blessed me with a voice to touch the hearts of people. I'd been instructed to spread love, not lust. And in those days, my innocence kept me away from evil."[31]

---

[31] David Ritz, *Divided Soul: The Life of Marvin Gaye* (New York: Da Capo Press, 1985), 38.

David Ritz noted that this reflected a complex situation in his personal life:

> Pleasing women was a chore he approached with suppressed anger which manifested itself in his sadomasochism, in rituals which allowed him to inflict pain upon his sexual partners, thereby punishing them for their insatiable demands.[32]

We don't have enough information to comment on Gaye's own predilections and wouldn't want to judge any of the artists in this book by their works, but the song itself is an accurate enough (and interesting enough) portrayal of masochism, notwithstanding, and in fact *supported by*, its obvious tongue-in-cheek humor. There is certainly sadistic language in here, but as the song unfolds, we realize that we are witnessing a genuinely masochistic scene from the perspective of the "torturer" who is male, albeit feminized.

There are plenty of clues that we are not pedaling sadistic services to a masochist here. For a start, a true sadist would never refer to the victim as "masochistic beauty"—the sadist would flee the scene if s/he felt that the victim was enjoying him/herself. The sadist has a horror of the masochist, who undermines the entire authority of the sadist to inflict true pain. We can look at various features of the genuine masochistic experience outlined above—and we will do so—but these features will lead to perhaps the most profound psychoanalytic insights from Deleuze about the masochistic imagination—*the three mothers of the masochist*. But before we go there, Example 7.6 is a formal diagram of the song with an image of the wavefile beneath; it will prove useful to consult in the prose that follows.

What is abundantly clear from a Lacanian point of view is that the masochist is perverse in trying to please God by enacting his will. The torturer closes verses 5 and 6 by referring to God, firstly as arbiter of guilt, to whom the masochist turns, and secondly as a caution that if s/he can't face his "rod," then s/he can't "for God." This reminds us that the whole perverse act is being performed to please the big Other who lies outside of the situation. However, this is true of perversion generally, and not confined to masochism.

A clear indicator of the masochistic art is the complete atmosphere of nonteleological, nonaccelerating suspense that hangs across the work. Deleuze talks about the masochistic whip, punctuating occasional breaks from the scenario's air of suspense. The song closes itself with a whip-crack, as if we have been enjoying one long inventive scene of masochistic suspense—a frozen moment in time, which Gaye's funk-groove embodies beautifully. Perhaps groove, therefore, is the masochist's dream—a nonteleological suspense, an attempt to stretch out time.[33] Look at the lack of any dynamic variety in the wavefile of Example 7.6. This dynamic monotony is perfectly common in this genre, of course, but it here serves the darker forces of perversion particularly well.

---

[32] Ibid., 92.
[33] Aspects of repetition and masochistic suspense are considered in Anna-Elena Pääkkölä, "The Sublime Space of Male Masochism in Elvis Costello's 'When I Was Cruel No. 2,'" *Radical Musicology* 7 (2019). www.radical-musicology.org.uk/2019/Paakkola.htm.

S & M and Pop Perversion           211

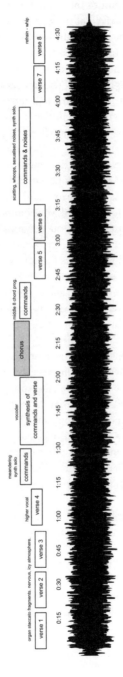

**Example 7.6** Formal wave diagram of "Masochistic Beauty" by Margin Gaye.

Humor is clearly lurking with Gaye's tongue firmly wedged into his cheek. Remember that the whole point of the masochistic scene is to make a display of the stupidness of the situation, arrived at through humor. The masochist's is a particular type of humor that follows the letter of the law, but shows the law to be mindless. Gaye adopts a rather bizarre, faux, upper-class-British, cockney accent from the outset. This sillyfied voice establishes comedy immediately; the ultracamp phrases such as "I love your booty" or "if you do it right, you get the pipe" are all quite close to Lehrer's parody. And masochism itself is by its very nature, to a certain extent, parody.

The language here is dirty enough to just about pass censorship, without being fully pornographic. Most of the instructions are fairly direct, but nothing like the language we'll encounter when we explore sadism in death metal. There are injunctions like "get down, get up, shut up"; there is talk of "cum," questions of "are you wet?" and so on, but the majority of language is masochistic in nature—injunctive and persuasive. While the torturer declares that he is "the masterman," we also learn that s/he is driven by duty, not pleasure—"It's my duty to spank your booty." The master/slave are constantly reversing as in the masochist's dialectical relationship. In sadism, there would be, no doubt.

Another aspect of masochism here is the search for an end point for the "victim" who wants the finite period of servitude to end in the hope of expiating guilt and undergoing rebirth. Likewise, the protagonist here is looking for a way "to close the gate," to be expunged. However, this doesn't happen through any kind of buildup and release of tension, but through a process articulated in the finite state of time denoted by the "contract."

We move now to thinking about the mother, or mothers. Remember that, for Deleuze, the torturer must represent the uncastrated mother who is fully powerful, wielding the law, beating the father (via the son) for trying to subvert her primal authority. Ritz referred to the song as "Marvin cursing and beating that mythical Evil Woman he so long sought to crush,"[34] but this glib remark does not do justice to the masochistic mindset, and we will find the opposite process at work. Gaye's ex-wife Janis reported a conversation around Gaye's other self-suppressed song "Sanctified Lady" (which was planned to be called "Sanctified Pussy," another outtake from the *Midnight Love* sessions), which is about the search for a perfect and incorruptible woman:

"Some say the song is beneath me," he explained. "And yes, there is humor implicit in the title. But it is no joke. To find a church girl, pure and innocent—as you were once innocent, Jan—"
"I was never innocent," I interrupted. "I lost my innocence when I was a child."
"When I met you—"
"When you met me, you imagined me to be someone I was not. When you met me, I had already been to hell and back. So had you. You forget those things."

---

[34] Cited in Lynn Van Matre, "How Sweet It Wasn't: The Tortured Life and Divided Soul of Marvin Gaye," *Chicago Tribune* (April 25, 1985). www.chicagotribune.com/news/ct-xpm-1985-04-28-850 1250764-story.html.

**Table 7.2** The three mothers of masochism, according to Deleuze: the Ideal must absorb characteristics of, and take over, the other two.

| Mother 1 | Masochistic Ideal | Mother 2 |
|---|---|---|
| Uterine *hetaeric* mother. Prostitute, self-assured, independent, powerful, modern woman: "For her the sexes are equal; she is a hermaphrodite"[a] | Oral mother. Nature. "The trinity of the masochistic dream is summed up in the words: cold-maternal-severe, icy-sentimental-cruel"[b] | Oedipal mother. Sadistic; actions always performed with a man "whose victim she is likely to become"[c] |

[a] Deleuze, *Sacher-Masoch*, 42.
[b] Ibid., 45.
[c] Ibid., 43.

"I remember everything," he said. "I remember too much. It's time to forget the past and turn back the hands of time. Time to meet that one woman, untainted and incorruptible—"

"Good luck on that journey," I said.

"I need a woman as flawless as my own mother."

"You'll never find that, Marvin. We only get one mother."

A week later, I was alarmed to learn that Marvin had gone to live with his mother. He had moved back to the rambling house on Gramercy Place. His father was there, living in a second-floor bedroom next to Mother's bedroom. Down the hallway was the room where Marvin slept. Back in his parents' home, Marvin grew more distant from reality. From what I heard, his paranoia grew alarmingly worse.[35]

There is so much wonderful Oedipal imagery here: the father and mother's separate rooms; the son's room equidistant between them; the son's attempt to find a mother replacement in his partner; his personal interest in sadomasochism as a way of beating the father. As is well known, Marvin Gaye was abused by his overbearing, loveless father. A preacher in public, a despot in private, and no stranger to whipping and beating his children, Gaye's father symbolized the law, God, and Satan in one. In fact, this father was responsible for Gaye's death, fatally shooting him during a domestic fight in which Marvin intervened as the father was beating the mother. Given that a fundamental premise of masochism is that the Oedipal mother punishes the father via the son, there is perhaps a particular poignance to this posthumous song, released from beyond the grave.

The brilliant mistake that Janis made was in her line "we only get one mother," when, of course, for the masochist, at least according to Deleuze, we have *three* mothers, or rather two mothers, each synthesizing and canceling each other to create the third—the masochist's ideal. Table 7.2 offers some characteristics of the three mothers: Mother 1, Mother 2, and the Masochistic ideal mother (our terms). Deleuze called these, respectively, the uterine mother, the oedipal mother, and the oral mother.

[35] Jan Gaye, *After the Dance: My Life with Marvin Gaye* (New York: Amistad, 2015), 281.

Let's do as the masochist does and take a tour around the revolving carousel of mothers who figure her/his imagination.

Mother 1 (the uterine mother) is described as a prostitute, a supremely confident modern woman who is thoroughly independent. In Gaye's song, we find this mother woven into the lyrical and musical fabric, rearing her head in combat with Mother 2. The first stanza closes with the line "like a whore" that positions us in this framework of nonsadistic but fairly independent "modern" sexuality. The sexy electro-funk-groove is also representative of this modern, fashionable, stylish woman. She is also described as hermaphroditic; she lacks nothing. Remember, she is not the castrated mother of "normal" people; the masochist disavows the mother's castration, so the mother lacks nothing and wants nothing for herself. But this *hetaeric* mother is very concerned with making the victim experience sexual pleasure, which would normally only happen *after* the masochistic experience. We do start to hear this in the pornosonic noises in the 3:15–4:00 section of commands and sexualized preorgasmic noises of shouts and pants. (Remember: in the masochistic imagination, the orgasm, if it happens, is a concern for afterward.)

Mother 2 wears a more sadistic face. It is she who cracks the whip; it is she who throws the victim to the floor and calls her victim her "slave." An interesting aspect of this mother is that she often works in tandem with another man. In Masoch's stories, the end of the tale often arrives when the torturer introduces a virile young Greek man into the masochistic scenario. And if we listen closely to Gaye's track, we can indeed hear this man. For one thing, there are the male backing vocals that interject throughout, but we also hear the hidden other in the voice of the vocoder that enters in the instruction scenario around the 1:30–2:00 mark. The vocoder voice was provided by Gordon Banks, Gaye's guitarist and producer, who Gaye referred to as "ID," standing for "The Indicator" (rather than the Freudian "id," but the connection may well still stand). This Other voice—the part of Mother 2 who is responsible for the sadistic drive—is thus twinned with the double action of the other man who brings about the conclusion of the masochistic relationship. For Masoch, this Greek figure found provision in the infamous masochistic "contract," but, in practice, his entry into the situation always expedited its end.

These two mothers are both unsatisfactory, and their alternation, fueled by dissatisfaction, produces only glimpses of the ideal mother—the third, "oral" mother. The beauty of Gaye's text is that this mother is not necessarily present in the lyrical content per se, but she can be discerned *through* it and has her real home in the *music itself*. This mother is the closest we can find to pure Nature. Nature is famously nurturing, fertile, rich, plentiful, but "she" is also harsh, cruel, punishing, and indiscriminate. So is the ideal other in the masochistic situation, who is responsible for the warmth and maternity as well as the coldness and cruelty of the masochistic situation.

From the very beginning of the track, the organ riff is intermittent, edgy, staccato, hesitant, ultraprecise. It pervades all of the verses with the same sense of nervous anxiety and icy coldness. But beneath this perpetual coldness, we can feel the maternal blanket of wonderfully rich bass and synth sounds. These enveloping warm sounds beneath the cold, chilling breath of the electric organ above give the present authors the feeling of sitting in an outdoor Icelandic spa: geothermal heat pushing upward; ice-cold air pushing downward—all natural. There is a form of maternal regularity to the whole groove—each two-measure hypermeasure of the verses emphasizes the final two beats with an all-unison, homophonic moment, as if we are constantly being let off our reigns for a moment, but always yanked back to the mother's knee at the end of each hypermeasure. In the left ear we can hear the occasional synthesized descending jagged sound like a long zip (of a leather outfit?) being pulled down—as if Mother 2 is overlapping in the soundscape with the Ideal mother. We think we also find the cold third mother in the meandering synth solo that emerges in 1:15–1:30 during those sections of maternal injunctions. The ideal mother is fundamentally disimpassioned, and this is typically also part of the masochistic suspense that does not seek any kind of generative momentum. With this, we can perhaps also equate Gaye's electro-(disimpassioned?) groove construction. Sure, there is repetition here (which Deleuze said was a characteristic of Sade), but repetition here serves a nongenerative function; it is how Deleuze describes it when he says that "repetition is what holds together the instant."[36] The layers of the groove do not pile up toward any kind of tense climactic point. The song merely stops when the whip is cracked. Example 7.6 shows the progression of verses and other material, but observe first how, even at the crudest level, the wavefile is constant, static with no dynamic growth, decline, or variety. Although we've noted a "chorus" at 2:00–2:30, this is hardly a typical chorus as it is only ever heard once; it has little of the *character* of a chorus as we find in Drew Nobile's recent book:

> Two particularly reliable chorus markers are text—choruses' lyrics tend toward summarizing, non-narrative content, whereas verses more often give detail or tell a story—and texture—choruses usually have a thicker texture than their corresponding verses, most commonly through the addition of backing vocals, a shift from hi-hat to ride cymbal in the drumbeat, and/or a general increase in "loudness." Other factors come into play as well, such as the length of melodic units (they tend to be shorter in choruses), the rhythm of the vocal line (choruses tend toward longer notes), or the presence of the title lyric (more often in the chorus).[37]

Gaye's "chorus," if there is one, is rather different. Sure, it has the "hook" of the key line, "I love you, my masochistic beauty," but otherwise the song is denuded of even the teleology of a returning refrain; we are in constant stasis. There is a brief move toward something that sounds like a middle eight, with its new temporary tonal region at 2:30–2:45. The song's form does move toward a period of audio collage of sex noises and whoops, as discussed, but this is no lurch toward a climax; rather, it is just another plastic part of the frozen masochistic scene. Neither is this the "Soul" music that Gaye

---

[36] Deleuze, *Sacher-Masoch*, 99.
[37] Nobile, *Form as Harmony in Rock*, 71.

was famous for; this is cold-blooded. Gaye doesn't sing, he raps; he doesn't vocalize, he gives us comedic poetry that he executes in the disimpassioned voice of a cockney toff. The ideal mother is impersonable; she is demonstrative and disavows sensuality. She has a coldness bordering on Sade's "apathy." And with this same apathy she neither enjoys nor begrudges her role as torturess.

## Pure Sadism

Sadism should be shocking. There's nothing liberal or permissive about it. Masochism has the saving grace of being consensual in the form of a contract. Sadism is much less practical to exercise (thankfully) because it breaks the law, and in the most horrific ways. Where masochism venerates the law, while subverting it through loopholes, the sadist tramples on it. The Sadean libertine, if genuine, would be jailed, removed from society. The infamous sadists of the twentieth century are people like Ted Bundy in the United States, or the "Moors Murderers" in the UK. The classic texts for graphic sadism are probably "120 Days of Sodom"—the Marquis de Sade's 1785 fantasy account of the exploits of four wealthy libertines, who share stories from brothel keepers in a secluded castle and then try to recreate them through orgies of sexual torture, pain, and murder that they inflict on the victims. We can also follow the accounts of the trial of Gilles de Rais, leader of the French army in the time of Joan of Arc, who was later to inspire the tale of "Bluebeard." Whether we believe to be genuine the accounts of the crimes described in the 1440 court that sentenced him, or whether we believe in a catholic conspiracy to remove him from office, there is certainly a sadistic imagination at work in whoever the source was for the recorded delight in child murder and sexual torture. Surprisingly enough, sadism in this form only exists in the darker corners of civilization as points of collective shock and shame, or in horror fiction—when the darkest phantasies that mankind can dream up for itself can flourish unfettered. And, of course, they come up in music like any other art. Cue "Death Metal," the dark pocket of sadism that music, insofar as it bears a trace of human society (or antisociety), *had* to construct for itself.

We're going to throw you in at the deep end and begin with Cannibal Corpse's "Entrails Ripped from a Virgin's C***" (*Tomb of the Mutilated*, 1992). You can probably get the measure of the song from its title; so if its subject matter is likely to disturb you as much as it should, please feel free to fast-forward to our analysis of Korn's "Lullaby for a Sadist," or Raw Rap's "sadomasochism," which you will find (marginally) more palatable.

**Cannibal Corpse, "Sadistic Embodiment"**

We're actually going to talk about "Entrails Ripped from a Virgin's C***," but we didn't want that to appear as our section heading (in case our parents are skim-reading through their courtesy copies of the book), so we deceived you slightly by advertising "Sadistic Embodiment" from *A Skeletal Domain* (2014). To honor our promise though, we will begin with this track as it will help us contextualize the genre of "Death Metal" in light of the sadistic imagination.[38]

The lyrics of "Sadistic Embodiment" don't exactly ring true. It's as if the writers had been instructed to write about sadism and embody it without really studying its workings. One thing that the band get wrong—let's begin with the *via negativa*—is anger. If there is a chorus in the song, it is the grunt/growl of four words: "anger," "released," "torture," and, "returning." Perhaps the word "anger" is what people might think of in terms of sadism—how can a torturer be level-headed and calm, unmotivated? And yet, this is the crux: the Sadean torturer-libertines are famous for their "apathy"— they conduct their activities without emotional investment and tell their tales in the most disimpassioned way. Indeed, one of the most sinister aspects of Sade's writing is the matter-of-fact tone of his descriptions. The other misnomer in the song is that the "mutilation leads to death" to the extent that "existence is now irrelevant." For the sadist's phantasy (rather than their reality), victims are rarely actually killed—they exist in a perfect suspension of life and death. In fact Lacan positioned such victims "between the two deaths," based on a line in Sade's *Justine*, when the torturer hesitates to kill the victim, insisting he wants to murder her twice—once on earth and once in the afterlife. Existence is, therefore, vital to sadism.

But there are musically sadistic elements too in the song, and which we find in the whole genre of "death metal," that do ring true. For one thing, there is the absolutely clinical control of the musicians. Say what you like about the sound they produce (it's fair to say that the present authors are not card-carriers), the musicianship is astounding. The four key members of the bands (like the four Sadean libertines?) are perfect executioners. Their guitar and drum techniques are phenomenal, particularly in the domain of rhythm, though the guitarists are real Baroque virtuosi with an absolute handle on their esoteric modes and scale patterns. Like "Math Rock" the rhythmical and metrical games played in this genre are fascinating, and the performances are always breathtakingly tight-knit. "Metric modulations" become a staple (where a constant subpulse that is not the main pulse acts as a bridge between two very different main pulses, effecting often radically different time signature changes). The musical control here is paramount, and yet the music created is designed to offend all but the genre's closest fans. The growling voices, the persistent distortion, the ludicrous speeds are all designed to inflict a kind of musical torture on the masses (who don't listen, of course, because in real life we have to consent to listen) through the ultimate control of the executors. One couldn't perform these intricate metric effects without really "having it together" musically—this is the ultimate in calculated precision from the sadistic torturer. Another genuine sadistic feature that Deleuze points out is the control of the passage of time; rather than remain frozen in time like the masochistic experience, the sadist takes control of time and, in fact, speeds it up through carefully controlled repetition. It is accelerative.

---

[38] Kenneth is greatly indebted to the work of his dear friend, music theorist (in metal, among other things) Ciro Scotto.

We'll focus a little now on "Entrails Ripped … " The lyrics are more sadistic than "Sadistic Embodiment" because they do indeed recount with some degree of clinical detachment the details of an entire disembowelment scene that is performed upon a virgin. To hear the detachment of the lyrics, listen to them being performed as a "poetry" recital by Big C from Metal Outlaw TV, with Boccherini and Strauss providing the soundtrack.[39] The lyrics come across here as passionless, entirely denuded of aggression. In the real song, we could never distinguish the lyrics without the CD booklet due to the metal "death growl," and we won't reproduce any of them here on account of their ultraviolent nature. They describe the whole scene in exacting detail, though largely without passion. It's a paradox that the most physically aggressive voices in music—the "death growl"—should be the most dispassionate; this is because all of the passion is enacted on a uniform level—it's perhaps not so much "dispassionate" as "indiscriminate." We can't hear any nuanced emotion in this growl; we can't discern any pleasure; we can't even discern any anger, despite anger being the prevailing emotional mask for the whole scene. And we think this anger-qua-mask is the ultimate disguise for the sadistic experience here. When asked about their disturbing lyrics, death metal bands will dismiss them as "fantasy," but Chris Barnes claimed that the song was loosely based on a real-life case of two brothers, one with a learning disability:

> They captured some girl, and the semi-retarded brother was talked into putting a coat hanger up her pussy to pull out her intestines.[40]

Barnes wants to have his entrails and eat them (it's real; it's fake; no it's real). It may be worth considering one of Deleuze's fundamental aspects of sadism, which is that the sadist needs to believe in reality even when they are dreaming, while the masochist needs to believe in phantasy even when facing reality. The graphic lyrics of the sadistic imagination are the corollary of the more reserved lyrics of the masochist. Remember also that, according to Deleuze, the graphic descriptions serve what he calls a "demonstrative" function—the sadist wants to describe, demonstrate, all with precision. Particularly toward the end of this song, there is a clear dichotomy between description and action. Look up the lyrics on google if you can bear to (and if your ISP will allow it), and you'll find fairly neutral descriptions of the acts—they aren't attempting to be "erotic" or sexualized; they are presented as a matter of fact, as if the group is describing the procedure required to make a cup of tea. The music says otherwise, though. Example 7.7 shows that, from about 3:30, there is a quickfire alternation between the vocals plus drums, which describe the actions (not to mince words: eating entrails), and the electric guitar riffs, which seem to accompany the actions themselves as if the sadist is caught between doing and saying.

---

[39] Metal Outlaw TV, "Cannibal Corpse: Entrails Ripped … (Metal Spoken Word)," *YouTube* (November 6, 2013). www.youtube.com/watch?v=TAX14VvP7ok.
[40] *Decibel* (June 2008): 71.

Notwithstanding this, there is a doubly accelerative momentum in the music and lyrics in the sadistic display. The lyrics move from meta-descriptions of "terrible scenes of agony" to the full graphic details of eating her insides and the brutal descriptions of her bodily excretions flowing as the narrator performs copra-necrophilia on "her emptied body." The cycles of repetitive moments of the sadist are embodied in every step. The sadist repeats and repeats in the pursuit of "over kill" (in an attempt to kill the victim in the next life)—hence going beyond murder to post-death acts of violence and necrophilia. An oddity about the lyrics of this song is the cold clarity of the Other's perspective that comes through, as if the torturer always realizes what the Other will say about his crimes. He recalls "orgies of sadism and sexual perversion"—the perpetrator knows the law of the father and commits the acts in an attempt to break that law. He even recalls his own unconscious memories as if he is his own psychoanalyst. He remembers former atrocities ("locked in my subconscious, obscene memories I thought I'd forgotten") as if he has gone through the talking cure and knows his own unconscious. This is the second point in the song when the pulse settles into a 6/8 meter of reverie. We might remember perhaps that the pervert "knows all" and refuses to cede power to an analyst, one of the key reasons that Lacan could not imagine a cure. Also, the singer lyrically begins the work of describing the whole scene ("Descriptions of my killings, bone chilling"). Remember that these graphic descriptions are vital to the sadist: one of Sade's libertines in *120 Days of Sodom* describes the ear as the most erotic organ.

Musically, the acceleration pushes through via a shifting carousel of repeated ostinati in different time signatures, each musical "block" being part of a particular scene. This is all part of the sadist's force of furious repetition, mechanization, and calculated acceleration. The first moment at which the drums start furiously whipping every eighth-note snare comes between thirty and forty seconds into the song when the vocalist describes the "orgies uncounted," giving us the scale of his crimes. You'll notice from Example 7.7 that there is an acceleration throughout; the brakes are squeezed on occasion, but only to make the acceleration more exacting. In the 6/8 passages that seem to describe the feminine element (the virgin tied to the sadist's bed), the tempo settles at ca. 110 bpm (eighth note = 330 bpm). A metric modulation maintains 110, now as a quarter-note pulse, emphasizing every eighth note in 2/4. There are constant distortions to the metrical flow to assault any pattern that is established, and these effects often accompany the lyrics, such as the moment the virgin is "devirginized" around the 1:30 mark as the sadist describes the flow of various bodily fluids. When the rounds of sadism pile up, we are somewhere nearer 240 bpm. Remember though that, for the sadist, this repetition/acceleration is all part of trying to make the scene resound through eternity (remember our discussion of Nietzsche and eternal recurrence?). The sadist wants his crimes to reverberate through the afterlife. In fact, this also explains the fact that in the text the victim seems to be constantly dying, or dead, and then dying again. Only once rigor mortis has actually occurred can the sadist accept that the victim is really dead, and the song come to an end.

We must ruminate on several other more general aspects of the sadistic imagination that are played out in the song. Firstly, remember Deleuze's analysis that

220  Listening to the Unconscious

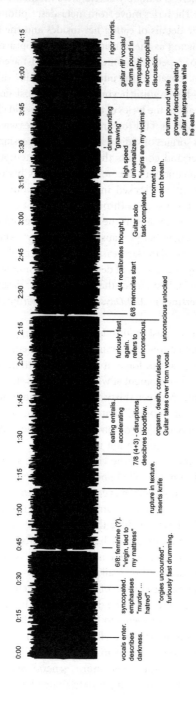

Example 7.7 Graph of "Entrails Ripped ..." by Cannibal Corpse.

the sadist is annihilating the mother. In Cannibal Corpse, this is clearly happening in the form of the virgin (the fantastical pure mother) whose womb is eaten via her vagina—the child is not being reborn; the mother is being symbolically killed in a grotesque parody of the scene of birth. And this is always happening musically in the song, too; the rocking 6/8 rhythms that offer the glimpse of femininity and maternal warmth and nature's pastoral aspects (the virgin tied to her bed; the sadist's long-forgotten memories) are always soon to be distorted by either 7/8 or 4/4 aggressive rhythms. There are no "dynamics" in this track (have a look at the wave diagram); Cannibal Corpse aren't renowned for their *sotto voce*. The whole thing, perhaps even the whole genre, is an annihilation of the maternal element through breaking of the paternal law.

A second more general aspect is the use of perverse (in the general sense) language. Compare this song with "Masochistic Beauty," or even "The Masochism Tango." Sade's use of language was intended to lie beyond censorship; his novel was never going to pass the censors, so he just hid it in his prison cell until the Bastille was stormed. That it was found and published is a curious historical accident. Cannibal Corpse's lyrics will pass the censors of any teenager's parents on account of them being completely hidden—only reproduced online or in the lyrics booklet. Thus, because no one is ever going to actually "hear" them as such, the group can be as deafeningly grotesque as possible—all hidden in plain sight. Part of sadistic irony is the way that it overreaches the law, always appealing to a higher principle of nature. And strange as it may seem, Nature is something that the sadist wants to bring to the cruel scene. Cannibal Corpse too. Their corpses are always decomposing; their humans are always monsters, acting according to their raw animal nature.

This also ties in with the lack of any aesthetic. Sure, heavy metal T-shirt designers care about aesthetics—but the gory death images are more like *annihilations* of beauty; black (nothing) backgrounds; half-rotted corpses (empty bodies). This is all worlds away from the exotic Mediterranean masochistic imagery of the boudoirs described by Masoch, or indeed by Tom Lehrer's exotic Latin American tango.

The sadist is also concerned with irony as an elevating form of demonstration to the Other. We think there are two major demonstrations in Cannibal Corpse: one is musical and relates to ironic musical proficiency; the other is lyrical and relates to the capacity for imaginative expression. First, the musical irony. If punk rock was an attempt to show that one can be musical and relevant without being "musical"— sticking two fingers up to the Western classical tradition while you do so—then death metal and related genres are an attempt to go beyond the Western classical tradition with ultracomplexity and precision in producing a similarly destructive sound. There is an appeal here to something more elevated. The most ardent Baroque fan might find difficulty in dismissing this music on the basis of its technical proficiency. It follows some Western musical laws, but produces an entire antilaw. This is thus an ironic form of demonstration upward. But the second form of ironic demonstration, as in Sade, is found in text. The group is lyrically trying to demonstrate how disgusting they can possibly be while still being regarded as human. To do this they demonstrate their adherence to deeper, more "natural" laws. They are demonstrating what potentially lurks beneath us all as a species. "Homo sum, humani nihil a me alienum puto," as Terence puts it: "I am human, and I think nothing human is alien to me."

## Korn, "Lullaby for a Sadist"

This is a good song to mull over when considering the incompatibility of the sadist and the masochist. In Korn's "Lullaby for a Sadist" from *The Paradigm Shift* (2013), we have a genuine sadist taking pleasure in hurting a victim. However, the victim is a "would-have-been" masochist who had originally wanted to be hurt, but the sadist has achieved a double success in *really* hurting them and is now celebrating their victory. It leads us to wonder whether, for a true sadist, there would be no more profound enjoyment than beating the masochism out of a masochist.

As a self-styled "nu metal" band, showing influences from a variety of other genres—grunge, funk, and hip hop—they are certainly less graphic in what they describe than Cannibal Corpse. They are also metrically less intricate and place less emphasis on virtuosity in their instrumental technique. Their instrumental (sadistic) mastery is shown as a precise and exacting control of their texture, with one of those block forms where a series of radical textural cuts demarcate different sections. The form of the song is actually a standard "cycle" of verse-prechorus-chorus, with a solo two-thirds of the way through and a final chorus as outro, though each section has a very different set of components, both musically and in terms of the sadistic ideas in the lyrics (see Example 7.8).[41]

Like Cannibal Corpse's 6/8 section that (within the parameters of "death metal") has a more "feminine" musical and lyrical subject, there is a clear lullabyesque arpeggiated acoustic riff from the beginning of "Lullaby for a Sadist," which underlies the verses and the opening reprise of the chorus. The lyrics here describe the voices inside that drive the sadist—the voices of the Big Other, which the pervert believes to be his own, allied with the words of God. This musically summons up the maternal world, though it is a maternal world that is crudely ripped apart in the prechorus and chorus. In the prechorus, the heavily percussive guitars act as the Sadean repeated crack of the whip, while the apathetic voice of the libertine-singer (semi-rapped) counts to five, each number followed by a declaration of his pleasure as sadist:

> One, I love hurting you; two, I love your pain; three, let's get together and play the sinner's game; four, is for the torture and five is for the shame, cos every time you want it I get off on this game.

Remember that, for Deleuze, the sadist held a specular and demonstrative aim. His aim is not just to commit acts of atrocity in dungeons behind closed doors but also to document, to recite, to demonstrate, to tabulate, to quantify them. Hence the "1-2-3-4-5" all the while we hear the sounds of screams and cries as the numbers

---

[41] Nobile discusses the formal functions of cyclic units and offers a particularly clear flow diagram in *Form as Harmony*, 123.

S & M and Pop Perversion  223

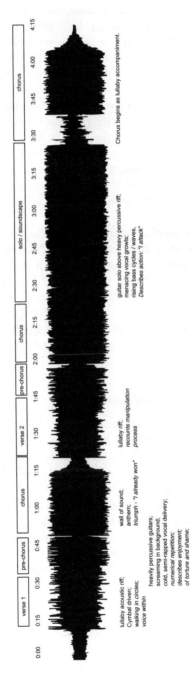

**Example 7.8** Graph of "Lullaby for a Sadist," Korn.

are articulated like brutal death strokes in a torture chamber. This is all serving to annihilate the innocent lullaby that had pervaded. Given that the sadist annihilates this maternal lullaby, we might question whether this lullaby is truly "for" a sadist or "for" a masochist? Probably the latter. Remember that the sadist believes in paternal law; the masochist in maternal law. The sadist beats the mother; the masochist beats the father.

It's notable that the chorus is beautifully produced in the Phil Specter "wall of sound" tradition—it is a celebration of refined power. The words may describe how the "coldness follows," but the music is a festival not of coldness but of warmth, enveloping the sadist. The would-be masochist has the coldness; the sadist now feels victorious, crowns himself, and wraps himself in the cloak of success. But the singer's voice becomes increasingly aggressive as he recalls how the victim thought s/he wanted it in the first place. Essentially the message is: "You wanted to play the game; it's not a game; and I won." We might also reflect that the subsequent verse describes how the sadist manipulated his victim from the beginning, now with the coldness and apathetic clarity of the libertine.

After the section that musically describes the "attack"—similar perhaps to the way that the musicians portrayed the action parts of "Entrails Ripped …"—the final chorus begins with a sudden return to that maternal chora, now with the words from the chorus about "the coldness" that "follows." The music box lullaby does, on reflection, sound "cold" and apathetic. Perhaps this would-have-been masochist was clinging to a cold and cruel nature, as is their wont? Either way, the masochist's internal maternal world is cruelly ripped apart once again and is hit with the wall of sound that, now more than before, parades the sadist's profound success over the masochist.

## "Sadomasochism," Raw Rap Relationship

For another manipulation of a would-be masochist into becoming the sadist's true victim (perhaps even more chillingly than Korn's), we have a portrayal of even purer sadism, though again billed as "Sadomasochism" by Raw Rap from their album *Antumbra: The Grim Adventures of TeWo and Mosi* (2017). With their lyrical references to demons and dungeons, the two rappers become the Sadean libertines and executioners par excellence. After portraying some generic masochistic elements, this track quickly descends into pure sadism. The sense of musical time is one of the primary ways in which this transformation is achieved. Revisiting the masochistic discussion above, we find many musical characteristics of the music being frozen in time early in the track, full of suspense. At the beginning, the rappers' lyrics question who is in charge—"Who decides the stupid time for when I'm supposed to be euthanized?" and the music portrays this timeless suspense wonderfully. The snare is mic'd up to sound like a regular whip; there is a wonderful chromatically descending sample that offers a deflating sound, and there are meandering, eerie, one-finger synth solos from around 1:15 in the track. This sonic freeze is the only masochistic element; from here it becomes clear that the *real* situation is purely sadistic. Time becomes repetitive and generative, working toward a particular climactic point at 1:48, which we will discuss in detail in a moment. And there will be no end to this: "You could never ever get me to stop." The sadistic aspect is confirmed in full when the libertines assert, "You simply are wrong, if you're thinking you could compete with a fucking malevolent God." The sadists now play their ace cards; there is no masochism here.

TeWo and Mosi are black and white rappers who trade throughout their lyrics on their "unity" as Yin and Yang. The opening lines show how they are unified and "UTI" ("under the influence," rather than suffering a urinary tract infection). These two rappers are not in competition like, say, Micky Avalon, Dirt Nasty, and Andre Legacy, discussed in Chapter 2; these are two libertines both working as one. They rap alternately, but always rap from the same hymn sheet. In verse 10, they begin to rap together in perfect synchronicity, coinciding in an alternative climax of "spinal pain" when they go on to consider their condition from a psychologically manipulative standpoint. The assurance that each voice sparks in the other leads us to the triumph of the pervert over the analyst. The rappers become manipulative psychoanalysts: "And psychiatrically analyze him, but actually plant an idea in him, inception to me comes naturally." This victory over the analyst is descriptive of the pervert's relationship with analysis in general. Remember that the pervert, and more so the sadist, *knows* what the other wants and can therefore not be analyzed; perverts such as these play cold, clinical games. The references early on in the song to "shape shifting" are typical in this respect.

This supreme arrogance of the sadist certainly spills over into the discourse of the rappers themselves. They make oblique references to Ray Bradbury's work and then comment outside of the fourth wall: "Did that fly over your head? Shit, everything we write does." The hubris of the sadist knows no boundaries, and the rappers posit themselves as all manner of gods—Krishna, Hades, Annanaki. Perhaps most poignantly for the sadist, who, for Lacan, assumes the power of the "gaze," we hear the sadist refer to seeing Krishna in the victim's iris. But at the moment of sublime acceleration and intensity, the torturers declare themselves to be "a fucking malevolent God."

The music is full of childish horror sounds, the kind of computer game samples that surround Super Mario in one of his "ghost" levels. These pervade the whole song, perhaps adding to the manipulative insistence that this is a game (which the sadists seem to use to lure their victims, before the torture becomes real). This 1980s Nintendo sound world becomes quite intense when the pair of libertines list 1980s horror film figures—Jason, Freddie, and so on. The references to zombie films, too, also help position us in the classically sadistic place of the "zone between two deaths"—these devils don't ever die; they just keep coming back for sequel after sequel. Similarly, the libertines conflate their various scenarios into one so that we're never really sure who, when, or what is happening.

Perhaps though, the aspect of this song that takes us further than Cannibal Corpse or Korn into the sadistic world is that the whole display is described as a "musical" itself. Mosi describes himself (themselves) as a "dark magician with the lyrics" and fills the "bridge" with the repeated line, "We hope you enjoyed this musical of sadomasochism." And yet, while there are undoubtedly musical sadistic aspects as described above—the generative acceleration, the libertines' vocal synergy, the manipulative game or movie atmosphere replete with interjections from synthetic sound effects—the music itself does not embody or enact the process as thoroughly as Cannibal Corpse, with their sadistic musical synthesis of nihilism and extraordinary technical control of their instruments (of torture).

## S & M and Generic Kinkiness

Early critics of E. L. James's *Fifty Shades of Grey* were quick to point out the acute dangers of romanticizing an abusive relationship.[42] There is also a danger in the public imagination with the conflation of sadism and masochism into one kinky soup. It's not the aim of this book to morally censure, but it should be clear by now that sadism in its genuine, pure form is a highly cruel and universally unethical practice that harms the other for the pleasure of the perverse self (though perceived as a big Other). Masochism at least is consensual and only potentially harms the person in charge (at least physically; if the masochist manipulated someone into harming him/her, then it could, of course, assume a more troublesome dimension). This isn't to say that there is "no such thing" as "S/M"—it's clear that the phenomenon exists, as attested by millions of couples (or triples, quadruples, etc.). But, really, what is happening here is that people sideline the dangerous aspects of the S in favor of the kinky aspects of the M and assume the equivalence or even interchangeability of roles. In clinical cases of these perversions, however, there is no such role reversal. Let's explore a few pop tracks in this light and look at the tension points between the clinical structure of perversion and the phantasy of S & M and also spare a thought for the possible routes by which we might traverse S & M.

### Rihanna, "S&M"

An internet blog by Emily Manbeck claims:

> After reading Freud and Deleuze's analyses on sadomasochism, I noticed some differences between its scholarly explanations and its depictions in creative self-expression. Freud and Deleuze describe S&M—especially as it relates to the libido and death drives—as not only a way of life but also a debilitating condition.[43]

Commenting further:

---

[42] See, for example, Sarah Ashton, Karalyn McDonald, and Maggie Kirkman, "Fifty Shades Darker: An Abusive Fairy Tale That Robs Women of Sexual Freedom," *The Conversation* (February 9, 2017). https://theconversation.com/fifty-shades-darker-an-abusive-fairy-tale-that-robs-women-of-sexual-freedom-72724.

[43] Blog post by Emily Manbeck: "S&M and Pop Culture: Has Pleasure through Pain Perpetuated through Art?" *Commonplace Book*, Georgetown University (October 30, 2013). https://blogs.commons.georgetown.edu/engl-355-fall2013/2013/10/30/sm-and-pop-culture-has-pleasure-through-pain-perpetuated-through-art/.

The heart-wrenching thing about Rihanna's song is that she is a victim of domestic abuse herself, yet she delights—or so she claims—to love "chains and whips" and "feeling bad."

The song "S&M" (*Loud*, 2010) appears to be, and may well be, tongue-in-cheek; the references to "sex in the air" and the overiteration of "S, S, S" and "M, M, M" show us that we are talking about an attempt to be ultrasexy here, rather than play a role in clinically exploring S or M as conditions. The imagery is more than whips and sexy leather, however; in the video, journalists are seen wearing mouth gag-balls;[44] one is even taken around on a leash. The bad-girl aesthetic comes very much to the fore and associates instantly with the menacing sawtooth growl of the bass in this up-tempo dance-pop song. Rihanna's persona-protagonist here is portrayed as the torturer, but she keeps insisting that she is in control; there doesn't seem to be a big Other outside of the situation controlling her actions. Or is there?

The role of the journalists in the video is telling; they first pin her to the wall and subsequently write down everything she says. There is certainly a master/slave dialectical role reversal taking place, which is more the domain of the masochist. Perhaps then, rather than the whips, chains, leather, and slowly chewed bananas, this is where the true masochism lies: the love–hate relationship to the media. Certainly a form of empowerment hovers above the whole proceedings; as one online commentator declared: "Rihanna turns the tables on abusive ex-lover Chris Brown in this heady dance club tribute to bondage—empowered, and as terrifyingly sexy as ever."[45]

### Christina Aguilera, "Masochist"

A more disturbing picture of a sadomasochistic complex is portrayed in Christina Aguilera's "Masochist" (*Liberation*, 2018), which gives a sorry picture of a mistreated woman. Although the whole frame is a state of emotional abuse rather than physical or sexual, its poignancy is perhaps all the greater as a result. The protagonist is clearly not happy in the relationship and knows that she should leave, a statement that she repeats. The accompaniment is afforded by a lush cushion of synthesized strings, so that when Aguilera sings, "I get all my pleasure in your bedroom, in your arms," we are not talking about kinky sex *a la* Rihanna here. But likewise the rejoinder—"You get all your pleasure from my torture, from my harm," all delivered in broken phrases—is full of pathos and signs of emotional scarring. And this very real sense of psychological manipulation is delivered in the chorus, whose touchingly dreamy, self-reproaching yet comforting melody expresses, "I must be some kind of masochist." Sure, the singer is being metaphorical here, but the very notion of the word implies that she thinks she must enjoy the situation somehow—that she *must* be taking some kind of pleasure.

---

[44] We, the authors, are proud to say that we don't know the technical term for these objects, nor do we wish to.
[45] Jake Conway, "Rihanna, 'S&M,'" *Q Magazine at Yale* (March 29, 2011). https://web.archive.org/web/20110713101456/http://www.qmagazineatyale.com/culture/music/rihanna-E2 80 9Csm E2 80 9D/.

All of the musical cues point to this not being the case—the strained, desperate sound of the voice; the warm, dreamy envelope of the synthesized strings the singer is cushioning herself in; the slow-moving harmony; the melodic sighs; the pleading broken phrases. She hates the situation but has been gaslighted into believing that, maybe, she loves it. The real tragedy here, then, is self-misdiagnosis. He is a sadist; she is a victim, not a masochist. But she claims that the longer she stays, the more "the hurt is my comfort and release": she is being conditioned to think she likes it, believing in "sadomasochism" when there is no such thing. She is merely taking on the social definitions that others might use to describe her.

### Pendulum's "Masochist" (*Jungle Sound Gold*, 2006)

Pendulum's "Masochist" is an oddity for a discussion of masochistic time, because Jungle is sometimes considered to be the paradigm of musical acceleration, not in literal musical terms but in philosophical terms. Members of famed unofficial cybernetic cultures research unit (CCRU) at Warwick University in the 1990s hailed Jungle as the music of the future, which they wanted to "accelerate" into. As one former philosopher in the group put it in 1996:

> Jungle functions as a particle accelerator, seismic bass frequencies engineering a cellular drone which immerses the body ... rewinds and reloads conventional time into silicon blips of speed ... It's not *just music*. Jungle is the abstract diagram of planetary inhuman becoming.[46]

Listening to parts of "Masochist," this might seem to be true. Looking at the waveform (Example 7.9), you can readily see the truly "accelerative" parts because we have indicated the blocks of speed underneath the diagram. Speed in this context seems to be always in direct proportion to overall volume. We find that in the main parts of the song the tempo is around 170 bpm, with high levels of quite violent and repetitive futuristic sounds (at least like the future sounded in 1990, a major theme of Mark Fisher's—one of the former CCRU members—philosophy, "hauntology").

First, we might wonder why the song is called "masochist." It may well be because the vocal samples, which form the narrative, are taken from *Death in the Jungle: Diary of a Navy Seal* by Gary Smith and Alan Maki. Published in 1995, the book forms an account of their experiences in Vietnam. Perhaps Pendulum's title is a comment on the authors? From the book's blurb:

> Though death reigned as king in the jungles of Vietnam, Gary Smith considered it a privilege and an honor to serve under the officers and with the men of Underwater Demolition Team Twelve and SEAL Team 1. Because he and his teammates, trained to the max, gave each other the courage to attain the unattainable.[47]

---

[46] CCRU, "Swarmachines," in *#accelerate: The Accelerationist Reader*, ed. Robin Mackay and Armen Avanessian (Falmouth: Urbanomic, [1996] 2014), 328.
[47] Gary Smith and Alan Maki, *Death in the Jungle: Diary of a Navy Seal* (New York: Ivy Books, 1995).

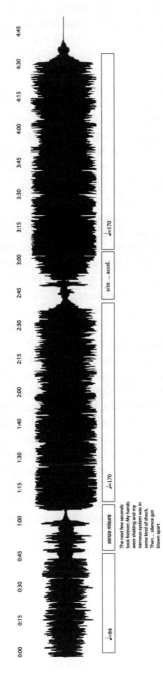

Example 7.9 Graph of "Masochist," Pendulum.

We can but speculate. However, what is sure is that masochism is not the whole story here. The book describes extremely cruel torture that borders on sadism, and to some extent, the music presented to us by Pendulum encapsulates both sadism and masochism in a more genuine way than we might expect and, in a more musically embodied way, with fewer lyrical cues than the tracks discussed above.

Looking at the annotated waveform diagram, we can see how the earliest part of the song is leisurely paced. We begin with piano and some light, gentle djembes beneath a spoken narrative that describes the sounds of the jungle. The samples, taken from a reading of the book, describe arriving from the boat and entering the jungle. "We cranked up the volume and marched to our own drummer" becomes the crucial line that directs tempo changes in the music. At this point, very early in the track, we hear mock "jungle drums" (or at least samples) that presents a rather more literal form of "Jungle" music than displayed in the sections that follow. At around 1:07, however, we drift into a timeless zone, marked *senza misura* on the graph, which employs a suspenseful augmented triad—like the opening of Hitchcock's *Vertigo* that we found sampled in Lady Gaga's "Born This Way." This accompanies the classic masochistic suspension of the accompanying words: "The next few seconds took forever." We can hear the aggression of a tiger's roar that punctuates the silence, and we get the feeling that this suspense, of not knowing where or when the next attack is coming from, is the suspended masochistic pleasure of the soldier.

But how do we figure that transition to the accelerative, sadistic passages, where the tiger's roar is sampled into a loud beat emphasizing thud that keeps repeatedly ripping away at us during the ultrafast drum and bass assault that follows at 1:07?

To be clear, we aren't going to seriously suggest that we are witnessing a single subject's point of view in this song, and that this point of view switches rapidly between acute masochism and acute sadism. This would be ridiculous. More likely, there is an inherent part of the love of the impending suspense that precedes that transforms into a hyperexaggerated pleasure in the adrenaline rush of a military offensive—even one against a tiger. We may even be witnessing the crossover between the masochistic love of danger from the soldier's perspective and the sadistic pattern of the tiger from its own perspective. While we would be technically wrong to call a tiger "sadistic," there is an element of the sadistic dream in the cold, apathetic purity of the feline nature. The sadist, remember, aims for a raw, brutal form of primal nature—not the beauty of the tropical jungle flowers, but the aggression of the tiger. While feline creatures are famous for playing with their food, bringing mice to the brink of death and leaving them as a performative gesture of approval for their "big Other" humans, this is unlikely a form of clinical sadism; however, enough of this idea survives in our human imaginations to associate the tiger with a wild, sadistic force of nature.

However we interpret this, we can at least talk of masochistic time and sadistic time in the track and explore the passage from one to the other within the music. The music, in this way, can also serve as a way of unpacking the passage from masochism to sadism that Deleuze does admit happens in rare cases, very less common than it was in Freud's limited conception.

Remember, Deleuze claimed that there is not an unavoidable transformation from one drive to the other—S and M are separate phenomena with their own economies. The only passage from one to the other is through a stage of "desexualization" and "resexualization"—a process Deleuze called "defusion." Earlier we likened this to a kind of "reboot" of the psyche, and this is what happens in the jungle track under discussion. At 1:00 we hear the augmented *Vertigo* motif disappear, and the track becomes a frozen jungle soundscape while we hear the words, "My hands were shaking and my nervous system was in some kind of shock. Then ... silence got blown apart." This brings in the eruption of the 170-bpm jungle beat, but it is notable for following a period of lyrical and musical "shock"—a completely "frozen" moment. We can surely imagine the moment in a Vietnam film when the music stops just before the tiger leaps out (it happens in *Apocalypse Now*); the subsequent gunfire becomes a raw expression of pure jouissance: a group of men—let's call them libertines, enacting the will of the big Other (justice, the state?)—firing their guns, well beyond all reason and necessity, into the unseen jungle. We find just such a moment in the first *Predator* film, where the platoon's display of acute profligacy with their ammunition in an attempt to "overkill" the predator is only matched by the director's desire to overspend his budget. But the point of this, when M transforms into S, is the shockforce of the reboot in-between these two scenarios. And the story continues.

At 2:00, we hear the augmented triad arpeggiations meandering through the complex of jungle/techno beats. There is a clear focus in the text on "discipline"— "noise discipline had to be maintained." But the crisp clarity of the speaking voice, with its wonderfully masochistic discipline of law, order, and decency begins to dissolve in time and pitch, as if the tape is being stretched, and it is then replaced by a wilder synthesizer solo. This is in some ways the height of sadistic escape from the law. The law returns again soon, however, as this solo and its entire texture collapses back into masochistic suspense at 2:40. This then begins to accelerate drastically back up to sadistic speed at 3:05, again adding a time/pitch distortion process to the voice of the law to eradicate it in favor of the chaos of the sadistic jungle.

This musical false passageway highlights one of the dangers that we face in this entire book—that music has no obligation to be loyal to the truth of the clinical situation. Worlds can be created that don't have to reflect our real situations. But this is also one of music's gifts, particularly for a discussion of sadism and masochism, which were both drawn from artistic expressions. While Masoch's art was extremely practicable in the way it laid out the conditions that he found in his own experiences, Sade used his entire imagination to create fantasies of things he might perhaps like to do in his ideal world beyond the law. Music serves as an ideal repository for these phantasmatic experiences and creates a rich counterpoint with reality. And, as we have found in every chapter of this book, the musical voice beneath the lyrics, as well as the very fabric of music's genres and practices, often shape, and distort the meanings that we can derive from them.

# 8

# Polly Jean Harvey Asks, "Is This Desire [Enough]?"

*While some have expressed the opinion that the many female characters who populate* Is This Desire? *represent different aspects of PJ's personality, proof of that theory remains a secret between the rather reticent songwriter and her therapist[1]*

## Summary: PJ Harvey's *Is This Desire?*

A fascinating aspect of the unconscious is that, however deeply we dig, there is always yet more mining to be done. Our reading of PJ Harvey's album *Is This Desire?* (1998) follows a fabulous Lacanian account of the album (with additional inspiration from Jean-Paul Sartre) by Lori Burns and Mélisse Lafrance in their book *Disruptive Divas: Feminism, Identity and Popular Music* (2001).[2] The authors evoke the Lacanian world of desire and its relations to the Other, focusing on the fundamental "lack" and "impossibility" that drive desire toward perpetual dissatisfaction. Lafrance describes the Lacanian-Sartrean axis of desire; Burns analyzes the musical detail, both fundamentally showing how desire accumulates, sustains, and fails to resolve. Essentially, this impossibility of desire's fulfillment is shown to be an aspect of micro detail throughout each song, each detail being an expression of a perhaps more rudimentary observation we might make, which is that all of the songs just kind of "stop"—each is left abruptly, without finding a place it can call home. As Lafrance notes, "Harvey challenges her listeners by refusing to resolve her songs, either musically or thematically."[3] This open-endedness, as both Burns and Lafrance forensically demonstrate, is distilled in each song of the album.

Of course, although, like ours, their chapter on PJ Harvey comes last in their book; theirs serves an introductory function to Lacanian desire as part of a much broader project of examining "disruptive divas"—Tori Amos, Courtney Love, Meshell Ndegeocello, Harvey—while ours is the final chapter of an exegesis of the Freudian-Lacanian unconscious. Thus, we are in the privileged (or otherwise) position of being

---

[1] "PJ Harvey—*Is This Desire?*—Classic Music Review," *altrockchick* (October 16, 2014). https://altrockchick.com/2014/10/16/classic-music-review-is-this-desire-by-pj-harvey/.
[2] Lori Burns and Mélisse Lafrance, *Disruptive Divas: Feminism, Identity, and Popular Music* (New York: Routledge, 2001).
[3] Ibid., 170.

able to delve further into the unconscious world of the album, with a body of additional concepts already unwrapped and ready for use at the conclusion of our book. While the theory we use in this chapter will not need reunpacking, we should make a few remarks by way of introduction to the album.

*Is This Desire?* is the fourth studio album by Harvey and marks one of the many changes in direction that have become her trademark.[4] As Lafrance puts it:

> While *Is this Desire?* turns away from more narrowly focused reflections on femininity, it expands the scope of Harvey's work to encompass issues related not only to women and their subjective and corporeal formation, but also to how heteronormative modalities of desire have both produced and relied upon an acutely cultural idea of "woman" and "man."[5]

The album is "peopled by a cast of women," with each song focusing on a unique female character, though with some male characters woven into their narratives.[6] Jennifer Rycenga writes that all twelve songs are "individual distillations of that moment in desire when something truly terrifying and/or truly exhilarating is about to happen."[7] A couple of songs have overt same-sex experiences, some less overtly gay or lesbian, and some heterosexual. Despite occasional cues, the highly empathetic songwriting makes the gender or sexuality of the singing persona difficult to discern. In any case ambiguity is an important dynamic,[8] and in some ways, this is the point we will be addressing. What is for certain, however, is that none of the relationships explored are 100 percent successful, certainly if we mark success as fulfilling of desire. And this is the point of Burns and Lafrance's line of enquiry, which we use as a starting point—desire cannot be fulfilled. However, we can certainly use this album and its microstories-in-music to examine the pitfalls that desiring couples seem to routinely fall into, and we have more than enough material in this album to look at some of the subterranean ways in which desire's impossibility cuts through a complex network of other (primarily Lacanian) concepts.

The first concept that we'd like to explore is the nature of the fundamental question that the album seeks to answer. Given that the whole edifice of Lacan's model of dialectical desire is framed around a question as we saw in Chapter 3, it will not be surprising that we return to this foundational question and see how the question PJ

---

[4] Harvey claimed: "When I'm working on a new record, the most important thing is to not repeat myself ... that's always my aim: to cover new ground and really to challenge myself. Because I'm in this for the learning." 50thirdand3rd, "Classic Music Review: *Is This Desire?* by PJ Harvey," Altrockchick, https://altrockchick.com/2014/10/.
[5] Burns and Lafrance, *Disruptive Divas*, 170.
[6] Ibid., 176.
[7] Jennifer Rycenga, "'It Tears My Heart Out Every Time!' PJ Harvey's *Is This Desire*," *GSLG Newsletter* 10, no. 1 (Spring 2000): 8–10.
[8] In "Catherine," for example, Lafrance reads the speaker as female, offering a lesbian perspective in that instance. We don't feel that things are this clear-cut here, but we certainly agree that it is a possibility, and as the reader will soon see, we figure this same Catherine figure, as she returns in a different song more decisively as a lesbian, albeit repressed.

Harvey poses is the same as Lacan's. We will also see how Harvey doesn't answer the question; she just purposefully reframes it.

The second angle we take is one of the central themes of the album, as outlined above—the cultural idea of "woman" and "man." We don't all live in a world of these binaries anymore in the twenty-first century (if we ever did), but it's worth remembering that pre-Lacanian psychoanalysis didn't even live in binaries; readers were assumed to be male; females were "other." Decentering Lacan's patriarchal language, Burns and Lafrance replace (in their own explanations) Lacan's "he/his" with "she/hers." This actually works well with much of Lacanian theory, for whom the Oedipus complex was universal, not, as in Freud, the dominant masculine mode, with the "negative" Oedipal attitude for girls, or, as Jung would theorize it—a little too symmetrically—the "Electra complex." But we can use this opportunity to reconsider the Lacanian theories of "sexuation" encountered in Chapter 4. What we'll find is that Lacan's "masculine" and "feminine" sexuations diverge more than ever from their "male" and "female" hosts, just as Lacan intended that they should. Furthermore, as we go through the songs, the "masculine" logic is always the problematic one (functionally and morally)—even when the tales are focused only on females, or even lesbian characters.

On the topic of the homosexual/queer inferences in the album, or at least the sense of gender and sexual fluidity, our third consideration is to tackle some of the perhaps more problematic ways in which homosexuality/queerness are portrayed by Harvey, ways symptomatic of psychoanalysis itself.[9] We examine the casually linked (not necessarily *causally* linked) concept of narcissism, which has long dogged cultural associations of "homosexuality," certainly in Freud's writings, and appears to pervade in some corners today.

Reigning ourselves back in to Burns and Lefrance's original premise—unsatisfiable desire—we reopen the case of *jouissance* for our fourth angle and examine three songs in which "joy" is portrayed, also looking, however, at how joy and "noise" intersect and how they scatter into drives.

## Che Vuoi? A Question to the Other

### "Is This Desire?"

We'll start with the last song on the album as this helps establish a key aspect of the album's entire "meaning." Coming right at the end, the song acts as what Lacan called a ***point de capiton***—a "quilting point" that fixes meaning (or seems to, at least) temporarily. It is the song in which Harvey asks the titular question: "Is this desire?" For Lacan, quilting points work retroactively. The meaning of a sentence isn't clear until we see the full stop. And even then, the next sentence can change the whole meaning radically. The final song now makes (more) sense of the full album's collection of songs.

[9] Although "queer" or "LGBTQ+" would be better terms for a contemporary reading, given the specific clinical usage of the term "homosexual" in our psychoanalytical references, even up to 2010, we retain it in our discussion.

We might also remember Lacan's *point de capiton* on a very granular level when we hear the word "enough" added to the end of the question, fundamentally transforming it into "Is this desire enough?" The question had seemed to be about whether the experiences concerned desire. Now, assuming that this *is* in fact desire, with that extra word, we now wonder "is it enough?" And there is still more to come. We might answer "enough for what?" And Harvey offers us more quilting points at the chorus's climax: "To lift us higher, to lift above?" But for us, this is not the whole story of the question; we need to know who it is addressed to. For that we need to listen more closely to the music.

Along with various other biblical figures that pepper the album, Joseph and Mary seem to be the main reference points in this final song, until we hear that Mary is in fact called "Dawn." Dawn, as Jennifer Rycenga rightly notes, is a form of the goddess Eos.[10] We might add, too, that Dawn held the key to the gates of heaven, which she unlocked each morning; she is also, therefore, a symbol of the endless repetition of the drive—the sun that rises in the morning only to set in the evening. When her name is evoked in the song, an organ accompanies the lines that allude to her "golden hair" (the symbol of feminine light). A lesser known fact about Dawn, however, is that she was sexually insatiable. Her appetite was a curse bestowed upon her by Aphrodite as punishment for sleeping with Aries. She therefore represents not only the interminable arousal of the sun but also the unrelenting arousal of desire. This all comes in the form of a curse, and a very human curse at that. And with Dawn's string of "unique" Greek figures who she took as lovers, we might recognize Lacan's feminine model of sexuation—she enjoys something about all of the individual members of the series; there is no imagined exception as in male-sexuated logic; there is no "one" who can break the spell. Through a twist of fate, though, the Joseph character is feeling particularly content—"I feel like a King," he declares, thus aligning himself, perversely perhaps, with the Freudian Father of *Totem and Taboo*—the imagined exception to the series of male sexuation, the guy who gets to enjoy everything. But (and it's a big but) Joseph and Mary are the most famously asexual couple in Christendom. Their very act of celibacy is the reason for the birth of Christ. And yet here they are: Mary now transformed into a frustrated nymphomaniac, asking Joseph whether their desire is enough to allow them to transcend. There must be more going on here.

For all the erotic words, the song is detumescent in the main. There are touches of desire emanating from the bare-blues guitar, and the cheeky emphasis on the "blue notes" offers a kind of flirtatious twinkling of the eye. In fact, the whole modern-blues aesthetic puts us in this heated libidinal sun, the bareness of the lone guitar accompaniment showing us the incompleteness of the singers who yearn to fill themselves with each other's desire. But it's a low level of tension. The song opens with the quietest possible sound of machine noise, before dirty drums and acapella singers enter the field. Before long we also muse on images of desire as a thermodynamic system: "The sunset went down and coldness cooled their desire." Dawn replies, "Let's build a fire," as a fairly direct attempt to reignite it, emphasized by the chugging guitar entry and bare drum track. Of course, this is a *thermodynamic* system (more

---

[10] Rycenga, "It Tears My Heart Out Every Time!" 8–10.

like the one that will begin Lyotard's "Libidinal Economy"), rather than a Freudian *hydraulic* one, where the libido flows from person to person, object to object, chamber to chamber; thermodynamics overlap with hydraulics, but concern *heat*. For us, the song's low-level tension, caught between hot and cold desire, is a reflection on how the state of desire is an untenable and unpleasant one; it is an arousal of an amount of tension that needs to be drained. Freud's "Nirvana principle" (the plane of consistency from Chapter 1) was a state of "zero" arousal, which is the only really satisfactory state to be in. The characters here want to escape this low level, however, and want to transcend and escape from the eternal repetition of the heating and cooling of desire. Neither is fulfilled, even through their nonfulfillment.

There are further musical cues that the couple desire to transcend and escape desire, even while questioning their very existence within it. As Harvey sings "Is this desire enough?" the guitar effects include long slides upward and downward (think of the "Beetlebum" slides by Blur), showing the musical aspiration to rise out of the earthy blues that keeps us tethered to despair. Like this gesture, Harvey also sings high notes at these stages of the song. However, within both musical versions of this attempted ascension, there is a clear fragility, both in her voice as it ascends and in the faltering, inaccurate guitar beneath.

In the text, Harvey describes the characters standing between two worlds before Joseph asks "is this desire enough?":

Hour-long, by hour, may we two stand
When we're dead, between these lands

The characters' *ennui* may be symptomatic of them being trapped in the zone between the two deaths—as Mother and Father of Christ, they are not allowed to Symbolically die, and Mary is to become a mediator between humans and the divine. There is a long, pregnant musical pause before the final chorus, which almost implies that the characters do not believe that their desire is enough. And the music gives the answer that the words can't find. The song, when it does end, ends abruptly. So, no.

OK, so who is the song's (and the album's) central question addressing? Are Mary and Joseph addressing each other? Sure, but there's more to it than that, because neither has the answer. Is Harvey addressing us? Of course, but we don't have the answer either. Nor are we supposed to answer. The question, like all questions to the big Other, is essentially rhetorical. The question seems to us to represent the fundamental address to the Big Other that aims to provoke an impossible answer. Consider how Žižek begins his essay on "Robert Schumann: The Romantic Anti-Humanist":

> What is music at its most elementary? An act of *supplication*: a call to a figure of the big Other (beloved Lady, King, God …) to respond, not as the symbolic big Other, but in the real of his or her being (breaking his own rules by showing mercy; conferring her contingent love on us …). Music is thus an attempt to provoke the "answer of the Real": to give rise in the Other to the miracle of which Lacan speaks apropos of love, the miracle of the Other stretching his or her hand out to me. The historical changes in the status of big Other … thus directly

concern music—perhaps, musical modernity designates the moment when music renounces the endeavour to provoke the answer of the Other.[11]

Remember that Lacan's fundamental question, asked by the neurotic (normal) subject, is: "What does the Other want from me?" But the neurotic (normal) subject fails to find the answer, because while they address the question symbolically, they want the answer to appear in the Real, which is impossible. Perhaps, then, "Is this desire enough?" asks a fundamental question that music itself is asking, one to which an answer cannot be forthcoming.

## Sexuation and the Nonsexual Relationship

Remember that "Is This Desire?" is the last song on the album. If we listen to the songs preceding it, we will doubtlessly come to the conclusion early on that desire is probably not enough for whatever is acting as the measure of success. All of the songs portray a human couple, sometimes heterosexual, sometimes with less clear genders or intimations of same sex, but all with essentially dysfunctional relationships. Even when characters are alone, they seem to be in a dysfunctional relationship with themselves, or with an image of themselves. And what we find in each case is that, whatever the actual genders of each relationship, the feminine desire that seems to function as a frame for the entire album is undone at micro level by an injection of masculine desire, which is more problematic because its ruling factors are envy of an imaginary "exception" to the Symbolic order, with a paradoxical blind faith in that same order. There are often lesbian allusions, and the album does not offer a "third" choice for sexuated desire, but rather draws in different and shifting amalgams of masculine and feminine sexuation, which help deconstruct the Lacanian binary rather more powerfully than in the basic way we demonstrated in Chapter 4, where we saw men adopting female sexuation and women adopting male sexuation. Here, Harvey paints a much richer picture of integration of both logics into more fluid scenarios, though, as we will see, the masculine logic is always a spanner in the works that seems to represent the entire human tragedy and the failure of the entire sexual relationship. One seemingly obvious answer to Lacan's binary logic of sexuation, which always yields failure of a sexual relationship, would be that homosexual relationships should work perfectly. The fact that such relationships can be just as fraught as heterosexual ones might seem to prove Lacan wrong, unless we take him at his word and see these two logics as dual structures that tend to form between two people of any gender and that prevent success. Let's first think about the frame of the album.

In the main, each song focuses on a female character who is essentially beautified by being held in the zone between two deaths.[12] As Lacan says, these fantasy female

---

[11] Žižek, *The Plague of Fantasies*, 245.
[12] See Lacan's work on Antigone, particularly "Antigone between Two Deaths," 270–90, in Lacan, *The Ethics of Psychoanalysis*, 212.

figures fascinate us, not only on account of the cinematic "male gaze" but also on account of their pity-inducing beauty within limbo. The list of limbo-locked women, given from Harvey's bird's-eye view, shows that each character—Dawn, Angelene, Catherine de Barra, Catherine, Leah, Elise—is just another character in the series, but each is unique (even the Mary-cum-Dawn character in the final summatory song). There is no exception to this series of female characters. And one thing that is clearly not exceptional about them is that they each suffer a condition of near fulfillment. This is a perfectly Lacanian feminine frame. If we took many of the lyrics of the album in isolation, we might imagine a series of pale pre-Raphaelite wraiths, engulfed in a fairy-tale world of forests, castles, and poetry, but the music adds a darkly gothic Poe-esque tinge to every song. We'll zoom in on examples as we progress, but, in general terms, the music's languorous, lugubrious nature vouchsafes an air of acceptance that these women have for their lot; each acknowledges that they are one of a series of unique beings, "without exception" as Lacan would say. And yet, the musical atmosphere of malaise and melancholy that hangs about their situations is always shown to stem from a failed attempt to integrate masculine logic into this world, a masculine logic that emanates either from the women themselves or from their partners (be they male or female). Let's take a couple of examples of songs in which, despite the macro-level feminine logic, the masculine force emerges as a disruptor, to be lamented, on the micro level.

## "Angelene"

This tale is imaginatively reimagined from the title of a J. D. Salinger short story, "Pretty Mouth and Green My Eyes," a story of ambiguous infidelity. Salinger's tale is quite a dispassionate and tawdry tale that describes a marriage breakdown.[13] Here, in Harvey's hands, the phrase becomes attached to a prostitute who describes accepting any man who offers her money while harboring the hope that there is someone special just around the corner who will save her. Lafrance concentrated on the open road and the lateral movement that symbolizes the unending process of desire. There is obviously this dimension, but for us, the whole "open road" aspect is infused with masculine-sexuated logic.

The first lines are accompanied by that dull, lazy, casual, empty sound of chugging minor-key guitar that lies at the heart of the album's sense of misery. The bass and drums play the bare minimum, giving a sense of fatigue and despondency. The atmosphere also rings of Nick Cave's "And no more shall we part" on account of its gentle but constant piano chords as if the pianist is falling asleep with each flop of his/her hand on the keys and waking her/himself up with surprise by the resulting sound. Everything described in the text is also mundane—"My first name Angelene / Prettiest mess you've ever seen." And every melodic line is basically the same for a while as she describes the

---

[13] In a nutshell, in Salinger's story, a guy rings his friend to complain that his wife is missing; a woman resembling the missing wife is actually with the friend who offers consolation on the phone.

men who she will work for ("any man [who] calls"). So far, she is drowned in feminine sexuation in regard to these men—every guy is the same, and so is she.

However—and here is the tragedy—she suddenly betrays a more deep-seated masculine logic, with the crucial line of Lacanian masculine exception: "But there'll be one" upon whom she pins all of her hopes. Her imagined exception will be a shining knight who will save her soul. We are also told that he will come from two thousand miles away. It's not difficult to read "2000 miles away" as "2000 years ago" and see the figure of Christ as this exception. This may also explain the sudden twist to the major and the sustained heavenly organ that enters. Is it possible, then, that Jesus himself is figured here as Freud's primeval father of *Totem and Taboo*—the exception to all mankind, the one that gets full enjoyment, who we kill and then feel guilty about and are therefore stopped from enjoying our lives? This is not far at all from Freud's original text, *Totem and Taboo*, that also considers the formation of early religion in its broader anthropological project, though he stops short of equating the "Father" with Christ (the son).

The energetic section of "hope," brought about from the image of the open road, and the pseudo-religious salvation collapse back into lifeless misery, though the organ is retained, now portraying more like the grim reality—offering a kind of Doors-esque "comedown" from a psychedelic trip. All becomes subdued again and we realize the improbability of things getting better any time soon, notwithstanding the hope-beyond-hope of an "exception." The name "Angelene" has the heavenly pretension and will become a link with another song on the album, "No Girl So Sweet," who suffers the similar problem of being viewed as an angel by her (masculinity fueled) lover.

### "No Girl So Sweet"

Notwithstanding its twee title, this is one of the edgiest songs on the album. A drum machine opens, offering up the impression of a four-to-the-floor EDM track. But the heavily distorted, angry blues singing makes for a very different aesthetic that depicts a far from healthy relationship despite the overtly romantic thrust of some of the lyrics ("took her from heaven and gave her to me"). The couple in this song seem to be heterosexual, and both have adopted their respective sense of sexuated logic—a rare coincidence in the album. They are also dysfunctional; without it being explicitly stated, he appears to be impotent toward her; she appears to be desperate for love and intimacy. She is "the girl with the sad eyes," who keeps asking "him" a question over and over again." And the questions she asks are all essentially forms of "Che vuoi?"—"What do you want from me?" She asks first: "Was I too weak?" Then "Was I a child?" "How much more can you take from me?" She is desperate—"I'd like to take you inside my head / I'd like to take you inside of me," confirming that the couple are not sexually engaged as yet. The heavy octaves here underscore her desires while showing the lack of fulfillment (there are no other tones to complete the chords). And impotent to offer any kind of answer (remember the Other can't actually tell us what S/He actually wants), he remains mute, or rather he cannot answer, but gives her the line, "You came from heaven." In this line he expresses the idea of her as the exception that has fueled him in the search for love. In the subsequent scene, she lies in the back of his car, with him being unable to touch her; he can only drive. She is presumably not actually from heaven (we suspect), but he thinks of her as such and places her on a pedestal, which actually renders her beyond his reach, or rather renders himself beyond the ability to reach her.

There is a deep irony here. As Žižek reminded us in the case of Sartre and de Beauvoir, the idea that a couple regard each other as the "exception" to everyone else was the justification for open marriage. "It's ok to have affairs," a lover might say, "as long as we know that *you* are the really special one." And yet, here we find the situation in which the exception is the one who escapes the series and prevents the relationship from functioning as it should. The response might come with something like, "You are so exceptional to me, that I can't see how to love you or desire you enough."

The male protagonist does declare "I love you," but this is almost entirely obliterated by high, distorted singing, as if either it is a repressed sentiment that is unconscious but inarticulable, or perhaps it is sayable but the musical unconscious undermines or at least distorts the meaning. Perhaps the "I love you" has become one of those meaningless statements that excuses all sins, like the central character of Richard Harris's play *Outside Edge*, who upsets his wife time and again, with the robotic *ex post facto* justification of "love you, fair enough? Ok?" Either way, it is clear that, just as we can't hear his answer to her perennial question ("What do you want from me?"), neither can she.

### "My Beautiful Leah"

"Beautiful Leah" is only clearly referred to in the title. Like several other songs on the album, her name, when mentioned, is distorted beyond recognition, as if the protagonist has repressed the word. The lover here is looking for her/his partner who has left in search of "it"—presumably love and fulfillment, which have otherwise been denied. The lover tragically confesses that "she said 'I have no one' even as I held her." The musical distortion here is almost overbearing, particularly in a high-bass instrument that seems to float in and out of phase with the heavier percussive rhythms. Just as the lover has failed to contain her/his partner to the extent that she has left in search of better luck, so the two streams of musical time are pulling against each other in the texture. Their incompatibility is also revealed in the quality of the voices deployed by Harvey. As s/he tries to remember her last words, a high feminine voice is double-tracked in the background, indicating the words kept alive in memory, reverberating in the present. In fact, the high female voice also sings "Late September, October, November, December," becoming more distant and disembodied as the memory fades each month. This also indicates the obsessive repetition of the lover who continues to punish her/himself over and over again, trying in vain to master the "death-drive." Perhaps, this also explains the incessant plodding rhythm, as s/he drags her/his feet from place to place in a futile search for something that will never return. The "out of sync" distorted bass also sometimes drives the vocal melody and sometimes falls behind it, begging the question of whether it is in control or being controlled. The answer, of course, is that the death-drive is both—it is here found at the steering wheel, but it plays itself out in the repeated actions performed by the host subject.

And repetition is central to the missing female's actions. It seems as though she has had several throws of the dice in the past and has never been happy: "If I don't find it this time, then I'm better off dead," she declared. And she has thus been structuring her happiness around a masculine logic of dream fulfillment in some exception to the series of experiences she has had thus far. This is never possible, hence the words "better off dead" that end the song abruptly, showing that the searching lover is in fear for her life. S/he knows that this form of logic does not bring fulfillment, and s/he searches for her with an unspoken expectation of hearing the news of her being found dead, rather than alive and fulfilled.

### "Catherine"

Whatever the gender of PJ Harvey's protagonist in this song, s/he is in love with someone named Catherine de Barra. Given the allusions at other points in the album to St. Catherine ("of the wheel"), we might consider a religious element to the romance. Lafrance proposes that Catherine may live alone on the isle of Barra, in the southern Hebrides. This is a very picturesque idea, perfectly compatible with the windy solitude described, but so is the idea of St. Catherine of Alexandria as venerated in isolated corners such as the popular pilgrimage site "Catherine's Hill" in Hampshire. We might also remember St. Catherine's mystical marriage to Christ, a possible explanation for the unattainability of PJ Harvey's Catherine.

The singing protagonist is clearly governed by masculine-sexuated desire; s/he is fueled by envy of the other who gets to enjoy Catherine (Christ?)—"I envy to murderous envy your lover." Catherine herself does not have a voice, and we don't know what motivates her, although we learn from the singer that Catherine's *jouissance* is scattered around her possessions that themselves act as fetishes for the singer. S/he envies the road Catherine walks on; s/he envies the pillow her head rests on; s/he envies the wind that blows through Catherine's hair. We haven't discussed fetishes much in this book, but these images are all substitutes for Catherine herself. For Freud, a fetish was an object that a male (almost exclusively) focuses on as a substitute for his mother's lack of a penis. In Lacan, things were a little different, where the penis isn't the important thing; the important thing is the "phallus"—the symbol erected to stand in place of our collective lack. In fact, for Lacan, the penis itself was a fetish for heterosexual women, standing in for the phallus. This also radically brought into question the whole perversion of fetishism, which, for Freud, had been far more prevalent in men; now the reverse was the case for Lacan. In essence, though, these items—including the lover himself, the last on the list of envied objects—are all the images of the little piece of Catherine that lie outside of the phallic function. Catherine's desire is feminine; the rejected singer's desire is masculine.

Musically this is all sung in Harvey's trademark blues-inflected melodic strains, with some quirky harmonic progressions emphasizing the twisted nature of the desire at play. The song also sounds as if it has been produced under water—perhaps making us feel somewhat uncanny—is this a demo? Am I listening to a bootleg? However, as the song draws to a close, an organ enters, and the melody becomes pure and liturgical, its descending lines creating the sensation that we are bowing down in reverence to [St.?] Catherine's beauty, looking at an icon: "For your eyes smilin', for your mouth singin'." But this music, albeit in a major key now, also adds a kind of funereal flavor, accompanying the words "in time I'd have won you," when we reflect on what might have been, with a clear implication of self-delusion. Again, this is all masculine-sexuated desire—Catherine is "the one"; she is placed on a pedestal (rather than her more readily associated *wheel*) and can't be approached in reality, only in a subjunctive memory of the future.

## Homosexuality, Narcissism, and Death-Drive: "The Wind" and "The Garden"

Finnish singer-songwriter Jukka Takalo titled one of his songs "Everyone's a Little Bit Gay" ("Jokainen on vähän homo," 2010), which was recently analyzed as a milestone in recent LGBTQ activism by Susanna Välimäki.[14] The song could be a reflection on one of the few Freudian ideas about "homosexuality" that could still resonate with the modern world. Freud claimed:

> In addition to their manifest heterosexuality, a very considerable measure of latent or unconscious homosexuality can be detected in all normal people. If these findings are taken into account, then, to be sure, the supposition that nature in a freakish mood created a "third sex" falls to the ground.[15]

From a Lacanian perspective, the idea of there being something gay about all of us would be structured as a feminine-sexuated piece of logic; the "homosexual" is not some imagined "exception" to sexual norms. The feminine logic of universal incompletion is what permeates Harvey's entire album, hindered only by the lingering vestiges of the masculine logic of the envied exception. The lines quoted above from Freud's essay, "The Psychogenesis of a Case of Homosexuality in a Woman," might elicit applause and cries of "Right on!" but his other views in this essay do not stand up to modern scrutiny, all being very much reflective of their time. In fact, Ronnie Lesser, in *That Obscure Subject of Desire Freud's Female Homosexual Revisited*, frames Freud's essay as the work of a Freud who was backtracking on his originally more liberal position in the 1905 *Three Essays on Sexuality*. The psychoanalytic tradition was certainly no kinder to "homosexuals" in the twentieth century than other social institutions, with a surprisingly late milestones being 1992, when the World Health Organization changed

---

[14] "'Everyone Is a Little Bit Gay': LGBTIQ Activism in Finnish Pop Music of the 21st Century," in *Popular Musicology and Identity: Essays in Honour of Stan Hawkins*, ed. Kai Arne Hansen, Eirik Askerøi, and Freya Jarman (Oxon: Routledge, 2020), 97–116.
[15] See Freud's "The Psychogenesis of a Case of Homosexuality in a Woman," in *That Obscure Subject of Desire Freud's Female Homosexual Revisited*, ed. Ronnie C. Lesser and Erica Schoenberg (New York: Routledge, [1920] 1999), 31.

its International Classification of Diseases to remove homosexuality.[16] But going back to Freud, we might ask, "Was Freud a positive force or a negative one for our understanding of 'homosexuality'?" This is a vexed question. Dreschner summarizes:

> Freud was tolerant for his time. He signed a 1930 petition to decriminalize homosexuality. Yet, although he did not consider homosexuality an illness, his theory did not quite constitute a clean bill of health—calling someone immature, rather than sick, is not as offensive, but neither appellation is particularly respectful.[17]

As we will see, some of Freud's views attempted to explain truisms of the time that we can no longer accept, one of which is highly relevant to this discussion: the "link" between narcissism and "homosexuality." We will explore this in depth as a kind of cautionary tale, and perhaps along the way we can replace some faulty Freudian footholds. Let's look at two of Harvey's songs— "The Wind" and "The Garden."

Jennifer Rycenga likens the two songs that feature Catherine to the "Kathryn" from K. D. Lang's "The Mind of Love" (*Ingénue*, 1992), thus deducing a "lesbian (sub)text." For us the subtext is certainly there for Catherine in the final lines of the song "The Wind." In this song, someone sings of a [St.?] Catherine who lives the life of a recluse. In the final lines, the singer suggests finding a husband for Catherine, to which we hear a whispered "shhh." Indeed, Harvey emphasizes the soft but penetrating "shhh" sound throughout the song (on words like "wash") as if there is a subliminal injunction to keep some sort of unspoken secret. Sure, Catherine may just prefer a life of solitude; in many ways she is spoken about with the reverence of Tennyson's "Lady of Shalott," who is condemned to live in a tower and never look out of the window. But the implication is that she is a lesbian, remaining outside of society, through either repression—that is, the inability to "come out"—or some other unknown reason, such as a vow of solitude and silence. But there are other associations woven into the song that problematize this portrayal somewhat. There are further references in the lyrics to torture: "She dreamt of children's voices and torture on the wheel." The first image may well represent a (perfectly healthy) yearning to bear children, but added to that image of torture, the children's voices adopt a more perverse, sadistic tone (given the association of "Catherine of the wheel," Catherine is more likely the tortured than the torturer). Perhaps it takes us from the "Lady of Shalott" to the castle of Gilles de Rais. This is a highly ambiguous image however, and we wouldn't want to suggest with any force that Harvey was associating "homosexuality" with perversion in the song, as Freud perhaps might have done in his own time. Our target is rather the association, played out elsewhere too, of homosexuality with narcissism, which is perhaps more subtle, but also more insidious. We are told that Catherine has built a chapel "with her own

---

[16] For a full history of psychoanalytic attitudes to homosexuality, see Jack Drescher, "A History of Homosexuality and Organized Psychoanalysis," *Journal of the American Academy of Psychoanalysis & Dynamic Psychiatry* 36 (2008): 443–60.
[17] Ibid., 446.

image on the wall," thus adding a clearly narcissistic component. We may well have images of the queen from Snow White ("Mirror, mirror on the wall …"), someone sinister, and possibly evil, but certainly in love with their image. It may even be that this love of the self is meant to be taken as synecdochical for "homosexuality" in the song. Let's explore this problematic possibility in the music.

The first verse, which sets the gothic scene of Catherine living on a high place, is whispered only. From the start, there is a sinister atmosphere, but one with a tongue-in-cheek "James Bond" musical topic creeping in. The song opens with one of those classic, jarring minor chords with a major seventh (think of the dissonant chord that ends the "007" theme), and part of the harmonic groove features the slow chromatic rise that also drives the "007" (then in E minor). Once the first verse and refrain are done, Harvey sings in full voice, high up in the register, seducing us with her lethargic, bluesy, chromatic melody like a siren. In the music video, this creates a doubly uncanny effect. We see Harvey lip-syncing, but we don't know whether she is syncing the whispering voice or the singing voice. The uncanniness is compounded further by the inclusion of a Doppelgänger. Harvey's urban video has focused our gaze on her walking around or being driven while she sings/whispers her story. Suddenly, however, the girl in the white fur coat is suddenly a different young woman, similar in appearance and identical in dress. The startling effect can only really refer to the axis between (i) the narcissistic aspect of the song and (ii) the lesbian subtext. Remembering Žižek's discussion of the object *a* as residing in the phantasy space between two articulations of the melodic line in Schumann (voice and piano), here rendered as the whisper and the singing, we now find two-people-in-one uttering them both, both objects of each other's lesbian gaze.

As Elizabeth Lunbeck puts it in "The Narcissistic Homosexual: Genealogy of a Myth":

> No one was more guilty of self-love in the minds of the first psychoanalysts than the homosexual, and narcissism was in consequence from the moment of its analytic debut until well into the 1970s inextricably intertwined with homosexuality.[18]

It might seem from Harvey's song that the associations pervade pop culture even today. In 2010, psychotherapist Gidi Rubinstein conducted a study that attempted to prove the link, concluding that

> the hypothesis, which is based on the Freudian connection between narcissism and homosexuality, is supported by the results, indicating that the homosexual students score higher in both measures of narcissism and lower on the self-esteem measure, compared to their heterosexual counterparts.[19]

---

[18] Elizabeth Lunbeck, "The Narcissistic Homosexual: Genealogy of a Myth," in *History and Psyche Culture, Psychoanalysis, and the Past*, ed. Sally Alexander and Barbara Taylor (New York: Palgrave, 2012), 49–70 (49).

[19] G. Rubinstein, "Narcissism and Self-Esteem among Homosexual and Heterosexual Male Students," *Journal of Sex and Marital Therapy* 36, no. 1 (2010): 24–34.

But his study was heavily criticized by Jack Drescher, who goes on to reflect on the study's "poor experimental design," showing also that narcissism is an extremely multivalent concept, which is reduced by Rubinstein beyond value:

> Consequently, the assertion of a linkage between homosexuality and narcissism is gratuitous and meaningless. To quote Gertrude Stein, "There is no there there."[20]

Freud's views of narcissism in connection with homosexuality were, however, quite fascinating in quite another sense in that he seems to convey a narcissistic moment as a kind of passageway to object choice. In "The Psychogenesis of a Case of Homosexuality in a Woman," Freud describes how:

> It is by no means rare for a love relation to be broken off by means of a process of identification on the part of the lover with the loved object, a process equivalent to a kind of regression to narcissism. After this has been accomplished, it is easy in making a fresh choice of object to direct the libido to a member of the sex opposite to that of the earlier choice.[21]

Freud posits this as hope of a "cure" for homosexuality, akin perhaps to so-called conversion therapy. Freud had been approached by the family of a girl who they wished to "cure." Freud insisted that a cure was not a likely outcome, but he agreed to analyze her and make further recommendations for treatment if he thought there was a possibility. In Freud's report, he posited narcissism at a key moment preceding object choice—allowing previous object choices to be undone (here in the clear "hope" that new object choice would be heterosexual). The idea of narcissism being a door to another object choice, and perhaps even another sexual position (a door that presumably opens both ways), is a concern of "The Garden"—a kind of partner song to "The Wind." Discussing this song, *Altrockchick* declares:

> Now we're looking at the possibility that the man was meeting with his Jungian shadow, the part of the self that is repressed ... making this a marvelously constructed tale of repressed desire. When PJ is on her game, her lyrics are akin to the experience of walking past the mirrors of the fun house—there are multiple interpretations possible, depending on your perspective. People who detest ambiguity will feel uncomfortable with such a poet, but I find PJ's work endlessly fascinating.[22]

Musing upon this song, Rycegna wonders whether it was "reinscribing antigay tropes by invoking sin, loneliness, and illicit temptation."[23] She redeems it, however, partly

---

[20] Jack Drescher, "There Is No There There: A Discussion of 'Narcissism and Self-Esteem among Homosexual and Heterosexual Male Students,'" *Journal of Sex & Marital Therapy* 36, no. 1 (2010): 38–47 (44).
[21] See Freud's "The Psychogenesis of a Case of Homosexuality in a Woman," 32.
[22] See note 1, above.
[23] Rycenga, "It Tears My Heart Out Every Time!" 9.

on account of its timbral richness, which offers a richer portrayal of sexuality. We might, though, reconsider again in light of the narcissistic association. The problematic Freudian relationship between narcissism and homosexuality is explored more explicitly in the only song focused solely on a male protagonist. This itself, given the album's focus on female vignettes in these songs, suggests yet another problematic aspect of Freud's theory of "homosexuality"—the association between homosexuality and gender characteristics of the opposite gender. Is this lone male protagonist included in the cycle because he is "homosexual," and therefore effeminate? In 1905, Freud, perhaps more "radically" than he would be in 1920,[24] suggested that there was no necessary connection between a person's gender and their sexual objects. The later Freud backed down from this and suggested, basically, that lesbians had masculine traits while gay men were effeminate. In truth, Freud kind of just gave up on the question: "It is not for psychoanalysis to solve the problem of homosexuality,"[25] a "problem" that he wanted to leave to the biologists.

> But psychoanalysis cannot elucidate the intrinsic nature of what in conventional or in biological phraseology is termed "masculine" and "feminine"; it simply takes over the two concepts and makes them the foundation of its work. When we attempt to reduce them further, we find masculinity vanishing into activity and femininity into passivity, and that does not tell us enough.

It is worth recalling, on the topic of masculine "homosexuality," that Freud posited an identification not only with the narcissistic self but also with the identification (rather than Oedipal love) for the mother. As Elizabeth Lunbeck reminds us, pertaining to Freud's essay "Leonardo":

> Recall that for the Freud of *Leonardo*, the boy becomes a homosexual in repressing his love of his mother and then identifying with her—putting "himself in her place"—and in taking "his own person as a model in whose likeness he chooses the new objects of his love."[26]

And this is how the central man of "The Garden" is framed. In many ways, the theme of this song is the Doppelgänger. We might recall Schubert's setting of Heinrich Heine's "Der Doppelgänger" (1827). In Schubert's hypermasculine setting, the former lover is established as "she" early on. The low partial triads, though ambiguous, are full of gravitas and solemnity as befits the occasion. The bass voice, intoning the melody like a tolling funeral bell, summons up the dark streets described in Heine's text and also offers a clear sign that this is a heterosexual experience. And the specular image the character sees, himself, is his Doppelgänger who leads to death, or at least to the death of love. PJ Harvey subverts this doubly, as we will see.

---

[24] Lesser and Schoenberg, *That Obscure Subject of Desire*, 7.
[25] Ibid., 31.
[26] Lunbeck, "The Narcissistic Homosexual," 49–70, 59.

Firstly, in this song, the character is wandering around a garden—instantly playing on the effeminate images of flowers and trees. The female voice too (high up, unlike some of Harvey's more masculine voices deployed in the album) adds to this. But the Doppelgänger does not just represent any kind of "Jungian shadow" (which basically equates to Freud's unconscious), but a clear narcissistic image that stimulates queer desire. From the start of the song, as Harvey narrates the situation, it is clear that the lone male who strolls the garden, inspired by his songbird (also male), is not alone. The deep, fat, distorted bass lazily trails Harvey's melodic line, indicating some kind of shadow or mirror image. In the second stanza, the full accompaniment of smokey lounge piano and sleazy night-club electric organ suffuse the whole atmosphere and submerge us into a fantasy space, as the character meets his Doppelgänger:

There inside the garden came another with his lips
Said, "Won't you come and be my lover? Let me give you a little kiss"

Subverting legend, wherein the meeting of one's Doppelgänger leads to death, this leads to sexual experience, though we are constantly reminded that "there was trouble taking place."

And at this sexual moment, almost every musical feature splits into its double. The piano melody is heavily delayed—syncopated as an echo between the beats. The vocal rise and fall is immediately repeated at a different pace (musicians would say it's "augmented"—stretched out in time: see Example 8.1). This all gives the impression that the self is breaking off into two separate parts, refracted narcissistically into a projected other.[27] This becomes clear in the lyrics when the protagonist realizes that he is alone, and "they kissed, and the sun rose and he walked a little further, and he found he was alone." A shouting voice that appears for a brief moment dissipates, and a few moments later, after his realization of being alone, the piano's Doppelgänger riff drops out. The scene becomes a kind of version of "La Belle Dame Sans Merci" with the lover left alone "on the cold hillside" after his fantasy of love, except that it seems clear that man is in love with his own image projection. Or, perhaps, the experience leaves him feeling as though it had been his own image, almost as if he is repressing his nature and fitting it into a Freudian category—"I'm gay?, no I'm probably just a narcissist?"

As Rycenga argues, due to Harvey's attempt to reimagine biblical themes, the garden depicted here, if not the garden of Eden, represents rather Gethsemane, where the disciples were gathered for the last supper, and where Judas betrayed Jesus (and himself) with a kiss, which now also serves as a kind of homoerotic turning point for Christian history.[28] The betrayal is now the unnamed "trouble" that takes place. This reference to Christ also takes us back to something we discussed before: the primeval father who is killed out of envy by all of the sons, who then cannot enjoy their new

---

[27] Burns notes this musical portrayal of Other too: "The lyrical Other is musically represented by the keyboard sound": Burns and Lafrance, *Disruptive Divas,* 197.
[28] Rycenga, "It Tears My Heart out Every Time!" 8–10.

**Example 8.1** Augmented "splitting" of the narcissistic vocal motif.

**Example 8.2** Album cover for PJ Harvey's *Is This Desire?*

freedom because of their collective guilt. Here, in Harvey's hands, this is combined with a more explicit double transgression—"homosexual" and narcissistic, both punishable in the fabula of the song and, taken together with "The Wind," possibly within the whole album's sexual tapestry. Framed within a feminine-sexuated desire, the masculine-sexuated micro-economy is punished. In essence, we might return to the album's cover—a double image of Harvey, asymmetrically split along a fault-line— one light, one dark (Example 8.2).

The verdict? We need to be careful not to wag our fingers too vigorously at PJ Harvey. In addition to making these two songs the most instrumentally lush, she also chooses the two songs about nature—"The Wind" and "The Garden"—to explore "homosexual" themes. She isn't suggesting that anything should be repressed or, following early psychoanalytic theory, that "homosexuality" was some kind of pathology. It's part of human nature. The album is far from any form of reactionary statement; rather, it's a moment to reflect on some of the problems inherent to psychoanalytic tradition, problems that also pervade almost any artwork, even in the ones that, on balance, do far more good than harm. Remember that the album is framed by the more open-minded and laudable feminine-sexuated logic, by which there is no imagined sexual or racial "other" (in the sense in which Edward Said used the term rather than Lacan) that the subject needs to pit themselves against (as in masculine-sexuated logic); there is a little pocket of "otherness" in all of the characters (and us), and this is to be accepted, normalized, and celebrated. If she fails to pick apart every outdated stereotype, let's be grateful for the overall celebration of sexual difference, acknowledge the remaining challenges, and be aware of them when we examine ourselves (in the mirror?).

## *Jouissance* and Its Impossibilities

### "Joy"

The song "Joy" seems to have been inspired by Flannery O'Connor's short story, "Good Country People" (1955), acting as a kind of comment on the central character, Joy, a young woman with a prosthetic leg and a philosophy doctorate. Joy is a confirmed atheist and attempts to seduce a bible salesman (who her family regard as one of the "good country people") in an act of protest against her family's conservatism. The salesman's "bible" is actually hollowed out, to stash his condoms, whiskey, and "nudie deck," and when Joy won't have sex with him in the barn, he steals her prosthetic leg and makes off. The tale is hardly one of joy; rather, it's a mixture of horrific extremes— the dream of biblical perfection versus nihilistic perversion.

*Jouissance*, in Lacanian theory, as discussed already, is the name for the otherwise unnamable intensity of pleasure experienced as pain. In the story, Joy herself changes her name to "Hulga" because it is the ugliest name she can think of and wants to spite her mother, creating an amalgam of ingredients of Lacanian *jouissance*. There are many perverse psychological angles to the story, not least the perversion of Joy herself, who only wants to have sex with the salesman on the condition that he doesn't really want to have it with her (like a sadist?). When he does want it, as it transpires, she refuses. But in PJ Harvey's hands, the pain of *jouissance* is rendered musically in some very clear ways.

One aspect of *jouissance* is captured by the use of "noise." Scott Wilson has written extensively about noise music from a Lacanian perspective, using it as a linchpin in his framing of what he calls the "audio unconscious."[29] At this point, we invite the reader to skim back to Chapter 3, where we explained the fourth level of Lacan's "graph of desire," illustrated through Bright Eyes' "The Road to Joy." Remember that the vector

[29] See chapter 4 of *Stop Making Sense: Music from the Perspective of the Real* (London: Karnac Books, 2015), 43–51. See also Scott Wilson, "Amusia, Noise and the Drive: Towards a Theory of the Audio Unconscious," in *Reverberations: The Philosophy, Aesthetics and Politics of Noise*, ed. Michael Goddard, Benjamin Halligan, and Paul Hegarty (London: Continuum, 2012), 15–25.

going from left to right in the upper portion of the graph crosses through the whole edifice of desire and marks the passage from *jouissance* to death. Remember also that Lacan places the "signifier of the lack in the Other"—the "S(*A*)"—in its path, and this signifier of the failure of the Other to answer the call of *jouissance* fragments *jouissance* into small pockets of drives. Well, in Wilson's version of this graph—a version in which he changes the Lacanian terms for musical ones, as explained in his chapter—he places "noise" in place of the S(*A*). Noise, therefore, becomes the symbol of failure in the big Other to absorb, articulate, comprehend, or accept primal articulations of pure *jouissance*. So noise is not quite *jouissance* itself, but it is a symbolic brick wall that *jouissance* hits up against. In a sense, though, the vector of *jouissance* is still part and parcel of the noises we hear in "Joy."

Indulge us. Play the track as you read this paragraph. And read at a rate of 2.8 words per second. Go. The first things you hear are jarring, mechanistic factory sounds. If we think of the pulse as a kind of moderato 4/4, somewhere between the second and third beats, you can hear some sort of mechanized growl—a byproduct of a machine with something stuck in it? As Harvey enters—more shouting than singing—with "Joy was her name," her utterances are punctuated with exhaustive breaths, deep physical cries of the anguish of expression. For a while, each of her lines has the same melody and rhythm—a little like those unanswered "Jody calls" (the military training calls; think *Full Metal Jacket*, "I don't know but I've been told …") in other songs on the album. These Jody calls are an appeal to the Big Other, whose failure to respond is marked symbolically by the noises *not* produced in response, where we hear only gaps—the empty sound of machines working, but simultaneously breaking. By the time you read this sentence, Harvey has probably just taken a break from singing, and the silence will have been filled with a heavy groove, reminiscent of futuristic jungle music with something like an ultradistorted cow-bell sample. Scott Wilson follows Oliver Sacks in discussing *amusia* (the condition of people being unable to enjoy music, or even being completely averse to it—Freud was one, Nabokov another). The sounds you're hearing now probably induce the same kind of feelings. They coincide with the discussion of Joy's "condition." Sure, in the short story that lies behind this song, the condition is an amputated leg, but the musical condition here is surely the inability to enjoy these ultraharsh sounds that stand as "noise"—the remainder that is left after we have absorbed everything "musical," remaining as symbol of impossibility to radically enjoy without pain. (Certainly we might well enjoy noise music; we like what we like! But within the fabula of the album here, these factory sounds seem, at least, to represent the unenjoyable and *a*musical.)

Around this point in your listening experience, you'll probably hear the next factory layer—the tubthumping sounds that lead to a sudden break in the whole texture at 2:17. The texture thins out a little afterward as the production line changes. Harvey has just reflected a little more on Joy's character—how she now doesn't have "a question." We might register this lack of a question again as the fact that the fundamental questioning of the psyche in Lacan's Level III ("Che vuoi?") gets replaced at Level IV by the line of *jouissance* that cuts through the system and leaves its quilting point of impossibility in its trail.

Listen to the factory layers pile up again, and listen to how Harvey's tale and Joy's ego disappear with a simple cry of "no." As Alex Ross would say, "The rest is noise." Until it just stops. Listen in your own time now until the wheels stop turning.

The whole position is impossible. Joy, we are told, "wants to go blind." This ushers in an alternative Oedipal narrative. After Oedipus has realized his familial *faux pas*— his moment of "anagnorisis" (the point in a Greek tragedy when a character realizes another's true identity, or indeed their own identity: think, "Luke, I am your father")— his action is to put out his own eyes. Once achieved, he becomes a successful and "visionary" king. Joy's problems are partly Oedipal; she wanted to wound her mother and strip her of her faith. Essentially, in choosing to seduce the unseducable bible salesman, she chooses to seduce the paternal representative of the law that she despised. The moment of transgression brings a trauma because she sees that the father figure wanted to abuse her all along. In essence, she comes to recognize herself in the mirror. The bible salesman, perverse though he is (he admits to having a collection of stolen prosthetics), is not so different from Joy herself; he is fundamentally bad but pretends to be good; she is fundamentally good but pretends to be bad. And this moment of Lacanian mirror recognition becomes her Oedipal moment of realization—"Into a hollow sky, [she] came face to face with her own innocence." Here the "noise" bass growl and the high pained singing create a kind of call-and-response contrapuntal flow that seems to be the double articulation of the self and the image. This must surely remind us of the "mirror" moments in the songs above—the queer encounters with the self—and here is another "unwed" woman—the missing leg, perhaps even representing her double-lack. The need to further weaken herself by putting out her Oedipal eyes is a way to keep her wounds open. The wound that had prevented her from completing her youthful Oedipal processes is now a double-wound (physically and metaphysically). Perhaps, as in Oedipus, the need to see in the darkness, through blindness, is a desire to see the unconscious. To see the unconscious is impossible, of course, but it is part of the drive toward *jouissance*.

## "A Perfect Day Elise"

The song "A Perfect Day Elise" is murderous or suicidal, so we can't talk about this as if it's a simple tale of everyday *jouissance*; we mustn't make it seem too normative. It seems to explore themes from "A Perfect Day for Bananafish" by Salinger, though with different characters and different sexual narratives. The tale is a far cry from Lou Reed's "Perfect Day." Joe picks up Elise as a "one night stand." She then jilts him, telling him not to come back. Essentially she stops him from repeating. We are told that he is burned by the sun and returns to her room with a gun, killing either Elise or himself.

It is clear from the refrain, which accompanies an affirmative G-Am progression (as ♭VI-♭VII) and a turn back into the B minor key on the words "perfect day Elise," that "Elise" is a form of "release" as the "aeolian cadence" (a rock version of the classic IV-V-I) turns to the "tonic" in the minor key. The "perfect day" was not, however, just the successful pickup; the whole drama is inscribed into the perfect day: (i) the pickup; (ii) the refused repeat-sex; (iii) the sunny day outside; (iv) the murder/suicide.

In refusing the repeat, Elise doesn't realize that she is denying the child's "fort-da"; like a parent refusing to pick up the child's rattle just thrown out of the pram, she tells him never to come back. And so Joe must master the situation another way. And this is all celebrated as Joe's *jouissance*. The image Harvey gives is that of Icarus, who flew too close to the sun and paid the price with melted wings. The same is true here of Joe, now scorched by the same sun. Perhaps it also speaks of the death-drive inherent within *jouissance*—the moment of destruction at the height of joy. (We might also think of the Manic Street Preachers' "Die in the Summertime," where the protagonist wants to die in the happiest time of year.)

*Jouissance* is inscribed in other, more musical ways. For one thing, as in the "mirror" moment of "Joy," there is a call and response going on between the perfect voice of Harvey and the noisy, fat-bass "noise" that repeats in its own octave. In fact, the verse unfolds with the same rhythmic pattern as the military "Jody call." Her words are the call, and his bass riffs descend in response, always threatening without ever actually becoming verbalized. Sure, we learn that this is a murderous undertone in the verses that propel the story, but in the chorus that reflects on the day's perfection, the bass and voice come together into an unholy amalgam of pleasure and pain.

We also hear Harvey release the *jouissance* of her voice in a rare moment of seemingly uncontrolled, primeval, unconscious expression. In the context of singing, a vocalized eruption sounds like ultimate pleasure; in the context of the shooting she describes, it sounds like sharp pain. Listen to it at 2:17. In the context of pop's propensity for vocalizing, this vocal enjoyment is a drop in the ocean, but in the context of PJ Harvey's carefully controlled libidinal flow, it is *everything*.[30]

## "The River"

"The River," the final song that we will discuss, offers great scope to explore a synthesis of the themes thrown up already by the other songs on the album and consequently, by this chapter. It also contains aspects of the "death-drive" that we explored in Chapter 5, but goes further by positing it as a holistic package of desire structured around the two sexuated logics of *jouissance*.

The song's lyrics describe two wanderers, both looking for a home. They come to a river—perhaps a good place to settle—but want to use the river to throw their pain into. The female voice as the storyteller and the silent male protagonist reflects on their incompatible desires, demonstrating the couple's inability to offer *jouissance* to the other. The music plods along slowly like a kind of funeral dirge, building slowly over the repeated B-F♯-E progression, occasionally varying to B-G-F♯ in refrains. The piano's activity seems to evoke the shimmering or flowing of the river, though the lethargic voice, drums, and guitars all point to the despondency of the characters,

---

[30] For more on the voice and *jouissance*, see Michel Poizat, *The Angel's Cry: Beyond the Pleasure Principle in Opera* (Ithaca, NY: Cornell University Press, 1992); Carlo Zuccarini, *Enjoying the Operatic Voice: A Neuropsychoanalytic Exploration of the Operatic Reception Experience* (Wilmington, DE: Vernon Press, 2018).

notwithstanding the slim rise in emotional texture as the song progresses toward a trumpet duet two-thirds of the way through.

It's hard not to think of Schubert's great contribution to the early art song tradition of "Die Schöne Müllerin" in which the male protagonist sets off on his nomadic wandering, falling for a young girl who, sadly, prefers an alternative suitor. The man then essentially drowns himself physically or metaphysically in the river. The gesture is usually viewed as a classic Freudian uterine fantasy—a return to the mother, but we might think of this more generally as a symbol of becoming one with nature's own flow. The river has always been a symbol of life's constant change and the acceptance of this change. Think of Heraclitus's famous maxim, "You can't stand in the same river twice," to which Cratylus replied that you can't even stand in the same river once. When the characters here gently dissolve themselves in the slow, solemn, weary music, they are essentially submitting their egos to the death-drive, but not a drive to "end it all"; this is not a suicide; this is a metaphysical alignment of life with the constant flow of time and change; it is a Nietzschean acceptance of repetition. The characters end by saying they want "to be washed away slow," and this is what the music achieves. It is one of the only songs on the album to fade out, rather than ending abruptly.

And this death-drive, explored through the song, becomes the linchpin of the other Lacanian concepts covered in this chapter. We learn in the lyrics that the incompatibility of the lovers is rendered clearly. He wants "the sun"; she wants "the whole." We might at first attribute this to the classic Lacanian failure of the sexual relationship, but let's think a minute. Him wanting the sun is a failing of masculine sexuation, sure enough. The sun is the ultimate "father of the primordial horde"; it represents the exception to the phallic order—the only thing that lies beyond it and yet controls it. The ultimate *jouissance*, we can fly toward it but we'll always get hurt; we can't even look at it too directly, lest we find ourselves blinded. This is masculine-sexuated desire. But the corollary is also masculine. Remember Lacan's phrase, that women are *not wholly* subject to the phallic symbol, by which he means they are not wholly subsumed in language, possessing reserved pockets of *jouissance* outside of it. Therefore, when PJ Harvey's "I" wants "the whole"—whatever gender the character might be—the sexuation of desire is also masculine. Therefore, we might naively think that the compatibility is assured—both want the same thing. But, of course, this is the real Lacanian tragedy: that identical sexuations are just as incompatible as opposites, particularly with the masculinized logic, by which everyone is envious of the imagined other that they want. Two people who essentially want *everything* are not going to work together. Would two people with feminine-sexuated logic fare better? The situation would certainly involve a double acceptance of the "not all" logic, where there are no imagined exceptions to the rule. Again, masculinized desire is the root cause of the problem in the album. Feminine sexuation is all about living with a certain pocket of *jouissance* that is just about enough. *That* desire, to answer Harvey, would be enough. But it's rare. Although it could happen in any relationship—heterosexual, homosexual, monogamous, polygamous, and so on—we don't come across it in the album.

The pseudo-homosexual masculine sexuation may also continue Harvey's problematic preservation of the narcissistic stereotype, although here we find it in a very different register. This is not literal "homosexuality," nor is it literal narcissism; rather, it is the recognition that the two people want the same thing; they want *more* than each other, and this will lead to destruction in the river, as surely as it did for Narcissus. We must also remember, though, that a narcissistic death drive is still an acceptance of change as a positive *ex nihilo* form of production. We must remember, too, that for most people Narcissus is a flower that returns each spring. For Narcissus himself, the flower was his next incarnation after his drowning. As the characters look in the river, we hear two trumpets playing a rather desultory duet, their melodic lines replicating each other, often bound up in unisons or the interval of a third. After several bars, we hear one trumpet has become distorted and seems to be getting stuck in a repeated, stuttering groove. The image thereby offered is a kind of musical narcissism, summoning up the image of reflection in the river, as if one image is running away from the other—Narcissus looking in a river rather than a static pool.

Remember that the path of *jouissance* in Lacan's fourth stage of desire breaks apart into the drives, where small pockets of *jouissance* become scattered and tied to different parts of the psyche. This is what seems to happen here. As well as the lovers throwing their pain in the river, we also realize that the river is a symbol of the Other's pain—"like a pain in the river"—a mark of the Other's failure to approach *jouissance*. At this point in the music, the ugly "noises" start up in the margins of the instrumental texture. Here the text also describes how the "white light scatters." The "white light" is itself a symbol of sexual *jouissance*—a state where all differentiation disappears into pure sensation, pure light. This now "scatters," broken through confrontation with the river as a symbol of lack in the Other—the "noise" for Scott Wilson. This scattering of white light is the scattering of *jouissance* into myriad "drives." And this breakdown of *jouissance* into the drives pollutes all of life, "like the way life scatters, to be washed away slow."

# Glossary of psychoanalytic terms

(Page numbers indicate first usage and definition of each term)

abject, 139
agent, 103
big Other, 104
castration, 99
cathexis, 16
*Che Vuoi?*, 98
chora, 139
condensation, 29
conditions of figurability, 32
conscious, 40
displacement, 29
drives, 100
economic hypothesis, 15
ego, 20
ego-ideal, 87
gaze, 90
graph of desire, 94
humor, 55
hysteria, 69
id, 20
ideal ego, 87
imaginary, 87
jouissance, 99
lack, 87
latent, 14
libido, 24
manifest, 14
master signifier, 104
matheme, 88
melancholia, 63
metaphor, 85
metonymy, 85
mirror stage, 87
narcissism, 45
need, 94
neurosis, 65

obscenity, 55
Oedipus complex, 50
Other, 95
perversion, 191
phallus, 57
phantasy, 106
pleasure principle, 20
*point de capiton*, 235
preconscious, 40
primary process, 40
principle of consistency, 21
production, 104
psychosis, 65
the Real, 87
reality principle, 19
repression, 17
secondary revision, 32
semiotic,139
signification of the Other, 95
signifier, 94
signifier of lack in the Other, 99
signifying chain, 94
split subject, 94
structural hypothesis, 40
sublimation, 32
superego, 38
symbolic, 87
topographical hypothesis, 36
truth, 103
unconscious, 40

# Bibliography

Abbate, Carolyn. *Unsung Voices: Opera and Musical Narrative in the Nineteenth Century.* Princeton: Princeton University Press, 1991.

Adorno, Theodor. *Mahler: A Musical Physiognomy.* Translated by Edmund Jephcott. Chicago: University of Chicago Press, 1992.

Altrockchick. "Classic Music Review: *Is This Desire?* by PJ Harvey." *50thirdand3rd* (October 2014). https://altrockchick.com/2014/10/.

Ashton, Sarah, Karalyn McDonald, and Maggie Kirkman. "*Fifty Shades Darker*: An Abusive Fairy Tale That Robs Women of Sexual Freedom." *The Conversation* (February 9, 2017). https://theconversation.com/fifty-shades-darker-an-abusive-fairy-tale-that-robs-women-of-sexual-freedom-72724.

Bailey, Robert. *Richard Wagner, Prelude and Transfiguration from "Tristan and Isolde."* New York: Norton, 1985.

Bard-Schwarz, David. *Listening Awry: Music and Alterity in German Culture.* Minneapolis: University of Minnesota Press, 2006.

Bauer, Nancy. *How To Do Things with Pornography.* Cambridge, MA: Harvard University Press, 2015.

Bottge, Karen. "Brahms's 'Wiegenlied' and the Maternal Voice." *19th-Century Music* 28, no. 3 (2005): 185–213.

Brittan, Francesca. "Berlioz and the Pathological Fantastic: Melancholy, Monomania, and Romantic Autobiography." *19th-Century Music* 29, no. 3 (2006): 211–39.

Brooks, Daphne A. "Amy Winehouse and the (Black) Art of Appropriation." *The Nation* (September 10, 2008). www.thenation.com/article/archive/amy-winehouse-and-black-art-appropriation/.

Burns, Lori, and Mélisse Lafrance. *Disruptive Divas: Feminism, Identity, and Popular Music.* New York: Routledge, 2001.

CCRU. "Swarmachines." In *#accelerate: The Accelerationist Reader*, edited by Robin Mackay and Armen Avanessian, 321–34. Falmouth: Urbanomic, [1996] 2014.

Chion, Michel. *The Voice in Cinema.* Translated by Claudia Gorbman. New York: Columbia University Press, 1999.

Cohn, Richard. "Uncanny Resemblances: Tonal Signification in the Freudian Age." *Journal of the American Musicological Society* 57, no. 2 (2004): 285–324.

Conway, Jake. "Rihanna, 'S&M.'" *Q Magazine at Yale* (March 29, 2011). https://web.archive.org/web/20110713101456/http://www.qmagazineatyale.com/culture/music/rihanna-E2 80 9Csm E2 80 9D/.

Cybulska, Eva. "Nietzsche's Eternal Return: Unriddling the Vision, a Psychodynamic Approach." *Indo-Pacific Journal of Phenomenology* 13, no. 1 (May 2013): 1–13.

Deleuze, Gilles. *Difference and Repetition.* London: Continuum, 2001.

Deleuze, Gilles. *Sacher-Masoch: An Interpretation.* London: Faber, 1971.

Deleuze, Gilles, and Felix Guattari. *Anti-Oedipus.* Translated by Robert Hurley, Mark Seem, and Helen R. Lane. Minneapolis: University of Minnesota Press, [1972] 1983.

Deleuze, Gilles, and Felix Guattari. *A Thousand Plateaus.* London: Continuum, 2004.

Densmore, John. *Riders on the Storm: My Life with Jim Morrison and the Doors*. New York: Delacorte Press, 1990.

Dibben, Nicola. "Pulp, Pornography and Spectatorship: Subject Matter and Subject Position in Pulp's *This Is Hardcore*." *Journal of the Royal Musical Association* 126, no. 1 (2001): 83–106.

Donington, Robert. *Wagner's "Ring" and Its Symbols. The Music and the Myth*. London: Faber & Faber, 1963.

Drescher, Jack. "A History of Homosexuality and Organized Psychoanalysis." *Journal of the American Academy of Psychoanalysis & Dynamic Psychiatry* 36 (2008): 443–60.

Drescher, Jack. "There Is No There There: A Discussion of 'Narcissism and Self-Esteem among Homosexual and Heterosexual Male Students.'" *Journal of Sex & Marital Therapy* 36, no. 1 (2010): 38–47.

Feder, Stuart. *Charles Ives: My Father's Song: A Psychoanalytic Biography*. New Haven, CT: Yale University Press, 1992.

Fierman, Marci. "Neutral Milk Hotel." *Pitchfork* (February 1, 2002). https://pitchfork.com/features/interview/5847-neutral-milk-hotel/.

Fisher, Mark. *Ghosts of My Life: Writings on Depression, Hauntology and Lost Futures*. Winchester: Zero Books, 2014.

Footman, Tim. *Radiohead. Welcome to the Machine: OK Computer and the Death of the Classic Album*. New Malden: Chrome Dreams, 2007.

Forrest, David. "PL Voice Leading and the Uncanny in Pop Music." *Music Theory Online* 23, no. 4 (December 2017). https://mtosmt.org/issues/mto.17.23.4/mto.17.23.4.forrest.html.

Freud, Sigmund. "The Archaic Features and Infantilism of Dreams." In *The Standard Edition of the Complete Psychological Works of Sigmund Freud*, vol. XV, translated by James Strachey. London: Hogarth, 1963.

Freud, Sigmund. "An Autobiographical Study." In *The Standard Edition of the Complete Psychological Works of Sigmund Freud*, vol. XX, translated by James Strachey. London: Hogarth Press, [1925] 1959.

Freud, Sigmund. "Beyond the Pleasure Principle." In *The Standard Edition of the Complete Psychological Works of Sigmund Freud*, vol. XVIII, translated by James Strachey. London: Hogarth Press, [1920] 1955.

Freud, Sigmund. "Group Psychology and the Analysis of the Ego." In *The Standard Edition of the Complete Psychological Works of Sigmund Freud*, vol. XVIII, translated by James Strachey. London: Hogarth Press, [1921] 1955.

Freud, Sigmund. "Inhibitions, Symptoms and Anxiety." In *The Standard Edition of the Complete Psychological Works of Sigmund Freud*, vol. XX, translated by James Strachey. London: The Hogarth Press, [1926] 1959.

Freud, Sigmund. "The Interpretation of Dreams" (Part 1). In *The Standard Edition of the Complete Psychological Works of Sigmund Freud*, vol. IV, translated by James Strachey. London: The Hogarth Press, [1900] 1953.

Freud, Sigmund. "The Interpretation of Dreams" (Part 2). In *The Standard Edition of the Complete Psychological Works of Sigmund Freud*, vol. V, translated by James Strachey. London: The Hogarth Press, [1900] 1953.

Freud, Sigmund. "Jokes and Their Relation to the Unconscious." In *The Standard Edition of the Complete Psychological Works of Sigmund Freud*, vol. VIII, translated by James Strachey. London: The Hogarth Press, [1905] 1960.

Freud, Sigmund. "Letter to Arthur Schnitzler." May 8, 1906. Syndics of Cambridge University Library, MS.Schnitzler, B31.
Freud, Sigmund. "The Loss of Reality in Neurosis and Psychosis." In *The Standard Edition of the Complete Psychological Works of Sigmund Freud*, vol. XIX. translated by James Strachey. London: The Hogarth Press, [1924] 1961.
Freud, Sigmund. "Mourning and Melancholia." In *The Standard Edition of the Complete Psychological Works of Sigmund Freud*, vol. XIV, translated by James Strachey. London: The Hogarth Press, [1918] 1953.
Freud, Sigmund. "On Narcissism: An Introduction." In *The Standard Edition of the Complete Psychological Works of Sigmund Freud*, vol. XIV, translated by James Strachey. London: The Hogarth Press, [1914] 1957.
Freud, Sigmund. "The Psychogenesis of a Case of Homosexuality in a Woman." In *That Obscure Subject of Desire: Freud's Female Homosexual Revisited*, edited by Ronnie C. Lesser and Erica Schoenberg, 13–36. New York: Routledge, [1920] 1999.
Freud, Sigmund. "A Special Type of Choice of Object Made by Men." In *The Standard Edition of the Complete Psychological Works of Sigmund Freud*, vol. XI. London: The Hogarth Press, [1910] 1957.
Freud, Sigmund. "Three Essays on Sexuality." In *The Standard Edition of the Complete Psychological Works of Sigmund Freud*, vol. VII, translated by James Strachey. London: The Hogarth Press, [1905] 1955.
Freud, Sigmund. "The Unconscious." In *The Standard Edition of the Complete Psychological Works of Sigmund Freud*, vol. XIV, translated by James Strachey. London: The Hogarth Press, [1915] 1957.
Gaye, Jan. *After the Dance: My Life with Marvin Gaye*. New York: Amistad, 2015.
Harrison, Daniel. *Harmonic Function in Chromatic Music: A Renewed Dualist Theory and an Account of Its Precedents*. Chicago: University of Chicago Press, 1994.
Heims, Steve. *The Cybernetics Group*. Cambridge, MA: MIT Press, 1991.
Holland, Eugene. "Jazz Improvisation: Music of the People-to-Come." In *Deleuze, Guattari and the Production of the New*, edited by Simon O'Sullivan and Stephen Zepke, 196–205. Continuum: New York, 2008.
Jones, Ernest. *The Life and Work of Sigmund Freud*, vol. 2. New York: Basic Books, 1961.
Keller, Hans. *Music and Psychology: From Vienna to London, 1939–52*. London, Plumbago Books, 2003.
Klein, Melaine. "Infantile Anxiety Situations Reflected in a Work of Art and in the Creative Impulse." In *Psychoanalysis and Art: Kleinian Perspectives*, edited by Sandra Gosso, 33–41. London: Karnac, 2004.
Klein, Michael. *Music and the Crises of the Modern Subject*. Bloomington: Indiana University Press, 2015.
Korzybski, Alfred. "A Non-Aristotelian System and Its Necessity for Rigor in Mathematics and Physics." *Proceedings of the American Mathematical Society*, New Orleans, LA, December 28, 1931.
Korzybski, Alfred. *Science and Sanity. An Introduction to Non-Aristotelian Systems and General Semantics*. New York: The International Non-Aristotelian Library, 1933.
Kramer, Lawrence. *Music as Cultural Practice, 1800–1900*. Berkeley: University of California Press, 1990.
Kristeva, Julia. *Powers of Horror: An Essay on Abjection*. Translated by Leon S. Roudiez. New York: Columbia University Press, 1982.

Kristeva, Julia. *Revolution in Poetic Language*. New York: Columbia University, [1974] 1984.
Lacan, Jacques. *Écrits*. Translated by Bruce Fink. London: Norton, [1966] 2006.
Lacan, Jacques. "Kant with Sade." Translated by James Swenson. *October* 51 ([1963] 1989): 55–75, 61.
Lacan, Jacques. *The Seminars of Jacques Lacan, Book II: The Ego in Freud's Theory and in the Technique of Psychoanalysis 1954–1955*. Edited by Jacques-Alain Miller, translated by Sylvana Tomaselli. New York: Norton, 1988.
Lacan, Jacques. *The Seminars of Jacques Lacan, Book VII: The Ethics of Psychoanalysis 1959–60*. Edited by Jacque-Alain Miller, translated by Dennis Porter. New York: Norton, 1992.
Lacan, Jacques. *The Seminars of Jacques Lacan, Book XI: The Four Fundamental Concepts of Psychoanalysis*. Translated by Jacques-Alain Miller. London: Vintage, 1998.
Lacan, Jacques. *Seminar XVII: The Other Side of Psychoanalysis*. Edited by Jacques-Alain Miller, translated by Russell Grigg. New York: Norton, 2007.
Lacan, Jacques. *Seminar XX: Encore. On Feminine Sexuality: The Limits of Love and Knowledge*. Edited by Jacques-Alain Miller, translated by Bruce Fink. New York: Norton, 1998.
Lacan, Jacques. *Television: A Challenge to the Psychoanalytic Establishment*. Edited by Joan Copjec, translated by Denis Hollier, Rosalind Krauss, and Annette Michelson. New York: Norton, [1973] 1990.
Land, Nick. *Fanged Noumena: Collected Writings 1987–2007*. London: Urbanomic, 2011.
Leas, Ryan. *LCD Soundsystem's Sound of Silver, 33 ⅓*. New York: Bloomsbury, 2016.
Lehman, Frank. *Hollywood Harmony: Musical Wonder and the Sound of Cinema*. New York: Oxford University Press, 2011.
Lunbeck, Elizabeth. "The Narcissistic Homosexual: Genealogy of a Myth." In *History and Psyche Culture, Psychoanalysis, and the Past*, edited by Sally Alexander and Barbara Taylor, 49–70. New York: Palgrave, 2012.
Lynskey, Dorian. "The Manic Street Preachers: 'I'll Always Hate the Tory Party. But Now I Hate Labour, Too." *New Statesman* (July 8, 2014). www.newstatesman.com/culture/2014/07/manic-street-preachers-i-ll-always-hate-tory-party-now-i-hate-labour-too.
Lynskey, Dorian. "Readers Recommend: Songs about Sci-Fi and Space." *The Guardian* (January 27, 2006). www.theguardian.com/arts/filmandmusic/story/0,,1695555,00.html.
Lyotard, Jean-Francois. *Libidinal Economy*. Translated by Iain Hamilton-Grant. London: Athlone, 1993.
Mactaggart, Allister. "'Silencio': Hearing Loss in David Lynch's *Mulholland Drive*." *Journal of Aesthetics & Culture* 6, no. 1 (2014): 1–11.
Manbeck, Emily. "S&M and Pop Culture: Has Pleasure through Pain Perpetuated through Art?" *Commonplace Book*, Georgetown University (October 30, 2013). https://blogs.commons.georgetown.edu/engl-355-fall2013/2013/10/30/sm-and-pop-culture-has-pleasure-through-pain-perpetuated-through-art/.
Margulis, Elizabeth Hellmuth. *On Repeat: How Music Plays the Mind*. New York: Oxford University Press, 2014.
Matre, Lynn Van. "How Sweet It Wasn't: The Tortured Life and Divided Soul of Marvin Gaye." *Chicago Tribune* (April 25, 1985).

McGowan, Todd. "Lost on *Mulholland Drive*: Navigating David Lynch's Panegyric to Hollywood." *Cinema Journal* 43, no. 2 (Winter 2004): 67–89.
Moore, Allan. *Song Means: Analysing and Interpreting Recorded Popular Song*. Farnham: Ashgate, 2012.
Morrison, Jim. "Interview with Jerry Hopkins." *Rolling Stone* (July 26, 1969). www.rolli ngstone.com/music/music-news/the-rolling-stone-interview-jim-morrison-73308/.
Mulvey, Laura. "Visual Pleasure and Narrative Cinema." *Screen* 16, no. 3 (1975): 6–18.
Nietzsche, Friedrich. *Beyond Good and Evil: Prelude to a Philosophy of the Future*. Translated by Walter Kaufmann. New York: Vintage Books, 1966.
Nietzsche, Friedrich. *The Case of Wagner*. Translated by Walter Kaufmann. New York: Vintage, 1967.
Nietzsche, Friedrich. *The Gay Science*. Translated by J. Nauckhoff. Cambridge: Cambridge University Press, 2001.
Nietzsche, Friedrich. "Notes on the Eternal Recurrence." In *Oscar Levy Edition of Nietzsche's Complete Works*, vol. 16. Edinburgh: T. N. Foulis, 1909–13.
Nietzsche, Friedrich. *Thus Spoke Zarathustra*. Edited by R. Pippin, translated by A. del Caro. Cambridge: Cambridge University Press, 2006.
Nietzsche, Friedrich. "Why I Write Such Good Books: Thus Spoke Zarathustra." In *The Genealogy of Morals and Ecce Homo*, translated by Walter Kaufman, 295–309. New York: Vintage, 1989.
Nietzsche, Friedrich. *The Will to Power*, vol. II, bks. III and IV. Edited by Oscar Levy, translated by A. Ludovici. Edinburgh: T. N. Foulis, 1913.
Nobile, Drew. *Form as Harmony in Rock Music*. New York: Oxford University Press, 2020.
Osborn, Brad. "Subverting the Verse—Chorus Paradigm: Terminally Climactic Forms in Recent Rock Music." *Music Theory Spectrum* 35, no. 1 (2013): 23–47.
Overy, Stephen. "The Genealogy of Nick Land's Anti-Anthropocentric Philosophy: A Psychoanalytic Conception of Machinic Desire." PhD dissertation, University of Newcastle, 2015.
Pääkkölä, Anna-Elena. "The Sublime Space of Male Masochism in Elvis Costello's 'When I Was Cruel No. 2.'" *Radical Musicology* 7 (2019). www.radical-musicology.org.uk/2019/Paakkola.htm.
Peters, Mathijs. *Popular Music, Critique and Manic Street Preachers*. Switzerland: Palgrave Macmillan, 2020.
Poizat, Michel. *The Angel's Cry: Beyond the Pleasure Principle in Opera*. Ithaca, NY: Cornell University Press, 1992.
Richards, Arlene. "A Fresh Look at Perversion." *Journal of the American Psychoanalytic Association* 51, no. 4 (December 2003): 1199–218.
Risse, Mathias. "A Freudian Look at What Nietzsche Took To Be His Biggest Insight." In *Nietzsche on Freedom and Autonomy*, edited by Ken Gemes and Simon May, 223–45. Oxford: Oxford University Press, 2009.
Ritz, David. *Divided Soul: The Life of Marvin Gaye*. New York: Da Capo Press, 1985.
Rubinstein, Gidi. "Narcissism and Self-Esteem among Homosexual and Heterosexual Male Students." *Journal of Sex and Marital Therapy* 36, no. 1 (2010): 24–34.
Rycenga, Jennifer. "'It Tears My Heart Out Every Time!' P.J. Harvey's *Is This Desire*." *GSLG Newsletter* 10, no. 1 (Spring 2000): 8–10.
Sawa, Dale Berning. "Awkwafina: 'I Was Just Rapping about My Genitalia—Not Making a Feminist Message.'" *The Guardian* (December 28, 2017). www.theguardian.com/film/2017/dec/28/nora-lum-awkwafina-genitalia-feminist-message.

Schelling, Friedrich Wilhelm Joseph. *Sämmtliche Werke*, vol I/III. Edited by K. F. A. Schelling. Stuttgart: Cotta, 1856–61.

Schenker, Heinrich. "Schubert's 'Ihr Bild' (Heine)." In *Der Tonwille: Pamphlets in Witness of the Immutable Laws of Music*, vol. 1 (issues 1–5), edited by William Drabkin, 41–3. Oxford: Oxford University Press, [1921] 2004.

Schopenhauer, Arthur. *The World as Will and Presentation*, vol. 2. Translated by David Carus and Richard Aquila. London: Routledge, [1819] 2016.

Scruton, Roger. *Understanding Music: Philosophy and Interpretation*. London: Continuum, 2009.

Shana, Goldin-Perschbacher. "Icelandic Nationalism, Difference Feminism, and Björk's Maternal Aesthetic." *Women and Music: A Journal of Gender and Culture* 18 (2014): 48–81.

Shannon, Claude. "A Mathematical Theory of Communication." *Bell System Technical Journal* 27 (July 1948): 379–423; (October 1948): 623–56.

Singh, Amrit. "New Xiu Xiu Video—'Dear God, I Hate Myself.'" *Stereogum* (February 1, 2010). www.stereogum.com/112171/new_xiu_xiu_video_-_dear_god_i_hate_myself_stereog/news/.

Smith, Gary, and Alan Maki. *Death in the Jungle: Diary of a Navy Seal*. New York: Ivy Books, 1995.

Smith, Kenneth. "Formal Negativities, Breakthroughs, Ruptures and Continuities in the Music of Modest Mouse." *Popular Music* 33, no. 3 (2014): 428–54.

Smith, Kenneth. "Pulp: A Paradigm for Perversion in Pornosonic Pop." In *Popular Musicology and Identity: Essays in Honour of Stan Hawkins*, edited by Freya Jarman, Kai Arne Hansen, and Eirik Askeroi, 160–77. Oxford: Routledge, 2020.

Smith, Kenneth. "Vertigo's Musical Gaze: Neo-Riemannian Symmetries and Spirals." *Music Analysis* 37, no. 1 (2018): 68–102.

Spitzer, Michael. "Post Memory: Anne Frank in Neutral Hotel's *In the Aeroplane over the Sea*." In *The Routledge Companion to Popular Music Analysis: Expanding Approaches*, edited by Ciro Scotto, Kenneth Smith, and John Brackett, 400–15. New York: Routledge, 2018.

Stumme, Clifford. "What Does 'Bury a Friend' by Billie Eilish Mean?" *Pop Song Professor* (February 20, 2019). www.popsongprofessor.com/blog/2019/2/20/what-does-bury-a-friend-by-billie-eilish-mean-lyrics.

Tagg, Philip. *Music's Meanings: A Modern Musicology for Non-musos*. New York: MMMSP, 2013.

Temperley, David. *The Musical Language of Rock*. New York: Oxford, 2018.

Välimäki, Susanna. "'Everyone Is a Little Bit Gay': LGBTIQ Activism in Finnish Pop Music of the 21st Century." In *Popular Musicology and Identity: Essays in Honour of Stan Hawkins*, edited by Kai Arne Hansen, Eirik Askerøi, and Freya Jarman, 97–116. Oxford: Routledge, 2020.

Wilson, Samuel. Music-Psychoanalysis-Musicology. Oxford: Routledge, 2017.

Wilson, Scott. "Amusia, Noise and the Drive: Towards a Theory of the Audio Unconscious." In *Reverberations: The Philosophy, Aesthetics and Politics of Noise*, edited by Michael Goddard, Benjamin Halligan, and Paul Hegarty, 15–25. London: Continuum, 2012.

Wilson, Scott. *Music from the Perspective of the Real*. London: Karnac Books, 2015.

Wisgard, Alex. "'I Think My Brain Is Working on Another Level ...'—Grandaddy's Jason Lytle Revisits *The Sophtware Slump*." *Line of Best Fit* (August 31, 2011). www.thelineof bestfit.com/features/interviews/i-think-my-brain-is-working-on-another-level-gra ndaddys-jason-lytle-revisits-the-sophtware-slump-67011.
Wittgenstein, Ludwig. *Philosophical Investigations*. New York: Macmillan, 1953.
Wright, Danny. "10 of the Best." *The Guardian* (January 6, 2016). www.theguardian.com/music/musicblog/2016/jan/06/pavement-10-of-the-best.
Wu, Pokeung. "The Idea of Repetition in Marx, Nietzsche and Freud, and Problems of Modernity." MA dissertation, UC San Diego, 2010.
*Zen Motoring*. Written by Ivan Battaliero-Owen. BBC 3 (January 16, 2022).
Žižek, Slavoj. *Interrogating the Real: Selected Writings*. New York: Continuum, 2005.
Žižek, Slavoj. "'There Is No Sexual Relationship': Wagner as a Lacanian." *New German Critique* 69 (1996): 7–35.
Žižek, Slavoj, and Mladen Dolar. *Opera's Second Death*. New York: Routledge, 2002.
Zuccarini, Carlo. *Enjoying the Operatic Voice: A Neuropsychoanalytic Exploration of the Operatic Reception Experience*. Wilmington, VT: Vernon Press, 2018.

# Index

Abbate, Carolyn
   unsung voices 2
Adams, Ryan 30
Adorno, Theodor 5, 73
Against Me 47
Aguilera, Christina 227–8
Alt-J 48–9
anagnorisis 252
Anna Abreu 71
Antlers, The 105–18, 155, 158
Arcade Fire 9, 25
Ariel Rechtshaid 43
Avalon, Micky 56–7, 225
Awkwafina 57

Basinski, William 190
Beatles, The 29
Bega, Lou 124
Belle and Sebastian 144–6
Berlioz, Hector 66–7
Blur 237
Bonnie Prince Billy 53
Brand News 32
Breuer, Josef 69–70
Bright Eyes 20–2, 85–101, 111
Burial 33

Cannibal Corpse 216–22
Charli XCX 47, 125–8
Clinic 30
Count Five 77

David, F. R. 1–5
Dead Man's Bones (Ryan Gosling) 92
Def Leppard 71
Deleuze, Gilles
   Nietzsche 181–4
   Sado-masochicm / Sadism / Masochism 203–31
doo-wop 1, 62
Doors, The 50–2, 198

Dorrough 47
double tonic complex 15, 25, 168
Doves 26
Dr Dre 40

East 17 33
Eilish, Billie 198–200
Eminem 40, 56, 201–2
emo 32

Fichte 40
Flanders and Swann 59–60
Fleetwood Mac 28,
Freud, Sigmund
   amusia 251
   castration 200–1
   cathexis 15–17, 20–1, 26, 46, 52, 63
   censorship 22–3
   conditions of figurability and secondary revision 32–3
   death drive 143–8, 152, 164
   desire 13
   displacement / condensation 29–32, 34
   dreamwork 26–9
   drive 24, 54, 55, 144, 164
   economic hypothesis 13, 15–36
   ego 18, 20–1, 36–8, 46, 48, 56, 64, 196–9
   hysteria 69–77
   id 38, 41
   libido 24, 46, 64, 236
   manifest / latent 14, 23, 28
   mourning / melancholia 63–5
   narcissism 45–50
   neurosis 65–9
   obscenity and jokes 55–63
   Oedipus complex 50–2, 102, 164
   paranoia 78–83, 166–9
   phallus 57
   pleasure principle 20–1, 144
   primary process 40
   principle of consistency 19–22

psychosis 77–81
reality principle 19–22, 38
regression 52–5
repetition compulsion 144, 147, 164, 254
repression 17–19, 37–8, 76
structural hypothesis 13
sublimation 32
superego 38, 62
topographic hypothesis 13

Gaye, Marvin 209–16
Girl Talk 33
Grandaddy 159–64
Green, Tom 42

Harouki Zombi 88–93
Harvey, P. J. 234–55
Heaven 17 190
Hegel, Georg Wilhelm Friedrich
  master-slave dialectic 133
Hitchcock, Alfred
  "Vertigo" 90, 135
Hopkins, Jon 16–17

Imbruglia, Natalie 117

Jay Z 125–8
Jewel 117
Julee Cruise 53
Jung, Carl Gustav 6, 24, 142
Just Kiddin' 71

Kant 40
Keller, Hans 6
Ken Kaniff 56
Klein, Melanie 5
Korn 222–4
Kristeva, Julia
  abject 139–42
  chora 139–42
  semiotic 139
  symbolic 139

Lacan, Jacques
  agent 103
  analyst discourse 113–15
  castration 99
  che vuoi? 98, 238

cybernetics 155–9
death drive 149–55, 254
desire 85, 98, 106–7, 122, 130–2, 233–2
drives 100, 141–2
ego-ideal / ideal-ego 87, 95–8
four discourses 101–18
graph of desire 93–101
hysteric discourse 107–11
jouissance 99, 106, 113–16, 122, 235, 250, 253
lack 87, 233
master discourse 105–7
master signifier 104, 130
mathemes 88
metaphor / metonymy 85
mirror Stage 87–8
need 94
objet petit a 88–93, 106, 122, 192, 196
Oedipus complex 102, 115, 235, 252
Other (big Other) 86, 91, 96, 104, 108, 233
perversion 138, 191–204
phallocentrism 124–8, 136, 242
phantasy 91, 106, 192
*point de capiton* 95, 235
production 104
real, symbolic, imaginary 86–8, 91, 93, 127, 148, 155, 157–8, 199–200
sexuation 124–8
signification of the Other 95
signifier 94
signifier of the lack in the Other 99, 251
split subject 94, 108
the gaze 90–91
truth 103
university discourse 111–13
woman, the; Woman 122–3
zone between two deaths 91–3
Lady Gaga 129–36, 146–8
LCD Soundsystem 18, 64–5, 184–9
Lehrer, Tom 204–9
Libertines, The 63–64
Lynch, David 90
Lyotard, Jean-Francois 157, 236

Madonna 49, 67
Manic Street Preachers 193–8
Mash-up 33

Mercury, Freddie and Montserrat
    Caballé 103
Metric modulation 217
Mitchell, Joni 136–8
Mitski 47
Modest Mouse 68–9
Morissette, Alanis 76–7, 117
Mulvey, Laura
    male gaze 48, 90, 91, 122, 131–2,
    239

National, The 47
Neutral Milk Hotel 34
Newsom, Joanna 35–6
Nicki Minaj 47
Nietzsche, Friedrich
    eternal recurrence 177–84
Nine Inch Nails 37, 149–51

Odd Future 56
Okkervil River 8

Pallett, Owen 17–18
Panda Bear 28
Pavement 31–3, 64, 198
Pearl Jam 38
Pendulum 228–31
Pictureplane 43
Pixies, The 68–69
Poe, Edgar Allen 92–3
Previn, Dory 80–81
Prince 36–7, 49, 136–7, 176
Pulp 38, 52, 193

Radiohead 9, 37, 81–2, 165
Ravel, Maurice 5, 26, 74, 186
Raw-Rap Relationship 224–6
Reed, Lou 252
REM 39
Rihanna 226–7
Richards, Arlene 200–2
Riley, Terry 189
Robyn 39, 67

Sade, Marquis de 216
Said, Edward 250
Salinger, J. D. 239
Sartre, Jean-Paul 90
Schelling, Friedrich 40, 178
Schenker, Heinrich 132
Schoenberg, Arnold 70, 170
Schopenhauer, Arthur 5, 9, 15, 24, 40,
    124, 177
Schubert, Franz 247, 254
Scud Mountain Boys 18–19
Scuzz Twittly 60–1
Smiths, The 47
Soft Cell 151–2
Soundforge 33
Sprechgesang 31
Springsteen, Bruce 22, 151
St Vincent (Annie Clark) 74–6
Steinfeld, Hailee 128–9
Strauss, Richard 70, 177, 218
Stravinsky, Igor 166
Suede 26, 74
Sufjan Stevens 9

terminal climax 25, 37, 55, 109, 151
Tilly and the Wall 54
Tindersticks, The 53, 78–80

Vampire Weekend 23

Wagner, Richard 15, 70, 124, 168, 177, 190
Welldon, Estela 201
Williams, Pharrell 173
Winehouse, Amy 152–5
Wolf, Patrick 72–4

Xiu Xiu 9, 28

Yeah Yeah Yeahs 29

Zappa, Frank 58–9, 61–3
Žižek, Slavoj 8, 89–91, 125, 128, 237,
    241, 245